THE PEOPLE SPEAK

Compiled and Edited by:

Colin Firth is a BAFTA- and Academy Award-winning actor. His films include *The English Patient, Fever Pitch, Bridget Jones's Diary, Girl with a Pearl Earring, A Single Man* and *The King's Speech.* Alongside Anthony Arnove, he was instrumental in bringing a televised stage performance of *The People Speak* to the UK in 2010.

Anthony Arnove is the author of *Iraq: The Logic of Withdrawal,* editor of *Iraq Under Siege, Howard Zinn Speaks* and *The Essential Chomsky,* and coauthor, with Howard Zinn, of *Voices of a People's History of the United States* and *Terrorism and War.* He is the co-director of *The People Speak* with Chris Moore and Howard Zinn.

With:

David Horspool is a historian and editor at the *Times Literary Supplement.* He is the author of two previous books: *Why Alfred Burned the Cakes* and *The English Rebel: One Thousand Years of Trouble-making from the Normans to the Nineties.* He writes for *The Times,* the *Guardian,* the *Telegraph* and the *New York Times.*

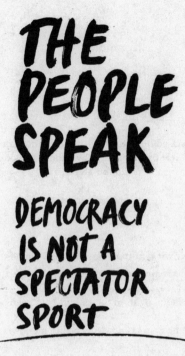

THE PEOPLE SPEAK

DEMOCRACY IS NOT A SPECTATOR SPORT

COLIN FIRTH &
ANTHONY ARNOVE

WITH
DAVID HORSPOOL

CANONGATE
Edinburgh · London

This paperback edition first published by Canongate Books in 2013
First published in Great Britain in 2012 by Canongate Books Ltd, 14 High Street,
Edinburgh EH1 1TE

www.canongate.tv

1

For permissions acknowledgements, please see page 503

British Library Cataloguing-in-Publication Data
A catalogue record for this book is available on
request from the British Library

ISBN 978 0 85786 448 2

Typeset in Stone Serif by Palimpsest Book Production Ltd,
Falkirk, Stirlingshire

Printed and bound in Great Britain by Clays Ltd, St Ives plc

In memory of Howard Zinn (1922–2010)

CONTENTS

An Eminently Skippable Introduction

If you studied O-level history in the 1970s, you probably know as much as I do about the achievements of kings, queens, archbishops and generals. My poor history teacher, Mr Cosgrove, occasionally used to try to liven things up by convincing us that they were all perverts. He'd bewitch us with extracurricular tales of inventive cruelties and obscure peccadilloes. It was often worth going to his class. This will have been offset with impersonal details of irrigation systems and mining utilities, bridges and steam engines – anything that testified to Britain's industrial, commercial or military prowess.

But whether we were given the official versions of these stories or not, whether they were edited, sanitised, bowdlerised, bare facts or outright lies, something was always missing. While it may be true that history, by which I mean the one we're actually living in, is full of kings, queens and politicians – written by them or for them (they also have a popular place in film lore, I'm told) – the absent component always seemed to be just about everybody else. The further back one looked in time, the more 'everybody else' was portrayed as a homogeneous mass: the multitude, the rabble, the people, crowd extras.

In order to give faces – or, rather, voices – to these people, I felt I had to look outside the classroom and perhaps outside the country.

I began to realise that many of the real stories of Britain revealed themselves through its guilty pleasures: the music I wasn't supposed to be listening to, or the jokes I wasn't supposed to be laughing at, or the books I wasn't supposed to be reading. Chief among the latter was Howard Zinn's *A People's History of the United States*: a book obviously not directly about Britain but which had an impact on the way I view my own country and the people who are left out of the textbooks. Zinn pointed out that these are the people who brought us democracy, that it works from the bottom up. That democracy's real protagonists are the troublemakers. He applied this conviction by living his life as a rampant troublemaker himself. And in so doing he changed a great many lives, including my own.

Another troublemaker, named Anthony Arnove, worked with Howard to develop that book into a series of readings celebrating the voices of such people around the United States. Aware of my enthusiasm for their project, they asked me if I would be interested in finding a British equivalent. This is the result of Anthony's and my exuberant and resounding failure to do that. In our attempt to include everything and everybody, we will have excluded whole centuries, whole issues, political movements, sections of the populace – and entire countries. There was a millennium or two to cover but we have to sign off at page 485. So, what we are offering you is a taster's menu.

I hope that these voices – whether they be socialists, anarchists, agitators, Chartists, suffragists, Lollards or Levellers – serve as a reminder that much of what we feel entitled to today, much of what we accept as civilised or decent, began as treason. Was fought for by men and women who weren't endowed with any political power, who were hanged for it, transported, tortured or imprisoned, until eventually their ideas were adapted to, adopted and handed down to us as basic rights. These freedoms are now in our care. And unless we act on them and continue to fight for them, they will be lost more easily than they were won.

Some of these words will be familiar to you. Some have been buried for years, words that might not have been heard aloud since they were first uttered. Some are the words of people whose lives overlap with our own.

Before gathering the voices you will encounter in this book, we had the great good fortune to bring together some of our friends and performers we admire to read a number of these selections on stage at a performance in 2010 that was filmed for and later broadcast by the History Channel. (Some day, we hope a DVD of the resulting film, *The People Speak* (UK), will be available, alongside the film of the same name that Howard and Anthony made in 2009, with Matt Damon, Josh Brolin and Chris Moore (www.thepeoplespeak.com).) This was not actorly activism: often implored to shut up about matters of consequence, actors were doing what they are trained and paid to do – act, interpret the voices of others.

It will not go unnoticed that, elsewhere, I have rather conspicuously embraced our monarchic narrative – and, in my haphazard professional capacity, also rendered the voice of a king. I can only say that I took great joy in the exercise and now revel in the contrariety. As Emerson would have it, 'A foolish consistency is the hobgoblin of little minds.'

Our exercise is a capricious one. We are not offering an objective version of history. It is not an attack on the many fine history teachers or their curricula (my father is a history teacher – the finest of all). It is simply an excursion beyond Mr Cosgrove's classroom. The pieces are chosen not necessarily because of their importance or because we feel any sense of responsibility, but because we liked them. Or they sound good out loud. We suggest you try them. We've cheated a little and added and subtracted from our event for the sake of shape. But not much. Vast quantities of rich and important material have been left out. Hopefully you'll feel indignant about that and feel impelled to point it out or, even better, compile another book . . . and then another.

   Most of all, we hope you might find some inspiration in these
pages to speak out yourself, and make your own voice heard on the
issues that move you. As Howard reminds us, democracy is not a
spectator sport, and history is not something on a library shelf, but
something in which each of us has a potentially critical role.

Colin Firth
London
May 2012

THE
PEOPLE
SPEAK

Note on the Text

While trying to be as faithful as we can to original texts, we have in some cases modernised spelling and punctuation to make the texts accessible. We have indicated omitted text within our selections by ellipses. But in all cases, it is our hope that you will see what we have presented here, which we do not claim to be authoritative, as a gateway to delving deeper into the original sources.

We have imposed a very loose and necessarily arbitrary order on the selections by dividing them into five chronological periods, with extracts that give an idea of the 'headlines' of those times. In between, there are thematic chapters, gathering together material on the environment, the nations of the British Isles, religion, empire and race, money and class, labour, war and peace, gender, and sexuality. For readers who prefer a purely chronological arrangement, there is a table at the end of the book (p. 509).

By Way of a Preface

Monty Python, *Monty Python and the Holy Grail* (1975)[1]

Arthur: Old woman!

Dennis: Man!

Arthur: Man. Sorry! What knight lives in that castle over there?

Dennis: I'm thirty-seven!

Arthur: What?

Dennis: I'm thirty-seven! I'm not old.

Arthur: Well, I can't just call you 'man'.

Dennis: You could say 'Dennis'.

Arthur: I didn't know you were called 'Dennis'.

Dennis: Well, you didn't bother to find out, did you? . . . What I object to is you automatically treating me like an inferior.

Arthur: Well, I am king.

Dennis: Ah, king. Very nice. And how'd you get that, eh? By exploiting the workers. By hanging on to outdated imperialist dogma, which perpetuates the economic and social differences in our society. If there's ever going to be progress . . .

Woman: Dennis, there's some lovely filth down here. Oooh, how do you do?

Arthur: How do you do, good lady? I am Arthur, King of the Britons. Whose castle is that?

Woman: King of the *who*?

Arthur: The *Britons*.

Woman: Who are the *Britons*?

Arthur: We all are. We are all Britons, and I am your king.

Woman: I didn't know we had a king. I thought we were an autonomous collective.

Dennis: You're fooling yourself. We're living in a dictatorship. A self-perpetuating autocracy in which the working classes—

Woman: Oh, there you go, bringing class into it again.

Dennis: That's what it's all about.

Arthur: Please, good people. I am in haste. Who lives in that castle?

Woman: No one lives there.

Arthur: Then who is your lord?

Woman: We don't have a lord.

Arthur: What?

1066–1450

———

COMMONERS AND KINGS

The story of medieval Britain, as it has come down to us, is mostly the story of kings, princes and high churchmen. But the dates in our history books – 1066, 1215, 1381 – mark events that happened for everybody, not just the privileged. What kings did affected commoners, and during this period, commoners began to discover that they could sometimes influence kings. The Norman Conquest was the greatest rupture in English (and eventually Welsh, Scottish and Irish) affairs since the Viking invasions. In many ways the Conquest, carried out by descendants of 'Northmen' who had colonised a region of France, *was* another Viking invasion, and the resentments it stirred lived long in folk memory. To this period, too, subsequent fighters for freedom owe the example of Magna Carta, the first attempt to rule without a king, by Simon de Montfort and his supporters, and the sacrifice of the peasants who followed Wat Tyler.

Orderic Vitalis on the Norman Conquest
(1066)[1]

Orderic Vitalis (1075–c.1142), the child of a Norman father and an English mother, was a Benedictine monk born in Shrewsbury. His twelfth-century account of the Norman conquest was far more critical of the Normans than earlier histories, and introduced the concept of the 'Norman yoke', the oppression of ordinary Englishmen by their conquerors, which would become a rallying cry in later centuries.

But meanwhile the English were groaning under the Norman yoke, and suffering oppressions from the proud lords who ignored the king's injunctions. The petty lords who were guarding the castles oppressed all the native inhabitants of high and low degress, and heaped shameful burdens on them. For Bishop Odo and William fitzOsbern, the king's viceregents, were so swollen with pride that they would not deign to hear the reasonable plea of the English or give them impartial judgement. When their men-at-arms were guilty of plunder and rape they protected them by force, and wreaked their wrath all the more violently upon those who complained of the cruel wrongs they suffered.

And so the English groaned aloud for their lost liberty and plotted ceaselessly to find some way of shaking off a yoke that was so intolerable and unaccustomed. Some sent to Swein, king of Denmark, and urged him to lay claim to the kingdom of England, which his ancestors Swein and Cnut had won by the sword. Others fled into voluntary exile so that they might either find in banishment freedom from the power of the Normans or secure foreign help and come back to fight a war of vengeance. Some of them who were still in the flower of youth travelled into remote lands and bravely offered their arms to Alexius, emperor of Constantinople, a man of great wisdom and nobility.

_____

Liber Eliensis on Hereward the Wake
(*c.* 1070)[2]

Hereward, later known as 'the Wake', became the most famous rebel against the Norman conquest when he led a force against William I from the fen country around Ely in 1070–71. This account, written about fifty years after the event, comes from Ely Abbey.

Morcar and the Bishop of Durham, Æthelwine, and Siward surnamed Barn, and Hereward, a most energetic man, along with many others, once again made for the Isle of Ely by boat. But, on hearing of this, the king with his boatmen blocked all means of exit for them on the eastern side of the Isle, and gave orders that a causeway two miles long be built on its western side. However, when the above-mentioned men saw that they had been blockaded this way, they raised a siege-work of peat-blocks in resistance to the stratagems of the king's army, and fought for many days. And when the king learnt that Hereward, that most brave warrior, was there, and mighty men with him, he gathered an exceedingly large force to fight against them and plotted evil against the holy place and thought of destroying it, because that place was by its intrinsic nature very well fortified, centrally situated in the country, and capable of being stormed. For it repeatedly caused the kingdom wearisome trouble and now it was bringing many insidious stratagems against the new king, because those who were fleeing from evils were added to their number and came to serve as reinforcements to them.

Hereward became leader and commander-in-chief to these men

and he said to them: 'Now, brothers, be zealous for the liberty of your country and give your souls for the heritage bequeathed to you by your fathers, since we have been made trash and an object of contempt in the sight of all neighbouring kingdoms and regions, and it is better for us to die in war than look upon the evil afflictions of our race and our saints.' And the king moved his camp towards the Isle near to the River Ouse, having in his company a large number of cavalrymen and foot-soldiers, and blockaded their escape-routes on all sides, with the aim of subjugating them to his rule. And it came to pass that, when the men on the Isle had lifted up their eyes at break of day – behold! – innumerable troops were carrying a heap of wood and sand in sacks, with the aim of making the bed of the swirling river fordable, and capturing siege-work. And the Isle was besieged in the 1069th year from the incarnation of the Lord, in the third year of the reign of this same King William. And Hereward with a few men went out to obstruct them, and they were overwhelmed by him. The others fled in order to escape.

But Hereward himself returned to Ely with his men, taking with them many spoils, and his name became known to all and people talked about his battles all around the kingdom. The king, on hearing those tales, angrily ordered brave and strong men to gather together from villages and cities with a view to taking them by storm. And Hereward sent men out to spy on the army, and they reported back to him, saying that an exceedingly numerous force had gathered from all over the kingdom to take them captive and kill them without mercy. And the men who had been with him took fright and kept crying out to him, 'How shall we few be able to fight continually against an unconquered multitude?' At this Hereward rose up and, confronting them head-on, fell upon them: some he struck down, others he dispatched to death in the water, and thus, that day, he rescued his men from fear and on the Isle people rejoiced, blessing the Lord who did great things in Israel and gave those men victory. And for a few days they kept quiet.

Extracts from Magna Carta (1215)[3]

The men who imposed the Great Charter on King John in 1215 were powerful landed barons. While their programme concentrated on advancing their own case, it also contained some of the earliest expressions of rights for all 'free men', on which later generations would come to rely. The Charter even offered a measure of protection to the unfree, the 'villein' who lived in bonded service to his master.

To all free men of our kingdom we have also granted, for us and our heirs for ever, all the liberties written out below, to have and to keep for them and their heirs, of us and our heirs: . . .

For a trivial offence, a free man shall be fined only in proportion to the degree of his offence, and for a serious offence correspondingly, but not so heavily as to deprive him of his livelihood. In the same way, a merchant shall be spared his merchandise, and a villein the implements of his husbandry, if they fall upon the mercy of a royal court. None of these fines shall be imposed except by the assessment on oath of reputable men of the neighbourhood . . .

No free man shall be seized or imprisoned, or stripped of his rights or possessions, or outlawed or exiled, or deprived of his standing in any other way, nor will we proceed with force against him, or send others to do so, except by the lawful judgement of his equals or by the law of the land . . .

To no one will we sell, to no one deny or delay right or justice . . .

All these customs and liberties that we have granted shall be observed in our kingdom in so far as concerns our own relations with our subjects. Let all men of our kingdom, whether clergy or laymen, observe them similarly in their relations with their own men . . .

We will not seek to procure from anyone, either by our own efforts or those of a third party, anything by which any part of these concessions or liberties might be revoked or diminished. Should such a thing be procured, it shall be null and void and we will at no time make use of it, either ourselves or through a third party . . .

Given by our hand in the meadow that is called Runnymede, between Windsor and Staines, on the fifteenth day of June in the seventeenth year of our reign . . .

Extracts from *The Song of Lewes* (1264)[4]

The Song of Lewes was written by a Franciscan friar shortly after the victory of Simon de Montfort's forces against Henry III and his son at the Battle of Lewes. The long poem is mostly a religious celebration of the triumph of right over might, but it also sets out some very early examples of doctrines of resistance and popular rights that would come to be increasingly important in British history. During Simon's brief ascendancy, the first meeting of the House of Commons took place but, following the escape of Prince Edward, Simon and his sons were defeated and killed at the Battle of Evesham in 1265.

Now England breathes, hoping for liberty; may the grace of God grant England prosperity! The English were despised like dogs, but now they have raised their head above their beaten enemies . . .

In the year of grace one thousand two hundred and sixty-four . . . the English people endured the shock of a great fight by the castle of Lewes, when reason gave way to fury, and life was cut short by the sword . . .

May the Lord bless Simon de Montfort, and his sons and followers! Courageously risking death, they fought bravely, giving succour to the English in their wretched state. It is almost impossible to describe how downtrodden the people were, robbed of nearly all their freedoms, in effect of life itself, as they were crushed under flint-hearted rulers, just as the people of Israel suffered under Pharaoh, crying out under a tyrant's devastation. But seeing the agony of the people, God gives at last a new Matathias, and with his sons, with the zeal of a zealot for right, he takes no notice of insults or the king's fury . . .

The saying goes, 'Whatever the King wishes, is law,' but the truth is the other way round, for the law stands even if the King falls. The law is made up of truth and charity and the habits of virtue; truth, light, charity, warmth, enthusiasm catch alight; this kind of law makes crime vanish. Whatever the King legislates, let it be consistent with these principles. Otherwise the people will be miserable; and they will be betrayed if the King averts his gaze from the truth, or lacks charity, or if he does not always have the energy to do right . . .

The King should treat his people according to their due. If he doesn't, if he degrades his people and demotes them, there is no point in asking why men treated in this way disobey him. On the contrary, they would be mad not to do so.

VOICES FROM THE PEASANTS' REVOLT

Wat Tyler addresses King Richard II (15 June 1381)[5]

The Great Revolt of 1381 sprang up after repeated attempts by the government of the teenaged Richard II to levy a poll tax on the whole population. The leader of the thousands of rebels who marched on the capital for justice was Wat Tyler, from Essex, here shown in his extraordinary meeting with his sovereign at Smithfield in London. No English peasant had ever conversed with a king as Tyler did on 15 June that year.

Then the King caused a proclamation to be made that all the commons of the country who were still in London should come to Smithfield, to meet him there; and so they did. And when the King and his train had arrived there they turned into the eastern meadow in front of St Bartholomew's, which is a house of canons: and the commons arrayed themselves on the west side in great battles. At this moment the Mayor of London, William Walworth, came up, and the King bade him go to the commons, and make their chieftain come to him. And when he was summoned by the Mayor, by the name of Wat Tighler of Maidstone, he came to the King with great confidence, mounted on a little horse, that the commons might see him. And he dismounted, holding in his hand a dagger which he had taken from another man, and when he had dismounted he half bent his knee, and then took the King by the hand, and shook his arm forcibly and roughly, saying to him, 'Brother, be of good comfort and joyful, for you shall have, in the fortnight that is to come, praise from the commons even more than you have yet had, and we shall be good companions.' And the King said to Walter, 'Why will you not go back to your own country?' But the other answered, with a great oath, that neither he nor his fellows would depart until they had got their charter such as they wished to have it, and had certain points rehearsed and added to their charter, which they wished to demand. And he said in a threatening fashion that the lords of the realm would rue it bitterly if these points were not settled to their pleasure. Then the King asked him what were the points which he wished to have revised, and he should have them freely, without contradiction, written out and sealed. Thereupon the said Walter rehearsed the points which were to be demanded; and he asked that there should be no law within the realm save the law of Winchester, and that from henceforth there should be no outlawry in any process of law, and that no lord should have lordship save civilly, and that there should be equality among all people save only the King, and that the goods of Holy Church should not remain in the hands of the religious, nor of parsons and vicars, and other churchmen; but that clergy already in possession should have a sufficient sustenance from the endowments, and the rest of the goods should be divided among the people of the parish. And he demanded that there should be only one bishop in England and only one prelate, and all the lands and tenements now held by them should be confiscated, and divided among the commons, only reserving for them a reasonable sustenance. And he demanded that there should be no more villeins in England, and no serfdom or villeinage, but that all men should be free and of one condition.

John Ball, 'Until Everything Shall be in Common' (1381)[6]

The uprising's spiritual inspiration came from the radical preaching of John Ball, whom the rebels released from Maidstone jail.

My good friends, things cannot go on well in England, nor ever will until every thing shall be in common; when there shall be neither vassal nor lord, and all distinctions levelled; when the lords shall be no more masters than ourselves. How ill have they used us! and for what reason do they thus hold us in bondage? Are we not all descended from the same parents, Adam and Eve? and what can they show, or what reasons give, why they should be more the masters than ourselves? except, perhaps, in making us labour and work, for them to spend. They are clothed in velvets and rich stuffs, ornamented with ermine and other furs, while we are forced to wear poor cloth. They have wines, spices and fine bread, when we have only rye and the refuse of the straw; and if we drink, it must be water. They have handsome seats and manors, when we must brave the wind and rain in our labours in the field; but it is from our labour they have where-with to support their pomp. We are called slaves; and, if we do not perform our services, we are beaten, and we have not any sovereign to whom we can complain, or who wishes to hear us and do us justice. Let us go to the King, who is young, and remonstrate with him on our servitude, telling him we must have it otherwise, or that we shall find a remedy for it ourselves. If we wait on him in a body, all those who come under the appellation of slaves, or are held in bondage, will follow us, in the hopes of being free. When the King shall see us, we shall obtain a favourable answer, or we must then seek ourselves to amend our condition.

William Grindcobbe, 'I Shall Die in the Cause of Gaining our Liberty' (c. 1381)[7]

After the Revolt, the authorities hunted down ringleaders, including William Grindcobbe of St Albans. King Richard, who is supposed to have offered to be the rebels' captain when first confronted by them in London, had harsher words for them when they were defeated: 'You wretches, detestable on land and sea: you who seek equality with lords are unworthy to live. Give this message to your colleagues. Rustics you were and rustics you are still: you will remain in bondage not as before but incomparably harsher. For as long as we live we will strive to suppress you, and your misery will be an example in the eyes of posterity.' After his capture, Grindcobbe took a final chance to address his followers.

Fellow-citizens, grudging liberty has at long last set you free from the oppression of centuries. Only stand firm, while you have the chance, and do not have any anxiety about my punishment. If it is my lot to die, I shall die in the cause of gaining our liberty and think myself happy to be able to end my life in such martyrdom.

DISUNITED KINGDOMS

———

'OUR ENGLISH ENEMIES'

The formative relationship between England and the other nations of the British Isles is also its most complex. As well as tragedy, oppression and brutality, it has produced a rich and varied literature, unforgettable songs and compelling political drama. The histories of Wales, Scotland and Ireland in relation to England took different paths and moved at different speeds, but they have in common the fact that English rule was at various times forcibly imposed from without. Wales was the first 'Celtic' nation to be assimilated to England, beginning with the inroads made by Norman barons after the Conquest, consolidated under the medieval Marcher lordships, and formalised by Acts of Union in 1536 and 1543 during the reign of Henry VIII. Welsh attempts to regain independence were comprehensively foiled, but Wales reasserted its uniqueness long after the defeat of Owain Glyn Dwr.

In Scotland the independence so powerfully proclaimed in the 1320 Declaration of Arbroath was occasionally achieved (and may yet be again), but even after the Union of Crowns in 1603, when a Scottish king succeeded to the English throne, and the Act of Union in 1707, when Scotland was 'bought and sold for English gold', Scottish voices continued to be raised in defence of their status, and in remembrance of their past.

For the island of Ireland, the encounter with England has been the bloodiest and most protracted. Ireland was snapped up by Norman barons and 'planted' with Scottish and English settlers. The growth of Irish consciousness and the experience of English abuse have been complicated by divisions over religion, culture and language. In the twentieth century, after the achievement of independence in 1921, the focus of resentment moved to the six counties of Northern Ireland that remained under British sovereignty, where two communities battled over a tarnished inheritance, with sometimes calamitous interventions from British security forces. It is one of the ironies of history that such bitter, intractable struggles should have so often occasioned such inspired rhetoric.

The Declaration of Arbroath (6 April 1320)[1]

*Six years after his army had defeated that of the English King Edward
II at Bannockburn, Robert Bruce sent the Declaration of Arbroath to
Pope John XXII in Rome. It is a formal declaration of Scottish independence, which sets out to confirm Scotland's status as a sovereign state
and its use of military action when unjustly attacked. It was most likely
drafted at Arbroath Abbey by Bernard de Linton, Abbot of Arbroath
and Chancellor of Scotland. The Declaration was signed and bore the
seals of thirty-eight Scots lords. The Pope accepted the Scottish case.
In 1328, the English did too, sealing the Treaty of Northampton, which
formally recognised Scotland as an independent nation.*

But from these countless evils we have been set free, by the help of
Him who though He afflicts yet heals and restores, by our most tire-
less prince, King and lord, the lord Robert. He, that his people and
his heritage might be delivered out of the hands of our enemies, bore
cheerfully toil and fatigue, hunger and peril, like another Maccabaeus
or Joshua. Him, too, divine providence, the succession to his right
according to our laws and customs which we shall maintain to the
death, and the due consent and assent of us all have made our prince
and king. To him, as to the man by whom salvation has been wrought
unto our people, we are bound both by his right and by his merits
that our freedom may be still maintained, and by him, come what
may, we mean to stand.

Yet if he should give up what he has begun, seeking to make us or
our kingdom subject to the King of England or the English, we should
exert ourselves at once to drive him out as our enemy and a subverter
of his own right and ours, and make some other man who was well
able to defend us our King; for, as long as a hundred of us remain

alive, never will we on any conditions be subjected to the lordship of the English. It is in truth not for glory, nor riches, nor honours that we are fighting, but for freedom alone, which no honest man gives up but with life itself.

Owain Glyn Dwr, Letter to Henry Don (July 1403)[2]

Owain Glyn Dwr (c.1359–c.1416) sent this letter to Henry Don (another Welsh noble) in July 1403, after Owain's victory at Hyddgen. Glyn Dwr was the last native Welshman to hold the title Prince of Wales, proclaiming himself in September 1400. He led the Welsh rebellion against English overlordship over the next few years, but by 1408 he was on the run. He is last mentioned in government records in February 1416, where terms are offered for his surrender. It is thought that by this time he was already dead.

Greetings and love.

We hope that, by God's help and yours, we can deliver the Welsh race from the captivity of our English enemies, who have oppressed us and our ancestors for a long time now. You may have sensed yourself that their time draws to a close now, and it is our turn to triumph, according to God's decree from the beginning, so no one need doubt a good result, unless it is lost through sloth or strife; and because the whole Welsh race is hesitant and fears predicted reprisals against them by our enemies, we command, require and entreat that you will make sufficient preparation to come to us with the greatest force possible, to the place where you hear we are, burning our enemies, attacking them as they march; and this, with God's help, will happen shortly. And do not forget this, if you wish to have your freedom and honour in the future; and do not be surprised if you do not receive notice of the first rising, because from great fear and danger, we have had to rise without fore-warnings. Farewell, and God defend you from evil.

From *The Complaynt of Scotland* (1549)[3]

This anonymous work, probably printed in Scotland, was originally written in Middle Scots. It has been attributed to several different authors at different times – Robert Wedderburn, David Lyndsay, James Inglis – but never securely. The theme throughout is a response to the meddling of English politicians in Scottish affairs. Here, the only thing worse than English interference for a Scots peasant is his treatment by his own countrymen, who make up the other 'estates': the nobility and clergy.

I labour night and day with my hands to feed lazy and useless men, and they repay me with hunger and the sword. I sustain their life with the toil and sweat of my body, and they persecute my body with hardship, until I am become a beggar. They live through me and I die through them. Alas, oh my natural mother, you reproach and accuse me of the faults my two brothers commit daily. My two brothers, nobles and clergy, who should defend me, are more cruel to me than are my old enemies the English. They are my natural brethren, but they are my mortal enemies.

Jonathan Swift, *A Modest Proposal* (1729)[4]

Jonathan Swift (1667–1745) was the Anglo-Irish dean of St Patrick's Cathedral in Dublin. His most famous work is Gulliver's Travels *(1726), but he first gained literary fame with this savagely satirical pamphlet, which attacked the impoverishment and neglect visited on the Irish by successive English governments, and innocently proposed a gruesome 'solution'.*

It is a melancholy object to those who walk through this great town or travel in the country, when they see the streets, the roads, and cabin doors, crowded with beggars of the female sex, followed by three, four, or six children, all in rags and importuning every passenger for an alms. These mothers, instead of being able to work for their honest livelihood, are forced to employ all their time in strolling to beg sustenance for their helpless infants: who as they grow up either turn thieves for want of work, or leave their dear native country to fight for the Pretender in Spain, or sell themselves to the Barbadoes.

I think it is agreed by all parties that this prodigious number of children in the arms, or on the backs, or at the heels of their mothers, and frequently of their fathers, is in the present deplorable state of the kingdom a very great additional grievance; and, therefore, whoever could find out a fair, cheap, and easy method of making these children sound, useful members of the commonwealth would deserve so well of the public as to have his statue set up for a preserver of the nation.

But my intention is very far from being confined to provide only for the children of professed beggars; it is of a much greater extent, and shall take in the whole number of infants at a certain age who are born of parents in effect as little able to support them as those who demand our charity in the streets . . .

I am assured by our merchants, that a boy or a girl before twelve years old is no saleable commodity; and even when they come to this age they will not yield above three pounds, or three pounds and half-a-crown at most on the exchange; which cannot turn to account either to the parents or kingdom, the charge of nutriment and rags having been at least four times that value.

I shall now therefore humbly propose my own thoughts, which I hope will not be liable to the least objection.

I have been assured by a very knowing American of my acquaintance in London, that a young healthy child well nursed is at a year old a most delicious, nourishing, and wholesome food, whether stewed, roasted, baked, or boiled; and I make no doubt that it will equally serve in a fricassee or a ragout . . .

Supposing that 1,000 families in this city, would be constant customers for infants' flesh, besides others who might have it at merry meetings, particularly at weddings and christenings, I compute that Dublin would take off annually about 20,000 carcasses; and the rest of the kingdom (where probably they will be sold somewhat cheaper) the remaining 80,000.

I can think of no one objection that will possibly be raised against this proposal, unless it should be urged, that the number of people will be thereby much lessened in the kingdom. This I freely own, and 'twas indeed one principal design in offering it to the world. I desire the reader will observe, that I calculate my remedy for this one individual Kingdom of Ireland, and for no other that ever was, is, or, I think, ever can be upon Earth. Therefore let no man talk to me of other expedients: Of taxing our absentees at 5s. a pound: Of using neither clothes, nor household furniture, except what is of our own growth and manufacture: Of utterly rejecting the materials and instruments that promote foreign luxury . . .

Therefore I repeat, let no man talk to me of these and the like expedients, till he hath at least some glimpse of hope that there will ever be some hearty and sincere attempt to put them into practice.

But, as to my self, having been wearied out for many years with offering vain, idle, visionary thoughts, and at length utterly despairing of success, I fortunately fell upon this proposal, which, as it is wholly new, so it hath something solid and real, of no expence and little trouble, full in our own power, and whereby we can incur no danger in disobliging England. For this kind of commodity will not bear exportation, and flesh being of too tender a consistence, to admit a long continuance in salt, although perhaps I could name a country which would be glad to eat up our whole nation without it.

After all, I am not so violently bent upon my own opinion as to reject any offer proposed by wise men, which shall be found equally innocent, cheap, easy, and effectual. But before something of that kind shall be advanced in contradiction to my scheme, and offering a better, I desire the author or authors will be pleased maturely to consider two points. First, as things now stand, how they will be able to find food and raiment for 100,000 useless mouths and backs. And secondly, there being a round million of creatures in human figure throughout this kingdom, whose whole subsistence put into a common stock would leave them in debt 2,000,0000 pounds sterling, adding those who are beggars by profession to the bulk of farmers, cottagers, and labourers, with their wives and children who are beggars in effect: I desire those politicians who dislike my overture, and may perhaps be so bold as to attempt an answer, that they will first ask the parents of these mortals, whether they would not at this day think it a great happiness to have been sold for food, at a year old in the manner I prescribe, and thereby have avoided such a perpetual scene of misfortunes as they have since gone through by the oppression of landlords, the impossibility of paying rent without money or trade, the want of common sustenance, with neither house nor clothes to cover them from the inclemencies of the weather, and the most inevitable prospect of entailing the like or greater miseries upon their breed for ever.

I profess, in the sincerity of my heart, that I have not the least personal interest in endeavouring to promote this necessary work, having no other motive than the public good of my country, by advancing our trade, providing for infants, relieving the poor, and giving some pleasure to the rich. I have no children by which I can propose to get a single penny; the youngest being nine years old, and my wife past child-bearing.

Theobald Wolfe Tone, Speech from the Dock (10 November 1798)[5]

Theobald Wolfe Tone (1763–98) was a leader of the United Irishmen, who worked to unite Catholics and Protestants against British rule in Ireland. He spent two years as an officer in the French army of Napoleon and, in September 1798, took part in an invasion of Ireland, which was comprehensively thwarted by the British. He expected a death sentence, but when his request to be executed by firing squad was rejected (he was to be hanged), Tone took his own life, cutting his throat in his cell. Here is an excerpt from his trial in 1798.

Wolfe Tone: I mean not to give the court any useless trouble, and wish to spare them the idle task of examining witnesses. I admit all the facts alleged, and only request leave to read an address which I have prepared for this occasion.

Judge: I must warn the prisoner that, in acknowledging those *facts*, he admits, to his prejudice, that he has acted *traitorously* against his Majesty. Is such his intention?

Tone: Stripping this charge of the technicality of its terms, it means, I presume, by the word *traitorously*, that I have been found in arms against the soldiers of the King in my native country. I admit this accusation in its most extended sense, and request again to explain to the court the reasons and motives of my conduct . . .

Mr President and Gentlemen of the Court Martial, I mean not to give you the trouble of bringing judicial proof to convict me legally of having acted in hostility to the government of his Britannic Majesty in Ireland. I admit the fact. From my earliest youth I have regarded the connection between Great Britain and Ireland as the curse of the Irish nation, and felt convinced that, whilst it lasted, this country could never be free nor happy. My mind has been confirmed in this opinion by the experience of every succeeding year, and the conclusions which I have drawn from every fact before my eyes. In consequence, I was determined to employ all the powers which my individual efforts could move, in order to separate the two countries . . .

I have laboured to create a people in Ireland by raising three millions of my countrymen to the rank of citizens. I have laboured to abolish the infernal spirit of religious persecution, by uniting the Catholics and Dissenters . . .

I have courted poverty; I have left a beloved wife unprotected, and children whom I adored fatherless. After such a sacrifice, in a cause which I have always – conscientiously considered – as the cause of justice and freedom – it is no great effort, at this day, to add the sacrifice of my life . . .

I am aware of the fate which awaits me, and scorn equally the tone of complaint and that of supplication. As to the connection between this country and Great Britain, I repeat it – all that has been imputed to me (words, writings, and actions), I here deliberately avow. I have spoken and acted with reflection and on principle, and am ready to meet the consequences. Whatever be the sentence of the court, I am prepared for it. Its members will surely discharge their duty; I shall take care not to be wanting in mine.

Robert Emmet, Speech from the Dock
(19 September 1803)[6]

Robert Emmet (1778–1803) was one of the leaders of the re-formed United Irishmen after Wolfe Tone's death. In 1803, he took part in a rising in Dublin, which, despite detailed preparations, failed when its leaders were forced to act before the agreed time. Emmet was captured in Dublin, and his trial, conviction, sentencing and execution took place over only two days. The speech he made from the dock was taken up by Irish nationalists as a rallying call in the struggle for independence.

Robert Emmet: I am asked what have I to say why sentence of death should not be pronounced on me, according to law. I have nothing to say that can alter your predetermination, nor that it will become me to say, with any view to the mitigation of that sentence which you are to pronounce, and I must abide by . . . I only wish, and that is the utmost that I expect, that your lordships may suffer it to float down your memories untainted by the foul breath of prejudice, until it finds some more hospitable harbour . . . I wish that my memory and name may animate those who survive me, while I look down with complacency on the destruction of that perfidious government . . . which displays its power over man, as over the beasts of the forest, which sets man upon his brother, and lifts his hand, in the name of God, against the throat of his fellow who believes or doubts a little more or a little less than the government standard, a government which is steeled to barbarity by the cries of the orphans, and the tears of the widows it has made.

Lord Norbury: . . . the mean and wicked enthusiasts who feel as you do, [are] not equal to the accomplishment of their wild designs.

Emmet: I appeal to the immaculate God, I swear by the Throne of Heaven, before which I must shortly appear, by the blood of the murdered patriots who have gone before me, that my conduct has been, through all this peril, and through all my purposes, governed only by the conviction which I have uttered, and by no other view than that of the emancipation of my country from the superinhuman oppression under which she has so long and too patiently travailed; and I confidently hope that, wild and chimerical as it may appear, there is still union and strength in Ireland to accomplish this noblest of enterprises . . .

Norbury: [I] do not sit [here] to hear treason . . .

Emmet: My lords, it may be a part of the system of angry justice to bow a man's mind by humiliation to the purposed ignominy of the scaffold; but worse to me than the purposed shame, or the scaffold's terrors, would be the shame of such foul and unfounded imputations as have been laid against me in this court. You, my lord, are a judge; I am the supposed culprit. I am a man; you are a man also. By a revolution of power we might change places, though we never could change characters. If I stand at the bar of this court, and dare not vindicate my character, what a farce is your justice! Does the sentence of death, which your unhallowed policy inflicts on my body, condemn my tongue to silence and my reputation to reproach? Your executioner may abridge the period of my existence; but while I exist I shall not forbear to vindicate my character and motives from your aspersions . . .

I have been charged with that importance in the emancipation of my country, as to be considered . . . 'the life and blood of the conspiracy'. You do me honour over much . . . There are men engaged in this conspiracy who are not only superior to me, but even to your own conceptions of yourself, my lord – and who would think themselves disgraced by shaking your blood-stained hand . . .

What, my lord, shall you tell me, on the passage to the scaffold, which that tyranny (of which you are only the intermediary executioner) has erected for my murder, that I am accountable for all the blood that has and will be shed in this struggle? If it were possible to collect all the innocent blood that you have shed in your unhallowed ministry in one great reservoir your lordship might swim in it . . .

Norbury: [The prisoner's] sentiments and language [disgrace your] family . . .

Emmet: My lords, you are impatient for the sacrifice. The blood which you seek is not congealed by the artificial terrors which surround your victim, it circulates warmly and unruffled through the channels which God created for noble purposes, but which you are now bent to destroy, for purposes so grievous that they cry to heaven. Be yet patient! . . . I have but one request to ask at my departure from this world, it is – THE CHARITY OF ITS SILENCE. Let no man write my epitaph; let me rest in obscurity and peace; and my tomb remain uninscribed, and my memory in oblivion, until other times and other men can do justice to my character. When my country takes her place among the nations of the earth, *then* and *not till then*, let my epitaph be written.

Rev. John Blackwell, Eisteddfod Address in Beaumaris (19 August 1832)[7]

John Blackwell (1797–1840) was the son of a Welsh collier. His love of books, from an early age, and prizewinning essays and poems brought him to the attention of a group of gentlemen who paid for his formal education. He took a degree at Jesus College, Oxford, and was ordained. He was recognised as a gifted poet in the Welsh language, and carried off numerous prizes at eisteddfods. At Beaumaris Eisteddfod, he set out his defence of the importance of literature in his native language.

But an ancient Briton feels that he condescends rather low in arguing this point respecting the cultivation of his native literature upon utilitarian principles merely. Every nation has some distinct peculiarities. We have ours; and as long as the cultivation of these does not make us worse subjects or worse men, there can be no harm in maintaining them. Is not nationality, and even national vanity, very frequently the root of the patriotism: and if the maintenance of national peculiarity be allowed to any people, it must be allowed to ourselves. The mountaineers of every country are notoriously attached to the customs and even prejudices of their fathers. There throbs a heart and there beats a pulse in the mountains, far more warm and bounding than are to be found in the plains. This may be owing in some measure to physical situation: the light and shade, and mossy summit, the deep blue and clear sky, the curtain of white and trailing mist which evening draws round the couch of the mountain spirit, the dancing stream, the bounding waterfall; all these scenic witcheries must and do give a spring and elasticity to the soul not to be found in the lowlands. But this is not all: in these peculiarities, also, we find traditions which were fastened first and deepest upon our infant memories. In them, we find proof of the antiquity and distinctness of our race. The origin of the Cimbric nation and of the Cimbric language eludes the keenest glance of the antiquary . . . Other languages can be traced to their origins, other nations may have grown old, and her bards and minstrels were bald and blind with years, before history had ever commenced her chronicles of the Western World. And that which has not only its maturity, but its old age, beyond the perceptions of men and recollections of time, must be immortal.

Letters from the Rebecca Riots (16–19 June 1843)[8]

The Rebecca Riots were a series of night-time raids on tollgates in Wales. The name 'Rebecca Riots' comes from Genesis 24:60, 'And they blessed Rebekah, and said unto her, Thou art our sister, be thou the mother of thousands of millions, and let thy seed possess the gate of those which hate them.' The tollgates were tangible representations of a tax and Poor Law system that many Welsh farmers felt was unfair. The rioters, also known as Rebecca's Daughters or Rebeccaites, would dress themselves in women's clothing and blacken their faces before attacking the tollgates. 'Rebecca' would occasionally send threatening letters to landlords whose rents were thought to be too high.

June 16th, 1843

I have had a complaint about you from your parishioners that you oppress them with tithes, and now I give you warning to return that poor man's Bible which you sold in lieu of tithe, and be willing to take from those who have not paid, and those who have paid a big tithe as they call it, I warn you to send back to them all that they have paid this year, more than they paid before, and that without delay so that I shall know from them Friday in Newcastle. If you will not do as I ask you, next Monday night I and some of my children will visit you, perhaps three or four hundred, and remember to put everything ready. I will break two of your limbs one leg and one arm and I will put all your goods on fire and remember not to deceive yourself the above thing is as certain to take place as there is life in your body. D. S. A. is not the thing awful that a minister of the Gospel as you call yourself behaves in such a barbarous fashion. Alas! Alas! Alas! Alas!

'REBECCA'

June 19th, 1843

As thy soul and ours live, if thou comest not out, thou and the poor that are in thy care, before Wednesday next, we are determined to destroy everything; and woe to thy own body, for *WE* will take care that thou shalt not flee! (Beware!) We trifle no longer.

'REBECCA (L.S.)

'MISS BROWN (L.S.)'

June 19th, 1843

Reverend Sir,

I, with one of my daughters, have recently been on a journey to Aberayron, and amongst other things have heard many things respecting you, namely, that you have built a schoolroom in the upper part of the parish, and that you have been very dishonest in the erection of it, and that you promised a free school for the people, but that you have converted it into a church, and that you get 80 [pounds] by the year for serving it. Now, if this is true, you may give the money back, every halfpenny of it, otherwise if you do not, I with 500 or 600 of my daughters will come and visit you, and destroy your property five times to the value of it, and make you a subject of scorn and reproach throughout the whole neighbourhood. You know that I care nothing about the gates, and you shall be like them exactly, because I am averse to every tyranny and oppression.

'REBECCA AND HER DAUGHTERS'

———————————

Nicholas M. Cummins, The Irish Famine
(17 December 1846)[9]

*Among the disasters that inspired the struggle for Irish independence
was the Great Famine. Potatoes were the staple food of the Irish
poor, and when a blight on the crop caused it to fail in 1845, people
began to starve in their hundreds of thousands. During the Irish
famine, England exported wheat for sale, and other crops and live-
stock were available to feed the people, but without money, they
were unable to pay for them. John Mitchel, an Irish nationalist leader,
wrote afterwards, 'The Almighty, indeed, sent the potato blight. But
the English created the Famine.' In December 1846, Nicholas
Cummins, a justice of the peace in Cork, wrote a damning letter to
the Duke of Wellington, which was also published in* The Times,
*exposing these crimes. It is estimated that the Famine killed at least
a million Irish people, while at least a million more emigrated.*

My Lord Duke,

Without apology or preface, I presume so far to trespass on
your Grace as to state to you, and, by the use of your illustrious
name, to present to the British Public the following statement
of what *I have myself seen within the last three days*: –

Having for many years been intimately connected with the
western portion of the County of Cork, and possessing some
small property there, I thought it right personally to investigate
the truth of the several lamentable accounts which had reached
me of the appalling state of misery to which that part of the
county was reduced. I accordingly went on the 15th inst. to
Skibbereen, and . . . I shall state simply what I saw there . . . Being
aware that I should have to witness scenes of frightful hunger,
I provided myself with as much bread as five men could carry,
and on reaching the spot I was surprised to find the wretched
hamlet apparently deserted. I entered some of the hovels to

ascertain the cause, and the scenes that presented themselves were such as no tongue or pen can convey the slightest idea of. In the first six famished and ghastly skeletons, to all appearance dead, were huddled in a corner on some filthy straw, their sole covering what seemed a ragged horse-cloth, and their wretched legs hanging about, naked above the knees. I approached in horror, and found by a low moaning they were alive; *they were in fever* – four children, a woman, and what had once been a man. It is impossible to go through the details – suffice it to say that in a few minutes I was surrounded by a least 200 of such phantoms, such frightful spectres as no words can describe. By far the greater number were delirious, either from famine or from fever. Their demonic yells are still ringing in my ears, and their horrible images are fixed upon my brain. My heart sickens at the recital, but I must go on. In another case – decency would forbid what follows, but it must be told – my clothes were nearly torn off in my endeavours to escape from the throng of pestilence around, when my neck-cloth was seized from behind by a grip which compelled me to turn. I found myself grasped by a woman with an infant, *just born*, in her arms, and the remains of a filthy sack across her loins – the sole covering of herself and babe . . .

A mother, herself in fever, was seen the same day to drag out the corpse of her child, a girl about twelve, perfectly naked, and leave it half covered with stones . . .

To what purpose should I multiply such cases? If these be not sufficient, neither would they hear who have the power to send relief, and do not. Let them, however, believe and tremble that they shall one day hear the Judge of all the Earth pronounce their tremendous doom, with the addition, 'I hungered and ye gave Me no meat; thirsty and ye gave Me no drink; naked and ye clothed Me not.'. . .

[I]n the name of starving thousands, I implore you, break the frigid and flimsy chain of official etiquette, and save the land of your birth.

Captain John McClure, Speech from the Dock (25 May 1867)[10]

John McClure was an Irish-American, born in New York State in 1846; he fought for the Union in the Civil War. With others of his countrymen he took part in the Fenian rising in Ireland of March 1867, leading the attack and capture of Knockadoon coastguard station in County Cork. When the rising failed, he was captured and tried before the Special Commission at Cork. He was sentenced to death, later commuted to penal servitude for life.

My lords – In answer to the question as to why the sentence of the court should not now be passed upon me, I would desire to make a few remarks in relation to my late exertions in behalf of the suffering people of this country, in aiding them in their earnest endeavours to attain the independence of their native land. Although not born upon the soil of Ireland, my parents were, and from history, and tradition, and fireside relations, I became conversant with the country's history from my earliest childhood, and as the human race will ever possess these God-like qualities which inspire mankind with sympathy for the suffering, a desire to aid poor Ireland to rise from her moral degradation took possession of me. I do not now wish to say to what I assign the failure of that enterprise with which are associated my well-meant acts for this persecuted land. I feel fully satisfied of the righteousness of my every act in connexion with the late revolutionary movement in this country, being actuated by a holy desire to assist in the emancipation of an enslaved and generous people. I derive more pleasure from having done the act than from any other event that has occurred to me during my eventful but youthful life. I wish it to be distinctly understood here, standing as I do perhaps on the brink of an early grave, that I am no filibuster or freebooter, and that I had no personal object or inclination to gain anything in coming to this country. I came solely through love of Ireland and sympathy for her people. If I have forfeited my life, I am ready to abide the issue. If my exertions on behalf of a distressed people be a crime, I am willing to pay the penalty, knowing, as I do, that what I have done was in behalf of a people whose cause is just – a people who will appreciate and honour a man, although he may not be a countryman of their own – still a man who is willing to suffer in defence of that divine, that American principle – the right of self-government. I would wish to tender to my learned and eloquent counsel, Mr Heron and Mr Waters, and to my solicitor, Mr Collins, my sincere and heartfelt thanks for the able manner in which they have conducted my defence. And now, my lords, I trust I will meet in a becoming manner the penalty which it is now the duty of your lordship to pronounce upon me. I have nothing more to say.

Pádraig Pearse, Eulogy for Jeremiah O'Donovan Rossa (1 August 1915)[11]

The Fenian leader Jeremiah O'Donovan Rossa (1831–1915) devoted his life to the struggle for Irish independence. He spent six years in prison in England, as well as spending time in exile in the United States, where he died. His body was brought back to Ireland, and at his funeral in Dublin in 1915, Pádraig Pearse delivered this eulogy. With this speech Pearse, who had only recently become an active rebel himself, helped galvanise the spirit that led to the Easter Rising the following year.

It has seemed right, before we turn away from this place in which we have laid the mortal remains of O'Donovan Rossa, that one among us should, in the name of all, speak the praise of that valiant man, and endeavour to formulate the thought and the hope that are in us as we stand around his grave.

The clear true eyes of this man almost alone in his day visioned Ireland as we of today would surely have her: not free merely, but Gaelic as well; not Gaelic merely, but free as well.

In a closer spiritual communion with him now than ever before or perhaps ever again, in a spiritual communion with those of his day, living and dead, who suffered with him in English prisons, in communion of spirit too with our own dear comrades who suffer in English prisons today, and speaking on their behalf as well as our own, we pledge to Ireland our love, and we pledge to English rule in Ireland our hate.

This is a place of peace, sacred to the dead, where men should speak with all charity and with all restraint; but I hold it a Christian thing, as O'Donovan Rossa held it, to hate evil, to hate untruth, to hate oppression and, hating them, to strive to overthrow them.

Our foes are strong and wise and wary . . . They think that they have pacified Ireland. They think that they have purchased half of us and intimidated the other half. They think that they have foreseen everything, think that they have provided against everything; but the fools, the fools, the fools! – they have left us our Fenian dead, and while Ireland holds these graves, Ireland unfree shall never be at peace!

————————————

Lewis Grassic Gibbon, *Sunset Song* (1932)[12]

Lewis Grassic Gibbon was the pseudonym of the Scottish writer James Leslie Mitchell (1901–35). Sunset Song was the first volume in his Scots Quair trilogy, following the fortunes of Chris Guthrie, a woman torn between attachment to her Scottish peasant roots and a desire to expand her mind and explore the world away from the Highlands. Gibbon evokes the cycle of attachment to and displacement from the land that was the Scottish peasant experience from the time of the Highland Clearances in the eighteenth century. In this passage, the village minister speaks at the unveiling of a memorial to Ewan Tavendale, Chris's husband, killed with three comrades in the First World War.

In the sunset of an age and an epoch we may write that for epitaph of the men who were of it. They went quiet and brave from the lands they loved, though seldom of that love might they speak, it was not in them to tell in words of the earth that moved and lived and abided, their life and enduring love. And who knows at the last what memories of it were with them, the springs and the winters of this land and all the sounds and scents of it that had once been theirs, deep, and a passion of their blood and spirit, those four who died in France? With them we may say there died a thing older than themselves, these were the Last of the Peasants, the last of the Old Scots folk. A new generation comes up that will know them not, except as a memory in a song, they pass with the things that seemed good to them, with loves and desires that grow dim and alien in the days to be. It was the old Scotland that perished then, and we may believe that never again will the old speech and the old songs, the old curses and the old benedictions, rise but with alien effort to our lips. The last of the peasants, those four that you knew, took that with them to the darkness and the quietness of the places where they sleep. And the land changes, their parks and their steadings are a desolation where the sheep are pastured, we are told that great machines come soon to till the land, and the great herds come to feed on it, the crofter is gone, the man with the house and the steading of his own and the land closer to his heart than the flesh of his body. Nothing, it has been said, is true but change, nothing abides, and here in Kinraddie where we watch the building of those little prides and those little fortunes on the ruins of the little farms we must give heed that these also do not abide, that a new spirit shall come to the land with the greater herd and the great machines. For greed of place and possession and great estate those four had little heed, the kindness of friends and the warmth of toil and the peace of rest – they asked no more from God or man, and no less would they endure. So, lest we shame them, let us believe that the new oppressions and foolish greeds are no more than mists that pass. They died for a world that is past, these men, but they did not die for this that we seem to inherit. Beyond it and us there shines a greater hope and a newer world, undreamt when these four died. But need we doubt which side the battle they would range themselves did they live today, need we doubt the answer they cry to us even now, the four of them, from the places of the sunset?

And then, as folk stood dumbfounded, this was just sheer politics, plain what he meant, the Highlandman McIvor tuned up his pipes and began to step slow round the stone circle by Blawearie Loch, slow and quiet, and folk watched him, the dark was near, it lifted your hair and was eerie and uncanny, the 'Flowers of the Forest' as he played it . . .

It rose and rose and wept and cried, that crying for the men that fell in battle, and there was Kirsty Strachan weeping quietly and others with her, and the young ploughmen they stood with glum, white faces, they'd no understanding or caring, it was something that vexed and tore at them, it belonged to times they had no knowing of.

He fair could play, the piper, he tore at your heart marching there with the tune leaping up the moor and echoing across the loch. Folk said that Chris Tavendale alone shed never a tear, she stood quiet, holding her boy by the hand, looking down on Blawearie's fields till the playing was over. And syne folk saw that the dark had come and began to stream down the hill, leaving her there, some were uncertain and looked them back. But they saw the minister was standing behind her, waiting for her, they'd the last of the light with them up there, and maybe they didn't need it or heed it, you can do without the day if you've a lamp quiet-lighted and kind in your heart.

Bernadette Devlin, Speech in Draperstown (13 April 1969)[13]

Bernadette Devlin stood in Mid Ulster for election to Parliament at Westminster at the age of twenty-one. She represented the Nationalist Independent Unity Party and, unusually, promised to take her seat in Westminster if she was successful, rather than abstain from the 'illegitimate' parliament. This speech was given on the eve of the election, which she won, to be returned as the youngest woman ever to serve as a British MP.

It's time that we decided, Catholic and Protestant, that our enemy is not the ordinary working man who differs in religion. Our enemy is the Ulster Unionist Party, and particularly the Ulster Unionist Party's insurance policy, the Loyal Orange Order. This vicious sectarian bully in the name of civil and religious liberty has divided this community into Catholic and Protestant. And the reason they divided us into two communities, was that if they could keep the ordinary man divided from his neighbour, we would have no strength to fight against our common enemy. The only time the people of this country ever could make a stand against the ruling minority that's kept us in oppression, was when Catholic and Protestant did stand together, was when Wolfe Tone took up the fight of the Irish people, when people like Tone and Emmet fought for the rights of the ordinary Irish people. There was no talk then about who was Catholic and who was Protestant;

the talk was who had money and who had none, and who was oppressed and who was oppressing. And in 1969 it's exactly the same old story. Only we have allowed the Unionists to win for far too long. We have allowed them to divide the ordinary working people. It is time that we stood up now and demanded the kind of society to which we, the people of this country, have a right.

Silvester Gordon Boswell, Address to Travellers on Appleby Hill (1967)[14]

Romany Gypsies have for centuries existed on the margins of British society. Silvester Gordon Boswell (1895–1977) belonged to a well-known extended Gypsy family. As he reached old age, he decided to use his prominent position to set up an organisation that would give Gypsies a voice. This speech was given at Appleby Horse Fair, the annual event in Cumbria at which thousands of Gypsies and travellers gather. The National Gypsy Education Council was formed in 1970, later renamed as the Gypsy Council, which represents Gypsies throughout Britain.

I'm not an educated man, but I'm a man of experience and I do know the way these things are done. Some of us have been talking this over – the travelling people who are on this ground – and we say and agree that we are willing to form this Travelling Traders' Association (suppose that will be the name). You may not see the results right away, in the first year . . . but there's got to be a beginning to all things, and this would go – it's a great idea. Because you are driven from pillar to post, out of one district to another and you have no rest on the road. There is a remedy for our people; we are British subjects; we are entitled to justice. Other minorities in this country, even those who come from abroad, are looked after and their human rights respected, but you've got nothing, nor nobody to care, nor no place to live, nor even to rest. You are technically a people 'of no fixed abode'. I have told the authorities and all concerned that you have the abodes, but you've nowhere to put them.

But you're doing nothing. I am an old man: I'm seventy-three years old. If it doesn't come by my day, it'll come in the time of some of you youngsters. And what I would like to see is some camps up and down the country. I'd like to see three types: a permanent camp where old people can go and stop and rest and be left in peace; a transit camp where you can come from one town to another and pay to go in and travel the country from North to South if you wish; and camps where you cans stop in decent comfortable conditions in the winter months. I want to know if you are going to remain silent like we have done all these years – like my grandfather, and great-grandfather who put his tent on this very hill in Appleby with packhorse and rods. We are in 1967, and with these facilities when we get them, I'm not thinking about you men. I'm thinking about your little children. The time has come when they should all be able to go to school and get some education. We all hear plenty in the news these days about education, new schools, bigger colleges, new universities, not one mention of the Romany, the gypsy, the traveller in regard to all this – and it's up to you to get it for your children too. They are the people I'm concerned with. That's all I've got to say. The rest is up to you.

Silvester Gordon Boswell, *The Book of Boswell: Autobiography of a Gypsy* (1970)[15]

In his memoir, Silvester Gordon Boswell recalled the nomadic lifestyle of the traditional Gypsy, and the difficulties of coping with the

encroachments of modern life. Boswell died in 1977; later, his son
turned his scrap-metal yard into the Gordon Boswell Romany
Museum.

The next stopping place I remember was Welshpool. It was considered a good market town for horses and ponies, and hawking and all that. But we were moving all over. Aberystwyth – where we saw more ponies on the mountains than we ever saw in our lives – Abergavenny and Hereford. And then we left the West Country: we moved right over to the London area: to such places as Wanstead Flats, Woolwich Common, Blackheath and Romford.

And there everything was free.

Old England was a wonderful place then, but now it seems to me like a police state. Wherever you go nowadays you're doing wrong, or you're attempting to do wrong, or you're about to do wrong and what then? When we've done all these wrong things we are just going where we should go, where we have a right to be. People have commandeered our common lands to build on. They've taken our by-ways, our lovely lanes away from us. And where are these people that's left on the roads today? They've got nowhere to go. You can't travel the roads. The traffic is too strong. So we've got to revert back to tin cans and iron trailers and that is everything on wheels. When we have an animal – and I still have them and I like them – we have to put it in a trailer to take it home to avoid accidents. It's all restrictions. Old England isn't like it was when I was a child.

———————————

Luke Kelly, 'For What Died the Sons of Róisín?' (c. 1970)[16]

Róisín, the Irish for Rosaleen, 'Little Rose', is a name used, following the poet James Clarence Mangan, to personify Ireland (''Tis you shall have the golden throne,/'Tis you shall reign, shall reign alone, My Dark Rosaleen!'). In this song, Luke Kelly of the Dubliners revisits the spirit of Nationalist rebellion, and asks what the sacrifice has been for.

For what died the sons of Róisín?
Was it fame?
For what died the sons of Róisín?
Was it fame?
For what flowed Ireland's blood,
And rivers that began when Brian chased the Dane,
And did not cease nor has not ceased,
With the brave sons of '16,
For what died the sons of Róisín?
Was it fame?

For what died the sons of Róisín?
Was it greed?
For what died the sons of Róisín?
Was it greed?
Was it greed that drove Wolfe Tone
To a martyr's death
In a cell of cold wet stone,
Will German, French or Dutch
Inscribe the Epitaph of Emmett
When we've sold enough of Ireland
To be but strangers in it?

For what died the sons of Róisín?
Was it greed?

To whom do we owe our allegiance today?
To whom do we owe our allegiance today?
To those brave men who fought and died
That Róisín live again with pride?
Her sons at home to work and sing,
Her youth to dance and make her valleys ring,
Or her faceless men, who for Mark and Dollar,
Betray her to the highest bidder?
To whom do we owe our allegiance today?

For what suffer our patriots today?
For what suffer our patriots today?
They have a language problem,
So they say,
How to write 'No Trespass'
Must grieve their heart full sore,
We got rid of one strange language
Now we're faced with many, many more,
For what suffer our patriots today?

Pauline M. Recounts Bloody Sunday
(30 January 1972)[17]

On 30 January 1972, thirteen Northern Irish civilians on a civil-rights march were shot by a detachment of British Army para-troopers. Bloody Sunday, as the day soon came to be known, did much to escalate the Troubles, sealing mistrust and hatred between the different communities in Northern Ireland. A judicial inquiry held by Lord Widgery shortly afterwards did nothing to ease the tensions. In 2010, after the most costly inquiry in British legal history, a new report, by Lord Saville, concluded that the 'unjustifiable firing' of 1Para, 'a force with a reputation for using excessive physical violence', was 'the cause of those deaths and injuries'. The prime minister, David Cameron, announced to the House of Commons that 'The conclusions of this report are absolutely clear. There is no doubt, there is nothing equivocal, there are no ambiguities. What happened on Bloody Sunday was both unjustified and unjustifiable. It was wrong.'

My husband and I started the march at Creggan which proceeded peacefully until we reached the alleyway beside Quinn's fish shop. At that moment the troops started firing tear gas (at close range). Everyone turned but we were blocked. Panic ensued and the army took advantage of this to use red dye from water cannon. At that moment Bernadette Devlin appeared and told everyone not to panic. We were forced down the alleyway. Now we were at waste ground and I was violently sick. It took me about twenty–twenty-five minutes to recover.

Then the Saracens were driven in along Rossville Street at an awful speed, towards the crowds which turned and ran. At that time rubber bullets were fired. We ran all the way to the High Flats. A man came round with a megaphone and told us to go to Free Derry Corner for the meeting.

We got to Free Derry Corner. The speakers were assembled on the platform and Miss Devlin said something to the effect, 'We will now have our meeting here peacefully if the British Army will allow us.'

The army then opened fire with live ammunition into the crowd to our consternation, without any provocation, as if under direct command of the CO.

My husband pushed me to the ground and lay over me. A young lad of about twelve lay on top of my head. The army continued to fire at the crowd on the ground. About twenty to thirty rounds were fired – then a lull (short).

We crawled to St Columb's Wells still under fire, and saw bodies on the ground at the barricade in front of Glenfada Park (directly in front of flats). All this time the army were firing at random towards the crowd. We ran from St Columb's Wells and found army firing from the Walls. We continued running to Stanley's Walk, and by this time the army had ceased fire.

At this point we were told that there were two dead and a boy shot through the cheek.

We decided to return home as quickly as possible.

I am an English Protestant living in Derry and was appalled by the brutality used indiscriminately by the British Army so wish to voice my protest.

Fo Halloo, Editorial on Isle of Man Tax Dodgers (4 June 1973)[18]

During the 1970s, the government of the Isle of Man introduced low rates of income tax and removed top rates altogether. The advent of wealthy mainlanders was not universally welcomed by the islanders. Fo Halloo, Manx for 'underground', was a Marxist group committed to resisting the takeover of the island by high finance, and by Britain.

As Tynwald Day approaches, Manxmen would do well to consider whether this ceremony any longer has any significance, when our claims to independence and national integrity have been reduced to mere pretence. Debased by successive governments, it remains today as little more than a commercialised tourist attraction, with Tynwald's puppets acting out the characters. A day of national bondage, when

Manxmen meet, not to celebrate their independence, but to pay homage to the British Crown and the almighty pound! The government's policy of selling the Island to the highest bidder has given financial control of Mann to a small band of capitalist manipulators, who invariably place profit before people. Our only natural resource, the land, is also rapidly falling under complete non-Manx control. Manxmen have been stripped of their pride and self-respect and forced to join the rat-race, chasing the proverbial 'quick buck' as an only means of survival.

The Isle of Man has become a pawn in the game of international finance, with the full backing of the Manx government! If this is allowed to continue, and if the number of immigrant tax-dodgers continues to spiral, then we can foresee only one eventuality . . . Full integration with the United Kingdom!

This would mean nothing to our present financial masters, as they will only move on to fresh pastures. But for the Isle of Man and genuine Manx people, such a move can only spell disaster.

Fo Halloo believes that the time has come for the Manxmen to fight back or for ever hold their peace!

We must fight the speculators; we must fight the developers; we must fight the manipulators; most of all we must fight the government. We must grasp every opportunity, however small, to prevent the ultimate takeover!

THE MANX CROSS IS BURNING! GET OFF YOUR KNEES NOW . . . GIVE TYNWALD DAY SOME MEANING. THE ANSWER LIES IN YOUR HANDS . . . STOP THE SELL-OUT TODAY!

Bobby Sands, Prison Diary (1–2 March 1981)[19]

Bobby Sands (1954–81) joined the Provisional IRA after he was driven from his birthplace in north Belfast, and his job there, by Loyalist paramilitaries. He served two terms in jail, the second in 1976 for his part in bombing a furniture store, for which he was sentenced to fourteen years' imprisonment at Long Kesh, later known as the Maze. For five years, he took part in the so-called dirty protest to win recognition for IRA inmates as political prisoners, not criminals. In March 1981, he began a hunger strike and, in the same month, succeeded in being elected as MP for Fermanagh-South Tyrone. The British government refused to concede to the hunger strikers' demands, and Sands died on 5 May 1981, after sixty-six days of fasting. A hundred thousand people attended his funeral. Nine more hunger strikers died. Most of their demands were subsequently granted.

Sunday, 1st

I am standing on the threshold of another trembling world. May God have mercy on my soul.

My heart is very sore because I know that I have broken my poor mother's heart, and my home is struck with unbearable anxiety. But I have considered all the arguments and tried every means to avoid what has become the unavoidable: it has been forced upon me and my comrades by four and a half years of stark inhumanity.

I am a political prisoner. I am a political prisoner because I am a casualty of a perennial war that is being fought between the oppressed Irish people and an alien, oppressive, unwanted regime that refuses to withdraw from our land.

I believe and stand by the God-given right of the Irish nation to sovereign independence, and the right of any Irishman or woman to assert this right in armed revolution. That is why I am incarcerated, naked and tortured.

Foremost in my tortured mind is the thought that there can never be peace in Ireland until the foreign, oppressive British presence is removed, leaving all the Irish people as a unit to control their own affairs and determine their own destinies as a sovereign people, free in mind and body, separate and distinct physically, culturally and economically.

I believe I am but another of those wretched Irishmen born of a risen generation with a deeply rooted and unquenchable desire for freedom. I am dying not just to attempt to end the barbarity of H Block, or to gain the rightful recognition of a political prisoner, but primarily because what is lost in here is lost for the Republic and those wretched oppressed whom I am deeply proud to know as the 'risen people'.

There is no sensation today, no novelty that 27 October [the starting date of the original seven-man hunger-strike] brought. The usual Screws were not working. The slobbers and would-be despots no doubt will be back again tomorrow, bright and early.

I wrote some more notes to the girls in Armagh today. There is so much I would like to say about them, about their courage, determination and unquenchable spirit of resistance. They are to be what Countess Markievicz, Anne Devlin, Mary Ann McCracken, Marie MacSwiney, Betsy Gray, and those other Irish heroines are to us all. And, of course, I think of Ann Parker, Laura Crawford, Rosemary Bleakeley, and I'm ashamed to say I cannot remember all their sacred names.

Mass was solemn, the lads as ever brilliant. I ate the statutory weekly bit of fruit last night. As fate had it, it was an orange, and the final irony, it was bitter. The food is being left at the door. My portions, as expected, are quite larger than usual, or those which my cell-mate Malachy is getting.

Monday, 2nd

Much to the distaste of the Screws we ended the no-wash protest this morning. We moved to B wing, which was allegedly clean.

We have shown considerable tolerance today. Men are being searched coming back from the toilet. At one point men were waiting three hours to get out to the toilet, and only four or five got washed, which typifies the eagerness of the Screws to have us off the no-wash. There is a lot of petty vindictiveness from them.

I saw the doctor and I'm 64 kgs. I've no problems.

The priest, Fr John Murphy, was in tonight. We had a short talk. I heard that my mother spoke at a parade in Belfast yesterday and that Marcella cried. It gave me heart. I'm not worried about the numbers of the crowds. I was very annoyed last night when I heard Bishop Daly's statement [issued on Sunday, condemning the hunger-strike]. Again he is applying his double set of moral standards. He seems to forget that the people who murdered those innocent Irishmen on Derry's Bloody Sunday are still as ever among us; and he knows perhaps better than anyone what has and is taking place in H Block.

He understands why men are being tortured here – the reason for criminalisation. What makes it so disgusting, I believe, is that he agrees with that underlying reason. Only once has he spoken out, of the beatings and inhumanity that are common-place in H Block.

I once read an editorial, in late '78, following the then Archbishop Ó Fiaich's 'sewer pipes of Calcutta' statement. It said it was to the everlasting shame of the Irish people that the archbishop had to, and I paraphrase, stir the moral conscience of the people on the H Block issue. A lot of time has passed since then, a lot of torture, in fact the following year was the worst we experienced.

Now I wonder who will stir the Cardinal's moral conscience . . .

Bear witness to both right and wrong, stand up and speak out. But don't we know that what has to be said is 'political', and it's not that these people don't want to become involved in politics, it's simply that their politics are different, that is, British.

My dear friend Tomboy's father died today. I was terribly annoyed, and it has upset me.

I received several notes from my family and friends. I have only read the one from my mother – it was what I needed. She has regained her fighting spirit – I am happy now.

My old friend Seanna [Walsh, a fellow blanket man] has also written.

I have an idea for a poem, perhaps tomorrow I will try to put it together.

Every time I feel down I think of Armagh, and James Connolly. They can never take those thoughts away from me.

Gwyn Alf Williams, *The Dragon Has Two Tongues* (1985)[20]

In 1985, HTV Wales produced The Dragon Has Two Tongues – A History of the Welsh, *a thirteen-part series broadcast on Channel 4. The programme was presented by the Welsh journalist Wynford Vaughan-Thomas (1908–87) and the historian Professor Gwyn Alf Williams (1925–95), of the University of Wales, Cardiff. They disputed their national history throughout. Vaughan-Thomas called Williams a 'Marxist magpie', who 'looked back into the past to select the bits that fit into the pattern of the future'. Williams responded that Vaughan-Thomas made the past into 'marmalade', and gave his own view of Welsh history.*

Today it looks to me as if the Welsh people have been declared redundant, as redundant as this pit, which after two hundred years is now a museum. This is a museum. Wales is being turned into a land of museums. Now what is shovelling into these . . . museums? History, they say. History. What is history?

We've been around for fifteen hundred years but our history has been an endless sequence of brutal ruptures, break after break after break, and with every break the Welsh people have been transformed. So far we have survived, but we've survived in crisis. For fifteen hundred years the Welsh people . . . have lived in a permanent state of emergency.

Welsh history has been nothing but change. The history of the Welsh has been a series of shocks inflicted on them from outside – shocks, breaks, ruptures. The Welsh in their history have suffered from so many ruptures, it's a wonder they haven't succumbed to multiple spiritual hernia.

FREEDOM OF WORSHIP

—————

'TOUCHING OUR FAITH'

Britain's political history has on many occasions been subsumed into its religious history. A Protestant Reformation was not what Henry VIII originally intended when he began his unilateral break from Rome in pursuit of his divorce from Catherine of Aragon. But the results of that momentous rupture were keenly felt across the country, and the so-called Pilgrimage of Grace was one consequence. As the Reformation took hold, ordinary people found that their faith could expose them to a martyr's terrible fate.

Even after the Reformation, with Protestantism secure in Britain, those Protestants outside the Established Church or Roman Catholics, who were allowed a measure of 'toleration', found themselves the target of official prejudice of the sort mocked by Daniel Defoe, or popular prejudice of the sort described by Ignatius Sancho.

Not everybody in Britain was a Christian, of whatever stripe. Queen Elizabeth I is recorded as complaining about 'the great number of negroes and blackamoores . . . carried into this realm . . . most of them are infidels having no understanding of Christ or his gospel'. This is an early indication of a Muslim presence, which would be greatly expanded hundreds of years later. A Jewish presence predated even that, as Jews are known to have come to Britain in the wake of the Norman Conquest; in 1290 Edward I forcibly expelled them, and they were not readmitted until 1656, under Cromwell.

While religious fervour was leading some to fight and die, there are occasional records of those brave enough to profess no faith at all. Atheism emerged as a reasoned philosophical position in Britain only in the eighteenth century, but the record of Matthew Hamont shows that some were being accused of it before then. While George Holyoake's trial as an atheist in 1842 was the last of its kind, the reaction of the people of Basingstoke to the perception of religious interference in everyday living is a sign of another view of the place of religion in British society.

By the twentieth century, religion might have seemed to have permanently slipped from its prime place in public affairs, but the events of the early twenty-first century ensured that attention was sharply refocused on one religion in particular – Islam.

THE PILGRIMAGE OF GRACE

The Examination of Nicholas Leche (1536)[1]

The popular uprising against Henry VIII's reforms to the Church that came to be known as the Pilgrimage of Grace began largely 'by means of the priests', as one rebel wrote later. One of the early rebels, Nicholas Leche, a priest of Belchford, took the initiative in raising the commons around Horncastle, Lincolnshire. After his arrest, this examination seems to show that the gentry abandoned their traditional role of suppressing rebellion, and actually assumed control. But it is likely, too, that Leche did his utmost to dissociate himself from the leadership of the rising. Nonetheless, he was tried for treason and executed at Tyburn in March 1537.

The gentlemen were always together, commonly a mile from the commons. What they did he knows not, but at length they brought forth certain articles of their griefs, of which one was that the King should not remit the subsidy, and another that he should let the abbeys stand, which articles George Stanes openly proclaimed in the field, and the sheriff and he, about Langwith field, said to the commons, 'Masters ye see that in all the time we have been absent from you we have not been idle. How like you these articles? If they please you say Yea. If not, ye shall have them amended.' The commons them held up their hands and said with a loud voice, 'We like them very well.'

Amongst other articles there declared, Mr Sheriff and other gentlemen said, 'Masters, there is a statute made whereby all persons be restrained to make their wills upon their lands, for now the eldest son must have all his father's lands, and no person to the payment of his debt, neither to the advancement of his daughters' marriages, can do nothing with their lands, nor cannot give his youngest son any lands.' Before this he thinks that the commons knew not what that Act of Uses meant. Nevertheless, when that article was read to them, they agreed to it as to all other articles devised by the gentlemen. He thinks all the exterior acts of the gentlemen amongst the commons were done willingly, for he saw them as diligent to set forward every matter as the commons were. And further, during the whole time of the insurrection, not one of them persuaded the people to desist or showed them it was high treason. Otherwise he believes in his conscience they would not have gone forward, for all the people with whom he had intelligence thought they had not offended the King, as the gentlemen caused proclamations to be made in his name. He thinks the gentlemen might have stayed the people of Horncastle, for at the beginning his parishioners went forward among the rebels only by command of the gentlemen. The gentlemen were first harnessed of all others, and commanded the commons to prepare themselves harness, and he believes the commons expected to have redress of grievances by way of supplication to the King.

The Pontefract Articles (2–4 December 1536)[2]

The rising spread to Yorkshire, and found a leader in a York lawyer, Robert Aske. It was Aske who devised an oath for the rebels, which cast them as 'pilgrims' against Church reform and the dissolution of the monasteries. At Pontefract, Aske and the pilgrims presented their demands to the King's commander in the field, the Duke of Norfolk.

1. The first touching our faith to have the heresies of Luther, Wycliffe, Huss, Melanchthon, Oecolampadius, Bucer, *Confessio Germaniae*, *Apologia Malancthionis*, The Works of Tyndale, of Barnes, of Marshall,

Rastell, St German [in Englisse] and such other heresies of Anabaptist, clearly within this realm to be annulled and destroyed.

2. The second to have the supreme head of the church touching *cura animarum* to be reserved unto the see of Rome as before it was accustomed to be, and to have the consecration of the bishops from him without any first fruits or pension to him to be paid out of this realm or else a pension reasonable for the outward defense of our faith.

3. Item we humbly beseech our most dread sovereign lord that the Lady Mary may be made legitimate and the former statute therein annulled, for the danger of the title that might incur to the crown of Scotland, that to be by parliament.

4. Item to have the abbeys suppressed to be restored unto their houses, lands and goods.

5. Item to have the tenth and first fruits clearly discharged of the same, unless the clergy will of themselves grant a rent charge in generality to the augmentation of the crown.

6 Item to have the Friar Observants restored unto their houses again.

7. Item to have the heretics, bishops and temporal of their sect, to have condign punishment by fire or such other, or else to try their quarrel with us and our party takers in battle.

8. Item to have the Lord Cromwell, the lord chancellor, and the Sir Richard Riche, knight, to have condign punishment, as the subverters of the good laws of this realm and maintainers of the false sect of those heretics and the first inventors and bringers in of them.

9. Item that the lands in Westmorland, Cumberland, Kendall, Dent, Sedbergh, Furness and the abbey lands in Mashamshire, Kirkbyshire, Nidderdale may be by tenant right, and the lord to have at every change, two years rent for gressum and no more, according to the grant now made by the lords to the commons there under their seal; and this to be done by act of parliament.

10. Item the statutes of handguns and crossbows to be repealed and the penalties thereof, unless it be in the king's forests or parks for the killing of his grace's deer red and fallow . . .

12. Item reformation for the election of knights of shire and burgesses, and for the uses among the Lords in the parliament house after their ancient custom.

13. Item statute for enclosures and intakes to be put in execution and that all intakes and enclosures since 4 Henry VII to be pulled down except mountains, forest and parks . . .

18. Item the privileges and rights of the church to be confirmed by act of parliament and priests not to suffer by sword unless he be disgraced, a man to be saved by his book, sanctuary to save a man for all causes in extreme need, and the church for 40 days and further according to the laws as they were used in the beginning of this king's days . . .

22. Item that the common laws may have place as was used in the beginning of your grace's reign and that all injunctions may be clearly decided and not to be granted unless the matter be heard and determined in the chancery.

The Examination of Robert Aske (1537)[3]

Aske was originally pardoned, but later arrested and examined about every aspect of his part in the Pilgrimage during his imprisonment in the Tower in April and May 1537. This is an extract from his replies to his interrogators, showing his belief that the suppression of the monasteries cut deep into the spiritual, aesthetic and economic life of the people of Tudor England. Aske was returned to York in July, where he was hanged.

[First] to the statut of subpressions, he dyd gruge ayenst the same and so did al the holl contrey, because the abbeys in the north partes gaf great almons to pour men and laudable servyd God; in which partes of laid dais they had but small comforth by gostly teching. And by occasion of the said suppression in the devyn service of almightie God is much minished, greate nombre of messes unsaid, and the blessed consecracion of the sacrement now not used and showed in thos places, to the distreas of the faith, and sperituall comforth to man soull, the temple of God russed and pulled down, the ornamentes and releques of the church of God unreverent used, the townes and sepulcres of honourable and noble men pulled down and sold, non hospitalitie now in thos places kept, but the fermers for the most parte lettes and taverns our the fermes of the same houses to other fermers, for lucre and advauntage to them selfes. And the profites of theis abbeys yerly goith out of the contrey to the Kinges highnes, so that in short space little money, by occasion of the said yerly rentes, tenementes and furst frutes, should be left in the said contrey, in consideracion of the absens of the Kinges highnes in thos partes, want of his lawes and the frequentacion of mechandisse. Also diverse and many of the said abbeys wer in the montaignes and desert places, wher the people be rud of condyccions and not well taught the law of God, and when the said abbeys stud, the said people not only had worldly refresshing in their bodies but also sperituall refuge both by gostly-liffing of them and also by speritual informacion, and preching; and many ther tenauntes wert her feed servauntes to them, and serving men, wel socored by abbeys; and now not only theis tenauntes and servauntes wantes refresshing ther, both of meat, cloth and wages, and knowith not now wher to have any liffing, but also strangers and baggers of corne . . .

Also the abbeys was on of the bewties of this realme to al men and strangers passing threw the same; also al gentilmen much socored in their nedes with money, their yong sons ther socored, and in nonries ther daughters brought up in vertue; and also ther evidenses and mony left to the usses of infants in abbeys handes, alwas sure ther; and such abbeys as wer ner the danger of see bankes, great mayntenours of see wals and dykes, mayntenours and bildres of briges and heghwais, and such other thinges for the comyn welth.

John Foxe, 'The Martyrdom and Suffering of Cicelie Ormes, Burnt at Norwich for the Testimonie and Witnes of Christes Gospell' (1557)[4]

The Reformation in England created martyrs on both sides of the religious divide. Cicelie Ormes (1525–57) was one of the victims of the Catholic Mary I recorded by John Foxe in his compendium of men and women who died for the new faith, known as Foxe's Book of Martyrs *(1563).*

About the xxiii. day of the said moneth of September, next after the other aboue mencioned, suffered at Norwich Cicelie Ormes, wyfe of Edmond Ormes worstedweuer, dwelling in S. Laurence parysh in Norwich. She being of thage of xxxii. yeres or more, was taken at the death of Simon Miller and Elisabeth Cooper aboue mentioned, in a place called Lollardes pyt, without byshops gate, at the said Norwiche, for that she said she wold pledge them of the same cuppe that they dranke on. For so saing, one maister Corbet of Sprowson, by Norwich, toke her, & sent her to the Chauncellor. when she came before him the Chauncellor asked her, what she said to the sacrament of Christes body. And she saide, she did beleue, that it was the sacramet of the body of Christ. Yea said e Chaucellor, but what is that e priest holdeth ouer his head? She answered him & said, it is bread: and if ye make it any better, it is worse. wherby at those wordes the Chaucellor sent her to the bishops prison, to the keper, called master Fellow, with many thretning & hote wordes, as a man being in a great chafe.

Then the xxiii. day of Iulye she was called before the Chauncellor again, who sat in iudgement wt maister Brigges & others. but she was most examined of Brigges. The Chauncellor offered her if she wold go to the church, & kepe her tongue, she shoulde be at libertie, and beleue as she would. But she told him she wold not consent to his wicked desire therein, do with her what he would: for if she shold, she said God wold surely plage her. The Chauncellor told her, he had shewed more fauour to her, then euer he did to any, & that he was loth to condene her, considering t she was an ignorat, vnlearned & folish woman. But she not weying his wordes, tolde him if he did, he shold not be so desirous of her sinful flesh, as she wold (by Gods grace) be cotent to geue it in so good a quarell. Then rose he & red the bloudy sentence of condenatio against her, & so deliuered her to e secular power, e sherifs of the city, maister T. Sutterton, & master Leonard Sutterto brethre, who immediatly caried her to e Gildhal in Norw. wher she remained vntil her death. This Cicely Ormes was a very simple woman, but yet zelous in the lordes cause, being borne in East Deram, & was ther e daughter of one T. Hawnd, tailor. She was taken e v. day of Iuly, & did for a xii. moneth before she was take, recat. but neuer after was she quiet in conscience, vntil she was vtterly driue from all their Poperie. betwene the time she recanted, & that she was taken, she had gotten a letter made, to geue to the Chaucellor, to let him know, that she repented her recantation from the bottom of her hart, & wold neuer do the like again while she liued: but before she exhibited her bill, she was take & sent to prison, as is before said. She was burnt the first day of Sept. betwene 7. & 8. of the clock in the morning, the said two sherifes being there, & of people to the nober of 200. When she came to the stake, she kneled down & made her praiers to God: that being done, she rose vp, & said. good people, I beleue in God the father, God the sonne, & God e holy ghost, thre persons & one God. This doe I not, nor will I recat, but I recat vtterly from the bottom of my hart, the doings of the Pope of Rome, & all his popish priests & shauelings. I vtterly refuse, & neuer wil haue to doe wt the again by gods grace. And good people, I wold you should not report of me, & I beleue to be saued in that I offer my selfe here vnto the death for the Lordes cause, but I beleue onely to be saued by the death of Christes passion: and this my death is & shalbe a witnes of my faith vnto you al here of the same. Good people: as many of you as beleue as I beleue, pray for me. then she came to the stake & laid her hand on it, & said: welcome the crosse of Christ, which being done, she loking on her hande, & seing it blacked with the stake, wiped it vpon her smock. for she was burnt at e same stake, that Symon Myller & Elisabeth Coper was burned at. The after she had touched it with her hand, she cam & kissed it, & said: welcom the swete cross of Christ, & so gaue her selfe to be bound therto. After the tormentors had kindled the fire to her, she said. My soule dothe magnifie the Lord, and my spirite reioyce in God my sauiour, and in so saying she set her hads together right against her brest, casting her eyes & head upward, and so stode heauing vp her hands by litle and litle, tyll the very synowes of her armes brast in sonder, & then they fel: but she yelded her life vnto the lord as quietly as she had been in a slomber, or as one feling no pain: so wonderfull did the Lord worke wt her. his name therfore be praysed for euer more, Amen.

Matthew Hamont, Trial for Heresy (1579)[5]

Matthew Hamont or Hamond of Hethersett, Norfolk, a wheelwright, was one of a handful of men burnt at the stake in Norwich during the reign of Queen Elizabeth I for heresy. These men were associated at the time with the extreme Protestant sect of Anabaptism, seen as a direct threat to both Church and secular authority. Some versions of Hamont's belief, however, seem those of an atheist, while others sound more like a forerunner of Unitarianism, the belief that only God, not Jesus Christ or the Holy Ghost, is divine.

1. That the New Testament and Gospel of Christ, are but mere foolishness, a story of man, or rather a mere fable.

2. That man is restored to grace by God's meer mercy, without the mean of Christ's blood, death, or passion.

3. That Christ is not God, nor the saviour of the world, but a meer man, a sinfull man, and an abominable idoll.

4. That all they that worship him are abominable idolaters, and that Christ did not rise again from death to life by the power of his godhead, neither that he ascended into heaven.

5. That the Holy Ghost is not God, neither is there any such Holy Ghost.

6. That baptism is not necessary in the church of God, neither the use of the sacrament of the body and blood of Christ.

For which he was burnt in the Castle Ditch on the 20th of May.

———————

John Mush, *The Life of Margaret Clitherow* (1586)[6]

*During the reign of Elizabeth I, an attempt was made to 'settle' the
English Reformation. Francis Bacon said of the Queen that her intention 'was not to make windows in men's souls'. But more ostentatious
defiance of Protestant norms was not tolerated. Margaret Clitherow
(1552/3–86) suffered most dreadfully for her adherence to her beliefs,
and her refusal to hide them. Her life was written up by the priest
she had sheltered, John Mush, and published in 1619.*

The judge, yet desirous to shift the thorn out of his own conscience
into the whole country, and falsely thinking that if the jury found
her guilty his hand should be clear from her blood, said again, 'Good
woman, I pray you put yourself to the country. There is no evidence
but a boy against you, and whatsoever they do, yet we may show
mercy afterward.' The martyr still refused. Then Rhodes [another
judge] said, 'Why stand we all the day about this naughty, wilful
woman. Let us despatch her.' Then the judge said 'If you will not put
yourself to the country, this must be – your judgment:

'You must return from whence you came, and there, in the lowest
part of the prison, be stripped naked, laid down, your back upon the
ground, and as much weight laid upon you as you are able to bear,
and so to continue three days without meat or drink, except a little
barleys bread and puddle water, and the third day to be pressed to
death, your hands and feet tied to posts, and a sharp stone under
your back.'

The martyr, standing without any fear or change of countenance,
mildly said, 'If this judgment be according to your own conscience,
I pray God send you better judgment before Him. I thank God heartily
for this.' 'Nay,' said the judge, 'I do it according to law, and tell you
this must be your judgment, unless you put yourself to be tried by
the country. Consider of it, you have husband and children to care

for; cast not yourself away.' The martyr answered, 'I would to God my husband and children might suffer with me for so good a cause.' Upon which words the heretics reported after, that she would have hanged her husband and children if she could.

After this sentence pronounced, the judge asked her once again, 'How say you, Margaret Clitherow? Are you content to put yourself to the trial of the country? Although we have given sentence against you according to the law, yet will we show mercy, if you will do anything yourself.' The martyr, lifting up her eyes towards heaven, said with a cheerful countenance, 'God be thanked all that He shall send me shall be welcome; I am not worthy of so good a death as this is: I have deserved death for mine offences to God, but not for anything that I am accused of.'

Daniel Defoe, *The Shortest Way with the Dissenters: Or, Proposals for the Establishment of the Church* (1702)[7]

Daniel Defoe (1660?–1731), who had fought with the Duke of Monmouth in his rebellion of 1685, was a Dissenter himself; that is, a Protestant who worshipped separately from the Church of England, and was consequently barred from many aspects of public life. In this satire, he takes the part of a High Tory churchman to suggest that the only solution to the problem of Dissent was mass murder. The essay, published in the first year of Queen Anne's reign, landed Defoe in prison, and in the pillory.

SIR ROGER L'ESTRANGE tells us a story in his collection of Fables, of the Cock and the Horses. The Cock was gotten to roost in the stable among the horses; and there being no racks or other conveniences for him, it seems, he was forced to roost upon the ground. The horses jostling about for room, and putting the Cock in danger of his life, he gives them this grave advice, 'Pray, Gentlefolks! let us stand still! for fear we should tread upon one another!'

There are some people in the World, who, now they are unperched, and reduced to an equality with other people, and under strong and very just apprehensions of being further treated as they deserve, begin, with ESOP'S Cock, to preach up Peace and Union and the Christian duty of Moderation; forgetting that, when they had the Power in their hands, those Graces were strangers in their gates!

It is now, near fourteen years, (1688–1702), that the glory and peace of the purest and most flourishing Church in the world has been eclipsed, buffeted, and disturbed by a sort of men, whom, GOD in His Providence, has suffered to insult over her, and bring her down. These have been the days of her humiliation and tribulation. She has borne with an invincible patience, the reproach of the wicked: and GOD has at last heard her prayers, and delivered her from the oppression of the stranger.

And now, they find their Day is over! their power gone! and the throne of this nation possessed by a Royal, English, true, and ever constant member of, and friend to, the Church of England! Now, they find that they are in danger of the Church of England's just resentments! Now, they cry out, 'Peace!' 'Union!' 'Forbearance!' and 'Charity!': as if the Church had not too long harboured her enemies under her wing! and nourished the viperous blood, till they hiss and fly in the face of the Mother that cherished them!

No, Gentlemen! the time of mercy is past! your Day of Grace is over! you should have practised peace, and moderation, and charity, if you expected any yourselves!

We have heard none of this lesson, for fourteen years past! We have been huffed and bullied with your Act of Toleration! You have told us, you are the Church established by Law, as well as others! have set up your canting Synagogues at our Church doors! and the Church and her members have been loaded with reproaches, with Oaths, Associations, Abjurations, and what not! Where has been the mercy, the forbearance, the charity you have shewn to tender consciences of the Church of England that could not take Oaths as fast as you made them? that having sworn allegiance to their lawful and rightful King, could not dispense with that Oath, their King being still alive; and swear to your new hodge podge of a Dutch Government? These have been turned out of their Livings, and they and their families left to starve! their estates double taxed to carry on a war they had no hand in, and you got nothing by!

What account can you give of the multitudes you have forced to comply, against their consciences, with your new sophistical Politics, who, like New Converts in France, sin because they cannot starve? And now the tables are turned upon you; you must not be persecuted! it is not a Christian spirit!

You have butchered one King! deposed another King! and made a Mock King of a third! and yet, you could have the face to expect to be employed and trusted by the fourth! Anybody that did not know the temper of your Party, would stand amazed at the impudence as well as the folly to think of it!

Your management of your Dutch Monarch, who you reduced to a mere King of Cl[ub]s, is enough to give any future Princes such an idea of your principles, as to warn them sufficiently from coming into your clutches; and, GOD be thanked! the Queen is out of your hands! Knows you! and will have a care of you!

There is no doubt but the Supreme Authority of a nation has in itself, a Power, and a right to that Power, to execute the Laws upon any part of that nation it governs. The execution of the known Laws of the land, and that with but a gentle hand neither, was all that the Fanatical Party of this land have ever called Persecution. This they have magnified to a height, that the sufferings of the Huguenots in France were not to be compared with them. Now to execute the known Laws of a nation upon those who transgress them, after having first been voluntarily consenting to the making of those Laws, can never be called Persecution, but Justice. But Justice is always Violence to the party offending! for every man is innocent in his own eyes.

The first execution of the Laws against Dissenters in England, was in the days of King JAMES I.; and what did it amount to? Truly, the worst they suffered was, at their own request, to let them go to New England, and erect a new colony; and give them great privileges, grants, and suitable powers; keep them under protection, and defend them against all invaders; and receive no taxes or revenue from them!

This was the cruelty of the Church of England! Fatal lenity! It was the ruin of that excellent Prince, King CHARLES I. Had King JAMES sent all the Puritans in England away to the West Indies; we had been a national unmixed Church! the Church of England had been kept undivided and entire!

To requite the lenity of the Father, they take up arms against the Son, conquer, pursue, take, imprison, and at last put to death the Anointed of GOD, and destroy the very Being and Nature of Government: setting up a sordid Impostor, who had neither title to govern, nor understanding to manage, but supplied that want, with power, bloody and desperate counsels and craft, without conscience.

Had not King JAMES I. withheld the full execution of the Laws: had he given them strict justice, he had cleared the nation of them! And the consequences had been plain; his son had never been murdered by them, nor the Monarchy overwhelmed. It was too much mercy shewn them that was the ruin of his posterity, and the ruin of the nation's peace. One would think the Dissenters should not have the face to believe, that we are to be wheedled and canted into Peace and Toleration, when they know that they have once requited us with a Civil War, and once with an intolerable and unrighteous Persecution, for our former civility.

Nay, to encourage us to be easy with them, it is apparent that they never had the upper hand of the Church, but they treated her with all the severity, with all the reproach and contempt as was possible! What Peace and what Mercy did they shew the loyal Gentry of the Church of England, in the time of their triumphant Commonwealth? How did they put all the Gentry of England to ransom, whether they were actually in arms for the King or not! making people compound for their estates, and starve their families! How did they treat the Clergy of the Church of England! sequester the Ministers! devour the patrimony of the Church, and divide the spoil, by sharing the Church lands among their soldiers, and turning her Clergy out to starve! Just such measures as they have meted, should be measured to them again!

Charity and Love is the known doctrine of the Church of England, and it is plain She has put it in practice towards the Dissenters, even beyond what they ought, till She has been wanting to herself, and in effect unkind to her own sons: particularly, in the too much lenity of King JAMES I., mentioned before. Had he so rooted the Puritans from the face of the land, which he had an opportunity early to have done; they had not had the power to vex the Church as since they have done.

Ignatius Sancho, Letter on the Gordon Riots (6 June 1780)[8]

Ignatius Sancho (1729–80) arrived in England from the West Indies as the orphaned two-year-old son of slaves, after his mother died of disease and his father committed suicide. A chance encounter with the Duke of Montagu led eventually to Sancho's freedom, and to employment as a servant, before he acquired enough money to set himself up in business as a grocer in Westminster. His shop was near the Houses of Parliament, and he witnessed the Gordon Riots, which began outside Parliament in June 1780. Lord George Gordon had put himself at the head of an anti-Catholic mob by protesting against a bill for Catholic 'relief'. Sectarian riots lasted for several days; dozens of buildings were set alight, Newgate Prison was thrown open and, after martial law was declared, more than two hundred rioters were shot dead. Sancho gave his views of the events in a letter to the banker John Spink.

In the midst of the most cruel and ridiculous confusion, I am now set down to give you a very imperfect sketch of the maddest people that the maddest times were ever plagued with. – The public prints have informed you (without doubt) of last Friday's transactions; – the insanity of L[or]d G[eorge] G[ordon] and the worse than Negro barbarity of the populace; – the burnings and devastations of each night you will also see in the prints: – This day, by consent, was set apart for the farther consideration of the wished-for repeal; – the people (who had their proper cue from his lordship) assembled by ten o'clock in the morning. – Lord N[orth], who had been up in council at home till four in the morning, got to the house before eleven, just a quarter of an hour before the associators reached Palace-yard: – but, I should tell you, in council there was a deputation from all parties; – the S[helburne] party were for prosecuting L[or]d G[eorge], and leaving him at large; – the At[torne]y G[enera]l laughed at the idea, and declared it was doing just nothing; – the M[inistr]y were for his expulsion, and so dropping him gently into insignificancy; – that was thought wrong, as he would still be industrious in mischief; – the R[ockingha]m party, I should suppose, you will think counselled best, which is, this day to expel him the house – commit him to the Tower – and then prosecute him at leisure – by which means he will lose the opportunity of getting a seat in the next parliament – and have decent leisure to repent him of the heavy evils he has occasioned. – There is at this present moment at least a hundred thousand poor, miserable, ragged rabble, from twelve to sixty years of age, with blue cockades in their hats – besides half as many women and children – all parading the streets – the bridge – the park – ready for any and every mischief. – Gracious God! what's the matter now? I was obliged to leave off – the shouts of the mob – the horrid clashing of swords – and the clutter of a multitude in swiftest motion – drew me to the door – when every one in the street was employed in shutting up shop. – It is now just five o'clock – the ballad-singers are exhausting their musical talents – with the downfall of Popery, S[andwic]h, and N[ort]h. – Lord S[andwic]h narrowly escaped with life about an hour since; – the mob seized his chariot going to the house, broke his glasses, and, in struggling to get his lordship out, they somehow have cut his face; – the guards flew to his assistance – the light-horse scowered the road, got his chariot, escorted him from the coffee-house, where he had fled for protection, to his carriage, and guarded him bleeding very fast home. This – this – is liberty! genuine British liberty! – This instant about two thousand liberty boys are swearing and swaggering by with large sticks – thus armed in hopes of meeting with the Irish chairmen and labourers – all the guards are out – and all the horse; – the poor fellows are just worn out for want of rest – having been on duty ever since Friday. – Thank heaven, it rains; may it increase, so as to send these deluded wretches safe to their homes, their families, and wives! About two this afternoon, a large party took it into their heads to visit the King and Queen, and entered the Park for that purpose – but found the guard too numerous to be forced, and after some useless attempts gave it up. – It is reported, the House will either be prorogued, or Parliament dissolved, this evening – as it is in vain to think of attending any business while this anarchy lasts.

I cannot but felicitate you, my good friend, upon the happy distance you are placed from our scene of confusion. – May foul Discord and her cursed train never nearer approach your blessed abode! Tell Mrs S[pink], her good heart would ache, did she see the anxiety, the woe, in the faces of mothers, wives, and sweethearts, each equally anxious for the object of their wishes, the beloved of their hearts. Mrs Sancho and self both cordially join in love and gratitude, and every good wish – crowned with the peace of God, which passeth all understanding, &c.

I am, dear Sir,

Yours ever by inclination,

IGN. SANCHO

Postscript

The Sardinian ambassador offered 500 guineas to the rabble, to save a painting of our Saviour from the flames, and 1,000 guineas not to destroy an exceeding fine organ: the gentry told him, they would burn him if they could get at him, and destroyed the picture and organ directly. – I am not sorry I was born in Afric. – I shall tire you, I fear – and, if I cannot get a frank, make you pay dear for bad news. – There is about a thousand mad men, armed with clubs, bludgeons, and crows, just now set off for Newgate, to liberate, they say, their honest comrades. – I wish they do not some of them lose their lives or liberty before morning. It is thought by many who discern deeply, that there is more at the bottom of this business than merely the repeal of an act – which has as yet produced no bad consequences, and perhaps never might. – I am forced to own, that I am for universal toleration. Let us convert by our example, and conquer by our meekness and brotherly love!

Eight o'clock. Lord G[eorge] G[ordon] has this moment announced to my Lords the mob – that the act shall be repealed this evening: – upon this, they gave a hundred cheers – took the horses from his hackney-coach – and rolled him full jollily away: – they are huzzaing now ready to crack their throats.

Huzzah.

William Blake, Selections (1793 to 1804)[9]

For more than thirty years, in his writing and his art, William Blake (1757–1827) elaborated a personal world view that was at once politically radical and religiously unique. In this selection from his verse, there are examples of his engagement with some of the tumultuous events of his lifetime, and the great inequalities he saw all around him, as well as his visionary response to them.

'America' (1793)

Let the slave grinding at the mill, run out into the field;
Let him look up into the heavens and laugh in the bright air;
Let the enchained soul shut up in darkness and in sighing,
Whose face has never seen a smile in thirty weary years,
Rise and look out – his chains are loose, his dungeon doors
    are open.
And let his wife and children return from the oppressors
    scourge –
They look behind at every step and believe it is a dream,
Singing, 'The sun has left his blackness, and has found a
    fresher morning
And the fair moon rejoices in the clear and cloudless night;
For empire is no more, and now the lion and wolf shall cease.'

Preface to *Milton* (1804)

Rouse up, O young men of the new age! Set your foreheads against the ignorant hirelings! For we have hirelings in the camp, the court, and the university, who would, if they could, for ever depress mental and prolong corporeal war. Painters, on you I call! Sculptors! Architects! Suffer not the fashionable fools to depress your powers by the prices they pretend to give for contemptible works or the

expensive advertising boasts that they make of such works; believe
Christ & his apostles that there is a class of men whose whole delight
is in destroying. We do not want either Greek or Roman models if
we are but just & true to our own imaginations, those worlds of
eternity in which we shall live for ever – in Jesus our Lord.

Preface to Book Two of *Jerusalem* (1804)

Spectre of Albion, warlike fiend,
In clouds of blood & ruin rolled,
I here reclaim thee as my own,
My selfhood, Satan, armed in gold.

Is this thy soft family love,
Thy cruel patriarchal pride
Planting thy family alone
Destroying all the world beside?

A man's worst enemies are those
Of his own house & family;
And he who makes his law a curse,
By his own law shall surely die.

In my Exchanges every land
Shall walk, & mine in every land,
Mutual shall build Jerusalem:
Both heart in heart & hand in hand.

———————————

Grace Aguilar, *History of the Jews in England* (1847)[10]

Grace Aguilar (1816–47) was a novelist born in Hackney, the daughter of a Sephardic merchant. She has been described as 'one of the few Victorian writers for a popular readership who attempted to defend Judaism and argue for religious tolerance'.[11] Her questioning of the stereotyping of Jews in England came ten years after Charles Dickens had introduced the character of Fagin to the reading public.

In the reign of George II., 1740, another act of parliament passed, recognising all Jews who resided in the American colonies, or had served as mariners during the war two years in British ships, as 'natural born subjects, without taking the sacrament'. Thirteen years afterwards, the naturalisation bill passed, but was repealed the year following, according to the petitions of the city of London, and other English towns. Since then the Jews have gradually gained ground in social consideration; but all attempts to place them on an exact equality with other British subjects of all religious denominations, by removing the disabilities which, the more fondly they cling to the land of their adoption, the more heavily oppress them, have as yet been unavailing.

By the multitudes, the Jews are still considered aliens and foreigners; supposed to be separated by an antiquated creed and peculiar customs from sympathy and fellowship – little known and still less understood. Yet they are, in fact, Jews only in their religion – Englishmen in everything else. In point of fact, therefore, the disabilities under which the Jews of Great Britain labour are the last relic of religious intolerance. That which they chiefly complain of is, being subjected to take an oath contrary to their religious feelings, when appointed to certain offices. In being called to the bar, this oath, as a matter of courtesy, is not pressed and a periodical act of indemnity shelters the delinquent. Jews, therefore, now practise at the bar, but only by sufferance. The same indulgence has not been extended to entering parliament, and consequently no Jew is practically eligible as a member of the House of Commons. Is it not discreditable to the common sense of the age that such anomalies should exist in reference to this well-disposed, and, in every respect, naturalised portion of the community? . . .

The domestic manners of both the German and the Spanish Jews in Great Britain are so exactly similar to those of their British brethren, that, were it not for the observance of the seventh day instead of the first, the prohibition of certain meats, and the celebration of certain solemn festivals and rites, it would be difficult to distinguish a Jewish from a native household. The characteristics so often assigned to them in tales professing to introduce a Jew or a Jewish family are almost all incorrect, being drawn either from the impressions of the past, or from some special case, or perhaps from attention to some Pole, Spaniard, or Turk, who may just as well be a Polish or Spanish Christian, or Turkish Mussulman, as a Jew. These great errors in delineation arise from the supposition, that because they are Hebrews they must be different from any other race. They are distinct in feature and religion, but in nothing else. Like the rest of the human race, they are, as individuals, neither wholly good nor wholly bad; as a people, their virtues very greatly predominate.

George Jacob Holyoake, Exchange with his Chaplain on Atheism (1850)[12]

George Holyoake (1817–1906) was a teacher and lecturer, and a socialist follower of the reformer Robert Owen. In 1842, after a remark made in a lecture on socialism given in Cheltenham, Holyoake was prosecuted for blasphemy. It is not clear that he was a confirmed atheist before the trial, but the prosecution itself seems to have made his mind up. He was imprisoned for six months, during which time his two-year-old daughter died. After his release, he founded and edited the Reasoner, *and developed his philosophy of 'secularism'. He published an account of his trial in 1850, including this conversation with the chaplain in Gloucestor gaol.*

Chaplain: Are you really an atheist, Mr Holyoake?

George Jacob Holyoake: Really I am.

Chaplain: You deny that there is a God?

Holyoake: No; I deny that there is sufficient reason to believe that there is one.

Chaplain: I am very glad to find that you have not the temerity to say that there is no God.

Holyoake: And I am very sorry to find that you have the temerity to say there is one. If it be absurd in me to deny what I cannot demonstrate, is it not improper for you to assert so dogmatically what you cannot prove?

Chaplain: Then where would you leave the question of atheism?

Holyoake: Just where it leaves us both. It is a question of probability.

Chaplain: Ah! the probabilities in favour of atheism are very few.

Holyoake: How know you that? Did you ever examine the question without prejudice, or read that written in its favour without fear? Those who dare not look at all never see far.

Chaplain: But if the atheist has so much on his side, why does he not make it known? *We* do not keep back *our* evidences.

Holyoake: Has the atheist an equal opportunity with you? Is it generous in you to taunt him with lack of evidence, when you are prepared to punish its production?

Chaplain: The reason is that your principles are so horrible; as Robert Hall has said, 'Atheism is a bloody and ferocious system.'

Holyoake: Permit me, sir, to return that gentle speech – to tell you that your principles are horrible, and that Christianity is a bloody and ferocious system.

Chaplain: Really I am shocked to hear you speak so dreadfully of Christianity.

Holyoake: Why should you be shocked to hear what you are not shocked to say?

Chaplain: But atheism is so revolting.

Holyoake: But Christianity is so revolting.

Chaplain: How dangerous is it for atheism to corrupt the minds of children?

Holyoake: How pernicious is it for Christian doctrines to corrupt the thoughts of infancy?

Chaplain: But you are only asserting.

Holyoake: Are you doing otherwise? I sometimes think that Christians would be more respectful in their speech if the same language could be applied to them with impunity which they apply to others.

Chaplain: But, my dear sir, the language of the atheist is so shocking to Christian feeling.

Holyoake: And, my dear sir, has it never occurred to you that the language of the Christian is shocking to atheistical feeling?

Chaplain: Atheists have a right to their opinions, I allow, but not to publish them.

Holyoake: I shall think you speak reasonably when you permit the same rule to be applied to the Christian.

Chaplain: But you really cannot be an atheist?

Holyoake: And you say this who have been a party to imprisoning me here for being one! If you believe yourself, go and demand my liberation.

Chaplain: Ah – when you come to die you will wish that you were a Christian.

Holyoake: Can it be that I shall wish to hold a creed that I distrust – one that leads me to deny another the liberty I claim for myself? If to be capable of looking back with satisfaction on conduct like this is to be a Christian, may I never die the death of the righteous, and may my last end never be like his.

Anonymous, Account of the Basingstoke Riots (28 March 1881)[13]

William Booth's Salvation Army, which began as the Christian Mission in Whitechapel in 1865, spread its revivalist message across the country, recruiting around a hundred thousand 'soldiers' by the end of the nineteenth century, and finding many supporters in high places. But it also invited resentment and, occasionally, ridicule, particularly for its temperance message. The Army's campaign against alcohol brought out the 'roughs' of Basingstoke, Hampshire, to march unsteadily for their rights in 1881. It was the last time the Riot Act was read in England.

Every contrivance which the ingenuity of the country bumpkins could suggest was employed to make a horrible discord. One man blew long blasts on a huge trombone, another clashed together as cymbals two tin can lids, a dozen played different tunes on as many tin whistles, one made hideous noises with a clarinet, and another rattled stones in the inside of a tin can. Those without instruments set up discordant howls and yells as they marched through the market-place amid the laughter and jeers of the groups gathered round . . .

On came the roughs clashing their cans and brandishing their sticks. They passed the 'Salvation Factory', but instead of proceeding along the street, they at once turned round and marched backwards and forwards immediately in front of the building so the Salvationists could not possibly begin their march. For twenty minutes this disorderly horde of vagabonds marched backwards and forwards under the eyes of the Mayor and the Specials, absolutely nothing being done, no attempt whatever being made to abate the nuisance or to allow the Army an opportunity of forming in the street. The thing was growing monotonous, when one of the roughs pushed another against the Captain of the Army, who was immediately seized by the Specials. As he shook himself loose, the police made a rush to the spot, crying, 'Violence' and the Mayor there and then, amid the jostling crowd, read the Riot Act . . . [T]he mob sang a stave of 'Rule Britannia' and the Specials exhorted one and all to clear the streets.

The Salvationists at once entered the building. The roughs, having achieved their purpose of 'arranging' a disturbance sufficient to afford a pretext for reading the Riot Act and preventing the Salvation Army from processing the streets, desisted from their clamour; and for the next hour Basingstoke was moved to fits of contemptuous laughter by watching the attempts of the special constables to clear the streets. Twenty mounted artillerymen rode hither and thither, and about forty others on foot marched backwards and forwards, driving the crowd before them . . . and the streets gradually cleared.

———————

Victoria Brittain, *The Meaning of Waiting* (2011)[14]

After the attacks on the United States of 11 September 2001, and the invasion of Afghanistan, several British citizens, as well as spouses of British citizens, were among those arrested and incarcerated without trial in the US prison camp in Guantánamo Bay, Cuba. Victoria Brittain's play is a work of 'verbatim theatre', using the words of eight Muslim women who are married to Guantánamo prisoners to show their experiences.

Inside I'm crying. I tell myself, don't be
sad, it's stupid, you have only one life, don't
throw it away in sadness.

I can only pray. I know Allah is doing this
test for me, for him, for a reason.

I read Koran, and read, and pray for
strength.

One time the lawyers arranged permission
so I could speak to my husband on the
telephone after all these years . . . There are
no words for the emotion when I heard his
voice . . .

CCTV of Sabah *walking in Grosvenor Square, then
inside the US embassy, then on the phone, first very
calm, then puts phone down, crying and crying.*

Afterwards I went home to the children and
I told them, 'Dad is fine, don't worry, he'll
come soon, he kisses you all, he knows you
are good children. You'll see him soon.'

Then in the mosque for Eid, people kept
coming to me and hugging me, saying
how good for the telephone call with your
husband. They were kind and happy for
me . . .

But no one knows except Allah what is
happening for me, what is in my heart.

CCTV Woman Z, *loose Indian scarf.*

Once, a long time ago, my husband wrote
this letter to me from Guantánamo:

'I am dying here every day, mentally and
physically. This is happening to all of us.
We have been ignored, locked up in the
middle of the ocean for years. Rather than
humiliate myself, having to beg for water,
I would rather hurry up the process that is
going to happen anyway. I would like to die
quietly, by myself. I was once 250 pounds.
I dropped to 150 pounds in the first hunger-strike.
I want to make it easy on everyone.
I want no feeding, no forced tubes, no
"help", no "intensive assisted feeding". This
is my legal right. The British government
refuses to help me. What is the point of my
wife being British? I thought Britain stood
for justice, but they abandoned us, people
who have lived in Britain for years, and
who have British wives and children. I hold
the British government responsible for my
death, as I do the Americans.'

My own husband wrote this . . .

Why do they not help him? Why have the
others come back and not him? Can you
tell me? Why can no one tell me? . . . I can't
believe my own husband wrote that letter
about wanting to die – he's not like that.
He's big, and strong, and talking, always
talking to everyone – people always love him. You
couldn't not love him.

I prayed when I went on the Hadj to let me
marry a man in white robes and a scarf like
those I saw – my prayer was answered back
home in Battersea – a young man from
Medina came to the mosque and someone
spoke to my mother. I liked him when I saw
him, though I did think at first he was just
too big . . . but he was too kind to me not to
love him.

You know, now I have dreams, I hear
voices, bad voices in my head, they tell me
he is dead, or that he has divorced me. I try
to tell them to go away, but they come back
again. They aren't true, are they?

What is happening to me?
You know, now he's been away from me in
Guantánamo longer than we were together
– eight years. And my youngest boy, he
never saw his dad, he doesn't even know
what a dad is.

Sabah: All those years and tests show things you'd not know before.

I see things with different eyes. If I see a carrot – I only see orange, orange, and what it means for me . . . for my husband.

Now I'm very tired and very sensitive. Allah knows how much I am exhausted. No one else can know these suffering years.

I love my husband so much, and I know he loves me, and our children, so much. Nothing has changed for us. When I see his letter, his writing, well, how to tell you how happy I am . . .

But, you know, he's changed too, he's written me poems, and for the children, something he never did before. When I read a letter from him, I can be so, so happy, he advises me, he has advice for each child, I can tell he is still strong after all these years and everything they did to him.

I pray to Allah, please help me, and help all those who are suffering and no one knows their story.

1642–1789

———

REPRESENTING THE PEOPLE

The Civil Wars, which began in 1642 and embroiled all four nations of the British Isles, came to a climax with the trial and execution of King Charles I in 1649. Kings had been deposed before in Britain, and the monarchy was eventually 'restored' in 1660, when Charles II took his father's throne. But the political landscape had been permanently reshaped by the events of the 1640s and 1650s. Radical groups such as the Levellers had openly discussed revolutionary ideas, including democracy. Ideas like that would not be forgotten.

In the eighteenth century, some areas of daily life, such as religious observance, benefited from increasing 'tolerance'. Others, such as the criminal law, were subject to ever more stringent penalties, with a group of innovations later known as the 'Bloody Code', which greatly expanded the number of crimes that carried the death penalty. In the world of popular politics, revolutions in America, in 1776, and France, in 1789, inspired some Britons as much as they frightened their masters.

Elizabeth Lilburne, *Appeal* (September 1646)[1]

The British Civil Wars, in which Parliament fought against, and eventually deposed and executed Charles I, coincided with an explosion in the dissemination of radical and popular voices, including those of women. The Levellers took their name originally from protesters who threw down, 'levelled', the hedges and fences of the enclosed fields, but 'levelling' came to be associated with all forms of equality. In this early Leveller petition, Elizabeth Lilburne, who was married to the Leveller leader John Lilburne, petitioned Parliament against his arrest and imprisonment.

That you only and alone, are chosen by the Commons of England to maintain their Lawes, and Liberties, and to do them Justice and Right which you have often before God and the World sworne to do yea, and in divers of your Declarations declared, it is your duty (in regard of the trust reposed in you) so to do without any private aimes, personall respects, or passions whatsoever and that you think nothing to good to be hazarded, in the discharge of your Consciences for the obtaining of these ends. and that you will give up your selves to the uttermost of your power and judgment to maintain truth, and conforme your selves to the will of God, (which is to do Iustice and right, and secure the persons estates and liberties of all that joyned with you, impricating the Iudgments of Heaven to fall upon you, when you decline from these ends, you judging it the greatest scandall that can be laid upon you, that you either do or intend to subvert the Lawes, Liberties, and Freedomes of the people, which freedomes . . . you your selves call, the Common Birthright of English-Men, who are borne equally free, and to whom the Law of the Land is an equall inheritance) . . . It is your duty to use your best endeavours, that the meanest of the Commonality, may enjoy their own birth-right, freedome, and liberty of the Lawes of the Land, being equally (as you say) intituled thereunto With the greatest subject, The knowledge of which as comming from your own mouths and pen, imboldneth your Petitioner (with confidence) to make her humble addresses to you, and to put you in mind that her husband aboue two moneths agoe made his formall and legall appeal to you against the injustice, and usurpation of the Lords acted upon him, which you received, read, committed, and promised him Iustice. But as yet no report is made of his businesse, nor any reliefe or actuall Iustice holden out unto him, although you have since found time to passe the Compositions as pardons, for the infranchising many of those that your selves have declared Traytors, and Enemies to the Kingdome, which is no small cause of sorrow to your Petitioner, and many others, that her Husband who hath adventured his life, and all that he had in the World, in your lowest condition for you, should be so sleighted and disregarded by you, as though you had forgot the duty you owe to the Kingdome, and your many oaths, vowes, and Declarations, which neglect hath hastned the almost utter ruine of your Petitioner her husband, and small Children: For the lords in a most Tyrannicall and barbarous manner, (being incouraged by your neglect) have since committed her husband for about three Weeks close prisoner to Newgate, locked him up in a little roome, without the use of pen, inke or paper (for no other cause but for refusing to kneel at the Bar, of those, that by Law are none of his Iudges) the cruell Iaylers all that time refusing, to let your Petitioner, or any of his friends, to set their feet over the threshold of his Chamber dore, or to come in to the prison yard to speak with him, or to deliver unto his hands, either meat, drink, mony, or any other necessaries; A most barbarous and illegall cruelty!

Wherefore your Petitioner humbly prayeth to grant unto her husband the benefit of the Law, and to admit him to your Bar himselfe, to plead his own cause, if you be not satisfied in the manner of his proceedings, or else according to Law, justice, and that duty and obligation that lieth upon; forthwith to release him from his unjust imprisonment, and to restrain and prohibit the illegall and arbitrary proceedings of the lords; according to that sufficient power enstated upon you; for the enabling you faithfully to discharge the trust reposed in you, and to vacuate this his illegall sentence and fine; and to give him just and honourable repairations, from the Lords, and all those that have unjustly executed their unjust commands, It being a rule in law, and a Maxim made use of by your selves in your Declaration 2. 1642. That the Kings illegall commands, though accompanied with his presence, doe not excuse those that obey them much lesse the Lords, with which the Law accordeth; And so was resolved by the Iudges, 16. Henr. 6, And that you will legally and judicially, examine the Crimes of the Earle of Manchester, and Col. King, which the Petitioners husband and others, have so often complained to you off; and do examplary justice upon them actording to their deserts; or else according to Law and justice punish those (if any) that have falsly complained of them. And that you would without further delay give us relief by doing us Iustice. All which, she the rather earnestly desireth, because his imprisonment in the Tower is extraordinary chargeable and insupportable. Although by right, and the custome of that place, his fees, chamber, and diet ought to be allowed him and paid out of the treasure of the Crowne) he having wasted and spent himselfe with almost six yeares attendance, and expectation upon your honovrs for justice and repairations against his barbarous sentence . . . of the Star-Chamber, to his extraordinary charge and dammage, and yet never received a penny, and also lost divers hundreds of pounds, the yeare, he was a prisoner in Oxford Castle for you, neither can he receive his Arrears for his faithfull service with the Earle of Manchester, although he spent, with him, much of his own mony, And the last year, by the unadvised means of some Members of his Honourable House was committed prisoner for aboue 3. moneths, to his extraordinary charges and expences; and yet in conclusion, he was releast, and to this day knoweth not wherefore he was imprisoned, for which according to law and justice he ought to receive reparations, but he never yet had a penny, all which particulars being considered, do render the condition of your Petitioner, her husband, and children, to be very nigh ruine and destruction, unlesse your speedy and long-expected justice prevent the same, Which your Petitioner doth earnestly intreat at your hands as her right, and that which in equity honour and conscience cannot be denyed her.

And as in duty bound, she shall ever pray, that your hearts may be kept upright, and thereby enabled timely and faithfully to discharge the duty you owe to the Kingdome according to the Great Trust reposed in you, and so free your selves from giving cause to be judged men that seeke your selves more then the publique good.

Richard Overton, *An Arrow Against All Tyrants* (25 September 1646)[2]

Richard Overton was a Leveller and pamphleteer, and one of the principal theorists behind Leveller beliefs. He wrote prolifically on commoners' rights, the secularisation of government, and redistribution of land. He was concerned that the victory of the New Model Army would result in one tyranny, the monarchy, being replaced by another, the Presbyterian-dominated Parliament. He was also the first radical voice to refer to the historic oppressions of the 'Norman Yoke' (see Orderic Vitalis, p. 9). In this pamphlet, written while Overton was imprisoned in Newgate and addressed to the radical MP Henry Marten, Overton attacks the sources of hereditary power.

Sir – we desire your help for your own sakes as well as for ourselves, chiefly for the removal of two most insufferable evils daily encroaching and increasing upon us, portending and threatening inevitable destruction and confusion of yourselves, of us, and of all our posterities: namely the encroachments and usurpations of the House of Lords over the commons' liberties and freedoms, together with the barbarous, inhuman, blood-thirsty desires and endeavours of the . . . clergy.

For the first, namely the exorbitances of the Lords: they are to such an height aspired, that contrary to all precedents, the free commoners of England are imprisoned, fined and condemned by them (their incompetent, illegal, unequal, improper judges) against the express letter of Magna Carta . . . that no free man of England 'shall be passed upon, tried, or condemned, but by the lawful judgement of his equals, or by the law of the land'.

Be awakened, arise and consider their oppressions and encroachments and stop their lordships in their ambitious career. For they do not cease only here, but they soar higher and higher. For their proper station will not content them, but they must make incursions and inroads upon the people's rights and freedoms and extend their prerogative patent beyond their master's compass.

And . . . the oppressions, usurpations, and miseries from this prerogative head are not the sole cause of our grievance and complaint, but in especial, the most unnatural, tyrannical, blood-thirsty desires and continual endeavours of the clergy against the contrary-minded in matters of conscience – which have been so veiled, gilded and covered over with such various, fair and specious pretences that by the common discernings such wolfish, cannibal, inhuman intents against their neighbours, kindred, friends and countrymen, as is now clearly discovered was little suspected (and less deserved) at their hands. But now I suppose they will scarce hereafter be so hard of belief. For now in plain terms and with open face, the clergy here discover themselves in their kind, and show plainly that inwardly they are no other but ravening wolves, even as roaring lions wanting their prey, going up and down, seeking whom they may devour.

For never before was the like heard of in England. The cruel, villainous, barbarous martyrdoms, murders and butcheries of God's people under the papal and episcopal clergy were not perpetrated or acted by any law so devilish, cruel and inhumane as this.

Therefore what may the free people of England expect at the hands of their . . . clergy, who thus discover themselves more fierce and cruel than their fellows? Nothing but hanging, burning, branding, imprisoning, etc. is like to be the reward of the most faithful friends to the kingdom and parliament.

The Putney Debates (29 October 1647)[3]

Thomas and William Rainborough were brothers who fought for Parliament in the Civil Wars, but whose emerging radical sympathies put them in opposition to Oliver Cromwell's leadership. After the New Model Army's victory in the first Civil War, representatives of different strands of opinion about how to run the country came together at Putney to debate a new constitution, and to discuss a document drawn up in the name of the army rank and file, the Agreement of the People. Henry Ireton, Cromwell's son-in-law, defended the conservative parliamentary position. Thomas Rainborough set out in the clearest terms the idea of universal suffrage. He and his fellow Levellers were defeated then, but their principles would eventually be widely embraced.

Major [William] Rainborough: I desire we may come to that end we all strive after. I humbly desire you will fall upon that which is the engagement of all, which is the rights and freedoms of the people, and let us see how far we have made sure to them a right and freedom, and if anything be tendered as to that [in this paper]. And when that engagement is gone through, then, let us consider of those [things only] that are of greater weight . . .

[Henry] Ireton: The exception that lies in it is this. It is said, they are to be distributed according to the number of the inhabitants: 'The people of England,' &c. And this doth make me think that the meaning is, that every man that is an inhabitant is to be equally considered, and to have an equal voice in the election of those representers, the persons that are for the general Representative; and if that be the meaning, then I have something to say against it. But if it be only that those people that by the civil constitution of this kingdom, which is original and fundamental, and beyond which I am sure no memory of record does go—

[(Nicholas) Cowling, interrupting]: Not before the Conquest.

[Ireton]: But before the Conquest it was so. If it be intended that those that by that constitution that was before the Conquest, that hath been beyond memory, such persons that have been before [by] that constitution [the electors], should be [still] the electors, I have no more to say against it.

Colonel [Thomas] Rainborough objected: That others might have given their hands to it.

Captain Denne denied that those that were set of their regiment were their hands.

Ireton [asked]: Whether those men whose hands are to it, or those that brought it, do know so much of the matter [as to] know whether they mean that all that had a former right of election [are to be electors], or [that] those that had no right before are to come in.

Cowling: In the time before the Conquest. Since the Conquest the greatest part of the kingdom was in vassalage.

[Maximilian] Petty: We judge that all inhabitants that have not lost their birthright should have an equal voice in elections.

Rainborough: I desired that those that had engaged in it [might be included]. For really I think that the poorest he that is in England hath a life to live, as the greatest he; and therefore truly, sir, I think it's clear, that every man that is to live under a government ought first by his own consent to put himself under that government; and

I do think that the poorest man in England is not at all bound in a strict sense to that government that he hath not had a voice to put himself under; and I am confident that, when I have heard the reasons against it, something will be said to answer those reasons, insomuch that I should doubt whether he was an Englishman or no, that should doubt of these things.

John Lilburne, Appeal to Cromwellian Soldiers (29 August 1649)[4]

It became an accepted principle of Leveller thinking that the army provided the best hope of truly representative government in Civil-War era England, at a time when MPs were elected by a tiny proportion of the population (and for much of the Civil-War period did not stand for re-election at all). Here, in a pamphlet entitled 'The Young Men's and the Apprentices Outcry', the Leveller spokesman John Lilburne appeals to the army to choose its own leaders. Lilburne had published a stream of pamphlets and appeals, many of them from his prison cell, both under Charles I's government and the parliamentary government that succeeded it. This was his last.

You our fellow-countrymen, the private soldiers of the Army, alone are the instrumental authors of your own slavery and ours. Therefore as there is any bowels of men in you, any love to your native country, kindred, friends or relations, any sparks of conscience in you, any hopes of glory or immortality in you, or any pity, mercy, or compassion to an enslaved, undone, perishing, dying people: oh help! help! Save and redeem us from total vassalage and slavery; and be no more like brute beasts, to fight against us or our friends, your loving and dear brethren after the flesh – to your own vassalage as well as ours.

And as an assured pledge of your future cordialness to us and the true and real liberties of the land of your nativity, we beseech and beg of you (but especially those amongst you that subscribed the *Solemn engagement* at Newmarket Heath, 5 June 1647) speedily to choose out from amongst yourselves two of the ablest and constantest faithful men amongst you in each troop and company, now at last (by corresponding each with other and with your honest friends in the nation to consider of some effectual course beyond all pretences and cheats) to accomplish the real end of all your engagements and fightings, viz. the settling of the liberties and freedoms of the *people* – which can never permanently be done but upon the sure foundation of a popular agreement – who (viz. the people) in justice, gratitude, and common equity cannot choose but to voluntarily and largely make better provisions for your future subsistence by the payment of your arrears than ever your officers or this pretended parliament intends, or you can rationally expect from them: witness their cutting off three parts of your arrears in four for free-quarter and then necessitating abundance of your fellow-soldiers, now cashiered, etc., to fill their debentures at two shillings and six pence, three shillings, and at most four shillings per pound, by means of which you that keep your debentures are necessitated to vie with the greatest bidder in the purchase of the late king's lands, whilst they are able to give about thirty years' purchase for that you cannot give eight years' purchase for; and if you will not give with the most you must have no land – so that the most of your debentures are likely to prove waste papers; and those that purchase will have but a slippery security of their possessions by reason of general discontents amongst all sorts of people, and particularly by so extraordinarily disengaging and cheating so many soldiers (as they have done) of their just expected recompense of reward.

The Last Speech of Colonel Richard Rumbold at the Market Cross at Edinburgh (26 June 1685)[5]

Richard Rumbold (c. 1622–1685) fought for Parliament in the Civil War (when he lost an eye), stood guard at the execution of Charles I, and was one of the Rye House plotters against the restored Charles II. In 1685, he took part in the Earl of Argyll's rising against James II, which was timed to coincide with that of the Duke of Monmouth in England. Both risings failed, and Rumbold was captured and executed for treason at the Cowgate in Edinburgh. His final speech is an attack on the absolutism he had fought against all his life.

Gentlemen and Brethren, It is for all men that come into the world once to die; and after death the judgment! And since death is a debt that all of us must pay, it is but a matter of small moment what way it be done. Seeing the Lord is pleased in this manner to take me to Himself, I confess, something hard to flesh and blood, yet blessed be His name, who hath made me not only willing, but thankful for His honoring me to lay down the life He gave, for His name; in which, were every hair in this head and beard of mine a life, I should joyfully sacrifice them for it, as I do this. Providence having brought me hither, I think it most necessary to clear myself of some aspersions laid upon my name; and, first, that I should have had so horrid an intention of destroying the King and his brother . . .

It was also laid to my charge that I was antimonarchical.

It was ever my thoughts that kingly government was the best of all where justly executed; I mean, such as it was by our ancient laws – that is, a king, and a legal, free-chosen Parliament – the King having, as I conceive, power enough to make him great; the people also as much property as to make them happy; they being, as it were, contracted to one another! And who will deny me that this was not the justly constituted government of our nation? How absurd is it, then, for men of sense to maintain that tho the one party of his contract break all conditions, the other should be obliged to perform their part? No; this error is contrary to the law of God, the law of nations, and the law of reason.

But as pride hath been the bait the devil hath caught most by ever since the creation, so it continues to this day with us. Pride caused our first parents to fall from the blessed state wherein they were created – they aiming to be higher and wiser than God allowed, which brought an everlasting curse on them and their posterity. It was pride caused God to drown the old world. And it was Nimrod's pride in building Babel that caused that heavy curse of division of tongues to be spread among us, as it is at this day, one of the greatest afflictions the Church of God groaneth under, that there should be so many divisions during their pilgrimage here; but this is their comfort that the day draweth near where, as there is but one shepherd, there shall be but one sheepfold. It was, therefore, in the defense of this party, in their just rights and liberties, against popery and slavery— . . .

I die this day in defence of the ancient laws and liberties of these nations; and tho God, for reasons best known to Himself, hath not seen it fit to honor us, as to make us the instruments for the deliverance of His people, yet as I have lived, so I die in the faith that He will speedily arise for the deliverance of His Church and people. And I desire of all you to prepare for this with speed. I may say this is a deluded generation, veiled with ignorance, that tho popery and slavery be riding in upon them, do not perceive it; tho I am sure there was no man born marked of God above another, for none comes into the world with a saddle on his back, neither any booted and spurred to ride him. Not but that I am well satisfied that God hath wisely ordered different stations for men in the world, as I have already said; kings having as much power as to make them great and the people as much property as to make them happy. And to conclude, I shall only add my wishes for the salvation of all men who were created for that end.

Prison Torture Reports (1721)[6]

*Until 1772, defendants who refused to enter a plea in court were,
unless they were found mute 'by visitation of God', subject to the
ordeal of 'peine forte et dure'. In the case of William Spiggot (here
misnamed Thomas) and his fellow accused, the meaning of this
judgment was read out: '. . . he shall lie upon his Back, and his Head
shall be covered, and his Feet bare, and that one of his Arms shall
be drawn with a Cord to one side of the House, and the other Arm
to the other side, and that his Legs shall be used in the same manner,
and that upon his Body shall be laid so much Iron and Stone as he
can bear, and more, and that the first Day after he shall have three
Morsels of Barley Bread, without any Drink, and the second Day he
shall drink so much as he can three times of the Water which is next
the Prison Door, saving running Water, without any Bread: and this
shall be his Diet until he die' (Proceedings of the Old Bailey). After
1772, refusal to plead was deemed the same as pleading guilty. In
1827 the presumption of guilt was reversed and refusal to plead was
redefined as equivalent to pleading not guilty.*

A like method was pursued in 1721, with Nathaniel Hawes, a prisoner
who refused to plead; when the cord proved inefficacious, a weight
of 250 pounds was laid upon him, after which he decided to plead.
The same year seems prolific of cases of this character, there being
particulars of an instance in the *Nottingham Mercury* of 19 January
1721. They are included in the London news, and are as follow:
'Yesterday the sessions began at the Old Bailey, where several persons
were brought to the bar for highway robbery, etc. Among them were
the highwaymen lately taken at Westminster, two of whom, namely,
Thomas Green, *alias* Phillips, and Thomas Spiggot, refusing to plead,
the court proceeded to pass the following sentence upon them: 'that
the prisoner shall be,' etc. [the usual form, as given above]. The
former, on sight of the terrible machine, desired to be carried back
to the sessions house, where he pleaded not guilty. But the other,

who behaved himself very insolently to the ordinary who was ordered to attend him, seemingly resolved to undergo the torture. Accordingly, when they brought cords, as usual, to tie him, he broke them three several times like a twine-thread, and told them if they brought cables he would serve them after the same manner. But, however, they found means to tie him to the ground, having his limbs extended; but after, enduring the punishment for an hour, and having three or four hundredweight put on him, he at last submitted to plead, and was carried back, when he pleaded not guilty.'

The Rev. Mr Willette, the ordinary of the prison, in 1776, published the 'Annals of Newgate', and from these we learn further particulars of the torture of the highwayman, Thomas Spiggot. 'The chaplain found him lying in the vault upon the bare ground, with 350 pounds weight upon his breast, and then prayed with him, and at several times asked him why he should hazard his soul by such obstinate kind of self-murder. But all the answer that he made was, 'Pray for me; pray for me.' He sometimes lay silent under the pressure as if insensible to the pain, and then again would fetch his breath very quick and short. Several times he complained that they had laid a cruel weight upon his face, though it was covered with nothing but a thin cloth, which was afterwards removed and laid more light and hollow; yet he still complained of the prodigious weight upon his face, which might be caused by the blood being forced up thither and pressing the veins so violently as if the force had been externally on his face. When he had remained for half-an-hour under this load, and fifty pounds weight more laid on, being in all four hundred, he told those who attended him he would plead. The weights were at once taken off, the cords cut asunder; he was raised up by two men, some brandy put into his mouth to revive him, and he was carried to take his trial.' The practice of *peine forte et dure* gave the name of 'Press-yard' to a part of Newgate, and the terrible machine above referred to was probably in the form of a rack.

Anonymous, 'Idol Worship, Or, The Way to Preferment' (1740)[7]

This unsigned print from the beginning of the classic age of the scabrous caricature later epitomised by James Gillray and Thomas Rowlandson shows that travelling the route to political power has long been seen to be a dirty business.

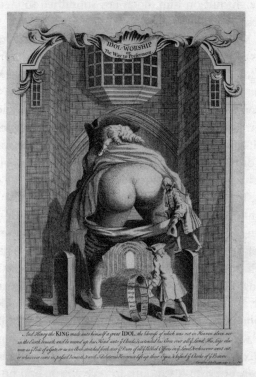

And Henry the KING made unto himself a great IDOL, the likeness of which was not in Heaven above, nor in the Earth beneath; and he reared up his Head unto the Clouds & and extended his Arm over all the Land; His legs also were as the Posts of a Gate, or as an Arch stretched forth over the Doors of all the Publick Offices in the Land, & whosoever went out or whosoever came in passed beneath, & with Idolatrous Reverence lift up their Eyes, & kissed the Cheeks of the Postern.

Thomas Paine, *Common Sense* (1776)[8]

One of the great denunciations of hereditary rule was written by Thomas Paine, who was born in Thetford, Norfolk, and emigrated to Pennsylvania in 1774. His pamphlets helped galvanise the movement of independence from Britain in the thirteen American colonies and inspired those fighting in other countries for popular government.

To the evil of monarchy we have added that of hereditary succession; and as the first is a degradation and lessening of ourselves, so the second, claimed as a matter of right, is an insult and imposition on posterity. For all men being originally equals, no *one* by *birth* could have a right to set up his own family, in perpetual preference to all others for ever, and though himself might deserve *some* decent degree of honors of his contemporaries, yet his descendants might be far too unworthy to inherit them. One of the strongest *natural* proofs of the folly of hereditary right in kings, is that nature disapproves it, otherwise she would not so frequently turn it into ridicule, by giving mankind an *Ass for a Lion*.

Secondly, as no man at first could possess more public honors than were bestowed upon him, so the givers of those honors could have no power to give away the right of posterity, and though they might say, 'We choose you for *our* head,' they could not, without manifest injustice to their children, say 'that your children and your children's children shall *reign* over *ours* for *ever*'. Because such an unwise, unjust, unnatural compact might (perhaps) in the next succession put them under the government of a rogue, or a fool. Most wise men in their private sentiments have ever treated hereditary right with contempt; yet it is one of those evils, which when once established is not easily removed; many submit from fear, others from superstition, and the more powerful part shares, with the King, the plunder of the rest.

This is supposing the present race of kings in the world to have had an honourable origin; whereas it is more than probable, that could we take off the dark covering of antiquity, and trace them to their first rise, we should find the first of them nothing better than the principal ruffian of some restless gang, whose savage manners or pre-eminence in subtlety obtained him the title of chief among plunderers; and who by increasing in power, and extending his depredations, overawed the quiet and defenceless to purchase their safety by frequent contributions. Yet his electors could have no idea of giving hereditary right to his descendants, because such a perpetual exclusion of themselves was incompatible with the free and unrestrained principles they professed to live by. Wherefore, hereditary succession in the early ages of monarchy could not take place as a matter of claim, but as something casual or complimentary; but as few or no records were extant in those days, and traditional history stuffed with fables, it was very easy, after the lapse of a few generations, to trump up some superstitious tale, conveniently timed Mahomet like, to cram hereditary rights down the throats of the vulgar. Perhaps the disorders which threatened, or seemed to threaten, on the decease of a leader and the choice of a new one (for elections among ruffians could not be very orderly) induced many at first to favor hereditary pretensions; by which means it happened, as it hath happened since, that what at first was submitted to as a convenience, was afterwards claimed as a right.

England, since the Conquest, hath known some few good monarchs, but groaned beneath a much larger number of bad ones; yet no man in his senses can say that their claim under William the Conqueror is a very honourable one. A French bastard landing with an armed banditti, and establishing himself King of England against the consent of the natives, is in plain terms a very paltry rascally original.

———————

Declaration of Independence (4 July 1776)[9]

The high point of idealism in the American Revolution was the writing of the Declaration of Independence in 1776, in which the fundamental principle of democracy is made clear: that government is secondary, and the people are primary.

When in the Course of human events, it becomes necessary for one people to dissolve the political bands which have connected them with another, and to assume among the powers of the earth, the separate and equal station to which the Laws of Nature and of Nature's God entitle them, a decent respect to the opinions of mankind requires that they should declare the causes which impel them to the separation.

We hold these truths to be self-evident, that all men are created equal, that they are endowed by their Creator with certain unalienable Rights, that among these are Life, Liberty and the pursuit of Happiness. – That to secure these rights, Governments are instituted among Men, deriving their just powers from the consent of the governed, – That whenever any Form of Government becomes destructive of these ends, it is the Right of the People to alter or to abolish it, and to institute new Government, laying its foundation on such principles and organizing its powers in such form, as to them shall seem most likely to effect their Safety and Happiness. Prudence, indeed, will dictate that Governments long established should not be changed for light and transient causes; and accordingly all experience hath shewn, that mankind are more disposed to suffer, while evils are sufferable, than to right themselves by abolishing the forms to which they are accustomed. But when a long train of abuses and usurpations, pursuing invariably the same Object, evinces a design to reduce them under absolute Despotism, it is their right, it is their duty, to throw off such Government, and to provide new Guards for their future security. – Such has been the patient sufferance of these Colonies; and such is now the necessity which constrains them to alter their former Systems of Government. The history of the present King of Great Britain is a history of repeated injuries and usurpations, all having in direct object the establishment of an absolute Tyranny over these States. To prove this, let Facts be submitted to a candid world.

Thomas Paine, *Rights of Man* (1791)[10]

Thomas Paine's revolutionary career continued after American independence was achieved. He turned his attention to the French Revolution, and to answering attacks on events in France published by the Whig politician Edmund Burke. Rights of Man *was a best-seller. As he did in America, Paine backed up words with action: a year after the publication of* Rights of Man, *he took up a seat as a deputy in the French National Convention, and less than a year after that, he was arrested and imprisoned, narrowly avoiding the guillotine.*

Titles are but nicknames, and every nickname is a title. The thing is perfectly harmless in itself, but it marks a sort of foppery in the human character which degrades it . . .

Hitherto we have considered aristocracy chiefly in one point of view. We have now to consider it in another. But whether we view it before or behind, or sideways, or anyway else, domestically or publicly, it is still a monster.

In France, aristocracy had one feature less in its countenance than what it has in some other countries. It did not compose a body of hereditary legislators. It was not '*a corporation of aristocracy*', for such

I have heard M. de la Fayette describe an English house of peers. Let us then examine the grounds upon which the French constitution has resolved against having such a house in France.

Because, in the first place, as is already mentioned, aristocracy is kept up by family tyranny and injustice.

2nd, Because there is an unnatural unfitness in an aristocracy to be legislators for a nation. Their ideas of *distributive justice* are corrupted at the very source. They begin life trampling on all their younger brothers and sisters, and relations of every kind, and are taught and educated so to do. With what ideas of justice or honor can that man enter a house of legislation, who absorbs in his own person the inheritance of a whole family of children, or metes out some pitiful portion with the insolence of a gift?

3rd, Because the idea of hereditary legislators is as inconsistent as that of hereditary judges, or hereditary juries; and as absurd as an hereditary mathematician, or an hereditary wise man; and as ridiculous as an hereditary poet-laureate.

4th, Because a body of men, holding themselves accountable to nobody, ought not to be trusted by anybody.

5th, Because it is continuing the uncivilized principle of governments founded in conquest, and the base idea of man having property in man, and governing him by personal right.

6th, Because aristocracy has a tendency to degenerate the human species.

Samuel Taylor Coleridge, 'Destruction of the Bastille' (1789–91)[11]

The Romantic poet Samuel Taylor Coleridge (1772–1834) held strong political views throughout his life, which extended to setting up a

'Pantisocratic' commune in New England. His first political inspiration
was the French Revolution. Written between 1789 and 1791, before
Coleridge turned twenty, this poem was first published in 1834, after
his death. It gives voice not only to the youthful optimism that greeted
the Revolution, but also the hope that freedoms won there could
inspire the peoples of other nations, including Britain. The manu-
script is incomplete.

I.

Heard'st thou yon universal cry,
And dost thou linger still on Gallia's shore?
Go, Tyranny! beneath some barbarous sky
Thy terrors lost, and ruin'd power deplore!
What tho' through many a groaning age
Was felt thy keen suspicious rage,
Yet Freedom rous'd by fierce Disdain
Has wildly broke thy triple chain,
And like the storm which Earth's deep entrails hide,
At length has burst its way and spread the ruins wide.

. . .

IV.

In sighs their sickly breath was spent; each gleam
Of Hope had ceas'd the long long day to cheer;
Or if delusive, in some flitting dream,
It gave them to their friends and children dear –
Awaked by lordly Insult's sound
To all the doubled horrors round,
Oft shrunk they from Oppression's band
While Anguish rais'd the desperate hand
For silent death; or lost the mind's controll,
Thro' every burning vein would tides of Frenzy roll.

V.

But cease, ye pitying bosoms, cease to bleed!
Such scenes no more demand the tear humane;
I see, I see! Glad Liberty succeed
With every patriot virtue in her train!
And mark yon peasant's raptur'd eyes;
Secure he views his harvests rise;
No fetter vile the mind shall know,
And Eloquence shall fearless glow.
Yes! Liberty the soul of Life shall reign,
Shall throb in every pulse, shall flow thro' every vein!

VI.

Shall France alone a Despot spurn?
Shall she alone, O Freedom, boast thy care?
Lo, round thy standard Belgia's heroes burn,
Thro Power's blood-stain'd streamers fire the air,
And wider yet thy influence spread,
Not e'er recline thy weary head,
Till every land from pole to pole
Shall boast one independent soul!
And still, as erst, let favour'd Britain be
First ever of the first and freest of the free!

Advertisement for Commemoration of the French Revolution (7 July 1791)[12]

Birmingham was an increasingly wealthy city in the late eighteenth century. But many of the wealthiest citizens were Dissenters, not members of the Church of England, and thus disbarred from taking a full part in the political process. Such men looked to the inspiration of the French Revolution to press for Parliamentary Reform. A group of Dissenters in Birmingham in 1791, some of them members of the prestigious scientific Lunar Society, announced that they would be celebrating the anniversary of the fall of the Bastille with a dinner.

Hotel, Birmingham, 7 July 1791.

Commemoration of the French Revolution.

A Number of Gentlemen intend DINING together on the 14th instant, to commemorate the auspicious day which witnessed the Emancipation of Twenty-six Millions of people from the Yoke of Despotism, and restored the Blessings of equal Government to a truly great and enlightened Nation, with whom it is our Interest, as a Commercial People, and our Duty as Friends to the general Rights of Mankind, to promote a free Intercourse, as subservient to a permanent Friendship.

Any Friend to Freedom, disposed to join the intended temperate Festivity, is desired to leave his Name at the Bar of the Hotel, where Tickets may be had at Five shillings each, including a Bottle of Wine, but no Person will be admitted without one.

Dinner will be on table at Three o'Clock precisely.

Anonymous Birmingham Handbill to Commemorate the French Revolution (July 1791)[13]

The proposed Birmingham dinner (see above) brought out strong 'loyalist' opposition. Whether it was these opponents who issued this handbill, with its uncompromisingly radical statements, as an act of provocation, or whether one of the diners themselves was the author, is not known. Whoever the real authors were, the results were dramatic. Three days of rioting and attacks on Dissenters, including the scientist Joseph Priestley, followed, perpetrated by 'Church and King' mobs that the authorities took little trouble to stop.

My Countrymen,

The second year of Gallic Liberty is nearly expired. At the commencement of the third, on the 14th of this month, it is devoutly to be wished, that every enemy to civil and religious despotism would give his sanction to the majestic common cause, by a public celebration of the anniversary. Remember, that on the 14th of July, the Bastile, that high altar and castle of despotism, fell. Remember the enthusiasm, peculiar to the cause of liberty, with which it was attacked. Remember that generous humanity that taught the oppressed, groaning under the weight of insulted rights, to save the lives of oppressors! Extinguish the mean prejudices of nations; and let your numbers be collected, and sent as a free-will offering to the National Assembly. — But is it possible to forget that your own Parliament is venal? Your minister hypocritical? Your clergy legal oppressors ? The reigning family extravagant? The crown of a certain great personage becoming every day too weighty for the head that wears it? Too weighty for the people who gave it? Your taxes partial and excessive? Your representation a cruel insult upon the sacred rights of property, religion, and freedom? — But on the 14th of this month, prove to the political sycophants of the day, that you reverence the olive branch; that you will sacrifice to public tranquillity, till the majority shall exclaim — 'The Peace of slavery is worse than the war of freedom. Of that moment let tyrants beware.'

LAND AND LIBERTY

―――――――

'THE EARTH IS A COMMON
TREASURY'

The Norman Conquest had concentrated land holdings in the hands of a tiny elite, but it was not until the sixteenth century that the land itself emerged as a popular issue on a national scale. The rich returns on wool led to the 'enclosure' of more and more common land for pasture. The rebels loyal to Robert Kett in Norfolk, in 1549, and the Diggers who camped with Gerrard Winstanley in Surrey a century later saw access to land and sharing the earth fairly as fundamental to their ideas of natural justice. Enclosure continued to take land out of commoners' use for around three hundred years, and the 'right to roam' protesters who joined the mass trespass on Kinder Scout in Derbyshire were a twentieth-century development of a centuries-old grievance. Though far fewer people relied on the land for their liveli-hood, the countryside had become a place of refuge from the indus-trialised cities, and walking through it became a political act.

The Industrial Revolution did not, however, turn the countryside into a playground. Agricultural workers experienced a revolution of their own and, like their urban counterparts, rural labourers fought against mechanisation, in the Captain Swing riots of 1830. They also fought for representation, achieved in the 1870s by Joseph Arch, who led his Agricultural Union in their 'Revolt of the Field'.

Some thinkers also began to question attitudes to other species, spawning the animal-rights and anti-vivisection movements. In our own time, environmentalists have campaigned locally against road-building, and as part of the global effort to draw attention to the human impact on climate change and the over-consumption of fossil fuels.

Robert Kett, 'Kett's Demands Being in Rebellion' (1549)[1]

In Norfolk, a popular insurrection to overturn landowners' enclosure of common land behind hedges for their own sheep to graze found a leader in one of the property owners they targeted. Robert Kett (c. 1492–1549) was persuaded of the justice of the rebels' cause and, in what became known as the 'camping tyme', led a large group of followers to Mousehold Heath outside Norwich. There, Kett presided over an alternative government. The government of the young Edward VI negotiated with the rebels at first, but then resolved to crush the rebellion by force. In the ensuing battle, as many as three thousand rebels were killed. Kett and his brother William were hanged.

1. We pray your grace that where it is enacted for inclosyng that it be not hurtfull to suche as have enclosed saffred groundes for they be gretly chargeablye to them, and that frome hensforth noman shall enclose any more.

2. We certife your grace that where as the lordes of ther manours hath byn charged with certen fre rent, the same lordes hath sought meanes to charge ther freholders to pay the same rights, contrarye to ryght.

3. We pray your grace that no lord of no mannor shall comon uppon the Comons.

4. We pray that prestes frome hensforth shall purchase no londes neyther fre nor Bond, and the londes that they have in possession

may be letten to temporall men, as they wer in the fyrst yere of
the reign of Kyng henry the viith.

5. We pray that Rede ground and medowe grounde may be at suche
price as they wer in the first yere of Kyng Henry the viith . . .

8. [W]e pray that [any prest] or vicars that be nat able to preche and
sett forth the woorde of god to hys parisheners may be clerly putt
from hys benyfice, and the parissheners there to chose an other
or elles the pateron or lord of the town . . .

11. We pray that all freholders and copieholders may take the
profightes of all commons, and ther to common, and the lordes
not to comon nor take profightes of the same . . .

16. We pray thatt all bonde men may be made fre for god made all
fre with his precious blode shedding.

17. We pray that Ryvers may be ffre and comon to all men for fyshyng
and passage.

Gerrard Winstanley, 'A Declaration from the Poor Oppressed People of England' (1649)[2]

*In the year that Charles I was executed and the Parliamentarians
took over the government of England and Wales, radical movements,
such as the Levellers, Ranters and Fifth Monarchists, started to gather
followers. Gerrard Winstanley (1609–76), a failed clothes merchant,
had a religiously inspired vision of communal living. On 1 April, he
led his followers to common land at St George's Hill in Surrey, where
they set up camp and sowed crops. Initially allowed to settle, they*

were eventually evicted by the army. Winstanley called his movement
the True Levellers, but they are better remembered as the Diggers.
St George's Hill now contains some of the most expensive property
in the country.

[W]e are resolved to be cheated no longer, nor be held under the
slavish fear of you no longer, seeing the Earth was made for us, as
well as for you: And if the Common Land belongs to us who are the
poor oppressed, surely the woods that grow upon the Commons
belong to us likewise: therefore we are resolved to try the uttermost
in the light of reason, to know whether we shall be free men, or slaves.
If we lie still, and let you steale away our birthrights, we perish; and
if we Petition we perish also, though we have paid taxes, given free
quarter, and ventured our lives to preserve the Nation's freedom as
much as you, and therefore by the law of contract with you, freedom
in the land is our portion as well as yours, equal with you: And if we
strive for freedom, and your murdering, governing Laws destroy us,
we can but perish.

Therefore we require, and we resolve to take both Common Land,
and Common woods to be a livelihood for us, and look upon you as
equal with us, not above us, knowing very well, that England, the
land of our Nativity, is to be a common Treasury of livelihood to all,
without respect of persons.

So, then, we declare unto you, that do intend to cut our Common
Woods and Trees, that you shall not do it; unlesse it be for a stock for
us, as aforesaid, and we to know of it, by a publick declaration abroad,
that the poor oppressed, that live thereabouts, may take it, and employ
it, for their publick use, therefore take notice we have demanded it in
the name of the Commons of England, and of all the Nations of the
world, it being the righteous freedom of the Creation . . .

For we say our purpose is, to take these Common Woods to sell
them, now at first to be a stock for our selves, and our children after
us, to plant and manure the Common land withal; for we shall

endeavour by our righteous acting not to leave the earth any longer intangled unto our children, by self-seeking proprietors; But to leave it in a free store-house, and common treasury to all, without respect of persons . . .

And further we intend, that not one, two, or a few men of us shall sell or exchange the said woods, but it shall be known publickly in Print or writing to all, how much every such, and such parcel of wood is sold for, and how it is laid out, either in victuals, corn, ploughs, or other materials necessary . . .

And thus in love we have declared the purpose of our hearts plainly, without flatterie, expecting love, and the same sincerity from you, without grumbling, or quarrelling, being creatures of your own Image and mould, intending no other matter herein, but to observe the Law of righteous action, endeavouring to shut out of the Creation, the cursed thing, called Particular Propriety, which is the cause of all wars, bloud-shed, theft, and enslaving Laws, that hold the people under miserie.

Signed for and in behalf of all the poor oppressed people of England, and the whole world.

Declaration of Wellingborough Diggers (1650)[3]

Winstanley's example inspired a short-lived following in different places across the country. The people of one Northamptonshire village explain here their reasons for digging.

1. We find in the Word of God, that God made the Earth for the use and comfort of all Mankind, and set him in to till and dresse it, and said, That in the sweat of his brows he should eat his bread; and also we find, that God never gave it to any sort of people, that

they should have it all to themselves, and shut out all the rest, but he saith, The Earth hath he given to the children of men, which is every man.

2. We find, that no creature that ever God made was ever deprived of the benefit of the Earth, but Mankind; and that it is nothing but covetousnesse, pride, and hardnesse of heart, that hath caused man so far to degenerate.

3. We find in the Scriptures, that the Prophets and Apostles have left it upon Record, That in the last days the oppressor and proud man shall cease, and God will restore the waste places of the Earth to the use and comfort of Man, and that none shall hurt nor destroy in all his holy Mountain.

4. We have great Encouragement from these two righteous Acts, which the Parliament of England have set forth, the one against Kingly Power, the other to make England a Free Common-wealth.

5. We are necessitated from our present necessity to do this, and we hope that our Actions will justifie us in the gate when all men shall know the truth of our necessity: we are in Wellinborrow in one Parish 1169 persons that receive Alms, as the Officers have made it appear at the Quarter Sessions last: we have made our Case known to the Justices, the Justices have given Order that the Town should raise a Stock to set us on work, and that the Hundred should be enjoyned to assist them; but as yet we see nothing is done, nor any man that goeth about it; we have spent all we have, our trading is decayed, our wives and children cry for bread, our lives are a burden to us, divers of us having 5, 6, 7, 8, 9 in Family, and we cannot get bread for one of them by our labor, rich men's hearts are hardened, they will not give us if we beg at their doors; if we steal, the Law will end our lives, divers of the poor are starved to

death already and it were better for us that are living to dye by the Sword than by Famine. And now we consider that the Earth is our Mother, and that God hath given it to the children of men, and that the common and waste Grounds belong to the poor, and that we have a right to the common ground both from the Law of the Land, Reason and Scriptures; and therefore we have begun to bestow our righteous labor upon it, and we shall trust the Spirit for a blessing upon our labor, resolving not to dig up any man's property, until they freely give us it; and truly we find great comfort already, through the goodnesse of our God, that some of those rich men amongst us, that have had the greatest profit upon the Common, have freely given us their share in it, as one Mr John Freeman, Thomas Nottingham and John Clendon, and divers others; and the Country Farmers have proffered divers of them to give us Seed to sow it, and so we find that God is perswading Japeth to dwell in the tents of Shem: and truly those that we find most against us are such as have been constant enemies to the Parliament's Cause from first to last.

Now at last our desire is, That some that approve of this work of Righteousnesse, would but spread this our Declaration before the great Councel of the Land, that so they may be pleased to give us more encouragement to go on, that so they may be found amongst the small number of those that considers the poor and needy, that so the Lord may deliver them in the time of their troubles, and then they will not be found amongst those that Solomon speaks of, which withhold the Corn (or the Land) from the Poor, which the people shall curse, but blessing shall be upon the heads of those Rulers that sell Corn, and that will let the poor labor upon the Earth to get them Corn, and our lines shall blesse them, so shall good men stand by them, and evil men shall be afraid of them, and they shall be counted the Repairers of our Breaches, and the Restorers of our Paths to dwell in. And thus we have declared the truth of our necessity; and whosoever will come in to us to labor with us, shall have part with us, and we with them, and we shall all of us endeavour to walk righteously and peaceably in the Land of our Nativity.

Anonymous, 'Bonny Portmore' (traditional, *c.* 1690)[4]

Portmore is in County Antrim in Northern Ireland; this ballad laments the destruction of the forest around Lough Beg, an area that passed out of the hands of the Irish O'Neill family into those of Lord Conway and his heirs. The third Viscount Conway built Portmore Castle in 1664, but the estate fell into disuse after his death without an heir, and the forest around it was cut down, to be used for shipmaking.

O bonny Portmore, you shine where you stand
And the more I think on you the more I think long
If I had you now as I had once before
All the lords in Old England would not purchase Portmore.
O bonny Portmore, I am sorry to see
Such a woeful destruction of your ornament tree
For it stood on your shore for many's the long day
Till the long boats from Antrim came to float it away.
O bonny Portmore, you shine where you stand
And the more I think on you the more I think long
If I had you now as I had once before
All the Lords in Old England would not purchase Portmore.
All the birds in the forest they bitterly weep
Saying, 'Where will we shelter or where will we sleep?'
For the Oak and the Ash, they are all cutten down
And the walls of bonny Portmore are all down to the ground.

O bonny Portmore, you shine where you stand
And the more I think on you the more I think long
If I had you now as I had once before
All the Lords of Old England would not purchase Portmore.

Thomas Spence, Spence's Plan for Parochial Partnerships in the Land (1816)[5]

Land was not only the source of most of Britain's wealth in the nine-teenth century, it was also the source of most of its political power. The radical bookseller Thomas Spence (1750–1814) proposed to take land out of the great landowners' hands and return it to the people. He envisaged parish corporations, made up of every person who lived within the parish boundaries, as the administrators of his plan. To the landowners, this was not only a radical but a fundamentally threatening proposal. Spence even wrote a 'Jubilee Hymn' to be sung to the tune of the National Anthem, 'HARK! how the trumpet's sound/ Proclaims the land around/The Jubilee!/Tell all the poor oppress'd, No more they shall be cess'd./Nor landlords more molest /Their property.' Spence himself, though frequently arrested, espoused non-violence. After his death his followers began to be associated with more direct revolutionary action, including the Cato Street conspiracy in 1820 (see William Davidson's speech, p. 230).

For Parochial Partnerships in the Land
Is the only effectual Remedy for the
Distresses and Oppressions of the People.
The Landholders are not Proprietors in Chief; they are but the
Stewards of the Public;
For the LAND is the PEOPLE'S FARM.
The Expenses of the Government do not cause the misery that

Surrounds us, but the enormous exactions of these
'Unjust Stewards.'
Landed monopoly is indeed equally contrary to the benign
Spirit of Christianity, and destructive of
The Independence and Morality of Mankind.
'The Profit of the Earth is for all;'
Yet how deplorably destitute are the great Mass of the People!
Nor is it possible for their situations to be radically amended, but
By the establishment of a system
Founded on the immutable basis of Nature and Justice.
Experience demonstrates its necessity; and the Rights of Mankind
Require it for their preservation.

John Clare, 'The Mores' (c. 1821–4)[6]

Enclosure only gathered pace in the centuries after Kett's rebels first challenged it. Between 1750 and 1920, more than a fifth of England was enclosed behind hedges and fences by Act of Parliament, and almost a third of agricultural land. The poet John Clare (1793–1864), deeply attached to the countryside of his native Northamptonshire, railed against the deprivation of liberty that enclosure entailed.

Far spread the moorey ground a level scene
Bespread with rush and one eternal green
That never felt the rage of blundering plough
Though centurys wreathed spring's blossoms on its brow
Still meeting plains that stretched them far away
In uncheckt shadows of green brown, and grey
Unbounded freedom ruled the wandering scene
Nor fence of ownership crept in between

To hide the prospect of the following eye
Its only bondage was the circling sky
One mighty flat undwarfed by bush and tree
Spread its faint shadow of immensity
And lost itself, which seemed to eke its bounds
In the blue mist the horizon's edge surrounds
Now this sweet vision of my boyish hours
Free as spring clouds and wild as summer flowers
Is faded all — a hope that blossomed free,
And hath been once, no more shall ever be
Inclosure came and trampled on the grave
Of labour's rights and left the poor a slave
And memory's pride ere want to wealth did bow
Is both the shadow and the substance now
The sheep and cows were free to range as then
Where change might prompt nor felt the bonds of men
Cows went and came, with evening morn and night,
To the wild pasture as their common right
And sheep, unfolded with the rising sun,
Heard the swains shout and felt their freedom won
Tracked the red fallow field and heath and plain
Then met the brook and drank and roamed again
The brook that dribbled on as clear as glass
Beneath the roots they hid among the grass
While the glad shepherd traced their tracks along
Free as the lark and happy as her song
But now all's fled and flats of many a dye
That seemed to lengthen with the following eye
Moors, loosing from the sight, far, smooth, and blea
Where swopt the plover in its pleasure free
Are vanished now with commons wild and gay
As poets' visions of life's early day
Mulberry-bushes where the boy would run

To fill his hands with fruit are grubbed and done
And hedgrow-briars – flower-lovers overjoyed
Came and got flower-pots – these are all destroyed
And sky-bound mores in mangled garbs are left
Like mighty giants of their limbs bereft
Fence now meets fence in owners' little bounds
Of field and meadow large as garden grounds
In little parcels little minds to please
With men and flocks imprisoned ill at ease
Each little path that led its pleasant way
As sweet as morning leading night astray
Where little flowers bloomed round a varied host
That travel felt delighted to be lost
Nor grudged the steps that he had ta'en as vain
When right roads traced his journeys and again —
Nay, on a broken tree he'd sit awhile
To see the mores and fields and meadows smile
Sometimes with cowslaps smothered – then all white
With daiseys – then the summer's splendid sight
Of cornfields crimson o'er the headache bloomd
Like splendid armys for the battle plumed
He gazed upon them with wild fancy's eye
As fallen landscapes from an evening sky
These paths are stopt — the rude philistine's thrall
Is laid upon them and destroyed them all
Each little tyrant with his little sign
Shows where man claims earth glows no more divine
But paths to freedom and to childhood dear
A board sticks up to notice 'no road here'
And on the tree with ivy overhung
The hated sign by vulgar taste is hung
As tho the very birds should learn to know
When they go there they must no further go

Thus, with the poor, scared freedom bade goodbye
And much they feel it in the smothered sigh
And birds and trees and flowers without a name
All sighed when lawless law's enclosure came
And dreams of plunder in such rebel schemes
Have found too truly that they were but dreams

W. G. Ward, 'The Battle, the Struggle, and the Victory' (10 May 1873)[7]

Following the lead of the agricultural workers' champion Joseph Arch, support for a union grew rapidly in the shires, and by 1873 the National Agricultural Labourers' Union had more than seventy thousand members. Employers and landowners decided to take on the union, and began refusing to hire men who 'combined' and sacking those who went on strike. W. G. Ward's article in the union's paper, the English Labourers' Chronicle, *set out the lines of the battle that would follow.*

The struggle of classes has commenced; the strife is deepening daily, and the battle is very near. The farmers have determined that the farm labourers shall not combine, that their serfs shall continue serfs, their claims to manhood crushed; that their wages shall not be a matter of mutual consideration or market value – the labourer shall have a maximum of wages at the dictation of a combination of farmers. He shall not be consulted, or his feelings and demands considered: submit or starve. And this tyranny in England in the year 1873!

Yes, today, while the tenant farmers are agitating for tenant rights, they are trampling upon the rights of their labourers; while they are combined to get legislative protection, and by legislation, public money to assist them in their business, they are bitterly indignant that their serfs should presume to combine, even to attain free agency to the simplest element of manhood – the right to say what their labour is worth . . .

Have the farmers no power of reflection, no memory of agrarian anarchy, no conception what manhood is, when tyranny is striving to crush out manliness, and tramples upon simple but hearty hopes, and leaves no alternative but slavish submission or manly rebellion? Cannot the farmers calculate the effects of their success in the exhaustion of Union funds, the prostration of the peaceable agitation, and the dispersion of the Union delegates and their leaders? Do they know so little of their men, know nothing of the character of Englishmen, that they believe that, silence the Union, and the men will tamely submit to the yoke of slavery; and that beat back Englishmen from the glimpse of freedom, tear up their Union cards, and unity is gone, starve them a week, and their submission is perfect? . . .

If our labourers inherit an atom of the spirit of their forefathers, of those who fought at Cressy and Waterloo, and struck for freedom at Naseby and Dunbar, they will not basely bend the neck to a farmer's yoke, let the consequences be what they may; if our labourers inherit within their breasts the hearts of iron of their forefathers, that gave them courage to face the battle with any odds, to bravely force the breach against any numbers, to win for their country in a hundred battles, surely now they will not sneak away at freedom's call, and rush to dishonoured graves, frightened at the frown upon a farmer's brow! Shall they, whose forefathers in the past gave their blood and lives freely for their country, not be able now to give all to win one battle for themselves? . . .

But if there is no alternative between submission to serfdom and starvation, if civilisation has no cheer, no comfort, no protection for the farm labourer, can he be expected to tamely lie down and die? No, no. Better to die in a noble struggle for freedom than linger out

a degraded life, a farmer's chattel, than creep on slowly, hunger-bitten
and tortured, to an ignominious pauper's grave.

Richard Barlow-Kennett, 'Address to the Working Classes' on Vivisection (1 August 1883)[8]

*The idea of the right of all living things to fair treatment has a long
tradition in England, including William Blake's poetic defence of
animal liberation ('A robin redbreast in a cage/Puts all heaven in
a rage') and Percy Shelley's justification of vegetarianism (A
Vindication of Natural Diet, 1813). The Victoria Street Society was
established to campaign against vivisection by Frances Power
Cobbe in 1875. The movement drew support from prominent figures,
but it also set out to appeal to the working classes, as this leaflet,
written by Richard Barlow-Kennett and first published in the
Society's newsletter, the* Zoophilist, *shows. Barlow-Kennett's contribution to animal welfare has its most lasting legacy in Battersea:
he donated £500 to the Dogs' Home on condition it opened its
doors to cats as well.*

Do you know of the un-English and cowardly sin practised in our
country, called VIVISECTION, which means cutting, mangling, and
torturing, sometimes for days and weeks together, LIVING animals?

Do you know that if a working man torture a horse or dog, he is
fined or imprisoned, while scientific torturers are by Law authorised
to carry on their vile pursuit?

Do you know that this debasing cruelty was introduced into
England from France, 200 years ago, under the pretence of alleviating
and curing the diseases of mankind, and do you not ask, in the name
of common sense, why all diseases are not banished by this time,
when millions of animals have been sacrificed; one human monster

having 'experimented' on 14,000 dogs in ten years?

Do you know that these torturers in pursuit of scientific discovery will never stop with animals, but will certainly try their experiments on men, women and children at the Hospitals – and indeed have done so already both abroad and at home? Do you see how this matter concerns you working men, who are so liable to accidents, and to be taken to some hospital in which 'experiments' are tried?

Do you see the power for GOOD you have, and how responsible you are to give your votes to those candidates only who will promise to support those who are labouring to abolish this diabolical Vivisection? You, working men, are freer to do this than those above you in station, who believe the mean denials of men, who visit them as friends, and whose hands are dyed with the blood of innocent, intelligent, faithful animals.

Do you know the hardening effect Vivisection has on poor young medical students – who will be the future doctors of your wives and children? – Do you wonder, Lord SHAFTESBURY said in reference to Vivisection, 'It is an abominable sin?'

Acquaint yourselves, working men, with this monster VIVISECTION! There are facts which will make your honest blood curdle, and stir your spirit to do something to protect the harmless brutes and the poor in our Hospitals; and to compel our Legislators to forbid a practice which disgraces old England herself, and every right-minded Englishman.

Henry S. Salt, *Animals' Rights Considered in Relation to Social Progress* (1892)[9]

Henry Salt was a public-school classics master, who left his job to devote himself to pamphleteering on behalf of radical causes,

including an attack on corporal punishment and a defence of vege-
tarianism. In Animals' Rights Considered in Relation to Social
Progress, *he set out the case against keeping, killing and hunting*
animals of all kinds.

That wild animals, no less than domestic animals, have their rights,
albeit of a less positive character and far less easy to define, is an
essential point which follows directly from the acceptance of the
general principle of a jus animalium. It is of the utmost importance
to emphasise the fact that, whatever the legal fiction may have been,
or may still be, the rights of animals are not morally dependent on
the so-called rights of property; it is not to owned animals merely
that we must extend our sympathy and protection.

   The domination of property has left its trail indelibly on the records
of this question. Until the passing of 'Martin's Act' in 1822, the most
atrocious cruelty, even to domestic animals, could only be punished
where there was proved to be an infringement of the rights of ownership. This monstrous iniquity, so far as relates to the domestic
animals, has now been removed; but the only direct legal protection
yet accorded to wild animals (except in the Wild Birds' Protection
Act of 1880) is that which prohibits their being baited or pitted in
conflict; otherwise, it is open for anyone to kill or torture them with
impunity, except where the sacred privileges of 'property' are thereby
offended. 'Everywhere,' it has been well said, 'it is absolutely a capital
crime to be an unowned creature.'

   Yet surely an unowned creature has the same right as another
to live his life unmolested and uninjured except when this is in
some way inimical to human welfare. We are justified by the
strongest of all instincts, that of self-defence, in safe-guarding
ourselves against such a multiplication of any species of animal
as might imperil the established supremacy of man; but we are
not justified in unnecessarily killing – still less in torturing – any
harmless beings whatsoever . . .

In the same way, while admitting that man is justified, by the exigencies of his own destiny, in asserting his supremacy over the wild animals, we must deny him any right to turn his protectorate into a tyranny, or to inflict one atom more of subjection and pain than is absolutely unavoidable. To take advantage of the sufferings of animals, whether wild or tame, for the gratification of sport, or gluttony, or fashion, is quite incompatible with any possible assertion of animals' rights. We may kill, if necessary, but never torture or degrade.

'The laws of self-defence,' says an old writer, 'undoubtedly justify us in destroying those animals who would destroy us, who injure our properties or annoy our persons; but not even these, whenever their situation incapacitates them from hurting us. I know of no right which we have to shoot a bear on an inaccessible island of ice, or an eagle on the mountain's top, whose lives cannot injure us, nor deaths procure us any benefit. We are unable to give life, and therefore ought not to take it away from the meanest insect without sufficient reason.'

I reserve . . . certain problems which are suggested by the wholesale slaughter of wild animals by the huntsman or the trapper, for purposes which are loosely supposed to be necessary and inevitable. Meantime a word must be said about the condition of those tamed or caged animals which, though wild by nature, and not bred in captivity, are yet to a certain extent 'domesticated' – a class which stands midway between the true domestic and the wild. Is the imprisonment of such animals a violation of the principle we have laid down? In most cases I fear this question can only be answered in the affirmative.

And here, once more I must protest against the common assumption that these captive animals are laid under an obligation to man by the very fact of their captivity, and that therefore no complaint can be made on the score of their loss of freedom and the many miseries involved therein! It is extraordinary that even humane thinkers and earnest champions of animals' rights, should permit themselves to be misled by this most fallacious and flimsy line of argument. 'Harmful animals,' says one of these writers, 'and animals with whom man has to struggle for the fruits of the earth, may of course be so shut up: they gain by it, for otherwise they would not have been let live.'

And so in like manner it is sometimes contended that a menagerie is a sort of paradise for wild beasts, whose loss of liberty is more than compensated by the absence of the constant apprehension and insecurity which, it is conveniently assumed, weigh so heavily on their spirits. But all this notion of their 'gaining by it' is in truth nothing more than a mere arbitrary supposition; for, in the first place, a speedy death may, for all we know, be very preferable to a protracted death-in-life; while, secondly, the pretence that wild animals enjoy captivity is even more absurd than the episcopal contention that the life of a domestic animal is 'one of very great comfort, according to the animal's own standard'.

To take a wild animal from its free natural state, full of abounding egoism and vitality, and to shut it up for the wretched remainder of its life in a cell where it has just space to turn round, and where it necessarily loses every distinctive feature of its character – this appears to me to be as downright a denial as could well be imagined of the theory of animals' rights. Nor is there very much force in the plea founded on the alleged scientific value of these zoological institutions, at any rate in the case of the wilder and less tractable animals, for it cannot be maintained that the establishment of wild-beast shows is in any way necessary for the advancement of human knowledge. For what do the good people see who go to the gardens on a half-holiday afternoon to poke their umbrellas at a blinking eagle-owl, or to throw dog-biscuits down the expansive throat of a hippopotamus? Not wild beasts or wild birds certainly, for there never have been or can be such in the best of all possible menageries, but merely the outer semblances and simulacra of the denizens of forest and prairie – poor spiritless remnants of what were formerly wild animals.

To kill and stuff these victims of our morbid curiosity, instead of immuring them in lifelong imprisonment, would be at once a humaner and a cheaper method, and could not possibly be of less use to science.

But of course these remarks do not apply, with anything like the same force, to the taming of such wild animals as are readily domesticated in captivity, or trained by man to some intelligible and practical purpose. For example, though we may look forward to the time when it will not be deemed necessary to convert wild elephants into beasts of burden, it must be acknowledged that the exaction of such service, however questionable in itself, is very different from condemning an animal to a long term of useless and deadening imbecility. There can be no absolute standard of morals in these matters, whether it be human liberty or animal liberty that is at stake; I merely contend that it is as incumbent on us to show good reason for curtailing the one as the other. This would be at once recognised, but for the prevalent habit of regarding the lower animals as devoid of moral purpose and individuality.

The caging of wild song-birds is another practice which deserves the strongest reprobation. It is often pleaded that the amusement given by these unfortunate prisoners to the still more unfortunate human prisoners of the sick-room, or the smoky city, is a justification for their sacrifice; but surely such excuses rest only on habit – habitual inability or unwillingness to look facts in the face. Few invalids, I fancy, would be greatly cheered by the captive life that hangs at their window, if they had fully considered how blighted and sterilised a life it must be. The bird-catcher's trade and the bird-catcher's shop are alike full of horrors, and they are horrors which are due entirely to a silly fashion and a habit of callous thoughtlessness, not on the part of the ruffianly bird-catcher (ruffianly enough, too often) who has to bear the burden of the odium attaching to these cruelties, but of the respectable customers who buy captured larks and linnets without the smallest scruple or consideration.

Finally, let me point out that if we desire to cultivate a closer intimacy with the wild animals, it must be an intimacy based on a
genuine love for them as living beings and fellow-creatures, not on
the superior power or cunning by which we can drag them from
their native haunts, warp the whole purpose of their lives, and
degrade them to the level of pets, or curiosities, or labour-saving
automata.

Ernest A. Baker, *The Forbidden Land* (1924)[10]

*The battle over access to public land did not with the industrial
revolution. Land came to be seen as a place where different classes'
idea of leisure activities – hunting and shooting for owners and their
friends, walking, 'rambling' and camping for others – were in opposition. Ernest Baker set out the problem that campaigners for access
to the countryside faced.*

Epping Forest was saved for the metropolis and the nation in 1871–4,
by simple assertion of the rights of common inhering in the local
inhabitants. But Kinder Scout, Bleaklow Head, the Langsett,
Saddleworth, and Yorkshire moors were in different case. Those
barren tracts never had the abundance of pasture, where the
commoner could graze his beasts, or of woods and spinneys, where
he had the right to gather firing; hence the claims to commonage
were unimportant. Thus, the moorlands remained waste lands out
and out, and nobody troubled much about them. So far as access to
them was concerned, no let or hindrance was interposed by heedless
landowners. Those who wanted to could cross them where they
pleased from village to village, but they were very few who did so
please; and as to recognised routes, the only ones of any extent were

the ways that followed in the time before railroads by the great droves of cattle that used to be sent from north to south.

Then, one unlucky day, grouse-shooting became a pastime with the idle rich, and the policy of shutting up the open wild gradually began. Nobody was as yet alive enough to the charm of these vast solitudes to raise objections. Only in the last few decades have the public realised the seriousness of their loss. Now, however, it is becoming at length an obvious fact, and we wonder how our fathers could have failed to appreciate it, that the open spaces of the Pennine are the back garden, the recreation ground, for the crowded millions of workers in the adjoining towns. They are to the big industrial cities of the north what the commons, heaths, and downs of the Home Counties are to London. Complete freedom of access may be delayed, but it will come inevitably; the day surely cannot be far off when every barrier must be removed, to meet the lawful necessities of the people.

Benny Rothman, The Kinder Trespass (24 April 1932)[11]

Kinder Scout is the highest point in the Peak District. In the 1930s, the land was in private ownership, and gamekeepers kept any trespassing walkers off, sometimes with violence. A young Communist car mechanic, Bernard 'Benny' Rothman (1911–2002), was inspired by his mistreatment at the gamekeepers' hands to lead a 'mass trespass' of about four hundred walkers. He was among six trespassers arrested and jailed for four months for their action. The campaign continued and gathered pace, with ten thousand walkers assembling the following week. Legislation to improve access to the countryside was first passed in 1949, but the 'right to roam' movement continued to press for more, a goal partly achieved with the

passage of the Countryside and Rights of Way Act 2000. This is
Rothman's testimony at his trial.

The prosecution has endeavoured to prove this charge of Unlawful
Assembly against myself and the other Defendants. For my defence
it is necessary to point out why this demonstration of April 24th was
held to explain what occurred. I don't want to waste your time but I
am just going to quickly examine this Access to Mountains business.
One of the remarkable things about Rambling at present is its tremendous growth during the last few years. More and more Ramblers are
leaving the towns and cities every week-end and going out for relaxation and for a change to the country. Unfortunately the big number
of restrictions placed on Ramblers fully prevent them enjoying the
country-side to their utmost. The biggest restriction placed on them
particularly so in Derbyshire is the fact that the majority of the Peaks
and big stretches of Moorland are closed to them. The Ramblers are
in the main forced to keep on footpaths where these exist and denied
the pleasure of Rambling over the Moorland or climbing on the tops.
In fact, at times, Rambling as it is as present, is a farce. In wet weather
the footpaths are like quagmires and in dry weather are more often
than not very much overcrowded. The whole enjoyment and change
is taken out of such Rambling, and as a means of relaxation for the
lads and girls who are really in need of a change from the drab and
monotonous conditions in cities such Rambling under these restrictions is of no use at all. It is true however, quite a big number of
Ramblers in spite of the fact that they are legally not allowed to walk
on the Moorland do so much to their sorrow if they are forced to
turn many miles back or are thrashed by Keepers as they sometimes
are. The justification of the simple demand to allow Ramblers the
privilege to walk over all uncultivated land is recognized at the present
day by thousands and tens of thousands of people who for this reason
are supporting the agitation for a piece of legislation generally known

as the Access to Mountains Bill. Quite apart from the fact that it is logically just for Ramblers to obtain access to mountains there is the historical fact which I want to dwell on; but to put it in a nutshell historians tell us that at one time the whole land belonged to the people and not to any one group or class. It was confiscated from the people by means of thousands of Inclosure Acts, passed by a Parliament which at that time only represented the Lords of the Manor and the Aristocratic class which became the land-owner. The British Workers Sports Federation like the many other organisations in existence believe and endeavour to obtain access to mountains for working class Ramblers.

Since 1884 different organisations and Societies have carried out agitation towards the passing of the Access to Mountains Bill. For year after year hopes have been raised only to be dashed down again when the Access to Mountains Bill has been rejected. What is this something that is preventing the Access to Mountains Bill being passed. The British Workers Sports Federation of which I am the Lancashire District Secretary believe that only by means of united action on the part of working class sportsmen can the demand for better facilities be obtained. We don't believe this in some religious kind but base our belief on actual instances of where this action of which we speak has been successful for Ramblers; the most striking example is that at Doctor's Gate. When this pass was closed to Ramblers by a land-owner action on the part of big numbers of Ramblers and Rambling clubs forced the land-owner to open the path to Ramblers. This took place in 1909, 1911 and [19]12 and again at a later date.

Similarly, action on the part of several thousand footballers in Tottenham last year under the leadership of the British Workers' Sports Federation obtained for these boys cheaper playing pitches and dressing accommodation. The mass trespass of April 24th was organised in this spirit and brought to light facts which nobody can mistake or misinterpret. It showed that the land-owners are not prepared to passively agree to allow rambling on the Moorland which they hold close; that the friendliness of many land-owners with the Ramblers Federation was not due to their sympathy to the Access to Mountains Bill but on the contrary, shewed that the land-owners recognised that the Ramblers Federation by acting to prevent mass action was assisting them to maintain the land which they had enclosed. I submit that the scuffle which ensued in April 24th was not the responsibility of the Ramblers who took part in this Mass Tresspass. I also suggest that the charges laid against myself and the Defendants here are an endeavour not to deliberately prevent breaches of the law but an attempt to prevent Ramblers from taking the mass action which will gain them access to mountains.

Let me examine in detail the facts of the case. The first piece of evidence brought against me was evidence in connection with the announcement of the demonstration. I submit that in every announcement made there was no suggestion to commit a breach of the peace but all our announcements, including the one made to the *Manchester Evening News* very briefly pointed out the reason why this demonstration was being held and announced our meeting place and time of meeting. In endeavouring to indicate that our intentions were violent this prosecution points out the article in the *Manchester Evening News* and stresses the words 'shock troops', words suggestive of the method used by the shock troops of the German Hitler party. I hope you will remember that the Reporter admitted that these were his own words. The first event that took place on April 24th is the meeting at the Recreation ground and I want to pass right off this and just comment on the fact that it is quite clear that there was nothing about that Meeting, to use the words of the witness Bradshaw, 'to cause any apprehension', and comment on the fact that we moved off actually before two o'clock in an endeavour to preserve the peace and prevent any disorder taking place. I want to comment on the fact that when requested we did not hold a meeting in the Puddle Field – again, a conscious endeavour on our part to maintain the Peace. We held a meeting at the Quarry where I spoke. Was my speech an inflammatory speech calculated to cause a breach of the peace? The very fact that no police interfered with me when I had finished speaking should indicate that my speech was just to explain the purpose of the demonstration, and to appeal for an orderly and disciplined ramble over Kinder. Let me comment here that almost every single newspaper reported that about the speech I made. Regarding the evidence of Messrs. Brailsford and Hudson who neither of them wrote down what I said and yet, remember the statements that they made here. I just ask you to take their evidence for what it is worth. Let me also comment on the fact that Hudson states quite definitively that he remembers me making the statement that I am the Secretary of the British Workers' Sports Federation and, in the second place, that I should lead the trespass; let me point out just this about those statements: that not one other witness can remember me making that statement and all the newspapers that commented on me making that speech at the Quarry simply referred to the Speaker; either as a young man or a Rambler, and that had I made the statement that I was the Secretary of the British Workers' Sports Federation it is quite evident that every newspaper would have mentioned it. Another point was brought out by the witness Hudson that many Ramblers at the meeting when they heard my speech became quite enthusiastic; I submit that this was only because I made it quite clear to everybody that we were not a mob of hooligans, that we were not there for the purpose of damaging either life or property. I submit that at this meeting I endeavoured to put to the Ramblers present there to keep together as a disciplined body and not as a mob.

The next point: the first thing I want to draw attention to is the manner in which we advanced. Every witness makes it quite clear that we advanced in open formation and I submit this was an endeavour on our part to avoid any possible scuffle. Regarding the scuffle itself – and I don't want to waste any time on the scuffle – I submit the different accounts given by the witnesses vary to such an extent that it is really difficult to get a true picture of what actually took place, but it seems remarkable that a cheerful body of young men and women who only a minute or two before had been singing should suddenly charge a small body of Keepers whom they have endeavoured to avoid, and drag them to the ground and assault them; I would like to submit that the Keepers who were pulled to the ground must have provoked the hostility of the Ramblers in question. It is curious, too, the Ramblers moved on immediately. Had it been their intention to assault the Keepers they certainly were in big enough numbers to do this. The demonstration of 24th April was a peaceful demonstration to gain support for our contention of the right to access to mountains. The assembly at the Quarry, if that is the assembly which is alleged to be an unlawful Assembly, gave no one reason to fear a breach of the Peace. If this is correct I simply plead not guilty to that charge.

Voices of the Kingsnorth Six Protest (October 2007)[12]

Greenpeace was founded as an environmental campaigning organ-isation in Canada in 1971, and its first British branch opened in 1976. Today it has 130,000 supporters in the UK and 2.8 million around the world. The documentary-maker Nick Broomfield made a film, A Time Comes, *about one of their most high-profile recent actions. The introduction explains: 'The UK government wants to reduce CO_2*

emissions 80 per cent by 2050. In 2007 it was considering building new coal-fired power stations across Britain. In protest, Greenpeace activists took direct action at Kingsnorth coal plant. This is their story.'

Will Rose: We had rope, water, paint, all of our supplies . . . We hadn't slept much the night before because we were nervous and in a strange place with a lot of other activists, and after a few hours of climbing, any adrenalin had worn off and we were dehydrated and exhausted. I felt as though I was going to collapse. My arms were aching from pulling on the ropes and my legs were aching from taking the strain. You'd get to a platform and rest for a minute and then have to pull up the bags. You can't stop because you can't let down the rest of the team.

Ben Stewart: It took nine hours . . . We were climbing up between the four flues. The CO_2 goes up at a temperature of 120 degrees and it was like climbing through a huge radiator. The hottest, dirtiest place you could imagine . . . And I do remember the sense of satisfaction coming out the top. It was just kind of pure, soaring joy. Like kind of endorphins exploding in the brain, like a firework of adrenalin. It was just insane . . .

Unfortunately we have a situation in Britain where our government simply isn't listening to reason. I'm standing right now on the chimney that belches out twenty thousand pounds of CO_2 every day. It's a shame on our nation. But what's a real shame is that Gordon Brown wants to build a new one of those carbon dinosaurs. And that's why we're up here. We're trying to stop that happening.

Narrator: How high is the chimney?

Hall: It's either 209 or 220 metres . . . I felt slightly nervous and afraid but I felt like this is something I've wanted to do for a long time, so

I felt, I felt quite honoured . . . Once I went over the side, it was not very nice at all. It was starting to get dark and I felt a bit lonely and exposed.

Narrator: And why did you feel it was necessary to do that action?

Hall: It emits nine million tons of carbon dioxide a year, and the fact that they're just trying to build a sicker one on the side is just completely outrageous.

Stewart: There was a very real danger, according to our lawyers, that we would go to jail . . . The moments the jury became most engaged was when the witnesses, the defendants, or the scientific witnesses were talking about the effects of climate change on our kids and on our grandchildren. And suddenly I think it put our actions into a different context. It made them look, quite frankly, proportionate and reasonable . . .

The guy stood up, and so much depended on that first utterance. Is it gonna be N or G? 'N' for not guilty or 'G' for guilty. As soon as the foreman went, 'N,' the court erupted . . . The verdict we think marks a tipping point for the climate change movement. When twelve normal people say that it is legitimate for a direct action group to shut down a coal-fired power station because of the harm that it does to the planet, then one has to ask where that leaves government energy policy.

———————————

EMPIRE AND RACE

'ALL SLAVES WANT TO BE FREE'

Britain's expansion overseas, beginning in the sixteenth century, brought new encounters and new injustices, and British relations with 'aliens' who settled in this country were always a complex combination of accommodation, toleration, suspicion and oppression. Foreigners within British shores were one thing. When it came to encounters with indigenous peoples in their own lands, Britain's record was often deplorable. Critics of the British Empire rose up even as its boundaries were being extended and its benefits extolled. That British imperial expansion was predicated in significant part on slavery, and in all cases on the imposition of the coloniser's rule on the colonised, was by no means universally celebrated, accepted or excused as the custom of the age.

The raising of native voices against the brutalities of empire and its intrinsic inequalities gave fuel to the abolitionist movement at home in the late eighteenth and early nineteenth centuries. In India, the so-called jewel in the imperial crown, men and women resisted British rule for more than a hundred and fifty years, from Mysore to Cawnpore. With Gandhi's non-violence *ahimsa* movement, an entirely new way of fighting oppression was born.

In the post-imperial age, the people of former colonies have brought their own perspective to life as immigrants in the 'mother country'. The old suspicions voiced by the first Elizabethans have also returned, while racial tension and prejudice have been widespread. But there has been more positive cross-cultural fertilisation, too, in areas as diverse as politics, literature, sport and music. In more recent years, migrant workers from the European Union and asylum seekers from around the world have become the latest immigrants to discover that Britain often gives a less than wholehearted welcome to 'outsiders'.

William Cecil, A Speech in Parliament, *anno* 1588, upon a Bill against Strangers and Aliens Selling Wares by Retail (1588)[1]

> *It is estimated that around fifty thousand immigrants settled in London between 1550 and 1585. William Cecil (1520–98), made Lord Burghley in 1571, was Elizabeth I's chief minister, lord treasurer, and her most trusted adviser. Not all business before the House was government business, however, and here Burghley speaks against a proposal to restrict the trade of these 'aliens'. As he argued, their effect on the capital's economy was mostly benign, but he also makes a moral case.*

This Bill, as I conceive, offereth to the consideration of this honourable House a controversy between the natural born subject of this realm, and a stranger inhabiting among us. Surely, before I proceed any further, I find myself doubly affected and doubly distracted. For, on the one side, the very name of my country and nation is so pleasant in mine ears and so delightful in my heart, that I am compelled to subscribe unto him who, having rehearsed all the degrees of conjunction and society, concludeth thus, *omnes omnium charitates una Patria complexa est.* Insomuch that in this case, wherein my country is a part, and especially that part of my country [London] which as it is the head of the body, so ought it by me to be most honoured and loved, methinks I might needs judge myself to be no competent judge in this cause. But on the other side, in the person of the stranger, I consider the miserable and afflicted state of these poor exiles, who, together with their countries, have lost all (or the greatest) comforts of this life, and, for want of friends, lie exposed to the wrongs and injuries of the malicious and ill-affected. The condition of strangers is that they have many harbours but few friends. In these respects I am moved with an extra ordinary commiseration of them, and feel in myself a sympathy and fellow-suffering with them . . .

And therefore I pray you that I may lay before you my judgment in the matter, as I have declared my affection to the parties. The bill requireth that it be enacted that no aliens-born, being neither denizens nor having served as apprentices by the space of seven years, should sell any wares by retail.

Because it is required that this be made a law, let us consider how it may stand, *first*, with the grounds and foundations of all laws (which are the laws of nature and the Law of God), and *secondly*, with the profit and commodity of the commonwealth.

I will not detain you with mathematical or philosophical discourses concerning the earth and man and man's residence thereon. The whole earth, being but a point in the centre of the world, will admit no division of dominions; *punctum est indivisibile*. Man (as Plato saith) is no earthly, but a heavenly creature, and therefore hath *caput tanquam radicem infixum caelo*. The residence or continuance of one nation in one place is not of the law of nature, which (being in itself immutable) would admit no transmigration of people or transplantations of nations. But I will propound unto you two grounds of nature, as more proper to this purpose. One is that we should give to others the same measure that we would receive from them, which is the golden rule of justice, and the other is that we ought by all good means to strengthen the links of society between man and man (*tum artibus, tum opera, tum facultatibus, devincire hominum inter homines societatem*), and that they wrench in sunder the joint society of mankind who maintain that the cause of a citizen should have that attention which is denied to the foreigner.

The law of God is next, which in infinite places commendeth unto us the good usage and entertainment of strangers; in Deuteronomy, *God loveth the stranger, giving him food and raiment. Therefore love ye the stranger*. In Leviticus, *if a stranger sojourn with yon in your land, ye shall not vex him. But the stranger which dwelleth with you shall be as one of yourselves, and ye shall love him as yourselves. For ye were strangers.* In Ezekiel, it appeareth that the land of promise was by God's appointment allotted as well to the stranger as to the Israelite . . . So that for this point I may well conclude with Mr Calvin, who saith that 'tis an inhospitality and ferocity worthy of a savage to oppress miserable strangers who take refuge in our safeguard . . .

Forsooth (it is said generally) by impoverishing the natural subject and enriching the stranger; by nourishing a scorpion in our bosoms; by taking the children's bread and casting it to dogs; and (more particularly), first, by multitude of retailers (for the more men exercise one trade, the less is every one his gain), and secondly, by the strangers policy, which consisteth either in providing their wares in such sort that they may sell better cheap than the natural subject, or else by persuading our people that they do so . . .

It cannot be denied that the number of retailers is somewhat increased by these denizens; but yet not so much, that the burden of them is so insupportable, as is pretended . . .

As touching their policy, which consists in drawing of customers to their shops or houses, either by selling cheap indeed, or else by persuading us that they sell their wares more cheap than our nation can do, I take it (saving reformation) very easy to be answered. For if the first be true that they do indeed sell better pennyworths, then we have no cause to punish but cherish them as good members of our commonwealth, which by no means can be better enriched than by keeping down the prices of foreign commodities, and enhancing the value of our own. Besides, the benefit of cheapness of foreign commodities by so much exceedeth the benefit of dear prices, by how much the number of buyers of them exceedeth the number of sellers, which is infinite. But if the second be true, that *it is but our error to believe that they sell their wares better cheap* than our nation doth, then surely I cannot but think it very great injustice to punish them for a fault committed by us.

It hath been further objected unto them in this house, that by their sparing and frugal living, they have been the better enabled to sell good pennyworths. It seems we are much straitened for arguments, when we are driven to accuse them for their virtues.

William Shakespeare, *Sir Thomas More*, Act II, Scene 4 (*c.* 1593)[2]

This scene from a play by several different hands is reliably attributed to Shakespeare. In it, Henry VIII's future chancellor, Thomas More, in his capacity as Sheriff of London, speaks to a riotous group of apprentices, who are about to attack foreigners in the city. It is one of the most eloquent statements of the grounds for multicultural living although, like many of Shakespeare's versions of history, it probably bears little relation to reality. Although More did address a crowd on the eve of May Day 1516 at St Martin's, his powers of persuasion were only temporary. A full-scale riot broke out, foreigners' houses were attacked, and order was brutally restored. Four men were hanged, drawn and quartered, and seven more hanged around the city. Three hundred who had been arrested were only spared by the King after Cardinal Wolsey and the Queen, Catherine of Aragon, appealed for their lives.

More: Grant them removed, and grant that this your noise
Hath chid down all the majesty of England;
Imagine that you see the wretched strangers,
Their babies at their backs with their poor luggage,
Plodding to the ports and coasts for transportation,
And that you sit as kings in your desires,
Authority quite silenced by your brawl,

And you in rough of your opinions clothed;
What had you got? I'll tell you: you had taught
How insolence and strong hand should prevail,
How order should be quelled; and by this pattern
Not one of you should live an aged man,
For other ruffians, as their fancies wrought,
With self same hand, self reasons, and self right,
Would shark on you, and men like ravenous fishes
Would feed on one another . . .
O, desperate as you are,
Wash your foul minds with tears, and those same hands,
That you like rebels lift against the peace,
Lift up for peace, and your unreverent knees,
Make them your feet to kneel to be forgiven!
Tell me but this: what rebel captain,
As mutinies are incident, by his name
Can still the rout? who will obey a traitor?
Or how can well that proclamation sound,
When there is no addition but a rebel
To qualify a rebel? You'll put down strangers,
Kill them, cut their throats, possess their houses,
And lead the majesty of law in line,
To slip him like a hound. Say now the king
(As he is clement, if th' offender mourn)
Should so much come to short of your great trespass
As but to banish you, whether would you go?
What country, by the nature of your error,
Should give you harbour? go you to France or Flanders,
To any German province, to Spain or Portugal,
Nay, anywhere that not adheres to England, –
Why, you must needs be strangers: would you be pleased
To find a nation of such barbarous temper,
That, breaking out in hideous violence,

Would not afford you an abode on earth,
Whet their detested knives against your throats,
Spurn you like dogs, and like as if that God
Owed not nor made not you, nor that the claimants
Were not all appropriate to your comforts,
But chartered unto them, what would you think
To be thus used? this is the strangers' case;
And this your mountainish inhumanity.

All: Faith a says true: let's do as we may be done to.

———————

Anna Barbauld, *Sins of Government, Sins of the Nation; Or, A Discourse for the Fast* (19 April 1793)[3]

The expansion of the British Empire was not met with universal approval at home. As Winston Churchill later admitted, 'We are not a young people with an innocent record and a scanty inheritance. We have engrossed to ourselves, in times when other powerful nations were paralysed by barbarism or internal war, an altogether disproportionate share of the wealth and traffic of the world . We have got all we want in territory, and our claim to be left in the unmolested enjoyment of vast and splendid possessions, mainly acquired by violence, largely maintained by force, often seems less reasonable to others than to us . . .'[4] The radical poet and essayist Anna Barbauld (1743–1825) here anticipates such self-knowledge by more than a century, in a sermon occasioned by Britain's entry into war against revolutionary France.

[W]ar may be said to be, with regard to nations, the sin which most easily besets them. We, my friends, in common with other nations, have much guilt to repent of from this cause, and it ought to make a large part of our humiliations on this day. When we carry our eyes back through the long records of our history, we see wars of plunder, wars of conquest, wars of religion, wars of pride, wars of succession, wars of idle speculation, wars of unjust interference; and hardly among them one war of necessary self-defence in any of our essential or very important interests. Of late years, indeed, we have known none of the calamities of war in our own country but the wasteful expense of it; and sitting aloof from those circumstances of personal provocation, which in some measure might excuse its fury, we have calmly voted slaughter and merchandised destruction – so much blood and tears for so many rupees, or dollars, or ingots. Our wars have been wars of cool calculating interest, as free from hatred as from love of mankind; the passions which stir the blood have had no share in them. We devote a certain number of men to perish on land and sea, and the rest of us sleep sound, and, protected in our usual occupations, talk of the events of war as what diversifies the flat uniformity of life.

We should, therefore, do well to translate this word war into language more intelligible to us. When we pay our army and our navy estimates, let us set down – so much for killing, so much for maiming, so much for making widows and orphans, so much for bringing famine upon a district, so much for corrupting citizens and subjects into spies and traitors, so much for ruining industrious tradesmen and making bankrupts (of that species of distress at least, we can form an idea), so much for letting loose the dæmons of fury, rapine and lust within the fold of cultivated society, and giving to the brutal ferocity of the most ferocious, its full scope and range of invention. We shall by this means know what we have paid our money for, whether we have made a good bargain, and whether the account is likely to pass – elsewhere . . .

In this guilty business there is a circumstance which greatly aggravates its guilt, and that is the impiety of calling upon the Divine Being to assist us in it. Almost all nations have been in the habit of mixing with their bad passions a show of religion, and of prefacing these their murders with prayers and the solemnities of worship. When they send out their armies to desolate a country and destroy the fair face of nature, they have the presumption to hope that the Sovereign of the Universe will condescend to be their auxiliary, and to enter into their petty and despicable contests. Their prayer, if put into plain language, would run thus: God of love, father of all the families of the earth, we are going to tear in pieces our brethren of mankind, but our strength is not equal to our fury, we beseech thee to assist us in the work of slaughter. Go out, we pray thee, with our fleets and armies; we call them Christian, and we have interwoven in our banners and the deco- rations of our arms the symbols of a suffering religion, that we may fight under the cross upon which our Saviour died. Whatever mischief we do, we shall do it in thy name; we hope, therefore, thou wilt protect us in it. Thou, who hast made of one blood all the dwellers upon the earth, we trust thou wilt view us alone with partial favour, and enable us to bring misery upon every other quarter of the globe. – Now if we really expect such prayers to be answered, we are the weakest, if not, we are the most hypocritical of beings . . .

Bad actions are made worse by hypocrisy: an unjust war is in itself so bad a thing, that there is only one way of making it worse – and that is, by mixing religion with it.

Robert Wedderburn, *The Axe Laid to the Root or A Fatal Blow to Oppressors, Being an Address to the Planters and Negroes of the Island of Jamaica* (1817)[5]

Slavery was an integral part of the expansion of the British Empire for more than two hundred years. When voices were raised against the slave trade in the late eighteenth century, some men of power began to admit as much. William Pitt the Younger declared in the House of Commons in 1792 that 'No nation in Europe . . . has . . . plunged so deeply into this guilt as Britain.' What gave the movement for abolition real force, however, were the voices of former slaves, such as Olaudah Equiano. Robert Wedderburn (1762–1835/6) was born free, but as the son of a slave, and a committed radical, he did much to popularise the cause of abolition among the working classes.

To the editor:

Be it known to the world, that, I Robert Wedderburn, son of James Wedderburn, esq. of Inveresk, near Musselborough, by Rosannah his slave, whom he sold to James Charles Shalto Douglas, esq. in the parish of St. Mary, in the island of Jamaica, while pregnant with the said Wedderburn, who was not held as a slave (a provision made in the agreement, that the whole when born should be free). This Wedderburn, doth charge all potentates, governors, and governments of every description with felony, who does wickedly violate the sacred rights of man – by force of arms, or otherwise, seizing the persons of men and dragging them from their native country, and selling their stolen persons and generations. – Wedderburn demands, in the name of God, in the name of natural justice, and in the name of humanity, that all slaves be set free; for innocent individuals are entitled to the protection of civil society; and that all stealers, receivers, and oppressors in this base practice be forgiven, as the crime commenced in the days of ignorance, and is now exposed in the enlightened age of reason.

Oh, ye oppressed, use no violence to your oppressors, convince the world you are rational beings, follow not the example of St Domingo, let not your jubilee, which will take place, be stained with the blood of your oppressors, leave revengeful practices for European kings and ministers.

My advice to you, is, to appoint a day wherein you will all pretend to sleep one hour beyond the appointed time of your rising to labour; let the appointed day be twelve months before it takes place; let it be talked of in your market place, and on the roads. The universality of your sleeping and non-resistance, will strike terror to your oppressors. Go to your labour peaceably after the hour is expired; and repeat it once a year, till you obtain your liberty. Union among you, will strike tremendous terror to the receivers of stolen persons. But do not petition, for it is degrading to human nature to petition your oppressors. Above all, mind and keep possession of the land you now possess as slaves; for without that, freedom is not worth possessing; for if you once give up the possession of your lands, your oppressors will have the power to starve you to death, through making laws for their own accommodation; which will force you to commit crimes in order to obtain subsistence . . . whilst the landholders, in fact, are surrounded with every necessary of life. Take warnings by the sufferings of the European poor, and never give up your lands you now possess, for it is your right by God and nature, for the 'earth was given to the children of men'.

Oh, ye Christians, you are convinced of the crime of stealing human beings; and some of you have put a stop to it. By law, give up the stolen families in possession, and perfect your repentance. I call on a mighty people, and their sovereign, to burst the chains of oppression, and let the oppressed go free, says 'the Lord'; and so says Wedderburn the deluded Spencean. Oh, ye Africans and relatives now in bondage to the Christians, because you are innocent and poor; receive this the only tribute the offspring of an African can give, for which, I may ere long be lodged in a prison, without even a trial; for it is a crime now in England to speak against oppression.

Dear countrymen and relatives, it is natural to expect you will enquire what is meant to be a deluded Spencean; I must inform you it is a title given by ignorant or self-interested men, to the followers of Thomas Spence, who knew that the earth was given to the children of men, making no difference for colour or character, just or unjust; and that any person calling a piece of land his own private property, was criminal; and though they may sell it, or will it to their children, it is only transferring of that which was first obtained by force or fraud; this old truth, newly discovered, has completely terrified the landholders in England, and confounded the Attorney General and the Crown Lawyers; and what is more alarming, it is not in the power of the legislature, with all their objections to the doctrines to make a law to prevent the publishing of self-evident truths, while a shadow of the British Constitution remains. The landholders, whose interest it is to oppose, are driven to the necessity of falsifying and misrepresenting the motives of the disciples of Spence; but truth once known, will dispel falsehood, as the rising sun excludes darkness.

Your humble servant being a Spencean Philanthropist, is proud to wear the name of a madman; if the landholders please, they may call me a traitor, or one who is possessed with the spirit of Beelzebub. What can the landholders, priests or laywers say, or do more than they did against Christ; yet his doctrine is on record, which says, 'Woe unto them that add house to house, or field to field.' When you are exhorted to hold the land, and never give it up to your oppressors, you are not told to hold it as private property, but as tenants at will to the sovereignty of the people.

Beware of the clergy of every description, they are bound by law and interest, in all countries, to preach agreeable to the will of the governor under whom they live; as proof of which, they must have a licence, if not of the established church. Listen to them as far as your reason dictates of a future state, but never suffer them to interfere in your worldly affairs; for they are cunning, and therefore are more capable of vice than you are; for instance, one was hung at Kingston, for coining; one in London, for forgery; one for a rape; one for murder; one was detected throwing the sleeve of his surplice over the plate, while he robbed it, even at the time he was administering

the Lord's supper, in the Borough; and Bishop Burn, of Kent, who
had 800l per annum, confessed on his death bed, he had practised
the same offence for over 40 years, and all these were college bred
men, and of course gentlemen. You know also they buy and sell your
persons as well as others, and thereby encouraging that base practice.
This is not doing as they would be done by.

Adieu, for the present, my afflicted countrymen and relatives yet
in bondage, though the prince, lords, and commons, are convinced
it is a crime deserving of death, to steal and hold a man in bondage.

I am a West-Indian, a lover of liberty, and would dishonour human
nature if I did not shew myself a friend to the liberty of others.

Mary Prince, *The History of Mary Prince, A West Indian Slave* (1831)[6]

*Mary Prince was born to slaves in Bermuda in 1788. She suffered
years of cruelty at the hands of different masters, but when her new
owners brought her to London in 1828, she was able to 'walk away'
and claim her freedom, though in effect she was confined to Britain,
where slavery was outlawed by this time. She went to the headquar-
ters of the Anti-Slavery Society, formed in 1823 to carry on the fight
against global slavery. She worked for its secretary, Thomas Pringle,
and his wife, Mary. It was in the Pringles' household that she dictated
her memoir, which was published in London in 1831. The book cata-
logues Prince's struggle to survive in Bermuda, Turks Island, Antigua,
and finally in England. It became a valuable document in the struggle
for the abolition of slavery.*

This was the first winter I spent in England, and I suffered much from
the severe cold, and from the rheumatic pains, which still at times
torment me. However, Providence was very good to me, and I got

many friends – especially some Quaker ladies, who hearing of my case, came and sought me out, and gave me good warm clothing and money. Thus I had great cause to bless God in my affliction.

When I got better I was anxious to get some work to do, as I was unwilling to eat the bread of idleness. Mrs Mash, who was a laundress, recommended me to a lady for a charwoman. She paid me very handsomely for what work I did, and I divided the money with Mrs Mash; for though very poor, they gave me food when my own money was done, and never suffered me to want . . .

I still live in the hope that God will find a way to give me my liberty, and give me back to my husband. I endeavour to keep down my fretting, and to leave all to Him, for he knows what is good for me better than I know myself. Yet, I must confess, I find it a hard and heavy task to do so.

I am often much vexed, and I feel great sorrow when I hear some people in this country say, that the slaves do not need better usage, and do not want to be free. They believe the foreign people, who deceive them, and say slaves are happy. I say, Not so. How can slaves be happy when they have the halter round their neck and the whip upon their back? and are disgraced and thought no more of than beasts? – and are separated from their mothers, and husbands, and children, and sisters, just as cattle are sold and separated? Is it happiness for a driver in the field to take down his wife or sister or child, and strip them, and whip them in such a disgraceful manner? – women that have had children exposed in the open field to shame! There is no modesty or decency shown by the owner to his slaves; men, women, and children are exposed alike. Since I have been here I have often wondered how English people can go out into the West Indies and act in such a beastly manner. But when they go to the West Indies, they forget God and all feeling of shame, I think, since they can see and do such things. They tie up slaves like hogs – moor them up like cattle, and they lick them, so as hogs, or cattle, or horses never were flogged; – and yet they come home and say, and make some good people believe, that slaves don't want to get out of slavery. But they put a cloak about the truth. It is not so. All slaves want to be free – to be free is very sweet. I will say the truth to English people who may read this history that my good friend, Miss S–, is now writing down for me. I have been a slave myself – I know what slaves feel – I can tell by myself what other slaves feel, and by what they have told me. The man that says slaves be quite happy in slavery – that they don't want to be free – that man is either ignorant or a lying person. I never heard a slave say so. I never heard a Buckra man say so, till I heard tell of it in England. Such people ought to be ashamed of themselves. They can't do without slaves, they say. What's the reason they can't do without slaves as well as in England? No slaves here – no whips – no stocks – no punishment, except for wicked people. They hire servants in England; and if they don't like them, they send them away: they can't lick them. Let them work ever so hard in England, they are far better off than slaves. If they get a bad master, they give warning and go hire to another. They have their liberty. That's just what we want. We don't mind hard work, if we had proper treatment, and proper wages like English servants, and proper time given in the week to keep us from breaking the Sabbath. But they won't give it: they will have work – work – work, night and day, sick or well, till we are quite done up; and we must not speak up nor look amiss, however much we be abused. And then when we are quite done up, who cares for us, more than for a lame horse? This is slavery. I tell it, to let English people know the truth; and I hope they will never leave off to pray God, and call loud to the great King of England, till all the poor Blacks be given free, and slavery done up for evermore.

Louis Asa-Asa, 'How Cruelly We Are Used' (31 January 1831)[7]

The appendix to Mary Prince's memoir included testimony by Louis Asa-Asa, a West African captured and sold into slavery around 1810. He was bought by French slave-traders, but regained his freedom when the ship on which he was confined was forced to put in at Cornwall. Like Mary Prince, Asa-Asa took advantage of the outlawing of slavery on British soil, but he spoke up for the abolition of slavery altogether.

My father's name was Clashoquin; mine is Asa-Asa. He lived in a country called Bycla, near Egie, a large town. Egie is as large as Brighton; it was some way from the sea. I had five brothers and sisters. We all lived together with my father and mother; he kept a horse, and was respectable, but not one of the great men. My uncle was one of the great men at Egie: he could make men come and work for him: his name was Otou. He had a great deal of land and cattle. My father sometimes worked on his own land, and used to make charcoal. I was too little to work; my eldest brother used to work on the land; and we were all very happy.

A great many people, whom we called Adinyés, set fire to Egie in the morning before daybreak; there were some thousands of them. They killed a great many, and burnt all their houses. They staid two days, and then carried away all the people whom they did not kill.

They came again every now and then for a month, as long as they could find people to carry away. They used to tie them by the feet, except when they were taking them off, and then they let them loose; but if they offered to run away, they would shoot them. I lost a great many friends and relations at Egie; about a dozen. They sold all they carried away, to be slaves. I know this because I afterwards saw them as slaves on the other side of the sea. They took away brothers, and sisters, and husbands, and wives; they did not care about this. They were sold for cloth or gunpowder, sometimes for salt or guns; some-times they got four or five guns for a man: they were English guns, made like my master's that I clean for his shooting. The Adinyés burnt a great many places besides Egie. They burnt all the country wherever they found villages; they used to shoot men, women, and children, if they ran away.

They came to us about eleven o'clock one day, and directly they came they set our house on fire. All of us had run away. We kept together, and went into the woods, and stopped there two days. The Adinyés then went away, and we returned home and found every thing burnt. We tried to build a little shed, and were beginning to get comfortable again. We found several of our neighbours lying about wounded; they had been shot. I saw the bodies of four or five little children whom they had killed with blows on the head. They had carried away their fathers and mothers, but the children were too small for slaves, so they killed them. They had killed several others, but these were all that I saw. I saw them lying in the street like dead dogs.

In about a week after we got back, the Adinyés returned, and burnt all the sheds and houses they had left standing. We all ran away again; we went to the woods as we had done before. – They followed us the next day. We went farther into the woods, and staid there about four days and nights; we were half starved; we only got a few potatoes. My uncle Otou was with us. At the end of this time, the Adinyés found us. We ran away. They called my uncle to go to them; but he refused, and they shot him immediately: they killed him. The rest of us ran on, and they did not get at us till the next day. I ran up into a tree: they followed me and brought me down. They tied my feet. I do not know if they found my father and mother, and brothers and sisters: they had run faster than me, and were half a mile farther when I got up into the tree: I have never seen them since. – There was a man who ran up into the tree with me: I believe they shot him, for I never saw him again.

They carried away about twenty besides me. They carried us to the sea. They did not beat us: they only killed one man, who was very ill and too weak to carry his load: they made all of us carry chickens and meat for our food; but this poor man could not carry his load, and they ran him through the body with a sword. – He was a neighbour of ours. When we got to the sea they sold all of us, but not to the same person. They sold us for money; and I was sold six times over, sometimes for money, sometimes for cloth, and sometimes for a gun. I was about thirteen years old. It was about half a year from the time I was taken, before I saw the white people.

We were taken in a boat from place to place, and sold at every place we stopped at. In about six months we got to a ship, in which we first saw white people: they were French. They bought us. We found here a great many other slaves; there were about eighty, including women and children. The Frenchmen sent away all but five of us into another very large ship. We five stayed on board till we got to England, which was about five or six months. The slaves we saw on board the ship were chained together by the legs below deck, so close they could not move. They were flogged very cruelly: I saw one of them flogged till he died; we could not tell what for. They gave them enough to eat. The place they were confined in below deck was so hot and nasty I could not bear to be in it. A great many of the slaves were ill, but they were not attended to. They used to flog me very bad on board the ship: the captain cut my head very bad one time.

I am very happy to be in England, as far as I am very well; – but I have no friend belonging to me, but God, who will take care of me as he has done already. I am very glad I have come to England, to know who God is. I should like much to see my friends again, but I do not now wish to go back to them: for if I go back to my own country, I might be taken as a slave again. I would rather stay here, where I am free, than go back to my country to be sold. I shall stay in England as long as (please God) I shall live. I wish the King of

England could know all I have told you. I wish it that he may see how cruelly we are used. We had no king in our country, or he would have stopt it. I think the King of England might stop it, and this is why I wish him to know it all. I have heard say he is good; and if he is, he will stop it if he can. I am well off myself, for I am well taken care of, and have good bed and good clothes; but I wish my own people to be as comfortable.

Joseph Sturge, Speech at the Baptist Missionary Society of Birmingham (July 1836)[8]

After the abolition of the slave trade in the British Empire, slavery itself continued in British overseas territories until 1833. Joseph Sturge (1793–1859), a Birmingham grain importer who devoted himself to the cause of emancipation, was among the more radical members of the Anti-Slavery Society. After 1833, he continued to campaign against the vestiges of slavery in the British Empire and slavery itself in the United States. A devout Quaker, he was also horrified by the way Christians had turned a blind eye to slavery and its pernicious effects in Africa.

If we turn our eyes for a moment to poor, unhappy Africa, we shall find that almost the whole of that continent may justly be said to be hermetically sealed against missionary efforts by this system, which, while it tears from its shores annually upwards of 100,000 victims, either to die amid all the horrors of the middle passage, or in hopeless, unmitigated toil and bondage, is supposed to destroy two or three times that number in the internal wars, fomented to the very heart of the continent, and the march of the slaves to the coast, to supply the white man's ships from the Christian country. What opinion, I would ask – were we Africans – should we form of such Christians as these? Can we wonder that, instead of receiving them as the messengers of peace and glad tidings, they should consider them as cannibals, and not unfrequently commit self-destruction, under the supposition that they shall be devoured when they arrive at the port of their destination? . . . To whom was it that the God of love used the severest language when personally upon earth? Not to the poor outcast of society, whatever his crimes might have been, but to the self-righteous, highly professing scribes and Pharisees; and such is the enormous guilt of the professing Christian Church in America with regard to slavery that if we were gifted with language powerful as an archangel, and strong and alarming as the most tempestuous billows of the Atlantic to the shipwrecked mariner, we ought to raise it to its highest emphasis on this occasion, under the persuasion that through the blessing of Heaven we should thus be most likely to encourage the faithful band of abolitionists, and carry dismay and ultimate conviction to their opponents, hasten the day of universal freedom, and the period when Christians of all nations shall show by deeds, not words, that they consider every country as their country and every man as their brother.

Anonymous Member of the Walthamstow Free Produce or Anti-Slavery Association, *Conscience Versus Cotton: Or, The Preference of Free Labour Produce* (1851)[9]

During the eighteenth and nineteenth centuries, campaigners tried to relate their causes to people's ordinary lives. In the 1790s, abolitionists encouraged a boycott of slave-grown West Indian sugar, which persuaded many consumers and sellers to get their sugar from what one trader called 'channels less contaminated, more

*unconnected with slavery, less polluted with human blood'. After
abolition in the British Empire, campaigners turned their attention
to slavery's persistence in other countries. This pamphlet, published
by the Newcastle Anti-Slavery Society, advocates the boycott of slave-
grown cotton from the southern United States.*

QUESTION. What undermines Slavery, and quietly lays the axe to its root?

Answer. A wide-spreading and thoughtful conviction, that the *unnecessary* purchase of one iota of slave labour produce, involves the purchaser in the guilt of the Slaveholder.

Every righteous man and every modest woman, who has not shrunk from the painful duty of contemplating Slavery in its inevitable inroads upon the purity and happiness of both sexes, and in its paralysing effect upon the noblest energies of our race, will be agreed in this; that, in the sad catalogue of deep human wrongs, this wrong is immeasurably the deepest, and that, in a word, Slavery is, of 'all villainies the sum and substance'. If, therefore, a number of intelligent and highly educated persons are, in various parts of this kingdom, pleading for the practical recognition of a principle, which they assert strikes at the very foundations of this sin, it would surely be as consistent with wisdom, as it would be with candour, to allow that this principle demands investigation from the pure minded and the just; more especially if it be further maintained, that every benevolent man and woman, whether on this side of the Atlantic or on that, could, if they willed it, help to develop this principle in action. It is, then, for a consideration of the 'Free Labour Movement', that we would earnestly solicit the attention of the reader. The claim of this Movement upon our sympathy for the benevolence of its end, no one will dispute; and the number is daily increasing of those from whom it commands respect for the rectitude of its means. For myself, I can, in all truth, affirm, that, in advocating the adoption, by an eminently practical people, of the

Anti-slave labour principle, I have far more confidence in the good-ness of my cause, than in any fancied ability to plead its merits, and am happy in a growing conviction, that by these merits it will be established, though my feeble efforts should fail, and be speedily among the things which have passed away, to be remembered no more.

What can I do to put down slavery? Should not this become an universal Conscience question; and, if it were so, should we not perceive greater readiness than is manifested at present to make trial of any auxiliary measure for the destruction of this wickedness, to which, in its moral and religious aspect, no exception could reason-ably be taken? That the Free Labour Movement is a peaceful one, is evident from its non-aggressive character. Its advocate simply discourages the slaveholder, by withdrawing his personal support from him; and will any one venture to assert, that we ought indi-vidually to encourage and stimulate a calling undeniably, and above all other callings, sinful? It is to be considered, moreover, that by the practical recognition of Free Labour produce principles, we afford a direct stimulus to the *honourable* vocation and *honest* enterprise of the Free Labour cultivator, throughout the globe; and, as this stim-ulus points unmistakeably to a plurality of free cotton growing coun-tries, the Anti-slave produce sentiment would work advantageously as regards *home* results. Our trade reports shew great pecuniary loss by such exclusive dealings with the slave cotton growers of the United States. We are too dependent upon America for the supply of this important article; and the remedy for this dependence is commercial encouragement held out to the free cotton growers of British India, the West Indies, Africa, and also the free cotton growers of the United States themselves, by an *organised* demand for the free article, as testified by the formation of Free Labour Associations. We attach importance to the growth of such Associations in this kingdom, because, as such, they are exponents of public sentiment, in regard to a preference of free labour merchandise, and must

therefore tell with considerable effect on the exertions already
making for the improvement and increase of cotton cultivation, not
merely in our colonial possessions, but in every land affording facilities for such cultivation. Satisfied as to the commercial advantages
to be derived from a firm and continued support of the Free Labour
Movement, it is chiefly the moral aspect of the whole question (an
aspect of which we ought never to lose sight) which we propose to
consider in the ensuing pages. To strengthen our position as
contenders for the abstract righteousness of the Anti-slave Produce
sentiment, we put the following case. Ignoring, for a moment, the
melancholy fact, that man stealing, woman whipping, and human
auction marts have existed long, we will suppose that twelve men
dare, in this year of our Lord eighteen hundred and fifty-one, to *begin*
Slavery, and to *begin* the Slave Trade. We will suppose that these men,
after having established the one with its adhesive pollutions, and
prosecuted the other with the barbarities ever enacted in that
'floating hell', the Slave-ship, bring into the British market, for the
first time, the fruits of their execrable dealings with mankind. We
only ask whether one human being, whose affections were holy, or
whose moral judgement was correct, would purchase one jot or one
tittle of such sin-begotten merchandise? No! is the instantaneous
and the righteous answer. Such merchandise would be immediately
put down by the moral sense of purchasers, and the vendors of it
exposed to well-merited scorn and indignant execration. But if the
above be granted, and beclouded indeed is the moral vision of those
who do not perceive that granted it must be, this inference is plain
– that, if it would be wrong to enter into commercial transactions,
even for an hour, with those who would begin slavery, it is wrong
to continue such transactions (one day longer than the intricacies
of the question absolutely demand) with those who would perpetuate it. Our position then is, that the advocates of the Anti-slave
Produce principle have the Right on their side. We may rest this
question on the safe ground of Conscience. Try this cause (we would

say to one and all) by a searching appeal to your moral sense: if you think it right to give the amount of your personal support to the slaveholder (which support you do give him by the purchase of his wares), go on to purchase them, without inquiring for, or taking any trouble to obtain, the free labour article; but if you do not think this quite right, but, on the contrary, deem it a holy thing in the sight of your Maker to wash your own hands clean from any *avoidable* participation in the sin of slaveholders, then do ye wash them clean, and, while your live, avow yourself to be in theory, and prove yourself in practice, a Preferrer of the Free to the Slave-grown article.

Ernest Jones, 'The Indian Struggle' (5 September 1857)[10]

The rebellion in India that began as a soldiers' mutiny and became a revolutionary uprising was greeted with horror by many Britons, especially after the account of the Cawnpore massacre of British civilians was publicized. Some observers, however, took up the case for Indian independence – none more passionately than Ernest Jones (1819–69), a veteran leader of the Chartist movement, who published this article in The People's Paper, *the periodical he edited from 1852–8. The 'Mutiny' was brutally crushed, and by 1858, India was under tighter British control than ever.*

There ought to be but one opinion throughout Europe on the Revolt of Hindostan. It is one of the most just, noble, and necessary ever attempted in the history of the world. We recently analysed and exposed the nature of England's Indian rule. We this week, in another column, give an episode referring to Oudh, and illustrating the nefarious, the infamous, the inexpressibly infamous conduct, of British domination. How any one can hesitate which side to take, is inconceivable to us.

England – the people, the English people – sympathise with liberty. On which side were they when Poland struggled for its freedom against Russia? On the side of Poland. On which side were they, when Hungary struggled for its rights with Austria? On the side of Hungary. On which side are they when Italy struggles for its life against the Germans, the French, the Papist, and the despot? On the side of Italy. Was Poland right? Then so is Hindostan. Was Hungary justified? Then so is Hindostan. Was Italy deserving of support? Then so is Hindostan. For all that Poland, Hungary, or Italy sought to gain, for that the Hindu strives. Nay! more. The Pole, the Hungarian, the Italian still own their own soil. The Hindu does not. The former have rulers of their own, or a kindred faith, above them. The Hindu has not. The former are still ruled by something like law, and by servants responsible to their masters. The Hindu is not. Naples and France, Lombardy and Poland, Hungary and Rome present no tyranny so hideous as that enacted by the miscreants of Leadenhall Street, and Whitehall, in Hindostan. The wonder is, not that one hundred and seventy millions of people should now rise—the wonder is that they should ever have submitted at all. They would not, had they not been betrayed by their own princes, who sold each other to the alien, and the base, truckling invader, that with his foul help they might cut each other's throats. Thus kings, princes, and aristocracies have ever proven the enemies and curses of every land that harboured them, in every age.

We bespeak the sympathy of the English people for their Hindu brethren. Their cause is yours – their success is, indirectly, yours as well. The fearful atrocities committed have nothing to do with the great cause at issue – that cause is just, it is holy, it is glorious. Englishmen, Scotchmen, Irishmen, what would you say if a colony of Dutch Jews came hither and asked permission to build a factory on Woolwich Marsh; if, after having gained that permission on promise of paying a yearly rental they intrigued with the French or Russians to let them into the country; if, after that, they promised to help you against the invader, in exchange for half of Kent; if, after having received the land, they betrayed both sides and sold you to the Yankees for a slice of Surrey; if, after eternal peace had been sworn to by all the contending parties, they set them all by the ears, and in the midst of the inextricable confusion they went on invading, conquering on their own account; if, being Protestants, they denounced and punished Protestantism to conciliate the Papists; if, again, they destroy Papists to conciliate Protestants; if, when weak and in danger, they swore to solemn treaties, on the faith in which you spared them when in your power; and if they thus, having gained time for strength and power, rushed upon you, unawares, sacked and burned your cities, outraged your women, and murdered your population, and thus, in the air of your surprise, dismay and weakness, subjugated you and your country – what would you say and do? If, still further, having thus enthralled you, they confiscated every acre of your own land; if, having thus confiscated it, they made you pay a rental for what had been your own freehold farms; if they then burdened those farms with such taxation, that the produce could not realise one half the amount; if, you being unable to pay, they seized your cattle, your farm implements, your very seed-corn; if, having thus stopped your means of production, they next year demanded the same rental and the same tax; if, because you could not pay it, they hung you with your heads downwards in the burning sun, lashed you, tortured you, tied scorpions to the breasts of your women, committed every atrocity and crime – what, we repeat, would you say and do? You would rise – rise in the holy right of insurrection, and cry to Europe and the world, to Heaven and earth, to bear witness to the justice of your cause.

Fellow countrymen! thus have the Hindus been treated at the hand of England; this is the cause of their insurrection, and every honest man throughout the world can pass but one judgement on the facts, and breathe but one aspiration for the issue.

———————————

Richard Cobden, Letter to John Bright on India
(22 September 1857)[11]

*The revenge of British forces, encouraged by the press at home,
horrified the radical MP and free-trade advocate Richard Cobden
(1804–65). Both Cobden and his fellow radical John Bright (1811–89)
had recently lost their seats in Parliament when Cobden wrote this
letter. It is an indication of the unpopularity of putting the Indian
case that although in private Bright shared Cobden's sentiments he
publicly supported suppression of the Mutiny when he stood for
election again the following year.*

These Indian horrors give me a perpetual shudder. The awful
atrocities perpetrated upon women and children almost give
rise to the impious doubt whether this world is under the government of an all-wise and just Providence. What crime had they
committed to merit the infliction of tortures and death? Verily
the sins of the fathers have been visited on the children to the
third and fourth generations! And how can it be otherwise in
the case of a nation? For if a collective crime be perpetrated, and
a community be visited with retributive justice, even an hour
after the commission of the deed, those who have entered life
in the interval must participate in the penalty. We can see that
it must be so, but not that it ought to be . . .

It is terrible to see our middle-class journals and speakers
calling for the destruction of Delhi, and the indiscriminate
massacre of prisoners. Leaving humanity out of the question,
nothing could have been more impolitic than the wholesale
execution of common soldiers with which we attempted from
the first to put down the rebellion. Had it been a mutiny of a
company or a regiment, it would have been of doubtful policy
to hang or blow from the guns all the *privates* concerned. But

when an entire army of 100,000 men have planted the standard of revolt, it is no longer a mutiny, but a rebellion and civil war. To attempt to hang all that fall into our power can only lead to reprisals and wholesale carnage on both sides . . .

To read the letters of our officers at the commencement of the outbreak, it seemed as if every subaltern had the power to hang or shoot as many natives as he pleased, and they spoke of the work of blood with as much levity as if they were hunting wild animals. The last accounts would lead one to fear that God is not favouring our cause, and that too many of our countrymen are meeting the fate which was intended for the natives.

But the future – what is in the distance? The most certain and immediate result is that we shall have a bankrupt empire of 150 millions of people on our backs . . . I now regard the task as utterly hopeless . . . It will be a happy day when England has not an acre of territory in Continental Asia. But how such a state of things is to be brought about, is more than I can tell. I bless my stars that I am not I a position to be obliged to give public utterance to my views on the all-absorbing topic of the day, for I could not do justice to my own convictions and possess the confidence of any constituency in the kingdom. For where do we find even an individual who is not imbued with the notion that England would sink to ruin if she were deprived of her Indian Empire? Leave me, then, to my pigs and sheep, which are not labouring under any such delusions.

Celestine Edwards, The British Empire (1892–4)[12]

Celestine Edwards (1857–94) was born in Dominica, the descendant of West Indian slaves, and settled in Britain after stowing away on a French ship and sailing the world for several years. He became a labourer and, after gaining a diploma in theology, a Methodist preacher. In speeches and journals, such as Lux *and* Fraternity, *he evangelised for black emancipation and against imperialism.*

[10 December 1892]

As long as such unrighteous deeds as cold-blooded murders are permitted under the British flag, as long as avarice and cupidity prompt the actions of a missionary nation . . . so long we shall protest against public money being spent in the interest of land-grabbers . . .

The injustice under which [the black man] is smarting will come home to his oppressors' children's children . . . He will surprise and disappoint those who never dreamt that the quiet happy-go-lucky Black would turn like the worm upon those who wronged him . . . If the British nation stole no more, they have stolen enough and have sufficient responsibility at home and abroad to occupy her maternal attention for the next hundred years. If the British nation has not murdered enough no nation on God's earth has.

[18 February 1893]

[T]he British Empire will come to grief unless it changes its methods for dealing with aboriginal races . . . The day is coming when Africans will speak for themselves . . . The day is breaking, and . . . the despised African, whose only crime is his colour, will yet give an account of himself . . . We think it no crime for Africans to look with suspicion upon the European, who has stolen a part of [their country], and deluged it with rum and powder, under the cover of civilisation.

[3 November 1894]

My ancestors proudly trod the sands of the African continent; but from their home and friends were dragged into the slave mart and sold to the planters of the West Indies . . . The very thought that my race should have been so grievously wronged is almost more than I can bear . . . Of the condition of my people today I but tarry to say that by diligence, thought, and care they have given the lie to many a false prophet who, prior to their Emancipation, sought to convince the world that the black man was in all respects unfit for freedom . . . Their position today is one over which I proudly rejoice. To their future I look with confidence.

'A Voice from the Aliens About the Anti-Alien Resolution of the Cardiff Trades Union Congress' (1895)[13]

In two successive meetings of the Trades Union Congress, in 1894 and 1895, delegates were persuaded to vote an 'Anti-Alien Resolution' against immigrant workers. The motion was put forward by the leaders of the National Union of Boot and Shoe Operatives, William Inskip and Charles Freak. In this pamphlet detailing the response of organised Jewish labour to the resolution, the prejudice and irrationality of 'Freakians and Inskipians' is laid bare.

We, the organised Jewish workers of England, taking into consideration the Anti-Alien Resolution, and the uncomplimentary remarks of certain delegates about the Jewish workers specially, issue this leaflet, wherewith we hope to convince our English fellow workers of the untruthfulness, unreasonableness, and want of logic contained in the cry against the foreign worker in general, and against the Jewish worker in particular.

It is, and always has been, the policy of the ruling classes to attribute
the sufferings and miseries of the masses (which are natural consequences of class rule and class exploitation) to all sorts of causes
except the real ones. The cry against the foreigner is not merely
peculiar to England; it is international. Everywhere he is the scapegoat
for others' sins. Every class finds in him an enemy. So long as the
Anti-Alien sentiment in this country was confined to politicians,
wire-pullers, and to individual working men, we, the organised aliens,
took no heed; but when this ill-founded sentiment has been officially
expressed by the organised working men of England, then we believe
that it is time to lift our voices and argue the matter out . . .

We will . . . prove to our English fellow workers that immigration
or emigration in no way affects the condition of the working men or
the state of the labour market . . .

[I]f the English worker has reason to be dissatisfied with his lot, let
him not blame his foreign fellow working man; let him rather study
the social and labour question and he will then find out where the
shoe pinches . . .

We, the Jewish workers, have been spoken of as a blighting blister
upon the English trades and workers, as men to whose hearts it is
impossible to appeal, and were it not for us, the condition of the
native worker would be much improved, he would have plenty of
work, good wages, and what not. Well, let us look into facts; let us
examine the condition of such workers with whom the Jew never
comes in contact, such as the agricultural labourer, the docker, the
miner, the weaver, the chain maker, ship builder, bricklayer and many
others. Examine their condition, dear reader, and answer: Is there
any truth in the remark that we are a 'blighting blister' upon the
English worker? . . .

[W]e appeal to our fellow-workers to consider whether there is any
justification whatever for regarding as the enemies of the English
workers the foreign workers, who, so far from injuring them, actually
bring trade here and develop new industries; whether, so far from

being the enemies of the English workers, it is not rather the capitalist class (which is constantly engaged in taking trade abroad, in opening factories in China, Japan, and other countries) who is the enemy, and whether it is not rather their duty to combine against the common enemy than fight against us whose interests are identical with theirs.

Henry Woodd Nevinson, 'The Slave-Trade of Today' (February 1906)[14]

Henry Nevinson (1856–1941) was a war correspondent for the Daily Chronicle *and the* Manchester Guardian. *He wrote this attack on slavery in Angola after travelling there in 1904–5. The slaves (known as 'indentured labourers') under Portuguese masters grew cocoa that was consumed in Britain, and his campaign persuaded British cocoa firms to boycott Portuguese-Angolan produce.*

I can imagine no more noble existence than has fallen to those poor and naked blacks, who have dared all for freedom, and, scorning the stall-fed life of slavery, have chosen rather to throw themselves upon such mercy as nature has, to wander together in nakedness and hunger from forest to forest and hut to hut, to live in daily apprehension of murder, to lurk like apes under the high branches, and at last to fall to the bullets of the Christians, dead, but of no further service to the commercial gentlemen who bought them and lose thirty pounds by every death.

Even to the slaves who remain on the plantations, not having the courage or good-fortune to escape and die like wild beasts, death, as a rule, is not much longer delayed in coming. Probably within the first two or three years the slave's strength begins to ebb away. With every day his work becomes feebler, so that at last even the ganger's whip or pointed stick cannot urge him on. Then he is taken to the hospital and laid upon the boarded floor till he dies. An hour or so afterwards you may meet two of his fellow-slaves going into the forest. There is perhaps a sudden smell of carbolic or other disinfectant upon the air, and you take another look at the long pole the slaves are carrying between them on their shoulders. Under the pole a body is lashed, tightly wrapped up in the cotton cloth that was its dress while it lived. The head is covered with another piece of cloth which passes round the neck and is also fastened tightly to the pole. The feet and legs are sometimes covered, sometimes left to dangle naked. In silence the two slaves pass into some untrodden part of the forest, and the man or woman, who started on life's journey in a far-off native village with the average hope and delight of childhood, travels over the last brief stage and is no more seen.

Laws and treaties do not count for much. A law is never of much effect unless the mind of a people has passed beyond the need of it, and treaties are binding only on those who wish to be bound. But still there are certain laws and treaties that we may for a moment recall: in 1830 England paid £300,000 to the Portuguese provided they forbade all slave-trade – which they did and pocketed the money; in 1842 England and the United States agreed under the Ashburton Treaty to maintain joint squadrons on the west coast of Africa for the suppression of the slave-trade; in 1858 Portugal enacted a law that every slave belonging to a Portuguese subject should be free in twenty years; in 1885, by the Berlin General Act, England, the United States, and thirteen other powers, including Portugal and Belgium, pledged themselves to suppress every kind of slave-trade, especially in the Congo and the interior of Africa; in 1890, by the Brussels General Act, England, the United States, and fifteen other powers, including Portugal and Belgium, pledged themselves to suppress every kind of slave-trade, especially in the Congo and the interior of Africa, to erect cities of refuge for escaped slaves, to hold out protection to every fugitive slave, to stop all convoys of slaves on the march, and to exercise strict supervision at all ports so as to prevent the sale or ship-ment of slaves across the sea.

If anyone wanted a theme for satire, what more deadly theme could he find?

To which of the powers can appeal now be made? Appeal to England is no longer possible. Since the rejection of Ireland's home-rule bill, the abandonment of the Armenians to massacre, and the extinction of the South-African republics, she can no longer be regarded as the champion of liberty or of justice among mankind. She has flung away her only noble heritage. She has closed her heart to compassion, and for ten years past the oppressed have called to her in vain. A single British cruiser, posted off the coast of Angola, with orders to arrest every mail-boat or other ship having serviçaes on board, would so paralyse the system that probably it would never recover. But one might as soon expect Russia or Germany to do it as England in her recent mood. She will make representations, perhaps; she will remind Portugal of 'the old alliance' and the friendship between the royal families; but she will do no more. What she says can have no effect; her tongue, which was the tongue of men, has become like sounding brass; and if she spoke of freedom, the nations would listen with a polished smile . . .

I am aware that, as I said in my first letter, the whole question of slavery is still before us. It has reappeared under the more pleasing names of 'indentured labor,' 'contract labor,' or the 'compulsory labor' which Mr Chamberlain has advocated in obedience to the Johannesburg mine-owners. The whole thing will have to be faced anew, for the solutions of our great-grandfathers no longer satisfy. While slavery is lucrative, as it is on the islands of San Thomé and Principe, it will be defended by those who identify greatness with wealth, and if their own wealth is involved, their arguments will gain considerably in vigor. They will point to the necessity of developing rich islands where no one would work without compulsion. They will point to what they call the comfort and good treatment of the slaves. They will protect themselves behind legal terms. But they forget that legal terms make no difference to the truth of things. They forget that slavery is not a matter of discomfort or ill treatment, but of loss of liberty. They forget that it might be better for mankind that the islands should go back to wilderness than that a single slave should toil there. I know the contest is still before us. It is but part of the great contest with capitalism, and in Africa it will be as long and difficult as it was a hundred years ago in other regions of the world. I have but tried to reveal one small glimpse in a greater battle-field, and to utter the cause of a few thousands out of the millions of men and women whose silence is heard only by God. And perhaps if the crying of their silence is not heard even by God, it will yet be heard in the souls of the just and the compassionate.

Ghadar Movement, 'An Open Letter to the People of India' (c. 1913)[15]

The Ghadar movement (from the Hindustani word for 'mutiny' or 'revolt') was an organisation dedicated to bringing down British rule in India, formed by Indian emigrants on the Pacific coast of the United States, with links across the Indian diaspora. The Ghadar newspaper was the mouthpiece of the movement. At the outbreak of the First World War, some Ghadar activists returned to India to begin an anti-British insurrection, but this was put down violently by colonial forces.

Dear Friends,
We do not have to remind you; you all know how much we have suffered under the British rule. We all wish to get rid of this foreign tyrant who has been bleeding us white. The time is

coming when our united efforts will be able to throw off the yoke of this aggressor.

Another world war is approaching. We must take advantage of this opportunity. England is sure to get involved in the coming war. Political wisdom demands that we must utilise this rare opportunity for our good. We must put forward our demand for complete independence when our enemy, British imperialism, is engaged in a life and death struggle.

To save her life, Britain will need India's friendship more than anything else. We must demand complete independence as the price of our friendship.

We must let the British rulers know in clear terms that if they care for the friendship of India, they must be prepared to give India full independence at once. Otherwise India will resist to limit their effort to get any help from India. It is beside the point how we will resist, but resist we will.

Complete independence means India's control over treasury, foreign affairs, and military forces. Nothing short of that will do.

We must remember that we can no longer trust any more promises from the British imperialists. To our sorrow, we have found out many times that we cannot reply upon their words. We must stand pat on our demands; we must one way or another unite until our demands are met.

The world situation is such that the British will think twice before refusing India's demand. We must not miss this golden opportunity.

To get full advantage of the situation, we must put up a strong united front. All those Hindustanis who really work for independence must come together in a united front. Personal differences must be forgotten. Unity of purpose is essential for our cause. All of us who hold India's freedom dear to us must work to establish a formidable united front. Our demands backed by our united front will have a telling effect.

Our demands must be popularised among our countrymen. Our people must be made to act in case our demands are not met.

Now is the time to educate our people: tomorrow may be too late. During the war, martial law will make things difficult. Unless the masses are made ready to act, our demands will not have much weight. The British imperialists care little for empty resolutions unless they are backed by the united might of the masses.

War may start any day. We have not a moment to lose. We must do our best to educate and organise the Indian masses while we have time. Our slogans must be such as:

Complete Independence or Non-cooperation! Freedom or Nothing Else! No Freedom, No Soldiers from India! No Freedom, No Money from India! Freedom or Resistance!

James Connolly, 'In Praise of the Empire' (9 October 1915)[16]

James Connolly (1868–1916) was the founder of the Independent Labour Party of Ireland. On the outbreak of war in 1914, he attempted to persuade Irishmen not to volunteer for the British Army. The campaign was not successful, and more than two hundred thousand Irishmen fought in the war, though Connolly kept up the pressure in satirical articles such as this one. Connolly later joined the revolutionary Irish Republican Brotherhood, and was a leader of the Easter Rising in Dublin in 1916. He was executed on 12 May 1916.

We want to say a few words in praise of the Empire. Now, do not get startled, or shocked, nor yet think that we are only sarcastic. We are not abandoning our principles, nor forgetting our wrongs, nor giving up as hopeless the fight for our rights, nor yet exercising the slave's last privilege – that of sneering at his masters.

We do not love the Empire; we hate it with an unqualified hatred, but, nevertheless, we admire it. Why should we not!

Consider well what this Empire is doing today, and then see if you can withhold your admiration.

At the present moment this Empire has dominions spread all over the seven seas. Everywhere it holds down races and nations, that it might use them as its slaves, that it might use their territories as sources of rent and interest for its aristocratic rulers, that it might prevent their development as self-supporting entities and compel them to remain dependent customers of English produce, that it might be able to strangle every race or nation that would enter the field as a competitor against British capitalism or assert its independence of the British capitalist.

To do this it stifles the ancient culture of India, strangles in its birth the new-born liberty of Egypt, smothers in the blood of ten thousand women and children the republics of South Africa, betrays into the hands of Russian despotism the trusting nationalists of Persia, connives at the partition of China, and plans the partition of Ireland.

North, south, east and west it has set its foot upon the neck of peoples, plundering and murdering, and mocking as it outraged. In the name of a superior civilisation it has crushed the development of native genius, and in the name of superior capitalist development it has destroyed the native industries of a sixth of the human race.

In the name of liberty it hangs and imprisons patriots, and whilst calling High Heaven to witness its horror of militarism it sends the shadow of its swords between countless millions and their hopes of freedom.

Despite all this, despite the fact that every day the winds of the earth are laden with the curses which its unwilling subjects in countless millions pray upon its flag, yet that flag flies triumphantly over every one of its possessions, even whilst its soldiers are reeling discomfited and beaten before the trenches of Turk and German.

The British Empire never fought a white European foe singlehanded, never dared yet to confront an equal unaided, yet it has laid upon its subjects everywhere from Ireland to India and from India to Africa, the witchcraft of belief in its luck, so that even whilst they see it beaten to its knees they are possessed with the conviction that it will pull through in some fashion. The devil's children have their father's luck!

Without that belief, without that conviction of the slaves that their master must remain in possession of his mastership, the British Empire would today be everywhere lit up with the fires of mutiny and insurrection.

In the labour movement we have long ago learned that it is the worker who is convinced of the power of the capitalist, who believes that 'the big fellows are sure to win', it is he who really keeps labour in subjection, defeats strikes and destroys Trade Unions. The problem before the labour movement is always to find out how this hopeless feeling can be destroyed, and confidence implanted in the bosom where despair usually reigns.

The moment the worker no longer believes in the all-conquering strength of the employer is the moment when the way opens out to the emancipation of our class.

The master class realise this, and hence all their agencies bend their energies towards drugging, stupefying and poisoning the minds of the workers – sowing distrust and fear amongst them.

The ruling class of the British Empire also know it, and hence they also utilise every agency to spread amongst the subject races a belief in the luck of England, in the strength of England, in the omnipotence of England. That belief is worth more to the British Empire than ten army corps; when it goes, when it is lost, there will be an uprising of resurgent nationalities – and a crash of falling empires.

Should we not therefore admire the Empire that in face of danger can yet fascinate and enthral the minds of its slaves and keep them in mental as well as physical subjection?

B. R. Ambedkar, 'India on the Eve of the Crown Government' (c. 1915)[17]

Much of the justification for colonial rule was based on the argument that it was an improvement on 'native' or even other foreign government. In this essay, probably written while he was a student in New York, Bhimrao Ambedkar (1891–1956), an activist of the Dalit ('Untouchable') caste, who would go on to write the constitution of an independent India, questions the tendentious history on which such theories were based.

More than anything else in the world, imperialism stands in greater need of defence and imperialists have not been wanting in their duty.

Unlike the Greeks who did not have even a word for imperialism nor knew the idea of the federation of city states, the Romans were the world's first and greatest imperial people and they coined a justification for imperialism that became the heritage of their successor.

They proclaimed that they were a people of superior race with a culture too high to be compared with any other, that they had a better system of administration, that they were versed in the arts of life. They also proclaimed that the rest were people of inferior race with a very low culture and were absolutely devoid of the arts of life, and that their administration was very despotic. As a logical consequence of this the Romans argued that it was their divine mission to civilise their low lying brethren, nay to conquer them and superimpose their culture in the name of humanity.

The British have justified their imperial policy in India by similar argumentation. The British historians of India have a kind of Leus Boswelliana – disease of admiration. Their optical vision somehow or other has magnified the vices, not the virtues, of the predecessors of the British in India. Not only have they been loud in their denunciation of the Moghul and the Maratha rulers as despots or brigands, they cast a slur on the morals of the entire population and their civilisation. This is but natural, for individuals as well as states can raise themselves only by lowering the merits of others.

Historians of British India have often committed the fallacy of comparing the rule of the British with their immediate or remote predecessors. In deference to historical methodology, they ought to compare the rulers of India with their contemporaries in England. Much of historical error will vanish if we closely follow this plan. It would no longer be a matter of contemptuous pity to read perhaps the abject condition of the Hindoos under the conquest of the Mohammedans when we will remember the pitiful condition of the Anglo-Saxons under their Norman conquerors when 'to be called an Englishman was considered as a reproach – when those who were appointed to administer justice were the fountains of all iniquity – when magistrates, whose duty it was to pronounce righteous judgements were the most cruel of all tyrants, and greater plunderers than common thieves and robbers . . .; when the great men were inflamed with such a rage for money that they cared not by what means it was acquired; when the licentiousness was so great that a Princess of Scotland found it necessary to wear a religious habit in order to preserve her person from violation'.[18]

The much spoken of Mohammedan cruelty could hardly exceed that committed by the first Crusaders on their conquest of Jerusalem. The garrison of 40,000 men 'was put to the sword without distinction; arms protected not the brave, nor submission the timid; no age or sex received mercy, and infants perished by the same sword that pierced their mothers. The streets of Jerusalem were covered with heaps of slain, and the shrieks of agony and despair resounded from every house.'[19]

If we thus run down through the history of India and history of England and compare contemporary events we will find that for every Native Roland we have an English Oliver. We must therefore repeat the warning of Sir Thomas Munro to English historians of India, who said, 'When we compare other countries with England, we usually speak of England as she now is, we scarcely ever think of going back beyond the Reformation and we are apt to regard every foreign country as ignorant and uncivilised, whose state of improvement does not in some degree approximate to our own, even though it should be higher than our own as at no distant period.'

Let us, therefore, turn to the 'Despots and Brigands' who ruled India before the British and let us review their deeds and the condition of the people during their respective rulers.

This knowledge is absolutely necessary in order to form a correct estimate of the economic condition of the people of India under the East India Company.

We need not wait to dilate upon the economic prosperity of India in ancient times since we have already dwelt upon it.

We have a consensus of opinion both Hindoo and Mohammedan as regards the prosperity of India when the Mohammedan conquest took place. The magnificence of Canouj and the wealth of the Temple of Somnath bear witness to it. It is a mistake to suppose that the Mussulman sovereigns of India were barbarous and despots. On the other hand the majority of them were men of extraordinary character. Mohammed of Guzni 'showed so much munificence, to individuals of eminence that his capital exhibited a greater assemblage of literary genius than any other monarch in Asia has ever been able to produce. If rapacious in acquiring wealth, he was unrivalled in the judgement and grandeur with which he knew how to expend it.' . . .

Clive described Bengal as a country of 'inexhaustible riches'. Macaulay said, 'In spite of the Mussulman despot and of the Maratha freebooter, Bengal was known through the East as the Garden of Eden – as the rich kingdom. Its population multiplied exceedingly; distant provinces were nourished from the overflowing of its granaries: and the noble ladies of London and Paris were clothed in the delicate produce of its looms.'

But with the advent of the English things began to change. Prosperity bade fair to India and perched itself on the Union Jack.

The evil forces were set forth both on the side of the Parliament and the East India Company.

The rule of the Company was anything but wise, it was rigorous, it gave security but destroyed property. The scheme of administration was far from perfect. Adam Smith characterises the 'Company of Merchants' as 'incapable of considering themselves as sovereigns, even after they have become such' and says, 'Trade or buying in order to sell again, they will consider as their principal business, and by a strange absurdity, regard the character of the sovereign as but an appendix to that of the merchants . . . as sovereigns, their interest is exactly the same with that of the country which they govern. As merchants, their interest is directly opposite to that interest.' . . .

In the local or Supreme Government of India, the native inhabitants had no voice. They were barred from all high paid offices and had no scope beyond the position of a petty clerk.

The internal administration was so devised that the Governors and the official staff in their capacity as advisers did or were compelled to do all the thinking for the inhabitants of the country. They enacted, true to a word, the part of Sir John Bowley or the 'Poor man's friend' so ably drawn by Charles Dickens: 'Your only business, my good fellow, is with me. You need not trouble yourself to think about anything. I will think for you; I know what is good for you; I am your perpetual parent. Such is the dispensation of all all-wise Providence . . . what man can do, I do. I do my duty as the Poor Man's Friend and Father, and I endeavour to educate his mind, by inculcating on all occasions the one great lesson which that class requires, that is entire dependence on myself. They have no business whatever with themselves.'

These Bowleys no doubt did the thinking as a divine mandate but unfortunately, none the less naturally, their thinking and enacting proved decidedly favourable to England and fatal to India.

John Archer's Presidential Address to the Inaugural Meeting of the African Progress Union (1918)[20]

John Archer (1863–1932) became the first person of African descent to hold civic office in London (and the second in the country) when he was elected Mayor of Battersea in 1913. In 1918, he became the first president of the African Progress Union, formed to promote 'the general welfare of Africans and Afro-Peoples' and to spread knowledge of black history, a post he held for three years. This is an extract from a speech he made at the first meeting of the Union.

The people in this country are sadly ignorant with reference to the darker races, and our object is to show to them that we have given up the idea of becoming hewers of wood and drawers of water, that we claim our rightful place within this Empire . . . That if we are good enough to be brought to fight the wars of the country we are good enough to receive the benefits of the country . . . One of the objects of this association is to demand – not ask, demand; it will be 'demand' all the time that I am your President. I am not asking for anything, I am demanding.

Manifesto of Bhagwati Charan Vohra (4 June 1928)[21]

Bhagwati Charan Vohra (1903–30) was a Punjabi revolutionary, a member of the Hindustan Socialist Republican Association, dedicated to overthrowing British rule by violent struggle. This manifesto was written for an Indian nationalist youth organisation, Naujawan Bharat Sabha. Vohra detonated a bomb under the viceroy's train in 1929. He died of wounds sustained while he was preparing a bomb in Lahore.

The historic question – 'Would you be governed by sword or pen?' – no more lies unanswered. Those who put that question to us have themselves answered it. In the words of Lord Birkenhead, 'With the sword we won India and with the sword we shall retain it.' Thanks to this candour, everything is clear now.

A word about the blessings of the British rule in India. Does it require any authorities to prove that India, with the richest soil and mine, is today one of the poorest countries, that India, which could be proud of so glorious a civilisation, is today the most backward country with only five per cent literacy? Do not the people know that India has to pay the largest toll of human life with the highest child death rate in the world? The epidemics, like plague, cholera, influenza and such other diseases are becoming commoner day by day. Is it not disgraceful for us to hear again and again that we are not fit for self-government? . . . Is this life worth living?

Does it require any revelation now to make us realise that we are enslaved and must be free? Shall we wait for an uncertain sage to make us feel that we are an oppressed people? Shall we expectantly wait for divine help or some miracle to deliver us from bondage? Do we not know the fundamental principles of liberty? 'Those who want to be free, must themselves strike the blow.' Young men, awake, arise; we have slept too long!

Mohandas Gandhi, Quit India Speech
(8 August 1942)[22]

With this speech, delivered to the All India Congress Committee, Mohandas Gandhi (1869–1948) launched the third of his satyagraha, or truth-force, campaigns to rid India of British rule. The principle of ahimsa, non-violence, was central to this effort. The circumstances of the speech were very different from the launch of previous campaigns in 1920 and 1930. Britain was in the midst of a world war, and Japanese forces were threatening India. They would find Indian support from Subhas Chandra Bose and his Indian National Army. Gandhi makes clear in this speech that welcoming the Japanese would merely replace one oppression with another.

Before you discuss the resolution, let me place before you one or two things. I want you to understand two things very clearly and consider them from the same point of view from which I am placing them before you. There are people who ask me whether I am the same man that I was in 1920 or whether there has been any change in me. You are right in asking that question. I may tell you that I am the same man today that I was in 1920. The only difference is that I am much stronger in certain things now than I was in 1920. I may explain it by pointing out that a man goes about heavily clothed in winter but the same man may be found without such clothing in summer. This outward change does not make any difference in the man. There are people who may say that I say one thing today and another thing tomorrow. But I must tell you that there is no change in me. I stick to the principle of non-violence as I did before. If you are tired of it then you need not come with me. It is not necessary or incumbent upon you to pass this resolution. If you want swaraj and independence and if you feel that what I place before you is a good thing and a right thing then only accept it. It is only that way you can give me complete support. If you do not do that I am afraid you will have to rue for what you do . . .

Your work does not finish with the attainment of freedom. There is no place for dictators in our scheme of things. Our object is to achieve independence and whoever can take up the reins may do so . . .

There are people who have hatred in their hearts for the British. I have heard people saying that they were disgusted with them. Common people's mind does not differentiate between British Government and British people. To them both are the same. They are the people who do not mind the advent of the Japanese. To them perhaps it would mean change of masters. But it is a dangerous thing. You must remove it from your mind. This is a crucial hour. If we keep quiet and do not play our part it would not be right on our part. If it is only Britain and the United States who fight this war and if our part, is only to give monetary help, whether given willingly or taken from us unwillingly, it is not a very happy proposition. But we can show our real grit and valour only when it becomes our own fight. Then even a child will be brave. We shall get our freedom by fighting. It cannot fall from the skies. I know fully well that the Britishers will have to give us freedom when we have made sufficient sacrifices and proved our strength. We must remove any hatred for the British from our hearts. At least in my heart there is no such hatred. As a matter of fact, I am a greater friend of the British now than I ever was. The reason for this is that at this moment they are in distress. My friendship demands that I must make them aware of their mistakes. As I am not in the position in which they are, I can point out their mistakes. I know they are on the brink of a ditch and about to fall into it. Therefore, even if they want to cut off my hands, my friendship demands that I should try to pull them out of that ditch.

This is my claim, at which many people may laugh, but all the same I say this is true. At a time when I am about to launch the biggest fight in my life there can be no hatred for the British in my heart. The thought that because they are in difficulties I should give them a push is totally absent from my mind. It never has been there. Maybe that in a moment of anger they might do things which might provoke you. Nevertheless you should not resort to violence and put non-violence to shame.

C. L. R. James, *Beyond a Boundary* (1963)[23]

C. L. R. James (1901–89), who was born in Trinidad and emigrated to Britain in 1932, was a novelist, historian, essayist, political activist, and writer on cricket. To the last of these callings he brought a new seriousness, partly informed by his Marxist and Trotskyist political affiliations, but also by his background as a West Indian. Beyond a Boundary *is a meditation on the meanings of cricket, and also a reflection of James's own experiences growing up in a British colony.*

It was only long years after that I understood the limitation on spirit, vision and self-respect which was imposed on us by the fact that our masters, our curriculum, our code of morals, *everything* began from the basis that Britain was the source of all light and learning, and our business was to admire, wonder, imitate, learn; our criterion of success was to have succeeded in approaching that distant ideal – to attain it was, of course, impossible . . .

We know nothing, nothing at all, of the results of what we do to children. My father had given me a bat and ball, I had learnt to play and at eighteen was a good cricketer. What a fiction! In reality my life up to ten had laid the powder for a war that lasted without respite for eight years, and intermittently for some time afterwards – a war between English Puritanism, English literature and cricket, and the realism of West Indian life. On one side was my father, my mother (no mean pair), my two aunts and my grandmother, my uncle and his wife, all the family friends (which included a number of headmasters from all over the island), some eight or nine Englishmen who taught at the Queen's Royal College, all graduates of Oxford or Cambridge, the Director of Education and the Board of Education, which directed the educational system of the whole island. On the other side was me, just ten years old when it began.

They had on their side parental, scholastic, governmental, and many other kinds of authority and, less tangible but perhaps more powerful, the prevailing sentiment that, in as much as the coloured people on the island, and in fact all over the world, had such limited opportunities, it was my duty, my moral and religious duty, to make the best use of the opportunities which all these good people and the Trinidad Government had provided for me. I had nothing to start with but my pile of clippings about W. G. Grace and Ranjitsinhji, my *Vanity Fair* and my Puritan instincts, though as yet these were undeveloped. I fought and won.

This was the battleground. The Trinidad Government offered yearly free exhibitions from the elementary schools of the islands to either of the two secondary schools, the government Queen's Royal College and the Catholic college, St Mary's. The number today is over four hundred, but in those days it was only four. Through this narrow gate boys, poor and bright, could get a secondary education and in the end a Cambridge Senior Certificate, a useful passport to a good job. There were even more glittering prizes. Every year the two schools competed for three island scholarships worth £600 each. With one of these a boy could study law or medicine and return to the island with a profession and therefore independence. There were at that time few other roads to independence for a black man who started without means. The higher posts in the government, in engineering and other scientific professions were monopolised by white people, and, as practically all big business was also in their hands, the coloured people were, as a rule, limited to the lower posts. Thus law and medicine were the only ways out. Lawyers and doctors made large fees and enjoyed great social prestige. The final achievement was when the Governor nominated one of these coloured men to the Legislative Council to represent the people. To what degree he represented them should not distract us here. We must keep our eye on the course: exhibition, scholarship, profession, wealth, Legislative Council and the title of Honourable. Whenever someone brought it off the local people were very proud of him.

That was the course marked out for me . . .

I had been brought up in the public-school code.

It came doctrinally from the masters, who for two generations, from the foundation of the school, had been Oxford and Cambridge men. The striking thing is that inside the classrooms the code had little success . . .

But as soon as we stepped on to the cricket or football field, more particularly the cricket field, all was changed. We were a motley crew . . . Yet rapidly we learned to obey the umpire's decision without question, however irrational it was. We learned to play with the team, which meant subordinating your personal inclinations, and even interests, to the good of the whole. We kept a stiff upper lip in that we did not complain about ill-fortune. We did not denounce failures, but 'Well tried' or 'Hard luck' came easily to our lips. We were generous to opponents and congratulated them on victories, even when we knew they did not deserve it. We lived in two worlds. Inside the classrooms the heterogeneous jumble of Trinidad was battered and jostled and shaken down into some sort of order. On the playing field we did what ought to be done . . .

Later, when reading elementary English history books, I became resentful of the fact that the English always won all, or nearly all, of the battles and read every new history book I could find, searching out and noting battles they had lost. I would not deny that early influences I could know nothing about had cast me in a certain mould or even that I was born with certain characteristics. That could be. What interests me, and is, I think, of general interest, is that as far back as I can trace my consciousness, the original found itself and

came to maturity within a system that was the result of centuries of
development in another land, was transplanted as a hothouse flower
is transplanted and bore some strange fruit.

––––––––––––

Peter Hain, Defence in Trial for Picketing Apartheid South African Cricket and Rugby (14–15 August 1972)[24]

*Peter Hain was born in Kenya and brought up in South Africa until
the age of ten. His parents were active in the campaign against
apartheid, and the regime's pursuit of them eventually forced them
to leave the country in order to earn a living. They settled in London,
and Hain attended Queen Mary College, University of London. As
a student, he began to lead a campaign against the sports tours
of all-white South African rugby and cricket teams. The Stop the
Seventy Tour campaign disrupted the Springboks' rugby tour, and
led to the cancellation of the cricket tour. In 1972 a private prosecution was brought against Hain for conspiracy by Francis Bennion,
a barrister and parliamentary draftsman. In the end Hain was
convicted and fined for invading the court during a Davis Cup match,
but the jury was unable to agree on the much more serious charge.
Hain went on to become an MP and a Labour cabinet minister.
South African teams did not play in Britain again until after the
end of apartheid.*

A famous writer once described a jury as the twelve persons chosen
to decide who has the better lawyer . . . I am sorry, in a way, that I
deprived you of this task because I am not a lawyer and after this
experience have no desire of ever becoming one. At times I have felt
like a chess novice, watched by a selected audience and the world
press as he plays a game against two grand masters simultaneously.
The reason I decided to defend myself was not taken lightly but

because I wanted to explain to you the reality of the case as I saw it, and I remind you that the phrase 'reality of the case' was the prosecution's and not mine. I don't have anything to hide and I don't have anything to regret about my activity in relation to the Stop the Seventy Tour campaign . . .

Direct action is essentially a personal form of action springing from a personal conscience.

Conspiracy is in a wholly different category from any of the things I say I did and which have been referred to to try and blur the issue. Mr Stable said that I had introduced direct action into Britain, but it has in its various forms a long honourable tradition in British society. The law of the land as it now stands contains many provisions as a result of direct action, notably the suffragettes . . .

I am not charged with climbing over the fence at Twickenham; I am charged with conspiracy to do some 208 particulars and it is that that I dispute very strongly and in my submission the evidence produced does not sustain the indictment. I think it is clear from the submissions I have made to you, and from one of the prosecution witnesses, Mr Gordon Winter, that the character of those activities was of an information and of a publicity nature, not of a conspiratorial nature . . .

It was an honest campaign and a book has been written about it by the defendant. It is very difficult to be more public than that. It was in my submission, open and above board, and the charge with which I am indicted, if it were to be sustained, would contradict that basic fact . . .

I hate apartheid. I have hated it ever since I woke up that morning in Johannesburg to find my parents missing – arrested by the South African Security Police who had come, like thieves in the night, and departed leaving me, a boy of eleven, to look after our home and two young sisters. My parents' crime? Belonging to the South African Liberal Party which had blacks as members. Just as you cannot play sport with black people in South Africa, neither can you belong to the same political party. It is against the law. And Mr Stable says we must always obey laws for no better reason, apparently, than that they are laws. So when the South African sportsmen came, of course I did what I could. I personally entered three sporting arenas – without agreeing with anyone to do so, and leaving without struggling and without being charged with a breach of the law. I debated with people like Wilf Wooller. I became spokesman for STST [Stop the Seventy Tour] and for reasons best known to the press was always quoted in these issues. Conspire, as alleged in this indictment, I did not.

Linton Kwesi Johnson, 'Inglan Is a Bitch' (1980)[24]

Linton Kwesi Johnson was born in 1952 in Chapelton, Jamaica. He moved to London in 1963 to be with his mother and read Sociology at Goldsmiths College, University of London. Although regarded as the father of dub poetry, a term he coined for the combination of reggae music and spoken word, he does not apply it to his own work, in which the words are always written before any musical background is added.

wen mi jus come to Landan toun
mi use to work pan di andahgroun
but workin pan di andahgroun
yu dont get fi know your way aroun

Inglan is a bitch
dere's no escapin it
Inglan is a bitch
dere's no runin whe fram it

mi get a likkle jab in a big otell
an awftah a while, mi woz doin quite well
dem staat mi aaf as a dish-washah
but wen mi tek a stack, mi noh tun clack-watchah!

Inglan is a bitch
dere's no escapin it
Inglan is a bitch
noh baddah try fi hide fram it

wen dem gi you di likkle wage packit
fus dem rab it wid dem big tax rackit
yu haffi struggle fi mek enz meet
an wen yu goh a yu bed yu jus can't sleep

Inglan is a bitch
dere's no escapin it
Inglan is a bitch fi true
a noh lie mi a tell, a true

mi use to work dig ditch wen it cowl noh bitch
mi did strang like a mule, but, bwoy, mi did fool
den awftah a while mi jus stap dhu owevahtime
den aftah a while mi jus phu dung mi tool

Inglan is a bitch
dere's no escapin it
Inglan is a bitch
yu haffi know how fi suvvive in it

well mi dhu day wok an mid dhu nite wok
mi dhu clean wok an mid dhu dutty wok

dem seh dat black man is very lazy
but it yu si how mi wok yu woulda seh mi crazy

Inglan is a bitch
dere's no escapin it
Inglan is a bitch
yu bettah face up to it

dem have a lickle facktri up inna Brackly
inna disya facktri all dem dhu is pack crackry
fi di laas fiteen years dem get mi laybah
now awftah fiteen years mi fall out a fayvah

Inglan is a bitch
dere's no escapin it
Inglan is a bitch
dere's no runnin' whey fram it

mi know dem have work, wok in abundant
yet still, dem mek mi redundant
now, at fifty-five mi gettin quite ole
yet still, dem sen mi fi goh draw dole

Inglan is a bitch
dere's no escapin it
Inglan is a bitch fi true
is whey wi a goh dhu bout it?

————————————

Sinéad O'Connor, 'Black Boys on Mopeds' (March 1990)[26]

Sinéad O'Connor (b. 1966) is an Irish singer-songwriter. This song has been associated with two deaths of black youths involving the police. One was Colin Roach, who died in Stoke Newington police station in 1983 after sustaining a gunshot wound that the police claimed was self-inflicted. The other was Nicholas Bramble, a seventeen-year-old who was chased by police on his motorcycle in 1987 and died when he lost control. The police believed that the motorcycle was stolen, but it belonged to Bramble.

Margaret Thatcher on TV
Shocked by the deaths that took place in Beijing
It seems strange that she should be offended
The same orders are given by her

I've said this before now
You said I was childish and you'll say it now
'Remember what I told you
If they hated me they will hate you'

England's not the mythical land of Madame George and roses
It's the home of police who kill black boys on mopeds
And I love my boy and that's why I'm leaving
I don't want him to be aware that there's any such thing as grieving

Young mother down at Smithfield
Five a.m., looking for food for her kids
In her arms she holds three cold babies
And the first word that they learned was 'please'

These are dangerous days
To say what you feel is to dig your own grave
'Remember what I told you
If you were of the world they would love you'

England's not the mythical land of Madame George and roses
It's the home of police who kill blacks boys on mopeds
And I love my boy and that's why I'm leaving
I don't want him to be aware that there's any such thing as
grieving.

Anonymous Tanzanian Asylum Seeker (October 2000)[27]

*An asylum seeker from Tanzania spoke at a meeting in Manchester,
as part of the Campaign against Racism and Fascism/National Civil
Rights Movement Caravan tour.*

On Wednesday, 2 February 2000, I was arrested in my house in
Salford, Manchester, and detained. I was deemed to have contravened
the laws of the land and I was specifically told that I belonged to
another land. It is from that day that my perception of life changed.
But more significantly my livelihood became contained and restricted;
and all in the name of immigration laws. Now, life is for me an intan-
gible reality in the hands of authorities and laws designed to withdraw
control of my own life. For the first time in my life, I can only see
but not participate in my own existence . . .

One morning in February 2000 there was a knock at the door and
the police and an immigration officer came in. I was told that I was

being detained under the Immigration Act. I was taken from my house to a police station where I was detained for one day before being taken to Manchester Airport Detention Centre. Many people are not aware that there is a prison at Manchester Airport. I was locked up there for five nights. You can only stay at Manchester Airport for a maximum of five nights, after which you have got two options. Either you are taken to a proper prison or you agree to be deported. I was told that I was going to be taken to Haslar. They did not say that Haslar was a prison.

First, they took me to another detention centre in Harmondsworth just outside London and I was detained there for a further night. Then I was told that I was to be taken to Haslar, which is a place of which I knew nothing. Somebody else, who was on the phone, was pleading not to be sent to Haslar and I did not know why. Then he said that he 'can't be going to Haslar because that is a prison'. I realised that I was going to be imprisoned. When I got to Haslar I was given prison uniform by prison guards and I was given a room to stay. It was a really terrible place, a completely different atmosphere from the other places I had been in.

In detention I was, like all the detainees, condemned to the lowest point of my life. Detention is where I spent the gloomiest weeks, experiencing all forms of despair. I cried a lot, believing that it is when you cry that you stumble on to a source of goodness. But when I called for goodness, goodness refused to come. Detention is where hope and inspiration are almost impossible to sustain. The cage is a place where sanity is a full-time job. I tried to keep going but I was very close to losing it. I saw fellow asylum seekers going clinically insane, trying to commit suicide and others, sadly, successful. You think that these are scenes which should trigger a human response, but not when it is asylum seekers. We never found out what happened to those who tried to hang themselves. They are simply taken away and the outside world never finds out. Asylum seekers faced open abuse from detention or prison officers who believe that all asylum seekers are scroungers and they should all be locked up.

I was detained in Haslar during the final year of my engineering degree at Manchester Metropolitan University. I tried to get out on bail to at least finish my degree. My application was not successful for the first time but eventually I was granted bail by the adjudicator.

The bail conditions were curious – I was told that I was not allowed to move from my house in Salford. Also, I was to appear at Manchester city centre police station three times a week. But at least I could avoid the cage. I have not been allowed to go to work so I have been condemned to use the voucher scheme . . .

The government's policies of dispersal, detention and vouchers are hugely traumatising for us. When we are dispersed, it is done without regard to any friends we may have around, places of social care, places of worship or even centres of legal representation. We find ourselves in places where there is no knowledge of us and absolutely no help waiting for us. For example, if a person is living in Manchester with a family member or friend and they apply for accommodation of their own, they could quite easily be dispersed to the north-east or somewhere equally distant . . .

It is painful to finally realise that you can be created as a human being and not be treated as such by fellow humans. Having come across a lot of fellow asylum seekers myself, some questions really bother me. Why would a wealthy Christian tortured by fundamentalist Muslims flee Egypt to be on vouchers? Why would a software engineer, persecuted for his political affiliation, flee Algeria to be on vouchers? Why would an established lawyer flee Nigeria to be on vouchers? . . .

The policy of detention is further proof that the authorities seriously disregard the welfare of asylum seekers and refugees. It is now possible to be arrested and detained in this country just for claiming asylum. It is now possible that a six-week-old baby can be detained. It is now possible that somebody is jailed for up to two years having committed no crime and certainly having not been convicted by the courts. Their only mistake is being a foreigner and claiming asylum in this country. Now let us ask ourselves a question. What crime would constitute a two-year jail term?

The immigration and asylum policy introduced by the government, the lies told about us by the racist and right-wing press, have made it possible to convince seven out of ten people in this country that we are over-helped and have overpopulated the land. It is quite clear to me that the authorities here have treated us as guinea pigs to see if their voucher system and their dispersal scheme will work.

We are accused of telling lies, stealing from the economy and exploiting the hospitality of the British people. We are treated as criminals. We do not get what we deserve but what we, or our supporters, negotiate and fight for. I truly believe that asylum should be a right not a fight. With relentless campaigning, we can show that the dangers to this society are not caused by refugees and asylum seekers but those who perpetuate their hate towards us.

Benjamin Zephaniah, 'What Stephen Lawrence Has Taught Us' (2001)[28]

Stephen Lawrence, a black teenager, was murdered by a group of white youths at a bus stop in Eltham in 1993. Two prosecutions, one private, were brought against three suspects, but the accused were acquitted after identification evidence was ruled inadmissible. The failings of the police investigation and the lack of convictions led to a public inquiry, and Lord Macpherson's report concluded that the

Metropolitan Police was 'institutionally racist'. Only after the principle
of 'double jeopardy' – not being tried for the same crime twice – was
scrapped in 2005 did it become possible for new forensic evidence
to be used to secure the conviction of two of the five alleged killers.
In January 2012, Gary Dobson and David Norris were found guilty of
murder. Benjamin Zephaniah's poem was commissioned by Channel
4 News.

We know who the killers are,
We have watched them strut before us
As proud as sick Mussolinis,
We have watched them strut before us
Compassionless and arrogant,
They paraded before us,
Like angels of death
Protected by the law.

It is now an open secret
Black people do not have
Chips on their shoulders,
They just have injustice on their backs
And justice on their minds,
And now we know that the road to liberty
Is as long as the road from slavery.

The death of Stephen Lawrence
Has taught us to love each other
And never to take the tedious task
Of waiting for a bus for granted.
Watching his parents watching the cover-up
Begs the question
What are the trading standards here?
Why are we paying for a police force
That will not work for us?

The death of Stephen Lawrence
Has taught us
That we cannot let the illusion of freedom
Endow us with a false sense of security as we walk the streets,
The whole world can now watch
The academics and the super-cops
Struggling to define institutionalised racism
As we continue to die in custody
As we continue emptying our pockets on the pavements,
And we continue to ask ourselves
Why is it so official
That black people are so often killed
Without killers?

We are not talking about war or revenge
We are not talking about hypothetics or possibilities,
We are talking about where we are now
We are talking about how we live now
In dis state
Under dis flag (God Save the Queen),
And God save all those black children who want to grow up
And God save all the brothers and sisters
Who like raving,
Because the death of Stephen Lawrence
Has taught us that racism is easy when
You have friends in high places.
And friends in high places
Have no use whatsoever
When they are not your friends.

Dear Mr Condon,
Pop out of Teletubby land,
And visit reality,
Come to an honest place

And get some advice from your neighbours,
Be enlightened by our community,
Neglect your well-paid ignorance
Because
We know who the killers are.

———————————

Two Reflections on Rock Against Racism and Love Music Hate Racism (2004)[29]

Roger Huddle helped co-found the anti-Fascist group Rock Against Racism. Here are two reflections from 2004 on the legacy and ongoing need for anti-racist cultural work, one by Huddle and the other by Lee Billingham, an organiser with the later group Love Music Hate Racism.

Roger Huddle

It is very important that we consider the establishment of Rock Against Racism in the wider political and historical context. 1976 was a year of major social upheavals, with the introduction by a Labour government of the Social Contract. It was also the year that saw a real rise of the Nazi National Front.

Red Saunders, a photographer and agitprop theatre performer, and I were both veterans of the 1960s cultural struggles, Vietnam, May 1968, hippies, the summer of love, Ginsberg, the Black Power movement. We were also big music fans, and loved great artists such as Dylan, Country Joe and the Fish, Otis Redding, Marvin Gaye and Aretha Franklin.

We had talked about the idea of a one-off gig against the rise of racism, and considered calling it Rock Against Racism. However, it remained just an idea until August 1976, when Eric Clapton made a sickening drunken declaration of support for Enoch Powell (the racist former Tory minister famous for his 'rivers of blood' campaign against immigration) at a gig in Birmingham.

Clapton's speech was all the more disgusting because he had his first hit with a cover of reggae star Bob Marley's 'I Shot The Sheriff'. In reply we wrote a letter to the *New Musical Express* and signed it, along with two members of Kartoon Klowns.

We finished the letter by saying that we were launching a movement called Rock Against Racism (RAR), and anyone outraged should write to us and join. We received hundreds of replies.

The founders of RAR were all soul fans, but what really propelled it into what became a mass movement was the explosion of punk. Our slogans were 'Reggae, Soul, Rock 'n' Roll, Jazz, Funk, Punk – Our Music' and 'NF = No Fun' (this in response to the Sex Pistols' record 'No Future').

What also gave RAR the political context to become much bigger was the establishment of the Anti-Nazi League in 1977. Together the ANL and RAR were able to build a really mass movement against the Nazis. The carnival in Victoria Park with the Clash, Tom Robinson and Steel Pulse attracted 85,000, and received fantastic coverage in *NME*. Twenty-five thousand came to the Northern Carnival in Manchester, which had The Buzzcocks, Graham Parker and the Rumour, and Misty in Roots. The Brockwell Park event with Elvis Costello and Aswad had 100,000, and 26,000 heard Aswad and the Specials in Leeds.

RAR also had a fanzine, *Temporary Hoarding*. It was the only really revolutionary cultural paper in Britain then or at any time. It included interviews with Johnny Rotten, the Clash and Aswad, it raised the issue of Ireland, and always argued against the despair that dominated punk music.

Today the Nazis in the BNP [British National Party] still see all popular music as 'jungle music', although they can't say that openly. It is still anathema to them because it's multiracial in its essence. As long as the Nazis exist we must challenge them. That is why it is critically important that Love Music Hate Racism (LMHR) and Unite Against Fascism are built, enjoyed and supported.

Lee Billingham

There were a couple of main inspirations behind launching the Unity festivals. Firstly, there's been an impressive tradition in Britain of music playing a significant part in the fight against Fascism – Rock Against Racism (RAR), for instance.

We also found – having launched Love Music Hate Racism (LMHR) – that there are hundreds of artists who are passionately anti-racist and anti-Fascist, and want to do something. And beyond them there are many music lovers who understand that what the BNP is about is a threat to everybody – that the multiracial, multicultural music scene is something through which we can express our unity, and which can isolate the Nazis.

The main carnival is taking place in London because we feel that this is where one of the greatest dangers is in terms of BNP electoral success. An election win in the London Assembly elections would obviously give them a platform from which to spout their filth and encourage racist violence.

We know that throughout Britain there is a mass movement of people opposed to the BNP that we can mobilise, in part through the music festivals. The public impact of these kinds of events will inspire people to get out and vote – because the BNP thrive on a low turnout.

In London the Libertines are headlining and David Gray is also playing. As well as these big names we really have something for everyone – the best in every type of music in Britain today. This again visibly emphasises our unity and our diversity.

We're also expecting Mick Jones from the Clash, Misty in Roots and Tom Robinson. We do want to explicitly link what we're doing today with what happened in the late 1970s. Part of what we want to encourage through LMHR is breaking down false barriers between musical genres put up by the music industry. Whereas RAR mixed with reggae, LMHR mixes grime and eski with indie punk, bhangra and hip-hop.

Part of the enthusiasm for the scene comes, I think, from the links people make to other movements – opposition to the war, and to this Labour government more generally. Without wanting to overstate it and to proclaim the birth of 'the new punk', acts like Dizzee Rascal, Wiley, or emerging new guitar bands out of London and elsewhere (like the Libertines) have an attitude of questioning authority, of anti-materialism, and there is something of a return to the idea of 'DIY culture' – whether that means forming a band in your garage or making tunes on a Sony PlayStation.

The other lead we want to take from RAR is that we want LMHR to be a vibrant movement from below – that people go away from the centrally organised carnivals inspired to set up their own gigs and events.

Chagos Protest by the People's Navy (11 March 2008)[30]

The Chagos archipelago is a chain of sixty-five small coral islands in the Indian Ocean, of which the largest is the island of Diego Garcia. In 1965, the archipelago formed part of the British colony of Mauritius. It had a settled population, descendants of former slaves and labourers from the Seychelles and Mauritius, and its own Creole language and culture. In 1966 The British government, led by Harold

Wilson, secretly agreed to lease Diego Garcia to the United States for fifty years. The US wanted an unpopulated island on which to build a huge military base, and the British obliged by evicting around two thousand islanders to Mauritius without consultation or appropriate compensation, and denying the fact for decades. For more than forty years, the Chagossians have been campaigning to return, resisted in the courts by successive British governments. After a law lords ruling overturning a Court of Appeal judgment in favour of the islanders, the Chagossians are now appealing to the European Court of Human Rights. In 2008 two activists, Jon Castle and Pete Bouquet, sailed their yacht from Thailand to Diego Garcia to highlight the islanders' treatment. They were arrested and their boat was impounded.

We have sailed our boat *Musichana* over two thousand miles to demonstrate to you the serious nature of our concerns about the plight of the Chagossians and about your military activities on Diego Garcia.

It is our duty as British citizens to challenge and expose these activities in a peaceful and responsible manner.

We represent a growing proportion of the world's population, who disagree with the treatment of the Chagossians and demand their right to return.

– The Chagos people were the legitimate inhabitants of the Chagos Archipelagos.

– Three generations of Chagossians are buried on the island.

– The UK courts have consistently supported the Chagossians in their right to return.

– While commendable, it is simply not good enough to allow some Chagossians to come back to clean and restore graveyards. When the work is finished they have to leave again.

We are disgusted by your military activities, because history has proven that violent military conflicts and all forms of terrorism solve nothing. Yet your actions and those of your respective governments, which corruptly entangle profit-making business with political and military decisions, continue to increase militarisation and the use of force as a first rather than a last option and only perpetuate global instability and terrorise innocent people.

Your base here is, together with the other US bases throughout the world, part of an axis of evil and represents all the corruption and subversion of human decency. From here your bombers have rained terror, horror and destruction, often on to the heads of innocent people. It has also been used for secretly transporting and holding prisoners without regard to even the most basic and accepted concepts of justice.

We urge you, in the name of humanity to cease your inhumane activities. You must leave Diego Garcia forthwith and end your shameful and harmful presence here, so that the rightful inhabitants, whom you exiled nearly forty years ago, can return to their homes and live in peace.

Mark Steel, 'The Poles Might be Leaving but the Prejudice Remains' (9 September 2009)[31]

Mark Steel is a British socialist, columnist, author and comedian. Steel wrote a column for the Guardian *between 1996 and 1999. In 2000 he started writing a weekly column for the* Independent, *where this article first appeared.*

Over the last few years it's become one of our quaint English tradi-tions that on any day following the announcement of immigration figures, certain newspapers display headlines such as 'TEN MILLION OR SOMETHING LIKE THAT POLES TO SWARM INTO BRITAIN LIKE PLUMBING LOCUSTS!!! And they plan to BUGGER OUR KITTENS!!!'

These newspapers would compete with each other until they

seemed to insist the number of Poles coming was more than the number of Poles in the world, but even then they'd have replied, 'Yes – well, that's because they're planning to bring ten million of their dead, to make use of our soft-touch spirit welfare scheme.'

But the latest figures, released yesterday, have spoilt this game because it turns out half the Poles who came here have gone back to Poland. Presumably these newspapers will get round that by screaming 'Poland on brink of disaster as it's invaded by millions of Poles!!!'

'Our hospitals simply can't cope with the numbers coming in,' said an unnamed doctor. 'I'm not racist but we're already full up.'

Like all panics about immigration, the anti-Polish version has created an almost artistic level of irrationality. A landlord of a pub in Lincolnshire who seemed otherwise charming and eloquent told me, 'The trouble with Poles is they walk in groups of four on the pavement, so you fall in the road trying to get round them.' I said, 'I'm sure just as many English people walk in groups of four on the pavement.' He said, 'Yes, but at least they do it in a language I can understand.' Which at least is an original way to be annoyed, to snarl: 'I don't mind falling in a puddle, as long as it's with the right mix of vowels and consonants, but when it's with three or even FOUR Zs it's time we took a stand.'

Now that more are leaving than coming, the anti-immigration newspapers have to revert to more traditional complaints. For example, one paper told us that, 'One immigrant is arrested every four minutes.' But they must have been short of space, because they left out how the average for the whole population is one arrest every THREE minutes. Now they'll print a story that: 'Immigrants are refusing to adapt to our way of life by only being arrested once every four minutes. If they don't want to follow our customs they should go back to where they came from.'

Even then it turned out these figures were taken disproportionately from London, where the immigrant population is higher than across Britain, and anyone arrested for murder who didn't fill in the box marked 'nationality' was assumed to be an immigrant. Because say what you like about a British murderer, at least they have the manners to complete a form in full afterwards.

But the most peculiar side of the obsession with foreigners coming over here disturbing our population figures is they have little to say about the British citizens living in other countries, the number of which has now passed five million. And yet they often have features about finding the perfect retirement home abroad: 'Judith and Roger eventually settled on their delightful rustic cottage in the heart of the Loire, complete with two acres of arable pastures and a goat, from where they could suck dry the overstretched resources of the long-suffering local council. "I'm a stranger in my own bleeding village," said one fed-up neighbour.'

There are 760,000 of us living in Spain, one-twelfth of the population of Cyprus is now British, five per cent of New Zealand and so on. And we can hardly claim that on our travels we 'adopt the customs of the local community', unless the travel companies claim: 'Our popular party game of seeing who's first to drink a bottle of absinthe and puke in an egg cup topless is not only lots of fun, but also a tribute to an ancient fertility ritual here in Crete, and as such enhances the tourists' understanding of regional history and culture.'

Most of the apocalyptic warnings of Eastern European takeover could be traced back to the organisation MigrationWatch, quoted uniformly by the most hysterical anti-immigration papers. But now the Poles are going the other way: instead of issuing a statement reading, 'Whoops, sorry,' they've declared the UK population is still destined to rise to an unsustainable 80 million in the next forty years, because millions are coming here from Africa. That's it – Africa, BILLIONS of them, and they're bringing Mount Kilimanjaro because of our soft-touch summit payments, and all their giraffes and the Sahara desert . . .

1790–1860

———

ONE MAN, ONE VOTE

In the late eighteenth century, radical political movements began to crystallise into campaigns for one specific goal: Parliamentary Reform. Initially, campaigners only agitated for an improvement to the often acutely unfair systems of patronage and under-representation that had long been the way Parliament operated. After the wounds of the Peterloo Massacre in 1819, and the disappointment of the Great Reform Act thirteen years later, the idea began to take hold that real progress would be made only when the people secured 'manhood suffrage', a vote for every adult man in the country (women were not yet part of most radicals' agenda). The nineteenth century's largest popular political movement, Chartism, aimed to deliver just that. Its failure delayed true democracy for another seventy years.

An Account of the Seizure of Citizen Thomas Hardy, Secretary to the London Corresponding Society (12 May 1794)[1]

Thomas Hardy (1752–1832) was a shoemaker who founded the radical London Corresponding Society to advocate parliamentary reform in January 1792. At this time, only a very small proportion of the population was eligible to vote, and while some 'rotten' boroughs represented a handful of constituents, large manufacturing towns, such as Manchester and Oldham, were unrepresented. The authorities took against the Society's plans to hold a popular convention to agitate for reform, affecting to believe that it constituted a threat to Parliament's role, and thus was an act of treason. Hardy and six others were arrested, and sent to the Tower of London charged with high treason. Eventually eleven separate trials were planned, with Hardy's the first to be heard. He was acquitted by a jury on 5 November. Two further trials, of fellow radicals John Thelwall and John Horne Tooke, also resulted in acquittals, before the Crown dropped the other prosecutions. The LCS continued until 1799, but Hardy was involved in radical causes for the rest of his life. He lived to see the Great Reform Act of 1832, which began the process of parliamentary reform, and the expansion of the electorate.

The house of Citizen Hardy was assailed about half an hour after six on Monday morning, the 12th May, 1794, by a messenger from one of the secretaries of state, accompanied by four or five runners, who, after securing his person, proceeded to his bed-room. Mrs Hardy having learned the occasion of the intrusion, requested them to withdraw while she put on some clothes: This they refused, and she anxious for an opportunity of sending for some friends, was obliged to dress herself in their presence, one of them walking about all the while with a pistol in hand. She was no sooner up than they proposed to search the bed, but on her expostulating sharply with them on the extreme indecency of such conduct they forebore. Mrs Hardy, however, found the purpose for which she had risen frustrated not only herself but even the lodgers being closely confined during the search. On their finding a considerable quantity of letters, one of them observed 'there was enough to send him abroad, if not to hang him.' This appeared to another too humane a way of speaking, therefore addressing himself to Mrs Hardy, he said 'I hope you will have the pleasure of seeing him hanged before your door.' Such discourse to an affectionate wife, considerably advanced in her pregnancy, evinced a large share of that humanity which characterises the present administration . . .

Fellow Citizens,

We have given you as above a detail of events, the most indecent, cruel and illegal, with which Britain has been disgraced, since the attack on Mr WILKES, which terminated in a decision of the Court of King's Bench, that general warrants were illegal.

Conscious that there did not exist any circumstances which could justify any such proceedings, and utterly disbelieving that government suspected the existence of any such; we were led to conclude that these outrages were only meant to agitate the public mind, and, give to ministers an opportunity of wresting from the people some of their yet remaining rights. The encroachments which we chiefly expected were a suspension of the Habeas Corpus Act, a Convention Bill and the introduction of a system of judicial proceedings similar to those usurped by the Court of Justiciary in Scotland, and it was our intention to warn our countrymen against such attempts, trusting their united efforts would have been able by constitutional means to rescue their country from the impending danger.

The precipitancy to administration has, however, prevented at least in part those salutary effects, and we now see the personal freedom of every individual Briton subjected to the malice of the king's ministers: but neither the terrors of this situation nor any other shall prevent our exposing to the just resentment of our countrymen, the falsehoods circulated by the ministerial newspapers, purporting to be the Report of the Secret Committee of the House of Commons, and Mr Pitt's speech on making that report. But first, we request the attention of every friend of truth and justice, nay, it may not be wholly useless, if some of the members of the secret committee will duly weigh the following circumstances. – It has long been notorious to the *London Corresponding Society*, that letters addressed to Citizen Hardy, and every other active member, were generally opened at the post-office, and that several have never been delivered. These letters it is reasonable to suppose have rested somewhere, and nowhere more reasonably than in the offices of the secretaries of state.

'Rules and Resolutions of the Political Protestants' (20 July 1818)[2]

'Political Protestants' was a name adopted by several northern local reform associations in cities such as Hull, York and Newcastle between 1818 and 1820. The groups varied in their approach, but all appealed to working-class men to campaign against a corrupt parliamentary system, and for universal suffrage.

We, the Members of this Institution, wishing not to invade the rights of any man, or set of men, are at the same time determined not to consent to the invasion of our own rights. Therefore, we do most solemnly protest against the scandalous, wicked, and treasonable influence, which the Borough Merchants have established in the People's House of Commons. Being firmly convinced, that if such corrupt and hateful influence had not existed; which has operated to the total subjugation of our rights in that House, and converted it into a perfect mockery of representation, our unfortunate country would not have been cursed with a twenty-five-years war – with a thousand millions of debt – with seventy millions of annual taxes – with ruined manufactories and commerce – with a standing army of one hundred and forty thousand men kept up in time of peace – with two millions of paupers, and twelve millions of annual Poor Rates – a Corn Bill, to prevent the people of England eating cheap bread; and thousands of British subjects perishing by hunger, and many thousands more escaping to America, to avoid such horrid misery! – A troop of Spies and Informers sent out to persuade a set of poor men who were but half fed, half clad, and consequently half mad, to commit acts of outrage, that they might have the advantage of hanging them! – With Gagging Bills – Dungeon Bills – Imprisonment without trial; – and lastly, an infamous Bill of Indemnity, to protect our seat-selling tyrants from being brought to justice for all their satanic deeds, these are the fruits of the Borough Mongering influence!

We, bitterly lamenting the condition of our plundered and insulted Country, have resolved to unite ourselves under the denomination of Political Protestants; for the purpose of sincerely protesting against the mockery of our indisputable right to a real Representation; and to use every means in our power, which are just and lawful, to rescue the House of Commons from the all-devouring influence of the Borough Merchants, and restore it to the people, agreeable to Magna Charta, and the spirit of the Constitution; and that nothing shall ever cause us to cease in our exertions, until we are fully and fairly represented in the People's House.

We sincerely believe that political ignorance has been the cause of all our national misery and degradation, and that nothing but a firm and extensive Union of the people to promote and diffuse a correct knowledge of our immutable rights can possibly protect our Country either from absolute despotism on the one hand or a dreadful

Revolution and anarchy on the other. We shall, therefore, meet once a week, in small classes, not exceeding twenty in each Class, and subscribe One Penny each, for the purpose of purchasing such means of information as may be required; in which way we exhort all Friends to radical Reform throughout the Kingdom to associate.

The Leaders of each Class shall hold a Meeting once a Month, to report the progress of the Institution; and in order to do away all ground of accusation against our proceedings, we declare that we will not have any secret transactions whatever, and that our Meeting, our Books and Accounts, of every description, shall at all times be laid open for the inspection of the Magistrates or others, who may request the same.

PETERLOO MASSACRE, ST PETER'S FIELDS, MANCHESTER (16 AUGUST 1819)

A mass meeting to advocate universal suffrage was called by the radicals Henry 'Orator' Hunt and James Watson to assemble at St Peter's Field in Manchester. A peaceful gathering of sixty thousand men, women and children was violently broken up first by local militia and then, as panic set in, by a detachment of Hussars. Eleven people died, and more than four hundred were wounded, included 140 cut with sabres. Four years after Waterloo, 'Peterloo' was cited as evidence that the government was willing to turn its armed forces on its own people.

Letter from Mr. W. R. Hay to Lord Sidmouth Regarding Peterloo (16 August 1819)[3]

This letter from a local magistrate to the home secretary shows some of the panic and antipathy that attended the massacre, and how little its potential impact was appreciated.

About eleven o'clock the magistrates, who were very numerous, repaired to a house, whence they might see the whole of the proceedings of the meeting. A body of special constables took their ground, about two hundred in number, close to the hustings; from them there was a line of communication to the house where we were. Mr Trafford was so good as to take the situation of attending Colonel L'Estrange, the commanding officer. – From eleven till one o'clock, the various columns arrived, attended by flags, each by two or three flags; and there were four, if not more, caps of liberty. The ensigns were of the same description as those displayed on similar occasions, with this addition, that one had a bloody pike represented on it; another, 'Equal Representation or Death'. There was no appearance of arms or pikes, but a great plenty of sticks and staves; and every column marched in regular files of three or four deep, attended with conductors, music, &c. The most powerful accession was in the last instance, when Hunt and his party came in.

But, long before this, the magistrates had felt a decided conviction that the whole bore the appearance of insurrection; that the array was such as to terrify all the king's subjects, and was such as no legitimate purpose could justify. In addition to their own sense of the meeting, they had very numerous depositions from the inhabitants, as to their fears for the public safety; and at length a man deposed as to the parties who were approaching, attended by the heaviest columns.

On a barouche-box was a woman in white, who, I believe was a Mrs Gant, from Stockport, and who it is believed had a cap of liberty. In the barouche were Hunt, Johnson, Knight, and Moorhouse, of Stockport: as soon as these four parties were ascertained, a warrant was issued to apprehend them. The troops were mustered, and Nadin, preceding the Manchester Yeomanry Cavalry, executed it. While the cavalry was forming, a most marked defiance of them was acted by the reforming part of the mob; however, they so far executed their purpose as to apprehend Hunt and Johnson on the hustings: Knight and Moorhouse in the moment escaped. They also took on the hustings, Saxton, and Sykes, who is the writer to the *Manchester Observer*, and which Saxton had before been addressing the mob. The parties thus apprehended were brought to the house where the magistrates were. In the mean time the Riot Act was read, and the mob was completely dispersed, but not without very serious and lamentable effects. Hunt, &c. were brought down to the New Bailey; two magistrates and myself, having promised them protection, preceded them; we were attended by special constables and some cavalry. The parties were lodged in the New Bailey; and since that have been added to them Knight and Moorhouse. On inquiry, it appeared that many suffered from various instances; one of the Manchester yeomanry, Mr Holme, was, after the parties were taken, struck by a brick-bat; he lost his power over his horse, and is supposed to have fractured his skull by a fall from his horse. I am afraid that he is since dead; if not, there are no hopes of his recovery. A special constable of the name of Ashworth has been killed – cause unknown; and four women appear to have lost their lives by being pressed by the crowd; these, I believe, are the fatal effects of the meeting.

A variety of instances of sabre wounds occurred, but I hope none mortal; several pistols were fired by the mob, but as to their effect, save in one instance deposed to before Colonel

Fletcher, we have no account. We cannot but deeply regret all this serious attendant on this transaction; but we have the satisfaction of witnessing the very grateful and cheering countenances of the whole town; in fact, they consider themselves as saved by our exertions. All the shops were shut, and for the most part continued so all evening. The capture of Hunt took place before two o'clock, and I forgot to mention, that all their colours, drums, &c. were taken or destroyed: since that I have been to the Infirmary, and found myself justified in making the report I have; but Mr Norris now tells me, that one or two more than I have mentioned may have lost their lives. The parties apprehended will have their cases proceeded on tomorrow; but it appears that there may arise difficulties as to the nature of some of their crimes, on which it may be necessary to consult government. The whole committee of magistrates will assemble tomorrow as usual.

During the afternoon, and part of the evening, parts of the town have been in a very disturbed state, and numerous applications made for military. These have been supplied, but in some cases have, in the Irish part of the town, been obliged to fire, I trust without any bad effect as to life, in any instance. At present every thing seems quiet; the reports agree with that, and I hope that we shall have a quiet night. I have omitted to mention, that the active part of the meeting may be said to have come in wholly from the country; and that it did not consist of less than 20,000 men, &c. The flag on which was 'Equal Representation or Death' was a black one; and in addition, on the same side, had 'No boroughmongering – Unite, and be Free'; at the bottom, 'Saddleworth, Lees, and Morley Union'; on the reverse, 'No Corn Laws; – Taxation, without Representation, is unjust and tyrannical.' On the Middleton flag was, 'Let us die like men, and not be sold like slaves'; reverse, 'Liberty is the birthright of man.'

Percy Bysshe Shelley, 'The Masque of Anarchy' (c. August 1819)[4]

Percy Bysshe Shelley (1792–1822) was committed to the cause of democracy. He was in Italy when he heard the news of Peterloo. His poem written in response was not published in his lifetime (he had tried to get his friend James Leigh Hunt to publish it earlier, but he felt it was too risky). The poem attacks Viscount Castlereagh, who introduced legislation banning large public meetings after Peterloo in the House of Commons, because the prime minister, Lord Liverpool, was in the House of Lords. For his part, Castlereagh claimed, 'I feel no wrath against the people, I am only doing my duty.' The journalist Paul Foot described 'The Masque of Anarchy' as 'without any doubt at all the finest poem of political protest ever written in our language', and it has been taken up by protesters from South Africa to Tiananmen Square.

LXXXIV

And if then the tyrants dare,
Let them ride among you there;
Slash, and stab, and maim, and hew;
What they like, that let them do.

LXXXV

With folded arms and steady eyes,
And little fear, and less surprise,
Look upon them as they stay
Till their rage has died away:

LXXXVI

Then they will return with shame,
To the place from which they came,
And the blood thus shed will speak
In hot blushes on their cheek:

LXXXVII

Every woman in the land
Will point at them as they stand –
They will hardly dare to greet
Their acquaintance in the street:

LXXXVIII

And the bold, true warriors,
Who have hugged Danger in wars,
Will turn to those who would be free
Ashamed of such base company:

LXXXIX

And that slaughter to the nation
Shall steam up like inspiration,
Eloquent, oracular,
A volcano heard afar:

XC

And these words shall then become
Like Oppression's thundered doom,
Ringing through each heart and brain,
Heard again — again — again.

XCI

Rise like Lions after slumber
In unvanquishable number!
Shake your chains to earth, like dew
Which in sleep had fall'n on you:
YE ARE MANY—THEY ARE FEW.

William Hone, *The Political House that Jack Built* (December 1819)⁵

The radical journalist William Hone (1780–1842) wrote this satire on the government of Lord Liverpool shortly after Peterloo. This verse focuses on the Prince Regent, the future George IV, whose indolence seemed to epitomise the contempt of the ruling class for the people. Hone spent much of his life in debt, but The Political House that Jack Built *was a hit, selling more than 100,000 copies and running into fifty-four editions.*

"Great offices will have
Great talents."

This is THE MAN—all shaven and shorn,
All cover'd with Orders—and all forlorn ;

This is THE MAN – all shaven and shorn,
All cover'd with Orders – and all forlorn;
THE DANDY OF SIXTY, who bows with a grace,
And has *taste* in wigs, collars, cuirasses and lace;
Who, to tricksters, and fools, leaves the State and its treasure,
And, when Britain's in tears, sails about at his pleasure:
Who spurn'd from his presence the Friends of his youth,
And now has not one who will tell him the truth;
Who took to his counsels, in evil hour,
The Friends of the Reasons of lawless Power;
That back the Public Informer, who
Would put down the *Thing*, that, in spite of new Acts,
And attempts to restrain it, by Soldiers or Tax,
Will *poison* the Vermin,
That plunder the Wealth
That lay in the House,
That Jack Built.

William Davidson, Speech to the Court in the Cato Street Conspiracy Trial (April 1820)[6]

William Davidson (1786–1820) was one of eleven men tried in connection with the Cato Street Conspiracy, a Spencean plot to blow up the cabinet. (For Spence and Spenceans, see p. 124.) The government became aware of the conspiracy in its early stages through a police spy who was instrumental in setting it up, but let it take shape so that the maximum number of conspirators could be arrested. Davidson was born in Jamaica of mixed race, the son of the island's attorney general and an unnamed black woman. On settling in London, he read Thomas Paine and joined the radical Marylebone Union Reading Society. The events of Peterloo convinced him that reform could not be achieved peacefully. He joined Arthur Thistlewood's revolutionary Spenceans, and was arrested as he stood guard outside the Cato Street attic. He and four others, including Thistlewood, were hanged on 1 May 1820, before a vast crowd. Their bodies were decapitated and buried in quicklime.

I appeal to any man that was in court, whether, in the summing up of the evidence, Judge Garrow did justice to me, as a prisoner at the bar. Was he not inveterate against me? did he not influence the minds of the jurymen, and almost insist upon their pronouncing me guilty? did any person identify me to be the identical person except those officers who, we all know, and every Englishman must know, have always been instrumental to the death of innocent men. I have never been in a public life. I appeal to all those gentlemen, whether I have ever engaged in any plot, if I had fifty lives, and they were wanting for the public good, they should have them; and if it were my blood, they should take every drop, and I would stand here while they took it, and fall a victim to my enemies; but in what manner is it I could ever be guilty of high treason? it was never pretended I had ever said any thing, directly or indirectly; I must have been a silent spectator from the nature of my colour. I should have been immediately remarked if I had taken an active part. I have got a deal to say for myself where I feel it to be proper; but there is not one single witness has ever said that I said any thing, consequently I could not be a person that was in the conspiracy; they have said, only that there was a man of colour, and, unfortunately, I was caught near the spot, and was fixed on by them; but still justice ought to be done to every man, and especially where it is done in the revered name of British justice . . .

[S]uppose I was found with a sword in my hand, who can prove that I meant to overturn the government? who can prove that I meant to assassinate the ministers? who can prove that I meant to lay my hand on my sovereign? Is my character so black as for it to be said in this country, or where I have travelled, that I am an assassin or a murderer? I appeal to every man who knows me, whether I am a man of that character or stamp directly or indirectly, to do such a thing; but even if the sword was in my hand; and my intention was even to join with those people, I do not see that it was a conspiracy against the lives of any ministers or of the King himself; because in the passages of Magna Carta, when King John granted that charter, the passage runs in this form; that the people should choose twenty-five barons from among them, with an intent that those twenty-five barons shall see that the acts of this charter are not violated by his majesty or any of his ministers; and if any of them be violated by the King or his ministers, four of those barons shall go and insist on redress; and if redress is not given within twenty-five days, they are to return and compel them to give it – how? with empty hands? no; with arms to stand and claim their rights as Englishmen; and if every Englishman felt as I do, they would always do that. But it goes on further to say; and if redress be not forthwith given, they shall seize on his revenues and his castles, and place such persons in his castles as will see and observe the duties imposed upon him by the barons. And our history goes on further to say, that when another of their majesties the kings of England tried to infringe upon those rights, the people armed, and told him that if he did not give them the privileges of Englishmen, they would compel him by the point of the sword; that is language never used by me, or those with whom I acted, and yet those persons were not considered as beneath the character of Englishmen, and to be condemned to death. Would you not rather govern a country of spirited men, than cowards? . . .

[T]hey have come forward to swear my life away on this charge, and I now tender my life to your service; I can die but once in this world, and the only regret left is, that I have a large family of small children, and when I think of that, it unmans me, and I shall say no more.

Mr Crawshay Recounts the Merthyr Uprising (1831)[7]

These accounts of an uprising in Merthyr Tydfil in South Wales show how strongly feelings ran for parliamentary Reform. A population that was ineligible to vote for a parliamentary candidate who might further their cause was enraged when local electors refused to support them.

On the 9th day of May, 1831, my miners had heard that Mr Stephens, a most respectable shopkeeper in Merthyr Tydfil, would not join me in supporting a Reform candidate for the county of Brecon, and such was their attachment to me, and such their feeling upon the subject of Reform, that, on that day, they, and other men, to the number of about 5,000 persons, met in the town of Merthyr, opposite the house of Mr Stephens, and commenced speaking on the subject of Reform. One of the orators, Thomas Llewellin by name, proclaimed, with a stentorian voice, that 'every one who was an enemy to Reform should be hung on the gallows', and he would be the man to do, it free of expense.

After a great deal of tumult and threat against Mr Stephens, the mob left that place, until about nine o'clock, when they again assembled, opposite Mr Stephens's house, and commenced an attack on his windows with stones and other missiles, Mr Stephens remaining in the back of his house, 'expecting plunder and murder to follow'. Some squares of glass were also broken at the Court, the residence of Mr Thomas, who was also considered to be inimical to Reform. On the following day Thomas Llewellin and another ringleader of the mob were apprehended upon Mr Stephens's deposition of the violence already committed upon, and feared by, him, and were examined, and committed to gaol for want of bail, by Mr Bruce, the stipendiary magistrate of Merthyr Tydfil, who sat in the Bush Inn. The mob, finding their companions were about to be sent to gaol, assembled round the Bush Inn, to the extent of about 3,000 in number, and openly stated to Mr Stephens, in Mr Bruce's presence, that unless Mr Stephens would forgive, and consent to the release of, the men in custody, they would rescue them, and burn his house and murder him. Mr Stephens, fearing that the threat would be instantly executed, consented to their release; upon which the mob declared they would not be satisfied unless they had a paper to that effect in writing from him, which Mr Stephens also consented to give them, Mr Bruce saying, that 'he did not know what else Mr Stephens had to do under the circumstances existing.' On receiving the paper from Mr Stephens, the mob raised 'hurrahs', and carried the two prisoners away on their shoulders with shouts of triumph, and subsequently dispersed. This was the commencement of the first overt act and tumultuous proceeding of the mob. But from that moment until Thursday, the 2nd day of June, no further outrage, or tumult, was known in Merthyr; but a general meeting of all the labouring classes, many miles round this extensive and populous mining and manufacturing district, was called, to take place on the top of a mountain, central to all parties; and, at this meeting, most numerously attended, no direct measure could be ascertained to have been determined upon. Petitioning the King for Reform, the abolition of the Court of Requests, the consideration of their own state of wages were equally attributed as the object; but those who attended on our behalf could not ascertain any particular point to have been considered, and the meeting dispersed without any resolution being come to, or any disturbance committed.

On the next Thursday a large number of riotous persons assembled at Merthyr, and went over the hill, to the residence of Mr Rowland Fothergill, managing partner of the Aberdare Iron Works, and, with clubs and menaces, compelled him, under penalty of his life, to sign a paper, stating that he had not declared that the miners of Mr Crawshay were getting five shillings per week more than his own.

Mr Fothergill's resistance was highly creditable to him, but, to save his life, he was compelled to sign the paper. They then demanded bread and cheese, and beer, which were divided to them, to the extent of all there was in the house. They next proceeded to the Aberdare shop, where Mr Scale also resisted, but the shopkeeper, more prudently, threw out of the windows all the bread and cheese he had. The mob then came back to Merthyr, and proceeded to the Bailiffs of the Court of Requests, whose houses they destroyed, and burnt their furniture; after which, they went to the house of Mr Coffin, Clerk of the Court of Requests, and demanded the books of the court, which, with all the other books in the house, were given them, and burnt in the street; the rioters then broke into the house, and dragged out, and burnt, every particle of furniture belonging to Mr Coffin, and left the house a complete wreck. The same persons then proceeded to the iron works of Mr Crawshay, and compelled all the men, except those employed in the blast furnaces, who were very few in number, to desist from working, and stopped 'fineries, forges, and mills. After this they proceeded to the Penydarren and Dowlais Iron Works, where they did the same. On the following morning a party of the ninety-third regiment of Highlanders arrived opposite the Cyfarthfa Iron Works, at ten o'clock, where Mr Crawshay joined them; and, very soon after, they were met by Messrs Bruce and Hill, acting magistrates for the county of Glamorgan. The soldiers, thus accompanied, proceeded to the town of Merthyr, followed by a large and tumultuous mob of rioters, armed with bludgeons of the most formidable description. At the Castle Inn, the Highlanders were drawn up in front of the house, where the High Sheriff and other gentlemen were met, and the mob immediately hemmed the soldiers in on all sides, so close that the soldiers and rioters were in actual contact; the most hardened and ferocious threats and defiance were uttered on all sides by the rioters to the soldiers, and bludgeons held up throughout the whole mob, and close to the faces of the soldiers. The High Sheriff mounted a chair, addressed them, and cautioned them, in the most earnest and feeling manner, as to the consequences of their illegal proceedings, and implored them to desist from violence. Mr Guest followed in the same strain, and was answered by a speech from a most daring rioter. Mr Crawshay followed, and added the most determined defiance to their attempts at extorting, by force and violence, any increase of their wages, while in a state of tumult: but promised that if they would return to their homes and work, and send a deputation from each mine level to him, in fourteen days after, he would investigate their complaints of distress, and do everything in his power to relieve them. All was vain.

CHARTISM

The Chartist movement was a popular response to the disappointment of parliamentary reform as it emerged in the Great Reform Act of 1832. Consciously invoking Magna Carta, the Chartists put forward their own People's Charter in 1838, advocating 'Universal Suffrage, No Property Qualifications, Annual Parliaments, Equal Representation, Payment of Members and Vote by [secret] Ballot'. Chartism was taken up across Britain and, at its height, was able to deliver petitions signed by millions to Parliament. Frustration with lack of progress, however, led some Chartists to more direct action, 'physical' as against 'moral' force.

Henry Vincent, Chartists in Wales (26 March 1839)[8]

Henry Vincent (1813–78), known within Chartism as 'the Demosthenes of the new movement' for his oratorical skills, was apprenticed as a printer in Hull before moving to London. He became the leading Chartist in the west of England and South Wales. He established the Western Vindicator, *based in Bath, in 1838, and included in it a weekly account of his 'Life and Rambles' between 26 February and 11 May 1839, from which these extracts are taken.*

Took a chaise in company with friend Edwards for Pontlanvraith, over the Monmouth hills. The morning fine. The scenery is very picturesque. Fine fertile hills rising in all directions. I could not help thinking of the defensible nature of the country in the case of foreign invasion! A few thousands of armed men on the hills could success-fully defend them. Wales would make an excellent Republic. The soil is exceedingly fertile. The working population are chiefly engaged in the iron and coal trade. They are said to have good wages; but I found this far from being the case. Work is very irregular, so what is gained in the wages is lost from the uncertain state of the labour market. We arrived at the Greyhound, Pontlanvraith, at twelve o'clock. A meeting was called for that hour. The Greyhound is a very comfortable house, and its inmates agreeably obliging. The working men hold their meetings in the house. A hustings was erected at the side of the buildings. After partaking of a good repast we went to the meeting and found above 1,000 sturdy men and women assembled. I ought to mention that the Radicals met us about a mile from the Greyhound, and conducted us into the village. On ascending the hustings I was loudly cheered. Mr Davis, a working man, was called to the chair. He explained the object of the meeting, and then introduced a thorough Radical Welchman (whose name I have unfortunately forgotten) to address the people in the Welch language. I regret my ignorance of the Welch. It appears to be a powerfully impressive language, and the people are passionately fond of their mother tongue. Mr Edwards was next introduced. He delivered an able speech, and was loudly cheered. A low fellow, evidently drunk, endeavoured to create a disturbance, but he was soon silenced, and 'taken care of' by a friend. Edwards was loudly cheered. I then arose amidst much cheering, and addressed the meeting for an hour and a half. In the course of which, after explaining the principles of the Charter, I showed the people how they would be bettered in circum-stances were they possessed of law-making powers. I also addressed the ladies, and proved to them their intimate connection with the

political interests of their country. My speech appeared to make a
very powerful impression, and at the conclusion I was cheered for
several minutes. Three cheers were given for the Chairman – three
for Vincent – three for Edwards – three for the Convention, Charter,
and the Ladies, and the meeting separated. Took tea, and walked on
to Blackwood, a small village about a mile from the Greyhound. The
evening mild. Within half a mile from Blackwood we were met by
about 100 little girls, dressed very neatly, carrying in front of them
a pretty device made up of flowers and three handsome flags upon
the top. On meeting us they curtsied, and then preceded us to
Blackwood, singing a Radical song with great skill; the chorus of
which was thus –

> Here's a health to Radical boys,
> Here's a health to Radical boys,
> May tyranny fall, and freedom prevail,
> That millions may share its joys.

It was a pleasing sight to see young children assembled to pray for
the success of a cause upon which their future happiness and freedom
depended. May God nerve our arms and strengthen our hearts, and
carry us triumphantly through the coming struggle! Our little
conductors halted at the Coach and Horses, the landlord and landlady
of which are good out-and-out Radicals. The meeting was held in
front of the house; a delightful place to speak from; for before us lie
a most beautiful prospect of hill and valley. The full-toned notes of
a blackbird were heard from a neighbouring cluster of trees. The
numbers present were about 1,500, amongst whom were a great
amount of females. Mr Burrell was called to the chair. Mr Edwards
spoke at some length in explanation of the Charter, and was warmly
applauded. I next addressed the meeting; shewed the people what
governments should exist for; and convinced them of the necessity
of having an equal share in the making of the laws and laying on of

the taxes. I spoke to the ladies at considerable length, arguing that they were more interested in a good state of government and society than the men; a fact of which they seemed fully convinced. I was pleased to notice several of the middle classes present, who appeared to take great interest in the proceedings. I was loudly cheered throughout my speech. A few words were spoken in Welch. Cheers innumerable were given in succession for Vincent, Edwards, the Charter, Convention, our sweethearts and wives, and the meeting separated. The people nearly all signed the petition. Sheets distinctly for the ladies were also signed. The most ardent enthusiasm prevailed.

Edward Hamer, 'The Chartist Outbreak in Llanidloes' (1839)[9]

During the year 1839, when Chartists were conducting a nationwide campaign to secure signatures for a petition to Parliament, there were several outbreaks of violence, in Longton, Devizes, Newport and the Montgomeryshire town of Llanidloes. Edward Hamer (1840–1911) was a local historian who wrote a pamphlet about the rising in Llanidloes.

Strengthened by the arrival of the men sent by the Home Secretary, the magistrates assembled at the hotel, and decided upon arresting the individuals against whom the warrants were out; and, to be prepared for the worst, had sent the town crier to request the immediate presence of the special constables then in the town. Between forty and fifty obeyed the call, and, loitering before the inn, watching the proceedings, were the identical men whom the authorities were so anxious to apprehend: they were pointed out to the police, who at once took them into custody, and secured them inside the hotel. Upon this the tocsin of alarm was given, and the news of the arrest reached those assembled at the bridge in a very short time. This crowd, with their numbers swelled on the way, soon arrived in sight of the hotel, where they saw the police and special constables drawn up to receive them. The sight took them aback, but it was only the momentary impediment that dammed up the waters for a more impetuous rush.

Without arms of some description, their great number was no match for the police and specials, armed with their staves of office. They accordingly withdrew for a few moments to procure whatever they could lay their hands on in the form of weapons — guns, staves, pikes, hay forks, sickles, and even spades were hastily seized by the excited and turbulent mob!

Some of the women who had joined the crowd kept instigating the men to attack the hotel – one old virago vowing that she would fight till she was knee-deep in blood, sooner than the Cockneys should take their prisoners out of the town. She, with others of her sex, gathered large heaps of stones, which they subsequently used in defacing and injuring the building which contained the prisoners. When the mob had thus armed themselves, the word 'Forward!' was given, and as soon as they were within hearing of the police, they imperatively demanded the release of their friends, which demand was of course refused. What took place during the next few minutes cannot be easily ascertained; both parties afterwards accused the other of commencing the fray. The special constables, many of whose acquaintances were among the crowd, were seen to give way on the approach of the Chartists, and to seek their safety either in the hotel, or by trusting to their legs. When their request was denied them, the mob set up a terrible shout, and pressed forward towards the door of the inn; the rioters asserting that the London police began the conflict by striking one of their number, which only exasperated them the more, and caused them to shout out for 'revenge!' as well as the release of the prisoners. They further state that the Ex-Mayor, on finding that he was locked out, to ensure his own safety, suddenly appeared to sympathise with the mob, by crying out 'Chartists for ever'; and, with a stick which he had in his hand, broke the first pane of glass, thus initiating the mob in the work of destruction.

The women followed the example thus set them by throwing stones at every window of the house, while the men pressed forward and tried to burst in the front door, through which the police had retired. The thought of their prey slipping through their fingers infuriated the mob, who sent repeated showers of stones at the door and windows; the latter were soon shattered into a thousand fragments. Guns were next fired through the door, which, after resisting all their efforts for some time, was ultimately burst open. The mob quickly spread themselves over the house in search of their comrades, whom they found handcuffed in the kitchen. They were at once led off to a smith's shop, where their gyves were knocked off. Finding themselves masters of the house, the rabble proceeded to hunt out the policemen, against whom alone their animosity was now directed. The Mayor with one of the police had retired to the bedrooms, but the latter (Blenkhorn) was soon found, and dragged from under a bed; his pistol and staff were wrested from him, and the former was presented at his head. He was then most savagely abused by all who were within reach of him, till his bruised and bleeding features moved the hearts of some of the most compassionate, who managed at great risk to save his life, for only with his life would some of the ruffians be appeased.

The Mayor (a surgeon by profession) was also discovered in one of the bedrooms. He was rather frightened when brought out into the street; but a happy idea occurred to him – he appealed to their better nature, by recalling to their memories how he had saved their mothers' lives in ushering them (the Chartists) into the world. He touched the right string; their hearts were softened, and they allowed him to proceed to his home without injuring him.

Chartist Protests in Newcastle (July 1839)[10]

This is an exchange between Chartists and the Newcastle city authorities.

Chartist Proclamation

MEN OF DURHAM AND NORTHUMBERLAND. – Your oppressors have set the majesty of the people at utter defiance. They have determined that you shall live a life of toil, and die a death of hunger when you can toil no more. If you do not submit to this, they will consign you to a bloody grave by the grand old argument[:] the bayonet, the bullet, the halter.

Corporation Proclamation

Whereas. Certain ill-disposed persons are in the habit of meeting within the limits of this borough and using inflammatory and seditious language, calculated to make Her Majesty's subjects discontented with their condition and to produce terror in the minds of the population.

This, therefore, is to give notice that these tumultuous assemblages will not be longer suffered to take place within the precincts of this borough.

JOHN FIFE, Mayor.
In the name of the Corporation
God Save the Queen

Chartist Counter-proclamation

Whereas. Certain men calling themselves the Corporation of Newcastle-on-Tyne, have presumed to call in question the inalienable right of Englishmen to meet, discuss and petition the Queen and Parliament for a redress of their grievances; and

Whereas. These men have presumed to forbid the exercise of a right founded in the Constitution, and have assumed the power which does not belong even to the Queen and the Parliament;

Now, therefore, we the council of the Northern Political Union, proclaim to the people of this Borough and the surrounding neighbourhood, that it is their duty to meet for the exercise of this Constitutional right, and show to the Corporation of Newcastle-on-Tyne that this assumed power of theirs is held in utter contempt by all good Englishmen.

God Save the People

POSTSCRIPT. – A meeting will be held in the Forth every evening at half past six.

Charles Dickens, 'The Fine Old English Gentleman: New Version' (7 August 1841)[11]

Dickens wrote this ballad for the Liberal journal the Examiner; *it was published during a time of economic depression, shortly after the Tories under Sir Robert Peel had been returned to government, and the Whigs, on whom hopes for more reform were pinned, had been ejected. It is a parody of a popular ditty about a Fine Old English Gentleman who, 'while he feasted all the great,/He ne'er forgot the small'.*

(To be said or sung at all Conservative dinners)

I'll sing you a new ballad, and I'll warrant it first-rate,
Of the days of that old gentleman who had that old estate;
When they spent the public money at a bountiful old rate
On ev'ry mistress, pimp, and scamp, at ev'ry noble gate,
  In the fine old English Tory times;
  Soon may they come again!

The good old laws were garnished well with gibbets, whips, and chains,
With fine old English penalties, and fine old English pains,
With rebel heads, and seas of blood once hot in rebel veins;
For all these things were requisite to guard the rich old gains
  Of the fine old English Tory times;
  Soon may they come again!

This brave old code, like Argus, had a hundred watchful eyes,
And ev'ry English peasant had his good old English spies,
To tempt his starving discontent with fine old English lies,
Then call the good old Yeomanry to stop his peevish cries,

    In the fine old English Tory times;
    Soon may they come again!

The good old times for cutting throats that cried out in their need,
The good old times for hunting men who held their fathers' creed,
The good old times when William Pitt, as all good men agreed,
Came down direct from Paradise at more than railroad speed . . .
    Oh the fine old English Tory times;
    When will they come again!

In those rare days, the press was seldom known to snarl or bark,
But sweetly sang of men in pow'r, like any tuneful lark;
Grave judges, too, to all their evil deeds were in the dark;
And not a man in twenty score knew how to make his mark.
    Oh the fine old English Tory times;
    Soon may they come again!

Those were the days for taxes, and for war's infernal din;
For scarcity of bread, that fine old dowagers might win;
For shutting men of letters up, through iron bars to grin,
Because they didn't think the Prince was altogether thin,
    In the fine old English Tory times;
    Soon may they come again!

But Tolerance, though slow in flight, is strong-wing'd in the main;
That night must come on these fine days, in course of time was
    plain;
The pure old spirit struggled, but its struggles were in vain;
A nation's grip was on it, and it died in choking pain,
    With the fine old English Tory days,
    All of the olden time.

The bright old day now dawns again; the cry runs through the
    land,
In England there shall be dear bread – in Ireland, sword and brand;
And poverty, and ignorance, shall swell the rich and grand,
    So, rally round the rulers with the gentle iron hand,
      Of the fine old English Tory days; Hail to the coming time!

Bilston South Staffordshire Rally (14 March 1842)[12]

*Chartism was a mass national movement, rallying support and
demonstrating ordinary people's capacity to organise across the
country. The South Staffordshire Rally was held in honour of the
Chartist leader Feargus O'Connor (c. 1796–1855).*

It was the largest concourse of people ever seen in this part of the
country. Bilston, Wolverhampton, Willenhall, Walsall, Wednesbury
and the surrounding villages were posted with large bills giving notice
of the procession and stating the time and manner of the various
processions to the railway station at Wolverhampton. At 5 a.m. the
Chartist band was in position in Bilston. Excellent arrangements had
been made by the Bilston Committee and at 10 a.m. an immense
concourse of brave, flannel-smocked colliers with 500 females with
splendid flags and banners and an excellent band set off from Bilston.
The lads of Walsall, Barlaston, Wednesbury, etc. were also stirring. It
was astonishing to behold the great concourse that poured into
Wolverhampton. O'Connor was expected at midday. The processions
met at Horseley Field. The road was completely blocked for two miles.
There was a warm response from the inhabitants. From Wolverhampton
to the railway station, which was two miles, the roads were completely
blocked. A carriage and four with two postillions in splendid livery

arrived at the station carrying Messrs Mogg, Stiran, Cook and Peplow
(of Stafford). There was a delay until 2.30 p.m. which was borne with
humour. The Chartist ladies of Bilston waved wands with cards
'Remember Frost, Williams and Jones.' Francis Langston was the
herald in a beautiful scarf, scarlet and green. The immense multitude
moved off in the following order: −

Herald and two flagbearers with motto
PEACE, LAW & ORDER.

Large green banner with motto
WELCOME TO THE DEFENDER OF THE PEOPLE'S RIGHTS −
O'CONNOR THE BRAVE.

Large flag with motto
WHAT IS LIFE WITHOUT LIBERTY?

Large concourse of Irishmen, motto
UNIVERSAL SUFFRAGE AND REPEAL OF THE UNION.

Reverse − green flags flying
CIVIL AND RELIGIOUS LIBERTY.

Large banner-motto
FEMALE CHARTIST ASSOCIATION, BILSTON
With a beautiful likeness of O'Connor.

Members of the Association 10 abreast.

Splendid silk banner, motto
NATIONAL CHARTER ASSOCIATION
COUNCIL OF BILSTON AND WOLVERHAMPTON NATIONAL
CHARTER ASSOCIATION.

Members of Association 10 abreast.

Splendid American Republican flag.

Members of Association 10 abreast.

Splendid green banner, motto
CIVIL AND RELIGIOUS LIBERTY: THE WHOLE CHARTER AND
NOTHING LESS.

Open carriage and 4 beautiful bays in which seated
FEARGUS O'CONNOR.

Members of Wolverhampton Association 4 abreast.

Splendid pink and white banner, motto
THE JUDGMENT OF HEAVENS IS LABOUR AND FOOD, THE
JUDGMENT OF KINGS IS TOIL AND STARVATION.

Band.

Members of Wolverhampton Association 4 abreast.

Splendid flag – WE KNOW OUR RIGHTS AND WILL DEFEND
THEM.

Large banner – THE WHOLE CHARTER AND NO SURRENDER.

Members of Wolverhampton Association 4 abreast.

Band.

Large silk flag.
THE PEOPLE'S CHARTER & NO SURRENDER
COUNCIL OF WALSALL ASSOCIATION.

Members of Walsall Association 10 abreast.

Large banner – THE SACRED WATCHWORD – LIBERTY.

Band.

Splendid large banner, motto
WELCOME BRAVE O'CONNOR
DEFENDER OF THE PEOPLE'S RIGHTS.

Council of Dudley Association, Members of Dudley Assn. 10
abreast.

Splendid banner – BEHOLD THE CONQUERING HERO COMES.

Large flag, motto – MORE PIGS AND LESS PARSONS.

Band.

Beautiful banner, motto
CHARTISTS NOW OR NEVER, NOW AND FOREVER,
ONWARD AND WE CONQUER, BACKWARD AND WE FALL,
THE PEOPLE'S CHARTER AND NO SURRENDER.

Council of Darlaston.

Members of Darlaston Association 10 abreast.

Green banner, motto
POOR TOILING SLAVES, HOW HARD YOUR FATE,
YOU'RE EATEN UP BY CHURCH AND STATE.

Large banner, motto
WE DO UNTO OTHERS AS WE WISH THEM TO DO UNTO US.

MONEY AND CLASS

―――――

'THE RANK IS BUT THE GUINEA'S STAMP'

In British history, the poor have often been ignored, taken for granted or simply squeezed for all they had. But from very early in that history, they have also made their voices heard.

The iron fetters of class hang heaviest on the poor, and the desperation of oppressed classes has led to uprisings in eras as different as the reign of Richard the Lionheart and the early nineteenth century. But the notion of the individual's capacity to transcend the destiny prescribed by money and class has inspired some of the most memorable British poetry, from the measured neoclassical cadences of Thomas Gray, to the fortifying Scots of Robert Burns or the plaintive Glaswegian 'Factory Girl' Ellen Johnston.

The effects of the industrial revolution on the labouring classes not only inspired great poetry. They also provided the evidence for the political and economic theories of two German immigrants, Frederick Engels and Karl Marx. Communism was in part codified and constructed in response to what Marx and Engels saw in Britain. The experiences of mass unemployment in the 1930s, and of homelessness and what the trade-union leader Jimmy Reid described as the alienation of 'victims of blind economic forces beyond their control' show that the conditions that Marx and Engels identified did not go away.

The Rebellion of William Fitz Osbert
(1196)[1]

William Fitz Osbert (d. 1196) led the first recorded popular uprising in English history, when he gathered a large following to protest at the burden of tax falling on the poor – and its evasion by the rich – for the ransom of Richard I (with whom he had served on crusade). Matthew Paris (c. 1200–59) was one of the few chroniclers to look sympathetically on his story, in the Chronica Majora.

About this time there arose a dispute in the city of London between the poor and the rich on account of the talliage, which was exacted by the King's agents for the benefit of the exchequer: for the principal men of the city, whom we call mayors and aldermen, having held a deliberation at their hustings, wished to preserve themselves free from the burden, and to oppress the poorer classes. Wherefore William Fitz Osbert, surnamed 'with the beard' because his ancestors in anger against the Normans never shaved, made opposition to the same, and called the mayors of the city traitors to our lord the King for the cause above-named; and the disturbances were so great in the city that recourse was had to arms.

William stirred up a large number of the middle and lower classes against the mayors and aldermen, but by their pusillanimity and cowardice the plans of William's confederates in resisting the injury done them were dissipated and defeated: the middle and lower classes were repressed, and the King, his ministers, and the chief men of the city, charged the whole crime on William. As the King's party were about to arrest him, he, being a distinguished character in the city, tall of stature and of great personal strength, escaped, notwithstanding their exertions, defending himself with nothing but a knife, and flying into the church of St Mary of the Arches, demanded the protection of our Lord, St Mary and her church, saying that he had resisted an unjust decree for no other purpose than that all might bear an equal share of the public burden, and contribute according to their means. His expostulations, however, were not listened to, the majority prevailed, and the archbishop, to the surprise of many, ordered that he should be dragged from the church to take his trial, because he had created a sedition and made such a disturbance among the people of the city. When this was told to William, he took refuge in the tower of the church, for he knew that the mayors, whom he had contradicted, sought to take away his life. In their obstinacy they applied fire, and sacrilegiously burnt down a great part of the church. Thus William was forced to leave the tower, almost suffocated with the heat and smoke. He was then seized, dragged out of the church, stripped, and, with his hands tied behind his back, conveyed away to the Tower of London. Soon after, at the instigation of the archbishop, the principal citizens, and the King's ministers, he was taken from the Tower, and dragged, tied to a horse's tail, through the middle of London to Tyburn, a pitiable sight to the citizens and to his own respectable relations in the city: after which he was hung in chains on a gallows. Thus William of the Beard was shamefully put to death by his fellow citizens for asserting the truth and defending the cause of the poor: and if the justice of one's cause constitutes a martyr, we may surely set him down as one. With him also were hanged nine of his neighbours or of his family, who espoused his cause.

George Manley, Defiance at Wicklow Gallows (1738)[2]

In 1738, George Manley was hanged in Wicklow for murder. Just before his execution, he addressed the public audience that had come to witness his death.

My friends, you assemble to see – what? A man leap into the abyss of death! Look, and you will see me go with as much courage as Curtius, when he leapt into the gulf to save his country from destruction. What will you see of me? You say that no man without virtue can be courageous! You see what I am – I'm a little fellow. What is the difference between running into a poor man's debt, and by the power of gold, or any other privilege, prevent him from obtaining his right, and clapping a pistol to a man's breast, and taking from him his purse? Yet the one shall thereby obtain a coach, and honours, and titles; the other, what? – a cart and a rope. Don't imagine from all this that I am hardened. I acknowledge the just judgment of God has overtaken me. My Redeemer knows that murder was far from my heart, and what I did was through rage and passion, being provoked by the deceased. Take warning, my comrades; think what would I now give that I had lived another life. Courageous? You'll say I've killed a man. Marlborough killed his thousands, and Alexander his millions. Marlborough and Alexander, and many others, who have done the like, are famous in history for great men. Aye – that's the case – one solitary man. I'm a little murderer, and must be hanged. Marlborough and Alexander plundered countries; they were great men. I ran in debt with the ale-wife. I must be hanged. How many men were lost in Italy, and upon the Rhine, during the last war for settling a king in Poland. Both sides could not be in the right! They are great men; but I killed a solitary man.

Thomas Gray, 'Elegy Written in a Country Churchyard' (1751)[3]

Thomas Gray (1716–71) wrote his most famous poem as a meditation on class and fate. It places value on the 'useful toil' of the poor and reminds the rich that all they can ultimately expect is a well-appointed grave (a 'storied urn or animated bust').

The curfew tolls the knell of parting day,
　The lowing herd wind slowly o'er the lea,
The ploughman homeward plods his weary way,
　And leaves the world to darkness and to me.

Now fades the glimmering landscape on the sight,
　And all the air a solemn stillness holds,
Save where the beetle wheels his droning flight,
　And drowsy tinklings lull the distant folds;

Save that from yonder ivy-mantled tower
　The moping owl does to the moon complain
Of such, as wandering near her secret bower,
　Molest her ancient solitary reign.

Beneath those rugged elms, that yew-tree's shade,
　Where heaves the turf in many a mouldering heap,
Each in his narrow cell for ever laid,
　The rude forefathers of the hamlet sleep.

The breezy call of incense-breathing morn,
　The swallow twittering from the straw-built shed,
The cock's shrill clarion, or the echoing horn,
　No more shall rouse them from their lowly bed.

For them no more the blazing hearth shall burn,
　Or busy housewife ply her evening care:
No children run to lisp their sire's return,
　Or climb his knees the envied kiss to share.

Oft did the harvest to their sickle yield,
　Their furrow oft the stubborn glebe has broke;
How jocund did they drive their team afield!
　How bowed the woods beneath their sturdy stroke!

Let not Ambition mock their useful toil,
　Their homely joys, and destiny obscure;
Nor Grandeur hear with a disdainful smile,
　The short and simple annals of the poor.

The boast of heraldry, the pomp of power,
　And all that beauty, all that wealth e'er gave,
Awaits alike the inevitable hour.
　The paths of glory lead but to the grave.

Nor you, ye proud, impute to these the fault,
　If Memory o'er their tomb no trophies raise,
Where through the long-drawn aisle and fretted vault
　The pealing anthem swells the note of praise.

Can storied urn or animated bust
　Back to its mansion call the fleeting breath?
Can Honour's voice provoke the silent dust,
　Or Flattery soothe the dull cold ear of Death?

Perhaps in this neglected spot is laid
　Some heart once pregnant with celestial fire;
Hands that the rod of empire might have swayed,
　Or waked to ecstasy the living lyre.

But Knowledge to their eyes her ample page
   Rich with the spoils of time did ne'er unroll;
Chill Penury repressed their noble rage,
   And froze the genial current of the soul.

Full many a gem of purest ray serene,
   The dark unfathomed caves of ocean bear:
Full many a flower is born to blush unseen,
   And waste its sweetness on the desert air.

Some village-Hampden, that with dauntless breast
   The little tyrant of his fields withstood;
Some mute inglorious Milton here may rest,
   Some Cromwell guiltless of his country's blood.

The applause of listening senates to command,
   The threats of pain and ruin to despise,
To scatter plenty o'er a smiling land,
   And read their history in a nation's eyes,

Their lot forbade: nor circumscribed alone
   Their growing virtues, but their crimes confined;
Forbade to wade through slaughter to a throne,
   And shut the gates of mercy on mankind,

The struggling pangs of conscious truth to hide,
   To quench the blushes of ingenuous shame,
Or heap the shrine of Luxury and Pride
   With incense kindled at the Muse's flame.

Far from the madding crowd's ignoble strife,
   Their sober wishes never learned to stray;
Along the cool sequestered vale of life
   They kept the noiseless tenor of their way.

Yet even these bones from insult to protect
   Some frail memorial still erected nigh,
With uncouth rhymes and shapeless sculpture decked,
   Implores the passing tribute of a sigh.

Their name, their years, spelt by the unlettered muse,
   The place of fame and elegy supply:
And many a holy text around she strews,
   That teach the rustic moralist to die.

For who to dumb Forgetfulness a prey,
   This pleasing anxious being e'er resigned,
Left the warm precincts of the cheerful day,
   Nor cast one longing lingering look behind?

On some fond breast the parting soul relies,
   Some pious drops the closing eye requires;
Ev'n from the tomb the voice of nature cries,
   Ev'n in our ashes live their wonted fires.

For thee, who mindful of the unhonoured dead
   Dost in these lines their artless tale relate;
If chance, by lonely Contemplation led,
   Some kindred spirit shall inquire thy fate,

Haply some hoary-headed swain may say,
   'Oft have we seen him at the peep of dawn
Brushing with hasty steps the dews away
   To meet the sun upon the upland lawn.

'There at the foot of yonder nodding beech
   That wreathes its old fantastic roots so high,
His listless length at noontide would he stretch,
   And pore upon the brook that babbles by.

'Hard by yon wood, now smiling as in scorn,
   Muttering his wayward fancies he would rove,
Now drooping, woeful wan, like one forlorn,
   Or crazed with care, or crossed in hopeless love.

'One morn I missed him on the customed hill,
   Along the heath and near his favourite tree;
Another came; nor yet beside the rill,
   Nor up the lawn, nor at the wood was he;

'The next with dirges due in sad array
   Slow through the church-way path we saw him borne.
Approach and read (for thou can'st read) the lay,
   Graved on the stone beneath yon aged thorn.'

Here rests his head upon the lap of earth
   A youth to fortune and to fame unknown.
Fair Science frowned not on his humble birth,
   And Melancholy marked him for her own.

Large was his bounty, and his soul sincere,
   Heaven did a recompense as largely send:
He gave to Misery all he had, a tear,
   He gained from Heaven ('twas all he wished) a friend.

No farther seek his merits to disclose,
   Or draw his frailties from their dread abode,
(There they alike in trembling hope repose)
   The bosom of his Father and his God.

Robert Burns, 'A Man's a Man for A' That' (January 1795)[4]

Robert Burns (1759–96) grew up on an Ayrshire farm, and knew poverty most of his life. He published this song, an appeal for universal brotherhood, in the Glasgow Magazine. *It is a hymn to common humanity, written in the wake of the French Revolution.*

Is there for honest poverty
    That hings his head, an' a' that;
The coward slave – we pass him by,
    We dare be poor for a' that!
For a' that, an' a' that.
    Our toils obscure an' a' that,
The rank is but the guinea's stamp,
    The man's the gowd for a' that.

What though on hamely fare we dine,
    Wear hoddin grey, an' a' that;
Gie fools their silks, and knaves their wine;
    A man's a man for a' that:
For a' that, an' a' that,
    Their tinsel show, an' a' that;
The honest man, tho' e'er sae poor,
    Is king o' men for a' that.

Ye see yon birkie ca'd a lord,
    Wha struts, an' stares, an' a' that;
Tho' hundreds worship at his word,
    He's but a coof for a' that;
For a' that, an' a' that,
    His ribband, star, an' a' that:

The man o' independent mind
    He looks an' laughs at a' that.

A prince can mak a belted knight,
    A marquis, duke, an' a' that;
But an honest man's aboon his might,
    Gude faith, he maunna fa' that!
For a' that, an' a' that,
    Their dignities an' a' that,
The pith o' sense, an' pride o' worth,
    Are higher rank than a' that.

Then let us pray that come it may,
    (As come it will for a' that,)
That Sense and Worth, o'er a' the earth,
    Shall bear the gree, an' a' that.
For a' that, an' a' that,
    It's comin yet for a' that
That man to man, the world o'er,
Shall brithers be for a' that.

———————

John Grimshaw, 'The Hand-loom Weavers' Lament' (*c.* 1810)[5]

John 'Common' Grimshaw was a radical ballad-singer and -seller from Gorton near Manchester. His version of this song was collected by a local antiquarian, John Higson. It bears witness to the impoverishment of ordinary workers and tradesmen at the time of the Napoleonic wars and the arrival of the power loom.

You gentlemen and tradesmen, that ride about at will,
Look down on these poor people; it's enough to make you crill;
Look down on these poor people, as you ride up and down,
I think there is a God above will bring your pride quite down.

Chorus – You tyrants of England, your race may soon be run,
You may be brought unto account for what you've sorely done.

You pull down our wages, shamefully to tell;
You go into the markets, and say you cannot sell;
And when that we do ask you when these bad times will mend,
You quickly give an answer, 'When the wars are at an end.'

When we look on our poor children, it grieves our hearts full
   sore,
Their clothing it is worn to rags, while we can get no more,
With little in their bellies, they to work must go,
Whilst yours do dress as manky as monkeys in a show.

You go to church on Sundays, I'm sure it's nought but pride,
There can be no religion where humanity's thrown aside;
If there be a place in heaven, as there is in the Exchange,
Our poor souls must not come near there; like lost sheep
   they must range.

With the choicest of strong dainties your tables overspread,
With good ale and strong brandy, to make your faces red;
You call'd a set of visitors – it is your whole delight –
And you lay your heads together to make our faces white.

You say that Bonyparty he's been the spoil of all,
And that we have got reason to pray for his downfall;
Now Bonyparty's dead and gone, and it is plainly shown
That we have bigger tyrants in Boneys of our own.

And now, my lads, for to conclude, it's time to make an end;
Let's see if we can form a plan that these bad times may mend;
Then give us our old prices, as we have had before,
And we can live in happiness, and rub off the old score.

———————

LUDDISM

'Luddite' uprisings were actions by groups of handloom weavers and framework knitters who saw mechanisation as a threat to their livelihoods. They took their name from a fictitious 'captain', Ned Ludd, in whose name anonymous letters and threats were issued. Luddites destroyed the new machinery and threatened owners, beginning in Nottingham in 1811, and spreading across Yorkshire and Lancashire.

John Sykes, Account of Machine-Breaking at Linthwaite, Yorkshire (6 March 1812)[6]

West Riding of Yorkshire

The complaint of John Sykes of Linthwaite in the said Riding clothdraper the servant of William Cotton of Linthwaite in the said Riding clothdraper taken upon oath this 6th day of March 1812 before me Joseph Radcliffe Esquire one of His Majesty's Justices of the Peace in and for the said Riding –

Who saith that between one and two o clock this Morning a number of people came to the door of his said Master's dwelling house and knocked violently at it, and demanded admittance or otherwise they would break the door open – to prevent which this Examinannt opened the door and 30 or more people with their faces blacked or disguised came in and asked if there were any ammunition guns or pistols in the house and where the Master was, on being told he was not at home they secured or guarded every person of the family and then a number of them took a pound of candles and began to break the tools and did break 10 pairs of shears and one brushing machine the property of his said Master, that one of them who seemed to have the command said that if they came again and found any machinery set up, they would blow up the premises, soon after which they all went away.

————————

Anonymous, 'An Address to Cotton Weavers and Others' (1812)[7]

This is from an unknown Luddite's speech.

Friends and fellow Mortals, long and tedious has been the oppression that you are labouring under, and the prospect before you only tends to embitter your days, your existence will be shortened, and your many children will become fatherless if you tamely submit much longer to wear that yoke, and to bear that Burden which is intolerable for human nature to endure, frequently you have uselessly applied to Government, to Magistrates, and to Manufacturers, but all to no purpose – what then is to be done – will you still calmly submit to endure that Arrogance Tyranny and Oppression that hath so long been exercised over you – Will you suffer your Children to be tortured out of existence, by bearing the slashes of hunger and nakedness, and yourselves insolently degraded by those very men that are living in luxury and Extravagance from the fruits of your labour – there is no doubt but many of you are well assured that the present unjust, unnecessary and destructive war is the Cause of your present Calamity – who are they then that have always been Stedfast and Constant advocates for this War – have not the greatest part of our Manufacturers, not to say Magistrates, who are they who have made themselves Rich since the War's Commencement, they are a few in every principal Town through this distressed Kingdom. From whence did their riches proceed? Methinks I hear a Voice say, all riches proceed from the servile and feeble hand of slavery. Who are they that are in the full enjoyment of their own Labour? None, for the Rich and artificial great, Labour not, nor do they ever intend to do, in consequence of which the just rights of the servile slave is innocently and unjustly taken from him – Friends and fellow sufferers, how must justice be trampled under foot – how long must he natural rights of moral man be held from your feeble sight, or how long will you bear your unparalleled suffering, and permit yourselves to be Robbed of more than four-fifths of the fruits of your labour – to solicit is in vain, to Petition is perfect Stupidity – as well might you solicit the Robber on the High way to give you back the property he had taken from you, or as well might you petition to head your Cause – You have but one life to lose. Death you must meet with, and to die with hunger is the most miserable, to Perish in the midst of that plenty that you have laboured for, is the most Dastardly – It is a Duty you owe to yourself and to the rising Generation, to put a stop to the unjust and lawless wheels of Tyranny – It is in your power and the immutable and unalterable Laws of Nature require it from your hands – It has often been said it is lawful and right for a Man to do what he will with his own – But this requires serious consideration, in the first place you must determine what is a man's own, you must lay aside all Artificial Tyrannical and unjust laws and simply look to the unerring Laws of Nature that are the same in all ages of the World. By so doing you will immediately see that nothing is justly a man's own but that he hath merited by his own industry – but if you shew Lenity and admit that all is a man's own that he is in possession of, you will soon see that it is not right for him to do what he pleaseth with it – admitting it doth no harm to any Creature. But if it can be proved that his proceedings are injurious to Society, then Society hath an undoubted right to put a sudden stop to his Vile proceedings – But every thing is out of order through the whole – and admission of one evil renders the Tyrant a pretence to plead the necessity of another – and thus the World has gone for numberless generations – till at last the insulted and degraded slaves of Britain are involved in the lawless and direful Whirlpool of Misery and Want. O, injured and degraded fellow sufferers, look around you and behold the rights you are deprived of – You who are as free born as your Vile oppressors – There was a fair Creation ready to receive you the moment you came into existence. A fertile Land that ought to have cost you nothing but the pains of Cultivating it. But not an Inch on the habitable Globe is yours. Tyranny hath deprived you of it. Nor have you time to behold the fair and free Creation of heaven the wide realms of necessary Care before you, and despair and destruction invades your wretched dwellings – Can you then any longer bear to hear your innocent and helpless Children crying to you for food, or to behold them Clothed in filthy rags – and yourself treated with disdain and ridicule and scorn by those very men that are unjustly feasting on the fruits of your slavery? Can you bear with impunity to see your rights and privileges thus trampled upon by a venal and profligate Band of Robbers? Insulted mortals, examine yourselves, and ask where are our rights that Bounteous Nature bestowed upon us. And you will see that they are fled from us for ever unless you Rise from your lethargy and Stupid Misery, and Boldly dare to tell your oppressors that you are determined to enjoy your natural rights – Viz – the fruits of your labour as these rights are founded in the unerring laws of the Great Creator.

———————

Anonymous, 'Hunting a Loaf' (1812)[8]

The image of the 'big loaf' was a common way of summing up the aspirations of the poor. This song from Derby refers to the forlorn hopes placed in politicians such as Sir Francis Burdett, who had been imprisoned for his views, and the prime minister, Spencer Perceval, who was assassinated in 1812.

GOOD people I pray give ear unto what I say,
And pray do not call it sedition,
For these great men of late they have cracked my pate,
I'm wounded in a woeful condition.
　　　　Fal al de ral, &c.
　For Derby it's true, and Nottingham too,
Poor men to jail they've been taking,
They say that Ned Ludd as I understood,

A thousand wide frames has been breaking.
>Fal al de ral, &c.
  Now it is not bad there's no work to be had,
The poor to be starv'd in their station;
And if they do steal they're straight sent to the jail,
And they're hang'd by the laws of the nation.
>Fal lal de ral, &c.
  Since this time last year I've been very queer,
And I've had a sad national cross;
I've been up and down, from town to town,
With a shilling to buy a big loaf.
>Fal lal, &c.
  The first that I met was Sir Francis Burdett,
He told me he'd been in the Tower;
I told him my mind a big loaf was to find,
He said you must ask them in power.
>Fal lal, &c.
  Then I thought it was time to speak to the prime
Master Perceval would take my part,
But a Liverpool man soon ended the plan,
With a pistol he shot through his heart.
>Fal lal, &c.
  Then I thought he'd chance on a rope for to dance,
Some people would think very pretty;
But he lost all his fun thro' the country he'd run,
And he found it in fair London city.
>Fal lal, &c.
  Now ending my journey I'll sit down with my friends,
And I'll drink a good health to the poor;
With a glass of good ale I have told you my tale,
And I'll look for a big loaf no more.
>Fal lal, &c.

George Gordon Byron's Speech on the Frame-Work Bill in the House of Lords (27 February 1812)[9]

As a poet and a peer, Lord Byron (1788–1824) was in the unusual position of being able to oppose injustice as an acknowledged and unacknowledged legislator (to use his friend Shelley's description of poets). Here is an extract from his maiden speech in the House of Lords, opposing legislation that would make the activities of Luddite felonies punishable by death.

My Lords; the subject now submitted to your Lordships for the first time, though new to the House, is by no means new to the country. I believe it had occupied the serious thoughts of all descriptions of persons, long before its introduction to the notice of that legislature, whose interference alone could be of real service. As a person in some degree connected with the suffering county, though a stranger not only to this House in general, but to almost every individual whose attention I presume to solicit, I must claim some portion of your Lordships' indulgence, whilst I offer a few observations on a question in which I confess myself deeply interested.

To enter into any detail of the riots would be superfluous: the House is already aware that every outrage short of actual bloodshed has been perpetrated, and that the proprietors of the Frames obnoxious to the rioters, and all persons supposed to be connected with them, have been liable to insult and violence. During the short time I recently passed in Nottinghamshire, not twelve hours elapsed without some fresh act of violence; and on the day I left the county I was informed that forty Frames had been broken the preceding evening, as usual, without resistance and without detection.

Such was then the state of that county, and such I have reason to believe it to be at this moment. But whilst these outrages must be admitted to exist to an alarming extent, it cannot be denied that they have arisen from circumstances of the most unparalleled distress: the perseverance of these miserable men in their proceedings tends to prove that nothing but absolute want could have driven a large, and once honest and industrious, body of the people, into the commission of excesses so hazardous to themselves, their families, and the community. At the time to which I allude, the town and county were burdened with large detachments of the military; the police was in motion, the magistrates assembled, yet all the movements, civil and military, had led to – nothing. Not a single instance had occurred of the apprehension of any real delinquent actually taken in the fact, against whom there existed legal evidence sufficient for conviction. But the police, however useless, were by no means idle: several notorious delinquents had been detected; men, liable to conviction, on the clearest evidence, of the capital crime of poverty; men, who had been nefariously guilty of lawfully begetting several children, whom, thanks to the times! they were unable to maintain. Considerable injury has been done to the proprietors of the improved Frames. These machines were to them an advantage, inasmuch as they superseded the necessity of employing a number of workmen, who were left in consequence to starve. By the adoption of one species of Frame in particular, one man performed the work of many, and the superfluous labourers were thrown out of employment. Yet it is to be observed, that the work thus executed was inferior in quality; not marketable at home, and merely hurried over with a view to exportation. It was called, in the cant of the trade, by the name of 'Spider work'. The rejected workmen, in the blindness of their ignorance, instead of rejoicing at these improvements in arts so beneficial to mankind, conceived themselves to be sacrificed to improvements in mechanism. In the foolishness of their hearts they imagined that the maintenance and well-doing of the industrious poor were objects of greater consequence than the enrichment of a few individuals by any improvement, in the implements of trade, which threw the workmen out of employment, and rendered the labourer unworthy of his hire. And it must be confessed that although the adoption of the enlarged machinery in that state of our commerce which the country once boasted might have been beneficial to the master without being detrimental to the servant; yet, in the present situation of our manufactures, rotting in warehouses, without a prospect of exportation, with the demand for work and workmen equally diminished, frames of this description tend materially to aggravate the distress and discontent of the disappointed sufferers. But the real cause of these distresses and consequent disturbances lies deeper. When we are told that these men are leagued together not only for the destruction of their own comfort, but of their very means of subsistence, can we forget that it is the bitter policy, the destructive warfare of the last eighteen years, which has destroyed their comfort, your comfort, all men's comfort? that policy, which, originating with 'great statesmen now no more' has survived the dead to become a curse on the living, unto the third and fourth generation! These men never destroyed their looms till they were become useless, worse than useless; till they were become actual impediments to their exertions in obtaining their daily bread. Can you, then, wonder that in times like these when bankruptcy, convicted fraud, and imputed felony are found in a station not far beneath that of your Lordships, the lowest, though once most useful portion of the people, should forget their duty in their distresses, and become only less guilty than one of their representatives? But while the exalted offender can find means to baffle the law, new capital punishments must be devised, new snares of death must be spread for the wretched mechanic, who is famished into guilt. These men were willing to dig, but the spade was in other hands: they were not ashamed to beg, but there was none to relieve them: their own means of subsistence were cut off, all other employments pre-occupied; and their excesses, however to be deplored and condemned, can hardly be subject of surprise . . .

I have traversed the seat of war in the Peninsula, I have been in some of the most oppressed provinces of Turkey; but never under the most despotic of infidel governments did I behold such squalid wretchedness as I have seen since my return in the very heart of a

Christian country. And what are your remedies? After months of inaction, and months of action worse than inactivity, at length comes forth the grand specific, the never-failing nostrum of all state physicians, from the days of Draco to the present time. After feeling the pulse and shaking the head over the patient, prescribing the usual course of warm water and bleeding, – the warm water of your mawkish police, and the lancers of your military, – these convulsions must terminate in death, the sure consummation of the prescriptions of all political Sangrados. Setting aside the palpable injustice and the certain inefficiency of the Bill, are there not capital punishments sufficient in your statutes? Is there not blood enough upon your penal code, that more must be poured forth to ascend to Heaven and testify against you? How will you carry the Bill into effect? Can you commit a whole county to their own prisons? Will you erect a gibbet in every field, and hang up men like scarecrows? or will you proceed (as you must to bring this measure into effect) by decimation? place the county under martial law? depopulate and lay waste all around you? and restore Sherwood Forest as an acceptable gift to the Crown, in its former condition of a royal chase and an asylum for outlaws? Are these the remedies for a starving and desperate populace? Will the famished wretch who has braved your bayonets be appalled by your gibbets? When death is a relief, and the only relief it appears that you will afford him, will he be dragooned into tranquillity? Will that which could not be effected by your grenadiers be accomplished by your executioners? If you proceed by the forms of law, where is your evidence? Those who have refused to impeach their accomplices when transportation only was the punishment, will hardly be tempted to witness against them when death is the penalty. With all due deference to the noble lords opposite, I think a little investigation, some previous inquiry, would induce even them to change their purpose. That most favourite state measure, so marvellously efficacious in many and recent instances, temporising, would not be without its advantages in this. When a proposal is made to emancipate or relieve, you hesitate, you deliberate for years, you temporise and tamper with the minds of men; but a death-bill must be passed off-hand, without a thought of the consequences. Sure I am, from what I have heard, and from what I have seen, that to pass the Bill under all the existing circumstances, without inquiry, without deliberation, would only be to add injustice to irritation, and barbarity to neglect. The framers of such a bill must be content to inherit the honours of that Athenian law-giver whose edicts were said to be written not in ink but in blood. But suppose it passed; suppose one of these men, as I have seen them, – meagre with famine, sullen with despair, careless of a life which your Lordships are perhaps about to value at something less than the price of a stocking-frame; – suppose this man surrounded by the children for whom be is unable to procure bread at the hazard of his existence, about to be torn for ever from a family which he lately supported in peaceful industry, and which it is not his fault that he can no longer so support; – suppose this man – and there are ten thousand such from whom you may select your victims – dragged into court, to be tried for this new offence, by this new law; still, there are two things wanting to convict and condemn him and these are, in my opinion, – twelve butchers for a jury, and a Jeffreys for a judge!

George Gordon Byron, 'An Ode to the Framers of the Frame Bill' (2 March 1812)[10]

Having failed to stop the Bill's passage into law, Byron wrote this Ode in response. In York in 1813, the new Act was put into effect when seventeen Luddites were hanged.

Oh well done Lord E——n! and better done R——r!
  Britannia must prosper with councils like yours;
Hawkesbury, Harrowby, help you to guide her,
  Whose remedy only must *kill* ere it cures:
Those villains, the Weavers, are all grown refractory,
  Asking some succour for Charity's sake –
So hang them in clusters round each Manufactory,
  That will at once put an end to *mistake.*

The rascals, perhaps, may betake them to robbing,
  The dogs to be sure have got nothing to eat –
So if we can hang them for breaking a bobbin,
  'Twill save all the Government's money and meat:
Men are more easily made than machinery –
  Stockings fetch better prices than lives –
Gibbets on Sherwood will *heighten* the scenery,
  Showing how Commerce, *how* Liberty thrives!

Justice is now in pursuit of the wretches,
  Grenadiers, Volunteers, Bow-street Police,
Twenty-two Regiments, a score of Jack Ketches,
  Three of the Quorum and two of the Peace;
Some Lords, to be sure, would have summoned the Judges
  To take their opinion, but that they ne'er shall,
For Liverpool such a concession begrudges,
  So now they're condemned by *no Judges* at all.

Some folks for certain have thought it was shocking,
  When Famine appeals and when Poverty groans,
That Life should be valued at less than a stocking,
  And breaking of frames lead to breaking of bones.

If it should prove so, I trust, by this token,
    (And who will refuse to partake in the hope?)
That the frames of the fools may be first to be *broken*,
    Who, when asked for a *remedy*, send down a *rope*.

'The Tradesman's Complaint'
(between 1802 and 1819)[11]

This is one of several versions of a ballad published around the end of the Napoleonic wars, when returning soldiers found that fighting for their country and defeating France had not improved their lot at home.

Draw near brother tradesmen, listen to my song,
Tell me if you can where our trade is all gone,
For long I have travelled but I can get none
        Oh! the dead time in Old England,
        In England what very bad times.

If you go to a shop and ask for a job,
The answer is no with a shake of the nob,
'Tis enough to make a man turn to and rob,
        Oh! the dead time in Old England,
        In England what very bad times.

There's many a tradesman you'll see in the street,
Walks from morning to evening employment to seek,
Till he has scarcely any shoes to his feet,
        Oh! the dead time in Old England,
        In England what very bad times.

There are sailors and soldiers returned from the wars,
Who bravely have fought in their country's cause,
To come home to be starved – better stayed where they was,
    Oh! the dead time in Old England,
    In England what very bad times.

Provision it is pretty cheap it is true,
But if you have no money there's none for you,
What is a poor man with a family to do?
    Oh! the dead time in Old England,
    In England what very bad times.

So now to conclude and finish my song,
Let's hope these dead times they will not last long,
That we may have reason to alter our tone,
    And sing O the good times in Old England,
    In England what very good times.

Thomas Carlyle, *Past and Present* (1843)[12]

In Past and Present, *Thomas Carlyle (1795–1881) addressed the 'condition of England'. In his first chapter, alluding to the legend of King Midas, he questioned the benefits of unbridled economic growth and productivity.*

To whom, then, is this wealth of England wealth? Who is it that it blesses; makes happier, wiser, beautifuller, in any way better? Who has got hold of it, to make it fetch and carry for him, like a true servant, not like a false mock-servant; to do him any real service whatsoever? As yet no one. We have more riches than any Nation ever had before, we have less good of them than any Nation ever had before. Our successful industry is hitherto unsuccessful; a strange success, if we stop here! In the midst of plethoric plenty, the people perish; with gold walls, and full barns, no man feels himself safe or satisfied. Workers, Master Workers, Unworkers, all men come to a pause; stand fixed, and cannot farther. Fatal paralysis spreading inwards, from the extremities, in St Ives workhouses, in Stockport cellars, through all limbs, as if towards the heart itself. Have we actually got enchanted, accursed by some god?

Frederick Engels, *The Condition of the Working Class in England* (1844)[13]

Frederick Engels (1820–95) was the son of a German factory owner. His experiences in supervising his father's business in Manchester led him to write his study of the effects of the industrial revolution on the working class. Here, he excoriates the moral bankruptcy of unfettered capitalism, 'our war of each against all'.

It is sufficiently clear that the instruction in morals can have no better effect than the religious teaching, with which in all English schools it is mixed up. The simple principles which, for plain human beings, regulate the relations of man to man, brought into the direst confusion by our social state, our war of each against all, necessarily remain confused and foreign to the working-man when mixed with incomprehensible dogmas, and preached in the religious form of an arbitrary and dogmatic commandment. The schools contribute, according to the confession of all authorities, and especially of the Children's Employment Commission, almost nothing to the morality of the working-class. So short-sighted, so stupidly narrow-minded is the

English bourgeoisie in its egotism, that it does not even take the trouble to impress upon the workers the morality of the day, which the bourgeoisie has patched together in its own interest for its own protection! Even this precautionary measure is too great an effort for the enfeebled and sluggish bourgeoisie. A time must come when it will repent its neglect, too late. But it has no right to complain that the workers know nothing of its system of morals, and do not act in accordance with it.

Thus are the workers cast out and ignored by the class in power, morally as well as physically and mentally. The only provision made for them is the law, which fastens upon them when they become obnoxious to the bourgeoisie. Like the dullest of the brutes, they are treated to but one form of education, the whip, in the shape of force, not convincing but intimidating. There is, therefore, no cause for surprise if the workers, treated as brutes, actually become such; or if they can maintain their consciousness of manhood only by cherishing the most glowing hatred, the most unbroken inward rebellion against the bourgeoisie in power. They are men so long only as they burn with wrath against the reigning class. They become brutes the moment they bend in patience under the yoke, and merely strive to make life endurable while abandoning the effort to break the yoke.

This, then, is all that the bourgeoisie has done for the education of the proletariat – and when we take into consideration all the circumstances in which this class lives, we shall not think the worse of it for the resentment which it cherishes against the ruling class. The moral training which is not given to the worker in school is not supplied by the other conditions of his life; that moral training, at least, which alone has worth in the eyes of the bourgeoisie; his whole position and environment involves the strongest temptation to immorality. He is poor, life offers him no charm, almost every enjoyment is denied him, the penalties of the law have no further terrors for him; why should he restrain his desires, why leave to the rich the enjoyment of his birthright, why not seize a part of it for himself? What inducement has the proletarian not to steal! It is all very pretty and very agreeable to the ear of the bourgeois to hear the 'sacredness of property' asserted; but for him who has none, the sacredness of property dies out of itself. Money is the god of this world; the bourgeois takes the proletarian's money from him and so makes a practical atheist of him. No wonder, then, if the proletarian retains his atheism and no longer respects the sacredness and power of the earthly God. And when the poverty of the proletarian is intensified to the point of actual lack of the barest necessaries of life, to want and hunger, the temptation to disregard all social order does but gain power. This the bourgeoisie for the most part recognises. Symonds observes that poverty exercises the same ruinous influence upon the mind which drunkenness exercises upon the body; and Dr Alison explains to property-holding readers, with the greatest exactness, what the consequences of social oppression must be for the working-class. Want leaves the working-man the choice between starving slowly, killing himself speedily, or taking what he needs where he finds it – in plain English, stealing. And there is no cause for surprise that most of them prefer stealing to starvation and suicide.

True, there are, within the working-class, numbers too moral to steal even when reduced to the utmost extremity, and these starve or commit suicide. For suicide, formerly the enviable privilege of the upper classes, has become fashionable among the English workers, and numbers of the poor kill themselves to avoid the misery from which they see no other means of escape.

But far more demoralising than his poverty in its influence upon the English working-man is the insecurity of his position, the necessity of living upon wages from hand to mouth, that in short which makes a proletarian of him. The smaller peasants in Germany are usually poor, and often suffer want, but they are less at the mercy of accident, they have at least something secure. The proletarian, who has nothing but his two hands, who consumes today what he earned yesterday, who is subject to every possible chance, and has not the slightest guarantee for being able to earn the barest necessities of life, whom every crisis, every whim of his employer may deprive of bread, this proletarian is placed in the most revolting, inhuman position conceivable for a human being. The slave is assured of a bare livelihood by the self-interest of his master, the serf has at least a scrap of land on which to live; each has at worst a guarantee for life itself. But the proletarian must depend upon himself alone, and is yet prevented from so applying his abilities as to be able to rely upon them. Everything that the proletarian can do to improve his position is but a drop in the ocean compared with the floods of varying chances to which he is exposed, over which he has not the slightest control. He is the passive subject of all possible combinations of circumstances, and must count himself fortunate when he has saved his life even for a short time; and his character and way of living are naturally shaped by these conditions. Either he seeks to keep his head above water in this whirlpool, to rescue his manhood, and this he can do solely in rebellion against the class which plunders him so mercilessly and then abandons him to his fate, which strives to hold him in this position so demoralising to a human being; or he gives up the struggle against his fate as hopeless, and strives to profit, so far as he can, by the most favourable moment. To save is unavailing, for at the utmost he cannot save more than suffices to sustain life for a short time, while if he falls out of work, it is for no brief period. To accumulate lasting property for himself is impossible; and if it were not, he would only cease to be a working-man and another would take his place. What better thing can he do, then, when he gets high wages, than live well upon them? The English bourgeoisie is violently scandalised at the extravagant living of the workers when wages are high; yet it is not only very natural but very sensible of them to enjoy life when they can, instead of laying up treasures which are of no lasting use to them, and which in the end moth and rust (*i.e.*, the bourgeoisie) get possession of. Yet such a life is demoralising beyond all others.

What Carlyle says of the cotton spinners is true of all English industrial workers:

> Their trade, now in plethoric prosperity, anon extenuated into inanition and 'short time' is of the nature of gambling; they live by it like gamblers, now in luxurious superfluity, now in starvation. Black, mutinous discontent devours them; simply the miserablest feeling that can inhabit the heart of man. English commerce, with its world-wide, convulsive fluctuations, with its immeasurable Proteus Steam demon, makes all paths uncertain for them, all life a bewilderment; society, steadfastness, peaceable continuance, the first blessings of man are not theirs. – This world is for them no home, but a dingy prison-house, of reckless unthrift, rebellion, rancour, indignation against themselves and against all men. Is it a green, flowery world, with azure everlasting sky stretched over it, the work and government of a God; or a murky, simmering Tophet, of copperas fumes, cotton fuz, gin riot, wrath and toil, created by a Demon, governed by a Demon?

And elsewhere:

> Injustice, infidelity to truth and fact and Nature's order, being properly the one evil under the sun, and the feeling of injustice the one intolerable pain under the sun, our grand question as to the condition of these working-men would be: Is it just? And, first of all, what belief have they themselves formed about the justice of it? The words they promulgate are notable by way of answer; their actions are still more notable. Revolt, sullen, revengeful humour of revolt against the upper classes, decreasing respect for what their temporal superiors command, decreasing faith for what their spiritual superiors teach, is more and more the universal spirit of the lower classes. Such spirit may be blamed, may be vindicated, but all men must recognise it as extant there, all may know that it is mournful, that unless altered it will be fatal.

Carlyle is perfectly right as to the facts and wrong only in censuring the wild rage of the workers against the higher classes. This rage, this passion, is rather the proof that the workers feel the inhumanity of their position, that they refuse to be degraded to the level of brutes, and that they will one day free themselves from servitude to the bourgeoisie. This may be seen in the case of those who do not share this wrath; they either bow humbly before the fate that overtakes them, live a respectful private life as well as they can, do not concern themselves as to the course of public affairs, help the bourgeoisie to forge the chains of the workers yet more securely, and stand upon the plane of intellectual nullity that prevailed before the industrial period began; or they are tossed about by fate, lose their moral hold upon themselves as they have already lost their economic hold, live along from day to day, drink and fall into licentiousness; and in both cases they are brutes. The last-named class contributes chiefly to the 'rapid increase of vice', at which the bourgeoisie is so horrified after itself setting in motion the causes which give rise to it.

Karl Marx and Frederick Engels,
The Communist Manifesto (February 1848)[14]

Published at a time when revolutions were sweeping across Europe, The Communist Manifesto *was the work of two expatriate Germans living in London. Together, Karl Marx (1818–83) and Engels set out in plain language their solution to the problems anatomised in Engels's* Condition of the Working Class *(and later theoretically elaborated in Marx's* Das Kapital.

A spectre is haunting Europe – the spectre of communism. All the powers of old Europe have entered into a holy alliance to exorcise this spectre: Pope and Czar, Metternich and Guizot, French Radicals, and German police-spies.

Where is the party in opposition that has not been decried as communistic by its opponents in power? Where the opposition that has not hurled back the branding reproach of communism, against the more advanced opposition parties, as well as against its reactionary adversaries?

Two things result from this fact.

I. Communism is already acknowledged by all European powers to be itself a power.

II. It is high time that Communists should openly, in the face of the whole world, publish their views, their aims, their tendencies, and meet this nursery tale of the spectre of communism with a manifesto of the party itself.

To this end, Communists of various nationalities have assembled in London and sketched the following manifesto, to be published in the English, French, German, Italian, Flemish, and Danish languages . . .

The theoretical conclusions of the Communists are in no way based on ideas or principles that have been invented, or discovered, by this or that would-be universal reformer.

They merely express, in general terms, actual relations springing from an existing class struggle, from a historical movement going on under our very eyes. The abolition of existing property relations is not at all a distinctive feature of communism.

All property relations in the past have continually been subject to historical change consequent upon the change in historical conditions.

The French Revolution, for example, abolished feudal property in favour of bourgeois property.

The distinguishing feature of communism is not the abolition of property generally, but the abolition of bourgeois property. But modern bourgeois private property is the final and most complete expression of the system of producing and appropriating products that is based on class antagonisms, on the exploitation of the many by the few.

In this sense, the theory of the communists may be summed up in the single sentence: Abolition of private property.

We communists have been reproached with the desire of abolishing the right of personally acquiring property as the fruit of a man's own labor, which property is alleged to be the groundwork of all personal freedom, activity, and independence.

Hard-won, self-acquired, self-earned property! Do you mean the property of the petty artisan and of the small peasant, a form of property that preceded the bourgeois form? There is no need to abolish that; the development of industry has to a great extent already destroyed it, and is still destroying it daily . . .

You are horrified at our intending to do away with private property. But in your existing society, private property is already done away with for nine-tenths of the population; its existence for the few is solely due to its non-existence in the hands of those nine-tenths. You reproach us, therefore, with intending to do away with a form of property, the necessary condition for whose existence is the non-existence of any property for the immense majority of society.

In one word, you reproach us with intending to do away with your property. Precisely so; that is just what we intend . . .

It has been objected that upon the abolition of private property all work will cease and universal laziness will overtake us.

According to this, bourgeois society ought long ago to have gone to the dogs through sheer idleness; for those of its members who work, acquire nothing, and those who acquire anything, do not work. The whole of this objection is but another expression of the tautology that there can no longer be any wage labour when there is no longer any capital.

All objections urged against the communistic mode of producing and appropriating material products have, in the same way, been urged against the communistic mode of producing and appropriating intellectual products. Just as, to the bourgeois, the disappearance of class property is the disappearance of production itself, so the disappearance of class culture is to him identical with the disappearance of all culture.

That culture, the loss of which he laments, is, for the enormous majority, a mere training to act as a machine . . .

Do you charge us with wanting to stop the exploitation of children by their parents? To this crime we plead guilty.

But, you will say, we destroy the most hallowed of relations when we replace home education by social.

And your education! Is not that also social, and determined by the social conditions under which you educate, by the intervention, direct or indirect, of society, by means of schools, etc.? The communists have not invented the intervention of society in education; they do but seek to alter the character of that intervention, and to rescue education from the influence of the ruling class.

The bourgeois clap-trap about the family and education, about the hallowed co-relation of parent and child, becomes all the more disgusting, the more, by the action of modern industry, all family ties among the proletarians are torn asunder, and their children transformed into simple articles of commerce and instruments of labour.

But you communists would introduce community of women, screams the whole bourgeoisie in chorus.

The bourgeois sees in his wife a mere instrument of production. He hears that the instruments of production are to be exploited in common and, naturally, can come to no other conclusion than that the lot of being common to all will likewise fall to the women.

He has not even a suspicion that the real point aimed at is to do away with the status of women as mere instruments of production.

For the rest, nothing is more ridiculous than the virtuous

indignation of our bourgeois at community of women which, they pretend, is to be openly and officially established by the communists. The communists have no need to introduce community of women; it has existed almost from time immemorial.

Our bourgeois, not content with having the wives and daughters of their proletarians at their disposal, not to speak of common prostitutes, take the greatest pleasure in seducing each other's wives.

Bourgeois marriage is in reality a system of wives in common and thus, at the most, what the communists might possibly be reproached with is that they desire to introduce, in substitution for a hypocritically concealed, an openly legalised community of women. For the rest, it is self-evident that the abolition of the present system of production must bring with it the abolition of the community of women springing from that system, i.e., of prostitution both official and unofficial.

The communists are further reproached with desiring to abolish countries and nationality.

The workers have no country. We cannot take from them what they have not got. Since the proletariat must first of all acquire political supremacy, must rise to be the leading class of the nation, must constitute itself *the* nation, it is, so far, itself national, though not in the bourgeois sense of the word.

National divisions and antagonisms between peoples are daily more and more vanishing, owing to the development of the bourgeoisie, to freedom of commerce, to the world market, to uniformity in the mode of production and in the conditions of life corresponding thereto.

The supremacy of the proletariat will cause them to vanish still faster. United action, of the leading civilised countries at least, is one of the first conditions for the emancipation of the proletariat.

In proportion as the exploitation of one individual by another is put an end to, the exploitation of one nation by another will also be put an end to. In proportion as the antagonism between classes within the nation vanishes, the hostility of one nation to another will come to an end . . .

In place of the old bourgeois society, with its classes and class antagonisms, we shall have an association in which the free development of each is the condition for the free development of all.

Henry Mayhew, 'Labour and the Poor' (23 October 1849)[15]

Henry Mayhew (1812–87) was a journalist and playwright. In 1849, as the Morning Chronicle's *'Special Correspondent for the Metropolis', he began a series of reports, or 'letters', on the poor in London. Mayhew continued his investigations and his writing after he left the* Chronicle *in 1850. He published them in what became the two volumes of* London Labour and the London Poor *in 1851, and updated them in the 1860s. The books are vital sources of information about hitherto unrecorded lives, as well as evidence of a growing recognition among the middle classes that 'the rich know nothing of the poor'.*

The causes of poverty among such as are willing to work, appeared to me to be two. 1. The workman might receive for his labour less than sufficient to satisfy his wants. 2. He might receive a sufficiency, and yet be in want, either from having to pay an exorbitant price for the commodities he requires in exchange for his wages, or else from a deficiency of economy and prudence in the regulation of his desires by his means and chances of subsistence. Or, to say the same thing in a more concise manner – the privations of the industrious classes admit of being referred either to (1) low wages, (2) high prices, or (3) improvident habits.

In opening the subject which has been entrusted to me, and setting

forth the plan I purpose pursuing, so as to methodise, and consequently simplify, the investigation of it, I stated it to be my intention
to devote myself primarily to the consideration of that class of poor
whose privations seemed to be due to the insufficiency of their wages.
In accordance with this object, I directed my steps first towards
Bethnal-green, with the view of inquiring into the rate of wages
received by the Spitalfields weavers. My motive for making this selection was, principally, because the manufacture of silk is one of the
few arts that continue localised – that is, restricted to a particular
quarter – in London. The tanners of Bermondsey – the watchmakers
of Clerkenwell – the coachmakers of Long-acre – the marine-store
dealers of Saffron-hill – the old clothes-men of Holywell-street and
Rosemary-lane – the potters of Lambeth – the hatters of the Borough
– are among the few handicrafts and trades that, as in the bazaars of
the East are confined to particular parts of the town. Moreover, the
weavers of Spitalfields have always been notorious for their privations, and being all grouped together within a comparatively small
space, they could be more easily visited, and a greater mass of information obtained in a less space of time, than in the case of any other
ill-paid metropolitan handicraft with which I am acquainted. In my
inquiry I have sought to obtain information from the artizans of
Spitalfields upon two points in particular. I was desirous to ascertain
from the workmen themselves, not only the average rate of wages
received by them, but also to hear their opinions as to the cause of
the depreciation in the value of their labour. The result of my inquiries
on these two points I purpose setting forth in my present communication; but, before entering upon the subject, I wish the reader
distinctly to understand that the sentiments here recorded are those
wholly and solely of the weavers themselves . . .

I will now proceed to give the result of my inquiries into the subject;
though, before doing so, it will be as well to make the reader acquainted
with the precautions adopted to arrive at a fair and unbiased estimate
as to the feelings and condition of the workmen in the trade. In the

first place, having put myself in communication with the surgeon of the district, and one of the principal and most intelligent of the operatives, it was agreed among us that we should go into a particular street, and visit the first six weavers' houses that we came to. Accordingly we made the best of our way to the nearest street. The houses were far above the average abodes of the weavers, the street being wide and airy, and the houses open at the back, with gardens filled with many-coloured dahlias. The 'long lights' at top, as the attic window stretching the whole length of the house is technically called, showed that almost the whole line of houses were occupied by weavers. As we entered the street, a coal cart, with a chime of bells above the horse's collar, went jingling past us. Another circumstance peculiar to the place was the absence of children. In such a street, had the labour of the young been less valuable, the gutters and door-steps would have swarmed with juveniles. We knocked at the door of the first house, and, requesting permission to speak with the workman on the subject of his trade, were all three ushered up a steep staircase, and through a trap in the floor into the 'shop'. This was a long, narrow apartment, with a window back and front, extending the entire length of the house – running from one end of the room to the other. The man was the ideal of his class – a short spare figure, with thin face and sunken cheeks. In the room were three looms and some spinning wheels, at one of which sat a boy winding 'quills'. Working at a loom was a plump, pleasant-looking girl, busy making 'plain goods'. Along the windows, on each side, were ranged small pots of fuchsias, with their long scarlet drops swinging gently back-wards and forwards, as the room shook with the clatter of the looms. The man was a velvet weaver. He was making a drab velvet for coat collars. We sat down on a wooden chair beside him, and talked as he worked. He told us he was to have 3s. 6d. per yard for the fabric he was engaged upon, and that he could make about half a-yard a day. They were six in family, he said, and he had three looms at work. He got from 20s. to 25s. for the labour of five of them, and that only when they all are employed. But one loom is generally out of work waiting for fresh 'cane'. Up to 1824, the price for the same work as he is now doing was 6s. The reduction, he was convinced, arose from the competition in the trade, and one master cutting under the other. 'The workmen are obliged to take the low prices, because they have not the means to hold out, and they knew that if they don't take the work others will. There are always plenty of weavers unemployed, and the cause of that is owing to the lowness of prices, and the people being compelled to do double the quantity of work that they used to do, in order to live. I have made a stand against the lowness of prices, and have lost my work through refusing to take the price. Circumstances compel us to take it at last. The cupboard gets low, and the landlord comes for his weekly rent. The masters are all trying to undersell one another. They never will advance wages. Go get my neighbour to do it, each says, and then *I'll* advance. It's been a continuation of reduction for the last 26 years, and a continuation of suffering for just as long. Never a month passes but what you hear of something being lowered . . . I was conducted, in the evening, to a tavern, where several of the weavers who advocated the principles of the People's Charter were in the habit of assembling. I found the room half full, and immediately proceeded to explain to them the object of my visit, telling them that I intended to make notes of whatever they might communicate to me, with a view to publication in the *Morning Chronicle.* After a short consultation among themselves, they told me that, in their opinion, the primary cause of the depression of the prices among the weavers was the want of the suffrage. 'We consider that labour is unrepresented in the House of Commons, and being unrepresented, that the capitalist and the landlord have it all their own way. Prices have gone down among the weavers since 1824 more than one-half. The hours of labour have decidedly increased among us, so that we may live. The weavers now generally work one-third longer than formerly, and for much less.' 'I know two instances,' said one person, 'where the weavers have to work from 10 in the morning till 12 at night, and then they only get meat once a week. The average time for labour before 1824 was 10 hours a day; now it is 14. In 1824 there were about 14,000 hands employed, getting at an average 14s. 6d. a week; and now there are 9,000 hands employed, getting at an average only 4s. 9d. a week, at increased hours of labour. This depreciation we attribute, not to any decrease in the demand for silk goods, but to foreign and home competition. We believe that the foreign competition brings us into competition with the foreign workman; and it is impossible for us to compete with him at the present rate of English taxation. As regards home competition, we are of opinion that, from the continued desire on the part of each trade to undersell the other, the workman has ultimately to suffer. We think there is a desire on the part of every manufacturer to undersell the other, and so get an extra amount of trade into his own hands, and make a large and rapid fortune thereby. The public, we are satisfied, do not derive any benefit from this extreme competition. It is only a few individuals, who are termed by the trade slaughterhouse-men – they alone derive benefit from the system, and the public gain no advantage whatever by the depreciation in our rate of wages. It is our firm conviction that if affairs continue as at present, the fate of the working man must be pauperism, crime, or death.'

Ellen Johnston, 'The Last Sark' (1859)[16]

Ellen Johnston (c. 1835–74) was a power-loom weaver from Lanarkshire who began to submit poems to weekly newspapers under the pseudonym 'Factory Girl'. Many were written in formal English, and her subjects ranged from international politics to everyday life in the factories and mills. She also published in dialect. This poem ('sark' means 'shirt') is an indictment of inequality. Johnston continued to go in search of manual labour in Glasgow, Belfast and Manchester

even after she had been published and found some small literary
fame.

GUDE guide me, are you hame again, an' ha'e ye got nae wark,
We've naething noo tae put awa' unless yer auld blue sark;
My head is rinnin' roon about far lichter than a flee –
What care some gentry if they're weel though a' the puir wad dee!

Our merchants an' mill masters they wad never want a meal,
Though a' the banks in Scotland wad for a twelvemonth fail;
For some o' them have far mair goud than ony ane can see –
What care gentry if they're weel though a' the puir wad dee!

This is a funny warld, John, for it's no divided fair,
And whiles I think some o' the rich have got the puir folk's share,
Tae see us starving here the nicht wi' no ae bless'd bawbee –
What care some gentry if they're weel though a' the puir wad dee!

Oor hoose ance bean an' cosey, John; oor beds ance snug an' warm
Feels unco cauld an' dismal noo, an' empty as a barn;
The weans sit greeting in oor face, and we ha'e noucht to gie –
What care some gentry if they're weel though a' the puir wad dee!

It is the puir man's hard-won toil that fills the rich man's purse;
I'm sure his gouden coffers they are het wi' mony a curse;
Were it no for the working men what wad the rich men be?
What care some gentry if they're weel though a' the puir wad dee!

My head is licht, my heart is weak, my een are growing blin';
The bairn is fa'en aff my knee – oh! John, catch haud i' him,
You ken I hinna tasted meat for days far mair than three;
Were it no for my helpless bairns I wadna care to dee.

———————————

Thomas Hardy, 'To an Unborn Pauper Child' (23 November 1901)[17]

In this poem, Thomas Hardy (1840–1928) expresses in the bleakest terms the kind of grip that class and lack of opportunity could have in turn-of-the-century Britain.

Breathe not, hid Heart: cease silently,
   And though thy birth-hour beckons thee,
       Sleep the long sleep:
       The Doomsters heap
   Travails and teens around us here,
And Time-wraiths turn our songsingings to fear.

Hark, how the peoples surge and sigh,
   And laughters fail, and greetings die:
       Hopes dwindle; yea,
       Faiths waste away,
   Affections and enthusiasms numb;
Thou canst not mend these things if thou dost come.

Had I the ear of wombèd souls
   Ere their terrestrial chart unrolls,
       And thou wert free
       To cease, or be,
   Then would I tell thee all I know,
And put it to thee: Wilt thou take Life so?

Vain vow! No hint of mine may hence
   To theeward fly: to thy locked sense
      Explain none can
      Life's pending plan:
   Thou wilt thy ignorant entry make
Though skies spout fire and blood and nations quake.

Fain would I, dear, find some shut plot
   Of earth's wide wold for thee, where not
      One tear, one qualm,
      Should break the calm.
   But I am weak as thou and bare;
No man can change the common lot to rare.

Must come and bide. And such are we –
   Unreasoning, sanguine, visionary –
      That I can hope
      Health, love, friends, scope
   In full for thee; can dream thou'lt find
Joys seldom yet attained by humankind!

———————————

Jack Dash, The Invasion of the Ritz Hotel
(c. 1938)[18]

In his 1969 memoir Good Morning Brothers, *Jack Dash (1907–89) of the National Unemployed Workers Movement, recalled a protest to expose the class divisions in Britain in the 1930s. Dash later became a docker and a union leader, and lived to see the docks disappear from east London. He said that his epitaph should be 'Here lies Jack Dash/All he wanted was /To separate them from their cash'.*

We decided to invade the Ritz Hotel in Piccadilly. Everything was well planned. The press – that is, the London and national newspapers (and in those days before the swallowing up of the little fish by the big 'uns under free enterprise there was quite a number of them) were all informed in advance. At the appointed time about 150 of our unemployed members, all dressed up in such remnants of our best suits as had escaped the pawnbroker, walked quietly into the Grill and sat down. This did not have the quite hoped-for effect, for due to a mistake – the only organizational mistake I can remember on the part of the campaign committee – we had overlooked the fact that the Grill was never open in the afternoons, only in the evenings. However, we continued as planned, took our places at the tables which were being set by waiters in readiness for the evening, and then pulled our posters from beneath our coats, with slogans calling for an end to the Means Test and more winter relief for the aged pensioners.

Can you imagine the looks on the faces of the waiters! They stood still in their tracks. Up rushed the management supervisor demanding to know what it was all about. He was politely told by our elected speaker, Wal Hannington, that we would like to be served with some tea and sandwiches because we were very tired and hungry, but he was not to be anxious and could present the bill which would be paid on the spot.

When the supervisor regained his breath he said, in a very cultured, precise Oxford-English voice: "I cannot permit you to be served. You are not our usual type of customer. You know full well that you are not accustomed to dine in an establishment of this quality. If you do not leave I shall have to send for the police." (This had already been done.) In reply, our spokesman informed him that many was the Saturday when wealthy clients of the Ritz would drive down to the East End workmen's caffs in their Rollses and Daimlers and have a jolly hot saveloy, old boy, what! Slumming, they called it, and they too were in unusual attire and frequenting establishments that were not accustomed to such a clientele; nevertheless, said our spokesman, these gentlemen were treated with courtesy and civility and nobody sent for the police. The Ritz, he added, was not a private members' club but a public restaurant; he requested the supervisor to give orders to the staff to serve us with the refreshment we had asked for.

The appeal might just as well have been addressed to the chandelier which hung from the ceiling. The supervisor stood there with a look of scorn, waiting for the police to come and throw us out. We refused to budge, insisting on our right as members of the general public, with legal tender in our pockets, to be served with what we had ordered. Meanwhile Wally had mounted the orchestra-platform to address us; waiters and kitchen staff stood around dumbfounded at our temerity. But our speaker was incensed and in good form, and the issue of class privilege was clearly put. I noticed several of the staff members nodding their heads as the speaker touched on salient points. His speech was never finished, however, for the Grill was soon surrounded by police. A couple of Inspectors came over and consulted our organizers; we were ordered to leave, and did so in an orderly manner. As we filed out several of the waiters came up to wish us luck in our campaign, and pressed money into our hands.

George Orwell, 'England, Your England' (1941)[19]

*Eric Blair (1903–50) took the pen name George Orwell for his work
as an essayist, novelist, and journalist. In this essay, Orwell writes
of the 'grip of the moneyed class' on British politics, including its
war aims and practices, and challenges the idea of shared sacrifice
in the war.*

England is a family with the wrong members in control. Almost
entirely we are governed by the rich, and by people who step into
positions of command by right of birth. Few if any of these people
are consciously treacherous, some of them are not even fools, but as
a class they are quite incapable of leading us to victory. They could
not do it, even if their material interests did not constantly trip them
up. As I pointed out earlier, they have been artificially stupefied. Quite
apart from anything else, the rule of money sees to it that we shall
be governed largely by the old – that is, by people utterly unable to
grasp what age they are living in or what enemy they are fighting.
Nothing was more desolating at the beginning of this war than the
way in which the whole of the older generation conspired to pretend
that it was the war of 1914–18 over again. All the old duds were back
on the job, twenty years older, with the skull plainer in their faces.
Ian Hay was cheering up the troops, Belloc was writing articles on
strategy, Maurois doing broadcasts, Bairnsfather drawing cartoons. It
was like a tea-party of ghosts. And that state of affairs has barely
altered. The shock of disaster brought a few able men like Bevin to
the front, but in general we are still commanded by people who
managed to live through the years 1931–9 without even discovering
that Hitler was dangerous. A generation of the unteachable is hanging
upon us like a necklace of corpses.

    As soon as one considers any problem of this war – and it does not
matter whether it is the widest aspect of strategy or the tiniest detail

of home organisation – one sees that the necessary moves cannot be made while the social structure of England remains what it is. Inevitably, because of their position and upbringing, the ruling class are fighting for their own privileges, which cannot possibly be reconciled with the public interest. It is a mistake to imagine that war aims, strategy, propaganda and industrial organisation exist in watertight compartments. All are interconnected. Every strategic plan, every tactical method, even every weapon will bear the stamp of the social system that produced it. The British ruling class are fighting against Hitler, whom they have always regarded and whom some of them still regard as their protector against Bolshevism. That does not mean that they will deliberately sell out; but it does mean that at every decisive moment they are likely to falter, pull their punches, do the wrong thing.

Until the Churchill Government called some sort of halt to the process, they have done the wrong thing with an unerring instinct ever since 1931. They helped Franco to overthrow the Spanish Government, although anyone not an imbecile could have told them that a Fascist Spain would be hostile to England. They fed Italy with war materials all through the winter of 1939–40, although it was obvious to the whole world that the Italians were going to attack us in the spring. For the sake of a few hundred thousand dividend drawers they are turning India from an ally into an enemy. Moreover, so long as the moneyed classes remain in control, we cannot develop any but a *defensive* strategy. Every victory means a change in the *status quo*. How can we drive the Italians out of Abyssinia without rousing echoes among the coloured peoples of our own Empire? How can we even smash Hitler without the risk of bringing the German Socialists and Communists into power? The left-wingers who wail that 'this is a capitalist war' and that 'British Imperialism' is fighting for loot have got their heads screwed on backwards. The last thing the British moneyed class wishes for is to acquire fresh territory. It would simply be an embarrassment. Their war aim (both unattainable and unmentionable) is simply to hang on to what they have got.

Internally, England is still the rich man's Paradise. All talk of 'equality of sacrifice' is nonsense. At the same time as factory workers are asked to put up with longer hours, advertisements for 'Butler. One in family, eight in staff' are appearing in the press. The bombed-out populations of the East End go hungry and homeless while wealthier victims simply step into their cars and flee to comfortable country houses. The Home Guard swells to a million men in a few weeks, and is deliberately organised from above in such a way that only people with private incomes can hold positions of command. Even the rationing system is so arranged that it hits the poor all the time, while people with over £2,000 a year are practically unaffected by it. Everywhere privilege is squandering good will. In such circumstances even propaganda becomes almost impossible. As attempts to stir up patriotic feeling, the red posters issued by the Chamberlain Government at the beginning of the war broke all depth-records. Yet they could not have been much other than they were, for how could Chamberlain and his followers take the risk of rousing strong popular feeling *against Fascism*? Anyone who was genuinely hostile to Fascism must also be opposed to Chamberlain himself and to all the others who had helped Hitler into power. So also with external propaganda. In all Lord Halifax's speeches there is not one concrete proposal for which a single inhabitant of Europe would risk the top joint of his little finger. For what war-aim can Halifax, or anyone like him, conceivably have, except to put the clock back to 1933?

It is only by revolution that the native genius of the English people can be set free. Revolution does not mean red flags and street fighting, it means a fundamental shift of power. Whether it happens with or without bloodshed is largely an accident of time and place. Nor does it mean the dictatorship of a single class. The people in England who grasp what changes are needed and are capable of carrying them through are not confined to any one class, though it is true that very few people with over £2,000 a year are among them. What is wanted is a conscious open revolt by ordinary people against inefficiency, class privilege and the rule of the old. It is not primarily a question of change of government. British governments do, broadly speaking, represent the will of the people, and if we alter our structure from below we shall get the government we need. Ambassadors, generals, officials and colonial administrators who are senile or pro-Fascist are more dangerous than Cabinet ministers whose follies have to be committed in public. Right through our national life we have got to fight against privilege, against the notion that a half-witted public-schoolboy is better fitted for command than an intelligent mechanic. Although there are gifted and honest *individuals* among them, we have got to break the grip of the moneyed class as a whole. England has got to assume its real shape. The England that is only just beneath the surface, in the factories and the newspaper offices, in the aeroplanes and the submarines, has got to take charge of its own destiny.

John Lennon, 'Working Class Hero' (11 December 1970)[20]

This song from is from John Lennon's first post-Beatles solo album, John Lennon/Plastic Ono Band. *Lennon (1940–80) commented in an interview, 'The thing about the "Working Class Hero" song that nobody ever got right was that it was supposed to be sardonic.'*

As soon as you're born they make you feel small
By giving you no time instead of it all
Till the pain is so big you feel nothing at all
A working class hero is something to be
A working class hero is something to be

They hurt you at home and they hit you at school
They hate you if you're clever and they despise a fool
Till you're so fucking crazy you can't follow the rules
A working class hero is something to be
A working class hero is something to be

When they've tortured and scared you for twenty odd years
Then they expect you to pick a career
When you can't really function you're so full of fear
A working class hero is something to be
A working class hero is something to be

Keep you doped with religion and sex and TV
You think you're so clever and classless and free
But you're still fucking peasants as far as I can see
A working class hero is something to be
A working class hero is something to be

There's room at the top they are telling you still
But first you must learn how to smile when you kill
If you want to be like the folks on the hill
A working class hero is something to be
A working class hero is something to be

If you want to be a hero well just follow me
If you want to be a hero well just follow me

———————————

Jimmy Reid, Inaugural Speech as Rector of Glasgow University (28 April 1972)[21]

Jimmy Reid (1932–2010), was a Clydeside trade-union activist. As an engineer at Upper Clyde Shipbuilders he emerged as one of the leaders of the occupation and work-in of 1971–2. It brought him to wide public attention, and he was elected Rector of Glasgow University in 1972. This speech was compared by the New York Times *(which printed it in full) to Abraham Lincoln's Gettysburg Address.*

Alienation is the precise and correctly applied word for describing the major social problem in Britain today. People feel alienated by society. In some intellectual circles it is treated almost as a new phenomenon. It has, however, been with us for years. What I believe is true is that today it is more widespread, more pervasive than ever before. Let me right at the outset define what I mean by alienation. It is the cry of men who feel themselves the victims of blind economic forces beyond their control. It's the frustration of ordinary people excluded from the processes of decision-making. The feeling of despair and hopelessness that pervades people who feel with justification that they have no real say in shaping or determining their own destinies.

Many may not have rationalised it. May not even understand, may not be able to articulate it. But they feel it. It therefore conditions and colours their social attitudes. Alienation expresses itself in different ways in different people. It is to be found in what our courts often describe as the criminal antisocial behaviour of a section of the community. It is expressed by those young people who want to opt out of society, by drop-outs, the so-called maladjusted, those who seek to escape permanently from the reality of society through intoxicants and narcotics. Of course, it would be wrong to say it was the sole reason for these things. But it is a much greater factor in all of them than is generally recognised.

Society and its prevailing sense of values leads to another form of alienation. It alienates some from humanity. It partially de-human-ises some people, makes them insensitive, ruthless in their handling of fellow human beings, self-centred and grasping. The irony is, they are often considered normal and well-adjusted. It is my sincere contention that anyone who can be totally adjusted to our society is in greater need of psychiatric analysis and treatment than anyone else. They remind me of the character in the novel, *Catch-22*, the father of Major Major. He was a farmer in the American Midwest. He hated suggestions for things like Medicare, social services, unemploy-ment benefits or civil rights. He was, however, an enthusiast for the agricultural policies that paid farmers for not bringing their fields under cultivation. From the money he got for not growing alfalfa he bought more land in order not to grow alfalfa. He became rich. Pilgrims came from all over the state to sit at his feet and learn how to be a successful non-grower of alfalfa. His philosophy was simple. The poor didn't work hard enough and so they were poor. He believed that the good Lord gave him two strong hands to grab as much as he could for himself. He is a comic figure. But think – have you not met his like here in Britain? Here in Scotland? I have.

It is easy and tempting to hate such people. However, it is wrong. They are as much products of society, and of a consequence of that society, human alienation, as the poor drop-out. They are losers. They have lost the essential elements of our common humanity. Man is a social being. Real fulfilment for any person lies in service to his fellow men and women. The big challenge to our civilisation is not *Oz*, a magazine I haven't seen, let alone read. Nor is it permis-siveness, although I agree our society is too permissive. Any society which, for example, permits over one million people to be unem-ployed is far too permissive for my liking. Nor is it moral laxity in the narrow sense that this word is generally employed – although in a sense here we come nearer to the problem. It does involve morality, ethics, and our concept of human values. The challenge we face is that of rooting out anything and everything that distorts and devalues human relations . . .

To the students I address this appeal. Reject these attitudes. Reject the values and false morality that underlie these attitudes. A rat race is for rats. We're not rats. We're human beings. Reject the insidious pressures in society that would blunt your critical faculties to all that is happening around you, that would caution silence in the face of injustice lest you jeopardise your chances of promotion and self-advancement. This is how it starts, and before you know where you are, you're a fully paid-up member of the rat-pack. The price is too high. It entails the loss of your dignity and human spirit. Or as Christ put it, 'What doth it profit a man if he gain the whole world and suffer the loss of his soul?'

Profit is the sole criterion used by the establishment to evaluate economic activity. From the rat race to lame ducks. The vocabulary in vogue is a give-away. It's more reminiscent of a human menagerie than human society. The power structures that have inevitably emerged from this approach threaten and undermine our hard-won democratic rights. The whole process is towards the centralisation and concentration of power in fewer and fewer hands. The facts are there for all who want to see. Giant monopoly companies and consortia dominate almost every branch of our economy. The men who wield effective control within these giants exercise a power over their fellow men which is frightening and is a negation of democracy.

Government by the people for the people becomes meaningless unless it includes major economic decision-making by the people for the people. This is not simply an economic matter. In essence it is an ethical and moral question, for whoever takes the important economic decisions in society *ipso facto* determines the social priorities of that society.

From the Olympian heights of an executive suite, in an atmosphere where your success is judged by the extent to which you can maximise profits, the overwhelming tendency must be to see people as units of production, as indices in your accountants' books. To appreciate fully the inhumanity of this situation, you have to see the hurt and despair in the eyes of a man suddenly told he is redundant, without provision made for suitable alternative employment, with the prospect in the West of Scotland, if he is in his late forties or fifties, of spending the rest of his life in the Labour Exchange. Someone, somewhere has decided he is unwanted, unneeded, and is to be thrown on the industrial scrap heap. From the very depth of my being, I challenge the right of any man or any group of men, in business or in government, to tell a fellow human being that he or she is expendable.

The concentration of power in the economic field is matched by the centralisation of decision-making in the political institutions of society. The power of Parliament has undoubtedly been eroded over past decades, with more and more authority being invested in the Executive. The power of local authorities has been and is being systematically undermined. The only justification I can see for local government is as a counter-balance to the centralised character of national government . . .

Everything that is proposed from the establishment seems almost calculated to minimise the role of the people, to miniaturise man. I can understand how attractive this prospect must be to those at the top. Those of us who refuse to be pawns in their power game can be picked up by their bureaucratic tweezers and dropped in a filing cabinet under 'M' for 'malcontent' or 'maladjusted'. When you think of some of the high flats around us, it can hardly be an accident that they are as near as one could get to an architectural representation of a filing cabinet.

If modern technology requires greater and larger productive units, let's make our wealth-producing resources and potential subject to public control and to social accountability. Let's gear our society to social need, not personal greed. Given such creative re-orientation of society, there is no doubt in my mind that in a few years we could eradicate in our country the scourge of poverty, the underprivileged, slums, and insecurity.

Even this is not enough. To measure social progress purely by material advance is not enough. Our aim must be the enrichment of the whole quality of life. It requires a social and cultural, or if you wish, a spiritual transformation of our country. A necessary part of this must be the restructuring of the institutions of government and, where necessary, the evolution of additional structures so as to involve the people in the decision-making processes of our society. The so-called experts will tell you that this would be cumbersome or marginally inefficient. I am prepared to sacrifice a margin of efficiency for the value of the people's participation. Anyway, in the longer term, I reject this argument.

To unleash the latent potential of our people requires that we give them responsibility. The untapped resources of the North Sea are as nothing compared to the untapped resources of our people. I am convinced that the great mass of our people go through life without even a glimmer of what they could have contributed to their fellow human beings. This is a personal tragedy. It's a social crime. The flowering of each individual's personality and talents is the pre-condition for everyone's development.

Dick Gaughan, 'Call It Freedom' (1988)[22]

Dick Gaughan is a folk singer and guitarist from Leith, Edinburgh, born in 1948. His song 'Call It Freedom', from an album of the same title, was inspired by the example of his parents. As Gaughan has written: 'My parents used to laugh cynically when they were told that, unlike the poor people in those horrible socialist countries, they had the freedom to travel anywhere they wanted. They laughed because they had hardly enough money to feed the children, let alone travel, and that was with both of them working around fifty hours a week each.

Glittering shop windows, sparkling commodities
Aladdin's caves of treasures, consumer's paradise
Patrolling the windows with clubs and uniforms
Security guards protect all this wealth

    And they call it 'Freedom', they call it 'Being Free'
    They call it 'Being Free', they call it 'Freedom'

Single woman with three children, living in a suitcase
Scared to go out at night, scared of pushers and muggers
Got no place to cook, lives on fish and chips and cornflakes
The doctor gave her Valium, said it would help her nerves

    And they call it 'Freedom', they call it 'Being Free'
    They call it 'Being Free', they call it 'Freedom'

Across there on the other side, behind the 'Iron Curtain'
People rise and go to work, they've got no unemployment
They've got nobody dying 'cause they can't afford to eat
They've got nobody dying 'cause they can't afford a home
They've got nobody dying 'cause they can't afford a doctor
They've got nobody dying 'cause they can't afford to live

    But they don't have 'Freedom', we're told that isn't
      being free
    We're told that isn't being free, we're told that isn't
      'Freedom'

So just remember if you're starving, you've got the freedom to
   starve
And if you're homeless, then you're free to have no home
And if you can't afford a doctor, well, you're free to die of
   sickness
You're just exercising free choice in the free world and
   having freedom

———————————

WORKERS UNITED

———————

'LABOUR'S "NO" INTO ACTION'

Labourers of all kinds did not always accept their treatment at the hands of their employers. As far back as the fourteenth century, the Statute of Labourers had been introduced to reinforce the medieval concept that the relationship between employers and employees was actually one between master and servant, and the latter could not be permitted to go looking for better terms elsewhere. One of the results of that repressive legislation was the Peasants' Revolt.

The beginnings of the industrial revolution began to shift the balance much further between workers and employers. In the eighteenth century, the earliest attempts to form trade unions and begin collective bargaining, not only for better pay but even more fundamentally for humane working conditions, were met by more harsh legislation, culminating in the Combination Acts passed between 1799 and 1825, which banned the practice of workers coming together to negotiate collectively.

Even before the Combination Acts were repealed, some workers had discovered the power of striking. With the growth of the legitimate trade-union movement, workers began to address a series of injustices through their own action.

In the twentieth century, there were economic arguments about coal, arguments about nationalisation and union power, but at their heart were human stories, about individuals and communities attempting to take their destinies into their own hands.

Glasgow Weavers, 'Address to the Inhabitants of Great Britain and Ireland' (1 April 1820)[1]

This proclamation was circulated around Glasgow and southwest Scotland by the 'Committee of Organisation for forming a Provisional Government', an organisation based in the trade-union movement in the area. An appeal to all workers of Britain, it precipitated the first general strike in British history. In Glasgow, the Lord Provost reported that 'almost the whole population of the working classes have obeyed the orders contained in the treasonable proclamation by striking work'. At the height of the strike, around 60,000 workers were reported to have withdrawn their labour. The anticipated next stage of this 'Radical War', a concerted rising in the North of England as well as Scotland, did not materialise, though there were some armed insurrections north of the border. Three men were executed, and many more were transported.

Friends and Countrymen – Roused from that torpid state in which we have been sunk for so many years, we are at length compelled, from the extremity of our sufferings, and the contempt heaped upon our petitions for redress, to assert our rights at the hazard of our lives, and proclaim to the world the real motives which (if not misrepresented by designing men, would have united all ranks) have reduced us to take up arms for the redress of our common grievances. The numerous public meetings held throughout the country have demonstrated to you that the interests of all classes are the same. That the protection of the life and property of the rich man is the interest of the poor man, and in return, it is the interest of the rich to protect the poor from the iron grasp of despotism; for, when its victims are exhausted in the lower circles, there is no assurance but that its ravages will be continued in the upper; for, once set in motion, it will continue to move till a succession of victims fall. Our principles are few, and founded on the basis of our constitution, which were purchased with the dearest blood of our ancestors, and which we swear to transmit to posterity unsullied, or perish in the attempt; – equality of rights (not of property) is the object for which we contend; and which we consider as the only security for our liberties and lives. Let us shew to the world that we are not that lawless sanguinary rabble, which our oppressors would persuade the higher circles we are, but a brave and generous people, determined to be free. Liberty or death is our motto; and we have sworn to return home in triumph, or return no more! Soldiers! shall you, countrymen, bound by the sacred obligation of an oath to defend your country and your King from enemies, whether foreign or domestic, plunge your bayonets into the bosoms of fathers and brothers, and at once sacrifice, at the shrine of military despotism, to the unrelenting orders of a cruel faction, those feelings which you hold in common with the rest of mankind? Soldiers! turn your eyes toward Spain, and there behold the happy effects resulting from the union of soldiers and citizens. Look to that quarter, and there behold the yoke of hated despotism broken by the unanimous wish of the people and the soldiery, happily accomplished without bloodshed – and shall you who taught those soldiers to fight the battles of liberty refuse to fight those or your own country? Forbid it, Heaven! Come forward then at once, and free your country and your king from the power of those that have held them too, too long in thraldom. Friends and countrymen, the eventful period has now arrived where the services of all will be required for the forwarding of an object so universally wished, and so absolutely necessary. Come forward then, and assist those who have begun in the completion of so arduous a task, and support the laudable efforts which we are about to make, to replace to Britons those rights consecrated to them by Magna Carta and the Bill of Rights, and sweep from our shores that corruption which has degraded us below the dignity of man. Owing to the misrepresentations which have gone abroad with regard to our intentions, we think it indispensibly necessary to declare inviolable all public and private property; and we hereby call upon all Justices of the Peace, and all others to suppress pillage and plunder of every description; and to endeavour to secure those guilty of such offences, that they may receive that punishment which such violation of justice demands. In the present state of affairs, and during the continuation of so momentous a struggle, we earnestly request of all to desist from their labour, from and after this day, the first of April, and attend wholly to the recovery of their rights, and consider it as the duty of every man, not to recommence until he is in the possession of those rights which distinguish the freeman from the slave; viz. that of giving consent to the laws by which he is to be governed. We, therefore, recommend to the proprietors of public works, and all others to stop the one, and shut up the other, until order is restored, as we will be accountable for no damages which may be sustained, and which, after this public intimation, they can have no claim to. And we hereby give notice to all those who shall be found carrying arms against those who intend to regenerate their country, and restore its inhabitants to their native dignity, we shall consider them as traitors to their country, and enemies to their king, and treat them as such. By order of the committee of organisation for forming a provisional government . . . Britons! God, Justice, the wishes of all good men, are with us; join together, and make it one cause, and the nations of the earth shall hail the day when the standard of liberty shall be raised on its native soil.

Richard Oastler, Letter to the
Leeds Mercury on Slavery (16 October 1830)[2]

Child labour was an accepted fact in nineteenth-century England,
but reformers whose attentions had concentrated on injustice outside
the country began to challenge inequity at home. The abolitionist
Richard Oastler (1789–1861) wrote this letter to the Leeds Mercury
after being told about conditions in the textile mills of Bradford. The
resulting campaign for 'factory reform' achieved some success after
three years, when an Act was finally passed in 1833, limiting the
working hours of underage workers. The 'Althorp Act' stipulated a
maximum twelve-hour day for those aged thirteen to eighteen, and
eight hours for those under thirteen years.

'It is the pride of Britain that a slave cannot exist on her soil;
and if I read the genius of her constitution aright, I find that
slavery is most abhorrent to it – that the air which Britons
breathe is free – the ground on which they tread is sacred to
liberty.' *Rev. R. W. Hamilton's Speech at the Meeting held in the*
Cloth-hall Yard, 22 September 1830.

Gentlemen, – No heart responded with truer accents to the
sounds of liberty which were heard in the Leeds Cloth-hall Yard,
on the 22d instant, than did mine, and from none could more
sincere and earnest prayers arise to the throne of Heaven, that
hereafter slavery might only be known to Britain in the pages
of her history. One shade alone obscured my pleasure, arising
not from any difference in principle, but from the want of application of the general principle *to the whole empire*. The pious and
able champions of *negro* liberty and *colonial* rights should, if I
mistake not, have gone farther than they did; or perhaps, to
speak more correctly, before they had travelled so far as the West
Indies, should, at least for a few moments, have sojourned in

our own immediate neighbourhood, and have directed the attention of the meeting to scenes of misery, acts of oppression, and victims of slavery, even on the threshold of our homes.

Let truth speak out, appalling as the statement may appear. The fact is true. Thousands of our fellow-creatures and fellow-subjects, both male and female, the miserable inhabitants of a *Yorkshire town* (Yorkshire now represented in Parliament by the giant of anti-slavery principles) are this very moment existing in a state of slavery, *more horrid* than are the victims of that hellish system '*colonial slavery*'. These innocent creatures draw out, unpitied, their short but miserable existence, in a place famed for its profession of religious zeal, whose inhabitants are ever foremost in *professing* 'temperance' and 'reformation', and are striving to outrun their neighbours in missionary exertions, and would fain send the Bible to the farthest corner of the globe – aye, in the very place where the anti-slavery fever rages most furiously, her *apparent charity* is not more admired on earth, than her *real cruelty* is abhorred in Heaven. The very streets which receive the droppings of an 'Anti-Slavery Society' are every morning wet by the tears of innocent victims at the accursed shrine of avarice, who are *compelled* not by the cart-whip of the negro slave-driver but by the dread of the equally appalling thong or strap of the over-looker, to hasten, half-dressed, *but not half-fed*, to those magazines of British infantile slavery – *the worsted mills in the town and neighbourhood of Bradford!!!*

Would that I had Brougham's eloquence, that I might rouse the hearts of the nation, and make every Briton swear, 'These innocents shall be free!'

Thousands of little children, both male and female, *but principally female*, from seven to fourteen years of age, are daily *compelled* to *labour* from six o'clock in the morning to seven in the evening, with only – Britons, blush while you read it! – *with only thirty minutes allowed for eating and recreation*. Poor infants! ye are indeed sacrificed at the shrine of avarice, *without even the solace of the negro slave*; ye are no more than he is, *free agents*; ye are compelled to work as long as the *necessity* of your needy parents may require, or the cold-blooded avarice of your worse than barbarian masters *may demand*! Ye live in the boasted land of freedom, and *feel* and mourn that *ye are slaves*, and slaves without the only comfort which the negro has. He knows it is his sordid, mercenary master's interest that he should *live*, be *strong* and *healthy*. *Not so with you*. Ye are doomed to labour from morning to night for one who cares not how soon your weak and tender frames are stretched to breaking! You are not mercifully valued at so much per head; this would assure you at least (even with the worst and most cruel masters) of the mercy shown to their own labouring beasts. No, no! your soft and delicate limbs are tired and fagged, and jaded, at only *so much per week*, and when your joints can act no longer, your emaciated frames are cast aside, the boards on which you lately toiled and wasted life away, are instantly supplied with other victims, who in this boasted land of liberty are hired – not sold – as slaves and daily forced to *hear* that they are free. Oh, Duncombe! Thou hatest slavery – I know thou dost resolve that 'Yorkshire children shall no more be slaves!' And Morpeth! who justly glorieth in the Christian faith – Oh, Morpeth! listen to the cries and count the tears of these poor babes, and let St Stephen's hear thee swear 'they shall no longer groan in slavery!' And Bethell, too! who swears eternal hatred to the name of slave, whene'er thy manly voice is heard in Britain's senate, assert the rights and liberty of Yorkshire youths. And Brougham! thou who are the chosen champion of liberty in every clime! oh bend thy giant's mind, and listen to the sorrowing accents of these poor Yorkshire little ones, and note their tears; then let thy voice rehearse their woes, and touch the chord thou only holdest – the chord that sounds above the silvery notes in praise of heavenly liberty, and down descending at thy will, groans in the horrid caverns of the deep in muttering

sounds of misery accursed to hellish bondage; and as thou sound'st
these notes, let Yorkshire hear thee swear, 'Her *children* shall be
free!'

George Loveless (August 1837)[3]

*George Loveless (1797–1874) was a Dorset ploughman and Methodist
lay preacher who formed a Friendly Society of Agricultural Labourers
in Tolpuddle in October 1833. Although the Combination Acts
outlawing trade unions had been repealed, landowners had Loveless
and his five fellow 'martyrs' prosecuted on the obscure grounds that
their Society had administered an illegal oath. They were sentenced
to seven years' transportation in Australia. A great public outcry led
to their pardon after two years, and Loveless returned to England in
1837. He wrote the pamphlet* The Victims of Whiggery *on his return
from transportation to support the relief and resettlement of the
returned convicts and their families. In 1846, he and his family
emigrated to Canada.*

I am told that the working man ought to remain still and let their
cause work its way – that God in his good time will bring it about
for him. However, this is not my creed; I believe that God works
by means and men, and that he expects every man who feels an
interest in the subject to take an active part in bringing about and
hastening on so important a period. Under such an impression, I
would call upon every working man in England, and especially the
agricultural labourers, who appear to be the lowest, degraded, and
the least active, to shake off that supineness and indifference to
their interests, which leaves them in the situation of slaves. Let
every working man come forward, from east to west, from north
to south; unite firmly but peaceably together as the heart of one

man; let them be determined to have a voice in, and form part of, the British nation; then no longer would the interests of the millions be sacrificed for the gain of a few, but the blessings resulting from such a change would be felt by us, our prosperity, even to generations yet unborn.

Arise, men of Britain and take your stand! Rally round the standard of Liberty, or forever lie prostrate under the iron hand of your land and money-mongering taskmasters!

Patience Kershaw, Testimony Before the Children's Employment Commission (1842)[4]

The limited achievements of the Althorp Act meant that children were still widely exploited. In 1842 the Children's Employment Commission heard the testimony of child workers in mines, and an Act of Parliament further limiting working hours followed. The Mines and Collieries Act also outlawed the employment of women and girls in mines. In 1870 it became compulsory for all children aged between five and thirteen to go to school. Patience Kershaw was a seventeen-year-old 'hurrier', employed to drag coal to to the surface. The board observed of her, 'This girl is an ignorant, filthy, ragged, and deplorable-looking object, and such an one as the uncivilised natives of the prairies would be shocked to look upon.' Her testimony inspired a song by Frank Higgins, in 1969 (see p. 340).

My father has been dead about a year; my mother is living and has ten children, five lads and five lasses; the oldest is about thirty, the youngest is four; three lasses go to mill; all the lads are colliers, two getters and three hurriers; one lives at home and does nothing; mother does nought but look after home.

All my sisters have been hurriers, but three went to the mill. Alice went because her legs swelled from hurrying in cold water when she was hot. I never went to day-school; I go to Sunday-school, but I cannot read or write; I go to pit at five o'clock in the morning and come out at five in the evening; I get my breakfast of porridge and milk first; I take my dinner with me, a cake, and eat it as I go; I do not stop or rest any time for the purpose; I get nothing else until I get home, and then have potatoes and meat, not every day meat. I hurry in the clothes I have now got on, trousers and ragged jacket; the bald place upon my head is made by thrusting the corves; my legs have never swelled, but sisters' did when they went to mill; I hurry the corves a mile and more under ground and back; they weigh 300 cwt.; I hurry eleven a-day; I wear a belt and chain at the workings, to get the corves out; the getters that I work for are naked except their caps; they pull off all their clothes; I see them at work when I go up; sometimes they beat me, if I am not quick enough, with their hands; they strike me upon my back; the boys take liberties with me; sometimes they pull me about; I am the only girl in the pit; there are about twenty boys and fifteen men; all the men are naked; I would rather work in mill than in coal-pit.

——————

Thomas Kerr, 'Aw's Glad the Strike's Duin' (1880)[5]

Thomas and George Allan, the folksong collectors who printed this song in an anthology, introduced its author as follows: 'Thomas Kerr, who was born in the Black Gate, under the shadow of the Old Castle, may justly claim to be a native of the old town . . . Leaving Newcastle, Mr Kerr settled in Blyth, where, his literary inclinations leading him to press work, he acted occasionally as reporter for the Blyth Weekly News. *To the* News *for some seven years he contributed the local letters of 'An Awd Trimmer' and during that time, in the letter, hundreds of songs appeared, most of them of a fugitive character, but some, taking the popular taste, became favourites and are still sung.'*

'Oh, aw's glad the strike's duin,' shooted lang Geordy Reed,
Ti the groop thit wis stanning iroond,
'Fur the care an' anxiety's ni' turned me heed,
An' am getting is thin is a hoond;
Fur ye knaw me an' Jenny had promist te wed
When the money te start hoose wis won,
But the unlucky stop cawsed wor sports te drop,
So aw's glad, very glad, the strike's duin.'

'Oh, aw's glad the strike's duin,' said a hawf-grown lad,
'Fur wor brass it wis getting' se short,
An' the boolin' an' runnin' wis gan te the bad,
An' we'd ni' sen a finish te sport.
Noo te Newcassel Races, se merry an' blate,
We'll yet start like shot iv a gun,
An' it's nyen ower late te back one fur the 'Plate',
So aw's glad, very glad the strike's duin.'

'Oh, aw's glad the strike's duin, for the sake o' my wife.'
Said a brave little man in the crood,
'Fur the pinchin' an' plannin' an sorrow an' strife
Neerly had her, poor lass, in her shrood.
Noo wor canny bit bairns ill luik tidy an' trim,
When te chapel on Sundays thor tuin;
An' hoo thenkful,' said he, 'iverybody shud be
That the unlucky strike is noo duin.'

'Oh, aw's glad the strike's duin,' cried oot shopkeeper Jack,
An' hes words they exprest awl he said,
Fur he's fyece wor a smile, an' hes lips gov a smack,
Is he tawkt o' 'the prospects o' trade'.
Hoo the business wid thrive is it yence did before,
An' the wheels iv prosprity run;
'Ay, an' awl get me whack,' said shopkeeper Jack,
'So aw's glad, very glad, the strike's duin.'

Then the crood awl agreed, wi' a nod o' the heed,
They war pleased the bad job wis put strite,
An' a wummin or two, is the crood they passed through,
Gae full vent te thor happy delite;
While the bairns in the street, wi' thor voices se sweet,
In the hite o' thor glory an' fun,
Shooted 'Hip, hip, horray!! it's settled the day,
An' wor glad, very glad, the strike's duin.'

William Morris, 'The Depression of Trade' (12 July 1885)[6] and 'Socialism: The Ends and the Means' (27 September 1886)[7]

The designer and socialist leader William Morris (1834–96) delivered his speech on 'The Depression of Trade' in Manchester and London to a new group, the Socialist League, who believed that Parliament was too corrupt to make any real improvement to the lives of ordinary working people. In 'Socialism, the Ends of the Means', a speech given in Manchester, Norwich and London, he set out his vision of an alternative, more democratic society.

The Depression of Trade

What is the essence of the society which took the place of feudalism: free competition – that is in other words a desperate war in which every man fights for his own hand; the aim of the struggle being to live free from labour at the expense of those that labour. This struggle results necessarily in the formation of two great classes, the successful and the unsuccessful, which in spite of minor divisions among them, have now taken the place of all the elaborate castes of feudality: the struggle therefore proposed for everyone born into the world of civilisation is the getting, or the keeping of a place in the class which lives on the labour of others.

In all codes of morals it is thought wrong to take away from an unwilling fellow-man the means of subsistence or enjoyment; this is commonly called stealing; and when practised by an individual in an unorganised manner if we catch him we think ourselves justified in torturing him in various ways in order to frighten others off from the like courses: for we call him a thief and his unorganised interference with other people's livelihood and pleasure we call stealing: nevertheless there is no man in any of the creeds so pious, there is none in any of the philosophies of such rigid morality that he does not with the approbation of all men do his very best to raise (as we call it) himself or at least his children into the class of . . . those who by force or fraud take away from their unwilling fellows the means of livelihood or pleasure: . . . only the commonness and the organisation of it . . . prevents this class from being called the class of thieves; so you see in spite of all our religion and all our morality we consider it a sacred duty to put those whom we love best, ourselves and our children into the position of thieves.

To put the matter shortly I should say of modern society that its aim is robbery and its instrument is war . . . and I must see to it myself and try to amend the state of things, or brand myself as a helpless slave.

In short what I want you to understand is that it is not as some people think, and as some people who know better say, that Socialists envy rich men because they are rich and live in enjoyment: if a man could be rich and do no harm with his riches it wouldn't matter: nay even if he had stolen his riches once for all we could put up with it and pass him by with no more active feeling than contempt: but unhappily riches always do . . . harm because they go on stealing day by day: riches on one side imply poverty on the other: the rich man has taken from the poor, and daily takes from him in order to be rich; what he gains we lose: therefore he is our enemy and cannot help being so in spite of any personal good will he has towards us or some of us; nor while the present system lasts can we relieve him of his false position: the rich man like the King never dies; another takes his place at once, and we can only change the tyrant and not the tyranny as long as the system of capital and wages lasts: it is the class, understand, that is our enemy and not the individual; although most unhappily these class divisions do create and cannot help creating vices in the individuals composing them which we cannot help noticing.

The monopolists who now live on the labour of the rest of mankind could never have sustained their position by their own mere force: Divide to Govern has been their rule: they have always by means of the instinctive cunning of an organism resisting destruction pitted one section of the workers against another, and so have held on precariously, depending always on the continued ignorance of those that they ruled over.

But the time for the end of this ignorance is drawing near: the workers have seen the wonderful effects of combination in increasing the productivity of labour, it remains for them only to shake off a few superstitions about the necessity of their retaining masters of a higher class of beings than themselves, and then they, the workers, will stand out as what they are – society itself – the old masters of society will also be recognised as what they are, mere useless hangers-on and clogs to life and the progress of humanity.

Socialism: The Ends and the Means

It is the custom of very practical people to taunt those whose end is or seems to be a long way off with being idealists: nevertheless I venture to think that without these idealists practical people would be in a much worse plight than they now are; they would have but a dull history of the past, a poor life in the present, and no hope for the future.

The wealth was made by all and should be used for the benefit of all; but we in our fear have forgotten what is meant by all. In this respect we have not gained but lost on the system we supplanted, the Feudal system of the Middle Ages: men did then feel themselves to be members each one of them of the great corporate body, the Church on earth and in Heaven. When we freed ourselves from their superstitions, we were not careful enough of the freedom of all men: the freedom that we claimed and got was the freedom of each to succeed at the expense of other people if only he were stronger and cleverer than they; that is, in other words, the freedom to enslave others . . . To such base courses has our one-sided freedom, our freedom to injure others brought us.

Now what are the conditions of an honest society? Surely to start with that every member of it should have a chance of a happy life, that is of a life which will develop his human faculties to the utmost, a chance which only his own will and not the will of anyone else can take away from him: and in order to have that chance he must be allowed to enjoy the fruits of his own labour.

Let us again then look at the end: it is a Community striving for the happiness of the human race: each man striving for the happiness of the whole and therefore for his own through the whole. Surely such a community would develop the best qualities of man, and make such a world of it as it is difficult to conceive of now: a world in which sordid fear would be unknown and in which permanent injustice defended by authority would not exist, and in which acts of wrong would be but the result of sudden outbursts of passion repented of by the actors, acknowledged as wrongs by all.

In spite of the disappointed hopes of the early part of the century we are forced to hope still because we are forced to move forward: the warnings of the past, the tales of bloodshed and terror and disorder and famine, they are all but tales to us and cannot scare us, because there is no turning back into the desert in which we cannot live, and no standing still on the edge of the enchanted wood; for there is nothing to keep us there, we must plunge in and through it to the promised land beyond.

Annie Besant, 'White Slavery in London' (23 June 1888)[8]

Annie Besant (1847–1933), free-thinker and Fabian socialist, reported in the paper she edited for the Law and Liberty League, the Link, *on the conditions endured by the non-unionised match workers of Bryant & May. As a result the 'matchgirls' (some of whom really were as young as twelve) were sacked and, with Besant's support, campaigned for reinstatement and improvements to their working conditions. After three weeks they succeeded, and also formed the Union of Women Matchworkers to represent them.*

At a meeting of the Fabian Society held on 15 June, the following resolution was moved by H. H. Champion, seconded by Herbert Burrows, and carried after a brief discussion:

'That this meeting, being aware that the shareholders of Bryant and May are receiving a dividend of over 20 per cent., and at the same time are paying their workers only 2d. per gross for making match-boxes, pledges itself not to use or purchase any matches made by this firm.'

In consequence of some statements made in course of the discussion, I resolved to personally investigate their accuracy, and accordingly betook myself to Bromley to interview some of Bryant and May's employees, and thus obtain information at first hand. The following is the outcome of my enquiries:

Bryant and May, now a limited liability company, paid last year a dividend of 23 per cent. to its shareholders; two years ago it paid a dividend of 25 per cent., and the original £5 shares were then quoted for sale at £18 7s. 6d. The highest dividend paid has been 38 per cent.

Let us see how the money is made with which these monstrous dividends are paid . . .

The hour for commencing work is 6.30 in summer and 8 in winter, work concludes at 6 p.m. Half-an-hour is allowed for breakfast and an hour for dinner. This long day of work is performed by young girls, who have to stand the whole of the time. A typical case is that of a girl of 16, a piece-worker; she earns 4s. a week, and lives with a sister, employed by the same firm, who 'earns good money, as much as 8s. or 9s. per week'. Out of the earnings 2s. is paid for the rent of one room; the child lives on only bread-and-butter and tea, alike for breakfast and dinner, but related with dancing eyes that once a month she went to a meal where 'you get coffee, and bread and butter, and jam, and marmalade, and lots of it . . .' The splendid salary of 4s. is subject to deductions in the shape of fines; if the feet are dirty, or the ground under the bench is left untidy, a fine of 3d. is inflicted; for putting 'burnts' – matches that have caught fire during the work – on the bench 1s. has been forfeited, and one unhappy girl was once fined 2s. 6d. for some unknown crime. If a girl leaves four or five matches on her bench when she goes for a fresh 'frame' she is fined 3d., and in some departments a fine of 3d. is inflicted for talking. If a girl is late she is shut out for 'half the day', that is for the morning six hours, and 5d. is deducted out of her day's 8d. One girl was fined 1s. for letting the web twist around a machine in the endeavour to save her fingers from being cut, and was sharply told to take care of the machine, 'never mind your fingers'. Another, who carried out the instructions and lost a finger thereby, was left unsupported while she was helpless. The wage covers the duty of submitting to an occasional blow from a foreman; one, who appears to be a gentleman of variable temper, 'clouts' them 'when he is mad'.

One department of the work consists in taking matches out of a frame and putting them into boxes; about three frames can be done in an hour, and 1/2*d*. is paid for each frame emptied; only one frame is given out at a time, and the girls have to run downstairs and upstairs each time to fetch the frame, thus much increasing their fatigue. One of the delights of the frame work is the accidental firing of the matches: when this happens the worker loses the work, and if the frame is injured she is fined or 'sacked'. 5*s*. a week had been earned at this by one girl I talked to.

The 'fillers' get 3/4*d*. a gross for filling boxes; at 'boxing,' i.e. wrapping papers round the boxes, they can earn from 4*s*. 6*d*. to 5*s*. a week. A very rapid 'filler' has been known to earn once 'as much as 9*s*.' in a week, and 6*s*. a week 'sometimes'. The making of boxes is not done in the factory; for these 21/4*d*. a gross is paid to people who work in their own homes, and 'find your own paste'. Daywork is a little better paid than piecework, and is done chiefly by married women, who earn as much sometimes as 10*s*. a week, the piecework falling to the girls. Four women day workers, spoken of with reverent awe, earn – 13*s*. a week.

A very bitter memory survives in the factory. Mr Theodore Bryant, to show his admiration of Mr Gladstone and the greatness of his own public spirit, bethought him to erect a statue to that eminent statesman. In order that his workgirls might have the privilege of contributing, he stopped 1*s*. each out of their wages, and further deprived them of half-a-day's work by closing the factory, 'giving them a holiday'. ('We don't want no holidays,' said one of the girls pathetically, for – needless to say – the poorer employees of such a firm lose their wages when a holiday is 'given'.) So furious were the girls at this cruel plundering, that many went to the unveiling of the statue with stones and bricks in their pockets, and I was conscious of a wish that some of those bricks had made an impression on Mr Bryant's conscience. Later on they surrounded the statue – 'We paid for it,' they cried savagely – shouting and yelling, and a gruesome story is told that some cut their arms and let their blood trickle on the marble paid for, in very truth, by their blood.

There seems to be a curious feeling that the nominal wages are 1s. higher than the money paid, but that 1s. a week is still kept back to pay for the statue and for a fountain erected by the same Mr Bryant. This, however, appears to me to be only of the nature of a pious opinion.

Such is a bald account of one form of white slavery as it exists in London. With chattel slaves Mr Bryant could not have made his huge fortune, for he could not have fed, clothed, and housed them for 4s. a week each, and they would have had a definite money value which would have served as a protection. But who cares for the fate of these white wage slaves? Born in slums, driven to work while still children, undersized because underfed, oppressed because helpless, flung aside as soon as worked out, who cares if they die or go on the streets, provided only that the Bryant and May shareholders get their 23 per cent, and Mr Theodore Bryant can erect statues and buy parks? Oh if we had but a people's Dante, to make a special circle in the Inferno for those who live on this misery, and suck wealth out of the starvation of helpless girls.

Failing a poet to hold up their conduct to the execration of posterity, enshrined in deathless verse, let us strive to touch their consciences, i.e. their pockets, and let us at least avoid being 'partakers of their sins', by abstaining from using their commodities.

Samuel Webber Recalls the Matchgirls' Strike
(*c.* 1888)[9]

Samuel Webber was born in Poplar, east London, in 1874, and moved to Birmingham in 1899. In 1971, the folklorist Roy Palmer recorded dozens of songs Webber remembered from his childhood, including this one from the matchgirls' strike.

When they went on strike, they walked up all the way from Bow, right up the Mile End Road, Whitechapel Road, up to Aldgate, Aldgate Pump, and up ... Leadenhall Street ... And as they went up Leadenhall Street they started singing:

> And we'll hang Old Bryant on the sour apple tree
> As we go marching on
> Glory glory Alleluia
> Glory glory Alleluia
> Glory glory Alleluia, and we all go marching on
>
> And we'll hang Old Bryant on the sour apple tree
> And we'll hang Old Bryant on the sour apple tree
> And we'll hang Old Bryant on the sour apple tree, as we go
>   marching on

Now these ladies ... they were shouting at the coppers, coming out of the office windows up above, and then they'd scramble for them, amongst them ... I seen these women fight out in the street like men.

Ben Tillett, The Dock Strike (1911)[10]

The success of the London dockers' strike of 1889 led to the relaunch of Benjamin Tillett's Dockers' Union, which was joined by thousands of workers. Tillett was also the moving force behind the creation of a National Transport Workers Federation. It was the Federation that took the lead in the next great confrontation between dockers and employers, part of what Tillett called in his memoir 'a series of strikes, entirely spontaneous in their origin, occurring in quick succession at most of the principal ports in the kingdom'. This account was published in The Clarion *in August of the year the strike took place.*

It just grew out of despair, the very madness of despair: almost hysterically the human cry of protest broke out. We smothered it for a month, we 'leaders,' we 'dictators' for we had not realised the hot resentment and stubborn determination of the men.

The employers scoffed at our exasperation. We simply told the men what the employers thought of them. The men grew restive, then angry, and then the thought came to them like an inspiration: they would no longer labour. Sulkily, by scores of thousands, they left their work. The work stopped – dead. Milk, ice, eggs, meat, vegetables, fruit, all manner of foods and necessaries lay there, out of the public reach. The stream of London's food supplies was stopped . . .

How often and with what a haughty unctuousness it had been demonstrated to Park Lane, and Change Alley, and Stockwell Park, and the New Cut, and the Mile End Road that Labour was dependent upon Capital; that the iron law of wages was as immutable as the force of gravity, and that the great and gifted captains of Industry could not set it going, but sat supine and sulky, looking exceedingly foolish. Labour had said, 'No.' Labour had put its 'No' into action, and the immutable laws of economics were as futile as the empty barrows, the unfired engines, and the moveless cranes along the blank sides of the deserted docks . . .

'Mob law in London! Police helpless! Government impotent! Demagogues as dictators! Wolf at our doors! Men compelled to leave their honest toil! Sufferings of the poor! Reign of terror! Where are the respectable leaders of Labour? Where is the Cabinet? Where are the troops?' Heaven in its mercy always leaves us the Press in all our afflictions.

But the action of the Press is typical. The Press might scold, and rant and sneer; but the Press wanted paper! What would the world do without its halfpenny oracles? What could the oracles do without paper? What would the advertiser say? The Press swanked and blustered and bluffed; but the Press did not go to the Government, nor to the troops, not to the captains of industry for its paper; it went to the Strike committee of the working men. The Press, being a thing of wind and words, understood that wind and words will not lift and load and carry tons of paper reels: that must be done by hands: common, hard, vulgar hands. So the Press ambled off to Tower Hill, and craved permission of Mob law. It was a lesson: it was a take down. It was, as the Press too well perceived, a portent. The Press swallowed the dose, but did not like it: made the most damnable faces, said rude words about the paid agitator, and the tyrannical Sansculotte, lording it on Tower Hill. But the Press had felt a draught.

A hard world, my masters, but we demagogues manage to live in it; and to live virilely, pugnaciously, agitating, and winning; to the disgusted amazement of hireling slanderers and refined futilities.

But the fight's the thing: the strike.

John Maclean, 'I Am Here as the Accuser' (9 May 1918)[11]

*John Maclean (1879–1923) was a revolutionary socialist in Glasgow,
whose opposition to the First World War, to conscription, and to the
exploitation of Glasgow workers were all seen as a threat to the war
effort. He had served a sentence of three years for offences such as
'appealing to soldiers to lay down their arms' when he was released
on parole. He made this speech after being rearrested, for sedition.
He was sentenced to six years in prison, but released at the end of
the war. Maclean is memorialised in the song 'The John Maclean
March' by Hamish Henderson (see p. 338).*

For the full period of my active life I have been a teacher of economics
to the working classes, and my contention has always been that
capitalism is rotten to its foundations, and must give place to a new
society. I had a lecture, the principal heading of which was 'Thou
shalt not steal; thou shalt not kill', and I pointed out that as a consequence of the robbery that goes on in all civilised countries today,
our respective countries have had to keep armies, and that inevitably
our armies must clash together. On that and on other grounds, I
consider capitalism the most infamous, bloody and evil system that
mankind has ever witnessed. My language is regarded as extravagant
language, but the events of the past four years have proved my
contention.

He [the Lord Advocate] accused me of my motives. My motives are
clean. My motives are genuine. If my motives were not clean and
genuine, would I have made my statements while these shorthand
reporters were present? I am out for the benefit of society, not for
any individual human being, but I realise this, that justice and
freedom can only be obtained when society is placed on a sound
economic basis. That sound economic basis is wanting today, and
hence the bloodshed we are having. I have not tried to get young

men particularly. The young men have come to my meetings as well as the old men. I know quite well that in the reconstruction of society, the class interests of those who are on top will resist the change, and the only factor in society that can make for a clean sweep in society is the working class. Hence the class war. The whole history of society has proved that society moves forward as a consequence of an under-class overcoming the resistance of a class on top of them. So much for that.

I also wish to point out to you this, that when the late King Edward the Seventh died, I took as the subject of one of my lectures 'Edward the Peacemaker'. I pointed out at the time that his 'entente cordiale' with France and his alliance with Russia were for the purpose of encircling Germany as a result of the coming friction between Germany and this country because of commercial rivalry. I then denounced that title 'Edward the Peacemaker' and said that it should be 'Edward the Warmaker'. The events which have ensued prove my contention right up to the hilt, I am only proceeding along the lines upon which I have proceeded for many years. I have pointed out at my economic classes that, owing to the surplus created by the workers, it was necessary to create a market outside this country, because of the inability of the workers to purchase the wealth they create. You must have markets abroad, and in order to have these markets you must have empire. I have also pointed out that the capi-talist development of Germany since the Franco-Prussian War has forced upon that country the necessity for empire as well as this country, and in its search for empire there must be a clash between these two countries. I have been teaching that and what I have taught is coming perfectly true.

I wish no harm to any human being, but I, as one man, am going to exercise my freedom of speech. No human being on the face of the earth, no government is going to take from me my right to speak, my right to protest against wrong, my right to do everything that is for the benefit of mankind. I am not here, then, as the accused; I am here as the accuser of capitalism dripping with blood from head to foot . . .

The country has been exploited by the capitalist in every sphere, to get the toilers to work harder to bring victory. I said at the commencement of the war that while this was being done, and while assurances were being given that at the end of the war the people would get back to normal, I said that circumstances would make such a return impossible. Now I have ample evidence to support that belief; I have used it at my meetings at Weir's of Cathcart – that they were asking the workers to work harder and harder, because there is going to be 'the war after the war', the economic war which brought on this war . . .

I have taken up unconstitutional action at this time because of the abnormal circumstances and because precedent has been given by the British government. I am a socialist, and have been fighting and will fight for an absolute reconstruction of society for the benefit of all. I am proud of my conduct. I have squared my conduct with my intellect, and if everyone had done so this war would not have taken place. I act square and clean for my principles. I have nothing to retract. I have nothing to be ashamed of. Your class position is against my class position. There are two classes of morality. There is the working class morality and there is the capitalist class morality. There is this antagonism as there is the antagonism between Germany and Britain. A victory for Germany is a defeat for Britain; a victory for Britain is a defeat for Germany. And it is exactly the same so far as our classes are concerned. What is moral for the one class is absolutely immoral for the other, and vice-versa. No matter what your accusations against me may be, no matter what reservations you keep at the back of your head, my appeal is to the working class. I appeal exclusively to them because they and they only can bring about the time when the whole world will be in one brotherhood, on a sound economic foundation. That, and that alone, can be the means of bringing about a re-organisation of society. That can only be obtained when the people of the world get the world, and retain the world.

An Ashton Sheet-Metal Worker Recounts the 1926 General Strike (1926)[12]

The notion of a nationwide 'general' strike was at least as old as the 'national holiday' once proposed by the Chartists. In 1926, a general strike became a reality after the Trades Union Congress called their 'front line' members out in sympathy for the mistreatment of miners whose wages were being reduced and conditions worsened. For nine days, more than 1.5 million workers struck. The government was well prepared, and the strike failed in its objectives, but the reversal of roles that took place during that May lived long in many strikers' memories.

Employers of labour were coming, cap in hand, begging for permission to do certain things, or, to be more correct, to allow their workers to return to perform certain customary operations. 'Please can I move a quantity of coal from such and such a place' or 'Please can my transport workers move certain foodstuffs in this or that direction . . .' Most of them turned empty away after a most humiliating experience, for one and all were put through a stern questioning, just to make them realise that we and not they were the salt of the earth.

I thought of the many occasions when I had been turned empty away from the door of some workshop in a weary struggle to get the means to purchase the essentials of life for self and dependents . . . I thought of the many occasions I had been called upon to meet these people in the never-ending struggle to obtain decent conditions for those around me, and its consequent result in my joining the ranks of the unemployed; of the cheap sneers when members of my class had attempted to rouse consciousness as to the real facts of the struggle . . . The only tactic practised by some of them was bullying, and that was no use in a situation such as this; some tried persuasion, referring to us as Mr Chairman and Gentlemen, but only a rigid examination of the stern facts of the case moved our actions. The cap-in-hand position reversed.

———————

Hamish Henderson, 'The John Maclean March' (1948)[13]

Hamish Henderson (1919–2002) wrote this song to commemorate the twenty-fifth anniversary of John Maclean's death in 1923. In November 1948 Henderson chaired a memorial meeting for Maclean (see p. 334) in Glasgow.

Hey, Mac, did ye see him as he cam doon by Gorgie
Awa ower the Lammerlaw an north o the Tay?
Yon man is comin an the haill toun is turnin oot
We're aa shair he'll win back tae Glasgie the day
The jiners an hauders-on are merchin fae Clydebank
Come on nou an hear him he'll be ower thrang tae bide
Turn out Jock an Jimmie, leave yer crans an yer muckle gantries
Great John Maclean's comin back tae the Clyde!

Argyll Street and London Road's the route that we're merchin
The lauds frae the Broomielaw are here, tae a man!
Hey Neil, whaur's yer hauderums, ye big Hielan teuchter

Get yer pipes, mate, an mairch at the heid o the clan
Hullo, Pat Malone, shair A knew ye'd be here, so,
The red an the green, lad, we'll wear side by side
Gorbals is his the day an Glasgie belangs tae him
Nou great John Maclean's comin hame tae the Clyde!

Forward tae Glasgie Green we'll mairch in guid order
Wull grips his banner weel, that boy isnae blate!
Aye, there, man, that's Johnnie nou, that's him there the
    bonnie fechter
Lenin's his feire, lad, and Liebknecht's his mate
Tak tent whan he's speakin, for they'll mind whit he said here
In Glesca, oor city, an the haill warld beside.
Och hey, lad, the scarlet's bonnie, here's tae ye Hielan Shony
Oor John Maclean's has come hame tae the Clyde!

Aweel, nou it's feenisht A'll awa back tae Springburn
Come hame tae yer tea, John, we'll sune hae ye fed
It's hard wark the speakin, och, A'm shair he'll be tired the nicht
A'll sleep on the flair, Mac, an gie John the bed
The haill city's quiet nou, it kens that he's restin
At hame wi' his Glasgie freens, thair fame an thair pride
The red will be worn, ma lads, an Scotlan will mairch again
Nou great John Maclean has come hame tae the Clyde.

Frank Higgins, 'The Testimony of Patience Kershaw' (1969)[14]

Frank Higgins, a folk singer from Liverpool, based this song on Patience Kershaw's evidence (see p. 320).

It's good of you to ask me, Sir, to tell you how I spend my days
Down in a coal black tunnel, Sir, I hurry corves to earn my pay.
The corves are full of coal, kind Sir, I push them with my hands
    and head.
It isn't lady-like, but, Sir, you've got to earn your daily bread.
I push them with my hands and head, and so my hair gets worn
    away.
You see this baldy patch I've got, it shames me like I just
    can't say.
A lady's hands are lily white, but mine are full of cuts and segs.
And since I'm pushing all the time, I've got great big muscles on
    my legs.
I try to be respectable, but, sir, the shame, God save my soul.
I work with naked, sweating men who curse and swear and hew
    the coal.
The sights, the sounds, the smells, kind Sir, not even God could
    know my pain.
I say my prayers, but what's the use? Tomorrow will be just the
    same.
Now, sometimes, Sir, I don't feel well, my stomach's sick, my
    head it aches.
I've got to hurry best I can. My knees are weak, my back near
    breaks
And then I'm slow, and then I'm scared these naked men will
    batter me.
But they're not to blame, for if I'm slow, their families will

starve, you see.

Now all the lads, they laugh at me, and, Sir, the mirror tells me why.

Pale and dirty can't look nice. It doesn't matter how hard I try.

Great big muscles on my legs, a baldy patch upon my head.

A lady, Sir? Oh, no, not me! I should've been a boy instead.

I praise your good intentions, Sir, I love your kind and gentle heart

But now it's 1842, and you and I, we're miles apart.

A hundred years and more will pass before we're standing side by side

But please accept my grateful thanks. God bless you, Sir, at least you tried.

———————————

Bobby Girvan and Christine Mahoney, The Miners' Strike (1984)[15]

The miners' strike of 1984, the 'Great Strike for Jobs', as the miners' leader Arthur Scargill called it, was the bitterest battle between the government and labour of modern times. It began after news that a pit in Cortonwood, South Yorkshire, was to be closed. These recollections are taken from an oral history of the pit villages and the miners' strike compiled in 1986 by Raphael Samuel, Barbara Bloomfield and Guy Boanas. Its title, The Enemy Within, *was taken from the prime minister Margaret Thatcher's notorious description of the miners' union. Bobby Girvan was a striking miner who travelled to Mansfield in Nottinghamshire, where many miners had continued working, for a demonstration. Christine Mahoney was a thirty-nine-year-old wife of a striking miner from Doncaster, and mother of three.*

Bobby Girvan

I think it was 14 May, it was a sunny day and we went down to Mansfield and it was a lovely carnival atmosphere if you like, it was brilliant. The thing that got me, the television cameras were there, there were a few drinks and that and singing and that. Arthur Scargill come on. We were told to get back to the buses pretty early, cos the one driving the bus wanted to go. But the thing about it was that the camera started setting up when half the people had gone and we went walking up the road towards the bus and the bus had gone and we were sitting on a grass verge and then I seen something and I couldn't believe it cos I'd had a few drinks and it was like watching one of these science-fiction movies, like a dark cloud coming over the place. You just saw the police coming out of the streets from every . . . you hadn't seen a policeman all day . . . on horseback, they were just getting anybody. It was pandemonium! And they were getting nearer and nearer to us and I thought, What's going to happen? Some of us went running down the road to see what the trouble was and I went to speak to this copper to see what were happening. One of them got me against the wall, another policeman grabbed him and asked him what were happening, and he says, oh he's all right this lad is. This copper went and stood with some of the women so they wouldn't get hit because they were just going mad. I see policemen get on buses, pulling people off, knocking hell out of them with sticks. As I went down the road I kept ducking and diving out of the way. I see a young schoolgirl coming round the corner with a satchel over her shoulder and a horse went flying by and knocked her flat. I went to pick her up and got kicked on the shoulder as a policeman were running past hitting people. And as I got up near the crowd there was people chucking stones and that. I never felt so frightened or so angry in my life when I seen what I seen. You've got horses, then policemen, then people chucking bricks and from what I could see in the middle of it, three or four, probably six policemen kicking hell out of a youth of probably seventeen or eighteen. He managed to stagger to his feet and his face was covered in blood and that and one of them . . . he got his stick out about a yard long and whacked him across the face with it and the ambulance men was angry and was effing and blinding to the police and they had to put that young lad in an oxygen tank for about twenty minutes before they even moved him and I've never seen a sight like it. And I never thought I would pick up a brick in anger but that day I did. I was totally disgusted with what the police were doing. I'd heard things that they'd do. I'd seen one or two incidents on the picket line but never anything like that.

Christine Mahoney

I've assisted the strike in every way. Collecting, picketing, fund-raising, dinners. I've been on everything that's going, all of it. You're that busy you don't really think about what stands out most. I've been one of about six women who've organised the food in the kitchen, getting it ready, putting it out, then you've got all the washing up and clearing up to do. It's not easy, you're doing more, a hell of a lot more, than before the strike, in fact I don't know what we're going to do when it's all over. It's going to be very quiet compared to what it is now.

When the strike first started I was chief fund-raiser, so I got a raffle going every week. I've seen me be out till eleven o'clock at night, it's been one or two in morning before I got to bed. I got a group of women and we'd do the whole village. As long as I saw money coming in I didn't mind. My daughter does her whack and my eldest son's done his bit, young 'un gives papers out, everyone's involved, the whole family, we're all in this.

Why am I doing it? It's not just for mine, we're all in this together, it's not like you've just got one husband, you look after everybody, and that's how it should be in a village. In a mining village everybody sticks together. I've found it has made a difference to the community in Armthorpe. I can remember when I was little, it was a mining village, then all of a sudden you got your hoity-toitys coming in and it sort of split. Well now everybody's back where they should be, there's no fences in village now. In my view that's some good that's come out of the strike, that's the only thing I'm really pleased about, everybody's back together the way they should be. Now, I've hundreds of friends round here, five of us may share one bag of flour, they're friends, but I've lost all previous so-called friends through strike. I've got no one to thank when this is over. My husband's family, not one's come forward to help, only my own mother, but she's worse off than us, my stepfather's a miner, they're on their own, so they get nothing. But best memory I'll have is way strike's brought everyone together and new friends I've made in the community.

Sacrifices, God, there's more than I can say. No coal for a start, no clothes, no shoes. I've got a whacking great big dog, he's on half food but I won't get rid of him, I've done without. There's been a lot of sacrifices, the kids doing without . . .

In my view, when all this is over, many attitudes will have been changed. I've been on picket lines with the other women and those women are never going to go back to the way they used to be. A lot of the men don't like it, and think a woman's place is in the home, but most of the women who had that old-fashioned attitude have changed now. Also, I think it's going to take a lot of years to get over the experiences we've had with the police. When all's said and done, they've got to live in this village and I don't think it will ever be the same again. My son was arrested a fortnight ago, he's not a miner but he's been helping out, and police came for him. I nearly got taken away with him. My worst memory of the strike will be when they fetched riot squad into village in August.

Sometimes we get fed up with the strike, but we're all in the same boat, we have to help each other out of the depressions. We sit down and talk it over with someone else. It's gone on a long time and it does cause tensions at home. We split up three weeks ago, but only for a few days, we've had twenty-one years and it's not first strike I've had. I mean we've argued before.

It's Christmas in a few days and the kids know it won't be the same. I can only get them one present each, they realise that, but as big as they are it still hurts. Still, we'll have our Christmas when they go back, they know that. They're not bothered, they haven't done bad. We'll have summat on table to eat.

———————

Mark Serwotka, 'Imagine Not Only Marching Together, But Striking Together' (26 March 2011)[16]

The announcement of large-scale cuts in public services by Prime Minister David Cameron and his coalition partner and Deputy Prime Minister Nick Clegg provoked an outcry by the country's biggest unions. Mark Serwotka, general secretary of the Public and Commercial Services Union (PCS), the trade union for British civil servants, made this speech to Jobs, Growth, Justice: March and Rally against the Cuts, in Hyde Park.

What a fantastic turnout. Now, let me start with a story. Before Christmas, I went with the leaders of the TUC to meet the government. Do you want to know something amazing about the government? Everyone on their side of the table was a multi-millionaire.

And these multi-millionaires, they tell us we're all in it together. But they don't use our services and they don't use all the things we care about in our community.

And let me tell you another thing, they have no mandate whatsoever for these cuts.

Nick Clegg – let's be straight talking – Nick Clegg lied to the people of Britain before the election. Now, my mother told me when I was young, when you lie you should be in the naughty corner. So let's send him off to the naughty corner.

Now listen. Let's be clear about this demonstration and something my union feels passionately about. And let the journalists and the media hear it loud and proud. We must oppose every single cut in public spending. No cuts. No cuts whatsoever.

And why do we oppose every cut? Because if we don't we will have to choose between young people and pensioners; between public sector and private sector; between those on welfare and those in work. We should defend every student, every pensioner and every worker wherever they are.

So, let's also be clear about two things to finish. There is an alternative to the cuts, and I'll tell you what the alternative is. Let's collect the tax that is avoided by the rich people in this country.

And while we're at it, while we're at it, let's start naming the scroungers. Sir Philip Green from Top Shop – what a scrounger he is. In one body swerve he avoided paying a quarter of a billion pounds in tax by investing it in Monaco. What an absolute scrounger and a disgrace.

But do you know what? What the government said is, 'We think you're good, Sir Philip, so we're bringing you in as an adviser to tell us how to make the cuts.' What shameful behaviour.

But let me finish on this last point. We know there's an alternative; we know how brutal this country will become if they make their cuts; so we've got to be prepared to stop it.

Now look around you in this park. Imagine what it would be if we didn't only march together, we took strike action together across all of our public services.

And let's be clear, whether you work in health, in schools, in the civil service, in private industry, wherever you work. We are stronger when we march together, so let's ensure that we strike together to let the government know we won't accept it.

So, just in case they are listening. If you want to take action together, make some noise . . . Right. If you want Sir Philip Green and the other scroungers to pay their tax, make some more noise . . .

And my last point is, if you want a society where we unite black and white, unemployed and workers, students and pensioners, public and private sector – proud of each other, proud to be diverse, make the biggest roar of all and stop the cuts.

———————————

1890–1945

EQUAL RIGHTS

The great achievements of the nineteenth century in expanding the vote and protecting workers' rights still left many sections of society excluded. The Irish writer Oscar Wilde decried the limits of charity in addressing such problems, instead calling for deeper changes to the social structure that could end poverty and other ills. The campaign to overturn the exclusion of women from the franchise spearheaded by Emmeline, Sylvia and Christabel Pankhurst was only delayed by the First World War. Domestic fascists sought to scapegoat Jews and immigrants for social problems and stirred up violence against these groups. But, as the Battle of Cable Street in 1936 demonstrated, people did not take such threats passively. George Orwell, witnessing the brutality of the British empire in Burma, expressed his opposition to capital punishment, which he felt diminished all of our humanity. After the Second World War, the introduction of the welfare state promised a new social settlement. But one of the architects of that reform, Aneurin Bevan, who as Minister for Health oversaw the introduction of the National Health Service, explained that the weight of established power and tradition was hard to shake off.

Oscar Wilde, 'The Soul of Man Under Socialism' (February 1891)[1]

The expansion of the right to vote and the growth of the trade-union movement had done little to solve the problems of the poorest in society. In this essay Oscar Wilde (1854–1900) wanted to show how socialism was not only a political or economic solution to inequality, but a moral and spiritual one. In attacking the effects of philanthropy, Wilde also called into question the whole basis on which Victorian social attitudes rested, that by fulfilling a 'duty' to alleviate the sufferings of the poor, the rich ensured their entitlement to their position in society.

The chief advantage that would result from the establishment of Socialism is, undoubtedly, the fact that Socialism would relieve us from that sordid necessity of living for others which, in the present condition of things, presses so hardly upon almost everybody. In fact, scarcely any one at all escapes.

Now and then, in the course of the century, a great man of science, like Darwin; a great poet, like Keats; a fine critical spirit, like M. Renan; a supreme artist, like Flaubert, has been able to isolate himself, to keep himself out of reach of the clamorous claims of others, to stand 'under the shelter of the wall', as Plato puts it, and so to realise the perfection of what was in him, to his own incomparable gain, and to the incomparable and lasting gain of the whole world. These, however, are exceptions. The majority of people spoil their lives by an unhealthy and exaggerated altruism – are forced, indeed, so to spoil them.

They find themselves surrounded by hideous poverty, by hideous ugliness, by hideous starvation. It is inevitable that they should be strongly moved by all this. The emotions of man are stirred more quickly than man's intelligence; and, as I pointed out some time ago in an article on the function of criticism, it is much more easy to have sympathy with suffering than it is to have sympathy with thought. Accordingly, with admirable though misdirected intentions, they very seriously and very sentimentally set themselves to the task of remedying the evils that they see. But their remedies do not cure the disease: they merely prolong it. Indeed, their remedies are part of the disease.

They try to solve the problem of poverty, for instance, by keeping the poor alive; or, in the case of a very advanced school, by amusing the poor.

But this is not a solution: it is an aggravation of the difficulty. *The proper aim is to try and reconstruct society on such a basis that poverty will be impossible.* And the altruistic virtues have really prevented the carrying out of this aim. Just as the worst slave-owners were those who were kind to their slaves, and so prevented the horror of the system being realised by those who suffered from it, and understood by those who contemplated it, so, in the present state of things in England, the people who do most harm are the people who try to do most good; and at last we have had the spectacle of men who have really studied the problem and know the life – educated men who live in the East-End – coming forward and imploring the community to restrain its altruistic impulses of charity, benevolence and the like. They do so on the ground that such charity degrades and demoralises. They are perfectly right. Charity creates a multitude of sins.

There is also this to be said. It is immoral to use private property in order to alleviate the horrible evils that result from the institution of private property. It is both immoral and unfair.

Under Socialism all this will, of course, be altered. There will be no people living in fetid dens and fetid rags, and bringing up unhealthy, hunger-pinched children in the midst of impossible and absolutely repulsive surroundings. The security of society will not depend, as it does now, on the state of the weather. If a frost comes

we shall not have a hundred thousand men out of work, tramping
about the streets in a state of disgusting misery, or whining to their
neighbours for alms, or crowding round the doors of loathsome shelters to try and secure a hunch of bread and a night's unclean lodging.
Each member of the society will share in the general prosperity and
happiness of the society, and if a frost comes no one will practically
be anything the worse.

Upon the other hand, *Socialism itself will be of value simply because
it will lead to Individualism.* Socialism, Communism, or whatever one
chooses to call it, by converting private property into public wealth,
and substituting co-operation for competition, will restore society to
its proper condition of a thoroughly healthy organism, and ensure
the material well-being of each member of the community. It will,
in fact, give Life its proper basis and its proper environment. But for
the full development of Life to its highest mode of perfection something more is needed. What is needed is Individualism. If the
Socialism is Authoritarian; if there are Governments armed with
economic power as they are now with political power; if, in a word,
we are to have Industrial Tyrannies, then the last state of man will
be worse than the first. At present, in consequence of the existence
of private property, a great many people are enabled to develop a
certain very limited amount of Individualism. They are either under
no necessity to work for their living, or are enabled to choose the
sphere of activity that is really congenial to them and gives them
pleasure. These are the poets, the philosophers, the men of science,
the men of culture – in a word, the real men, the men who have
realised themselves, and in whom all Humanity gains a partial realisation. Upon the other hand, there are a great many people who,
having no private property of their own, and being always on the
brink of sheer starvation, are compelled to do the work of beasts of
burden, to do work that is quite uncongenial to them, and to which
they are forced by the peremptory, unreasonable, degrading Tyranny
of want. These are the poor, and amongst them there is no grace of

manner, or charm of speech, or civilisation, or culture, or refinement
in pleasures, or joy of life. From their collective force Humanity gains
much in material prosperity. But it is only the material result that it
gains, and the man who is poor is in himself absolutely of no importance. He is merely the infinitesimal atom of a force that, so far from
regarding him, crushes him: indeed, prefers him crushed, as in that
case he is far more obedient.

Of course, it might be said that the Individualism generated under
conditions of private property is not always, or even as a rule, of a
fine or wonderful type, and that the poor, if they have not culture
and charm, have still many virtues. Both these statements would be
quite true. The possession of private property is very often extremely
demoralising, and that is, of course, one of the reasons why Socialism
wants to get rid of the institution. In fact, property is really a nuisance.
Some years ago people went about the country saying that property
has duties. They said it so often and so tediously that, at last, the
Church has begun to say it. One hears it now from every pulpit. It is
perfectly true. Property not merely has duties, but has so many duties
that its possession to any large extent is a bore. It involves endless
claims upon one, endless attention to business, endless bother. If
property had simply pleasures we could stand it; but its duties make
it unbearable. In the interest of the rich we must get rid of it. The
virtues of the poor may be readily admitted, and are much to be
regretted. We are often told that the poor are grateful for charity.
Some of them are, no doubt, *but the best amongst the poor are never
grateful.* They are ungrateful, discontented, disobedient and rebellious. They are quite right to be so. Charity they feel to be a ridicu-
lously inadequate mode of partial restitution, or a sentimental dole,
usually accompanied by some impertinent attempt on the part of the
sentimentalist to tyrannise over their private lives. Why should they
be grateful for the crumbs that fall from the rich man's table? They
should be seated at the board, and are beginning to know it. As for
being discontented, a man who would not be discontented with such

surroundings and such a low mode of life would be a perfect brute. Disobedience, in the eyes of any one who has read history, is man's original Virtue. It is through disobedience that progress has been made, through disobedience and through rebellion. Sometimes the poor are praised for being thrifty. But to recommend thrift to the poor is both grotesque and insulting. It is like advising a man who is starving to eat less. For a town or country labourer to practise thrift would be absolutely immoral. Man should not be ready to show that he can live like a badly fed animal. He should decline to live like that, and should either steal or go on the rates, which is considered by many to be a form of stealing. As for begging, it is safer to beg than to take, but it is finer to take than to beg. No: a poor man who is ungrateful, unthrifty, discontented and rebellious is probably a real personality, and has much in him. He is at any rate a healthy protest. As for the virtuous poor, one can pity them, of course, but one cannot possibly admire them. They have made private terms with the enemy, and sold their birthright for very bad pottage. They must also be extraordinarily stupid. I can quite understand a man accepting laws that protect private property, and admit of its accumulation, as long as he himself is able under those conditions to realise some form of beautiful and intellectual life. But it is almost incredible to me how a man whose life is marred and made hideous by such laws can possibly acquiesce in their continuance.

Emmeline Pankhurst, 'Kill Me Or Give Me My Freedom' (14 July 1913)[2]

The struggle for women's votes was for a long time overshadowed by the concentration of activists on the prospect of 'manhood suffrage'. Emmeline Pankhurst's Women's Social and Political Union

*represented the more radical end of the campaign to secure the vote
for one half of the population. In this speech, delivered in London
in 1913, when she was out on licence from prison after a deteriora-
tion in her health, she explained her views.*

It is a little over three months since I last stood on this platform, on
the eve of an Old Bailey trial. The outcome of that trial was I was sent
to three years' penal servitude, and in little over three months I stand
here again. At that last meeting I tried to make my audience understand the reason why women are rebels. We are rebels, and with greater
justification than my fellow-rebel – Sir Edward Carson. Sir Edward
Carson is a rebel as I am. He told us so in Ireland on Saturday. He is
at liberty while I am a felon, and yet I and all other women have
justification for rebellion which neither Sir Edward Carson nor any
other man in the so-called United Kingdom has. They have a constitutional means of obtaining redress for their grievances. Women have
no such means. I say we are rebels because there is no other way open
to us of obtaining redress for the grievances, the grave grievances
which women have . . .

You know there is something worse than apparent failure, and that
is to allow yourself to desist from doing something which you are
convinced in your conscience is right, and I know that women, once
convinced that they are doing what is right, that their rebellion is
just, will go on, no matter what the difficulties, no matter what the
dangers, so long as there is a woman alive to hold up the flag of rebellion. I would rather be a rebel than a slave. I would rather die than
submit; and that is the spirit that animates this movement. Well, we
are not going to die, at any rate the movement is not going to die,
and that is all that matters . . .

[W]e shall break laws in order to get our own way. They know
perfectly well that we are breaking the laws because we have had
no voice in making them; because, whether just or unjust, we have
to submit to them; because we are taxed without being represented.

I mean to be a voter in the land that gave me birth or that they shall kill me, and my challenge to the Government is this: kill me or give me my freedom: I shall force you to make that choice.

———————————

George Orwell, 'A Hanging' (1931)[3]

Capital punishment was an accepted part of the criminal justice system across the British Empire for hundreds of years. George Orwell, who was born in India and served as an imperial policeman in Burma during the 1920s, was unusual in questioning the morality of execution. Capital punishment was abolished in the UK in 1965.

It was about forty yards to the gallows. I watched the bare brown back of the prisoner marching in front of me. He walked clumsily with his bound arms, but quite steadily, with that bobbing gait of the Indian who never straightens his knees. At each step his muscles slid neatly into place, the lock of hair on his scalp danced up and down, his feet printed themselves on the wet gravel. And once, in spite of the men who gripped him by each shoulder, he stepped slightly aside to avoid a puddle on the path.

It is curious, but till that moment I had never realised what it means to destroy a healthy, conscious man. When I saw the prisoner step aside to avoid the puddle, I saw the mystery, the unspeakable wrongness, of cutting a life short when it is in full tide. This man was not dying, he was alive just as we were alive. All the organs of his body were working – bowels digesting food, skin renewing itself, nails growing, tissues forming – all toiling away in solemn foolery. His nails would still be growing when he stood on the drop, when he was falling through the air with a tenth of a second to live. His eyes saw the yellow gravel and the grey walls, and his brain still remembered, foresaw, reasoned – reasoned even about puddles. He and we were a party of men walking together, seeing, hearing, feeling, understanding the same world; and in two minutes, with a sudden snap, one of us would be gone – one mind less, one world less.

Voices from the Battle of Cable Street (4 October 1936)[4]

Oswald Mosley, leader of the British Union of Fascists (BUF), attempted in 1936 to lead a march of his followers into an area of east London with a large Jewish population. A group of around three thousand East Enders gathered to resist the march, and prevent it going through their neighbourhood. Despite the protection of the police, the Fascists were driven back around Cable Street in Wapping and forced to abandon their planned march.

William J. Fishman, Stepney Labour activist, aged 16

On 4 October 1936, an extraordinary political happening took place in the East End of London. The home-grown Fascist leader, Sir Oswald Mosley, had attempted to carry out his threat to lead a great march of his Blackshirt contingent through the Jewish quarter. It was an act of provocation, ostensibly aimed at the dual targets of Fascist attacks: Jews and Communists. Three thousand mobilised at their start line in Royal Mint Street flanked by over double their number of police who were to act as a protective shield. But they never set out. By late afternoon the Fascist 'army' was forced to turn about and march off in the opposite direction, through the deserted city, along the Embankment where, in the absence of an audience, they quickly dispersed. That night there was dancing in the pubs and in the side streets of the East End. And thus a legend was born.

Phil Piratin, Secretary of the Communist Party

East London was the centre of Mosley's activity. Branches were opened up at Bethnal Green, Shoreditch, Hackney and elsewhere. Full-time organisers, well-provided premises, all of these were paid for. The appeal was made to the worst elements and the basest sentiments. Jews were 'taking away your jobs'. Because of the Jews 'you had no home'. The Jews were the bosses and the landlords. The capitalist Jew exploited you – the Communist Jew was out to take your liberties, freedom and private property! It didn't make sense, but put over with flourish and showmanship it was propaganda calculated to gull the most backward section of the community.

Joe Jacobs, Stepney Communist Party member

In Stepney we heard a rumour that Mosley intended organising a mass march of uniformed Fascists through the heart of the Jewish area. In fact, the *Blackshirt* [a BUF newspaper] carried a notice saying full information about a proposed march and meetings would appear next week. The next week's issue announced a march . . . Before these announcements, the air was full of foreboding. Speculation was mounting. Rumour multiplied. The immediate response was that this could not be allowed to happen and that if it did the outcome would be disastrous . . .

A petition was being signed against Mosley's march all over the East End. Other organisations were organising and calling for opposition to the march. Others were telling people to stay at home and leave it to the police to see that Mosley's hordes behaved. We in the Communist Party were supposed to tell people to go to Trafalgar Square and come back in the evening to protest after Mosley had marched . . . How could they be so blind to what was happening in Stepney? The slogan 'They Shall Not Pass' was already on everyone's lips and being whitewashed on walls and pavements.

Fishman

October 4 opened with a bright autumnal morning, the weather was conducive for both sides to 'do battle'. Then an extraordinary scene took place. From out of the narrow courts, alleyways and main thoroughfares came the steady tramp of marching feet, growing in intensity as the columns were swelled by reinforcements. A forest of banners arose, borne aloft, with the watchwords THEY SHALL NOT PASS emblazoned in a multi-variety of colours, with red predominating. Youngsters clustered at the rear of the marchers chanting 'Mosley shall not pass!' and 'Bar the road to Fascism!' Loudspeaker vans patrolled the streets booming out the message for all to rally to the defence lines at Cable Street and Gardiners Corner. Mass battalions, mobilising spontaneously, from the ranks of many local folk.

Julie Gershon, Stepney resident

We stood at the corner of Leman Street and Whitechapel, and I think Mosley was supposed to come along at about eleven o'clock but thousands of people were there early in the morning. They might have reached the beginning of Cable Street but they didn't get down there. People were throwing things out of their windows, anything to build up the barricades so they couldn't pass. There were Jews and Irish, the lot. Everybody was down there.

Mr Ginsberg, Cable Street resident

People were knocked to the ground and the horses didn't care who they trod on. They tried to push them back. Of course, they went so far and no further. I went to help this chap who the horse had jumped on – his stomach see? He was in terrific pain. I went to help him but the police were saying, 'Get back, get back.' They were going to hit me, I had to go back, I couldn't help the man. But Mosley never got past. It was a heavy atmosphere. Many people were afraid, they stayed in their houses and wouldn't come out. But a lot of us did.

Jacobs

As the police withdrew their main forces and the crowds moved away from the major points of conflict, all the cafés and other public places were full of laughing people swapping stories of their own particular experience of the past few hours. As things turned out, there had been over eighty arrests and many of them had already begun to leave the police stations on bail. I would not like to estimate the number of injured. There were many people bandaged and bloody. The debris left after the fight was everywhere. The streets did not return to normal for some time.

Mrs Beresford, Lascombe's fish-and-chips shopkeeper

After the battle of Cable Street there was a feeling of relief. But there was a fear that it could all come up again. Why he went for the Jewish people I'll never know. They never interfered with anybody. If they started today, who would they go for?

Aneurin Bevan, *In Place of Fear* (1952)[5]

In his part autobiography, part political tract In Place of Fear, *the Labour politician Aneurin Bevan (1897–1960) set out how the challenges for a working-class person entering the august halls of Parliament.*

'The past lies like an Alp upon the human mind.' The House of Commons is a whole range of mountains. If the new Member gets there too late in life he is already trailing a pretty considerable past of his own, making him heavy-footed and cautious. When to this is added the visible penumbra of six centuries of receding legislators, he feels weighted to the ground. Often he never gets to his feet again.

His first impression is that he is in church. The vaulted roofs and stained-glass windows, the rows of statues of great statesmen of the past, the echoing halls, the soft-footed attendants and the whispered conversation, contrast depressingly with the crowded meetings and the clang and clash of hot opinions he has just left behind in his election campaign. Here he is, a tribune of the people, coming to make his voice heard in the seats of power. Instead, it seems he is expected to worship; and the most conservative of all religions – ancestor worship.

The first thing he should bear in mind is that these were not his ancestors. His forebears had no part in the past, the accumulated dust of which now muffles his own footfalls. His forefathers were tending sheep or ploughing the land, or serving the statesmen whose names he sees written on the walls around him, or whose portraits look down upon him in the long corridors. It is not the past of his people that extends in colourful pageantry before his eyes. They were shut out from all this; were forbidden to take part in the dramatic scenes depicted in these frescoes. In him his people are there for the first time, and the history he will make will not be merely an episode in the story he is now reading. It must be wholly different; as different as is the social status which he now brings with him.

To preserve the keen edge of his critical judgment he will find that he must adopt an attitude of scepticism amounting almost to cynicism, for Parliamentary procedure neglects nothing which might soften the acerbities of his class feelings. In one sense the House of Commons is the most unrepresentative of representative assemblies. It is an elaborate conspiracy to prevent the real clash of opinion which exists outside from finding an appropriate echo within its walls. It is a social shock absorber placed between privilege and the pressure of popular discontent.

WAR AND PEACE

———————

'WHAT PEOPLE HAVE YOUR
BATTLES SLAIN?'

There is scarcely a decade in British history without war at home or abroad. Britons are taught about the glories of their military history, but less widely celebrated are the voices that risked disapproval and worse by raising their objections to war.

Anti-war sentiments have tended to come from two camps. The first are the theorists of pacifism, such as the poet Thomas Hoccleve, who tried to prick a prince's conscience about the Hundred Years War. This is the tradition to which the Quakers of George Fox belong, whose pacifist principles Gandhi found 'glorious'. The second group who have spoken up against war are those who have seen action. From the First World War, which put so many Britons into uniform, emerged the first distinctive school of anti-war soldier poets, including Wilfred Owen and Siegfried Sassoon.

The atomic age changed the threat of war into the threat of annihilation. When Britain acquired its own nuclear capability in the 1950s, the Campaign for Nuclear Disarmament was set up in response. Britain's alliance with the United States also produced protests, from the anti-Vietnam war marchers of 1968 to the Greenham Common camp of the 1980s. In the past decade, Britain's decision to follow the US into war in Iraq sparked a protest that produced the biggest political demonstration in British history, with up to a million people marching against the war in London.

Thomas Hoccleve, 'An Appeal for Peace with France' (1412)[1]

These lines come from a long poem addressed to the future Henry V by the London poet and clerk Thomas Hoccleve (c. 1368–1426). Three years later, Henry led an invasion of France that reopened the Hundred Years War and resulted in the bloody siege of Harfleur and victory at Agincourt. Hoccleve's words, framed as a pacifist plea, turned out to be prophetic.

Allas! what peple hathe your werre slayne!
What cornes wastede, and doune trode and shent!
How many a wyfe and maide hathe be forlayne,
Castels doune bete, and tymbred houses brent
And drawen doune, and alle tortore and rent!
The harme ne may not rekened be ne tolde;
This werre wexethe alle to hore and olde . . .

Whan ye have stryven and foughten alle your fille,
Pees folwe mote; but goode were it or than
That pees were hade; what luste have ye to spille
The bloode that Crist with his bloode bought, whan
He on the crosse starfe? O lady seint Anne,
Thy doughter pray to besech hir sone
To stynte of werres the dampnable wone.

The booke of revelacions of Bride
Expressethe how Crist thus seide hir unto,
'I am pees verray, there I wole abide

Where as pees is, none other wole I do.
Of Fraunce and Engelonde the kynges two,
If they wole have pees, pees perpetuelle
They shulle have;' thus hir booke seithe wote I welle . . .

Now, pees, approche, and drive out werre and strife;
Frenship appere, and bannysshe thou hate;
Tranquillitee, thou reve ire hir lyfe,
That fervent is and leef to debate;
Ye thre virtues, now lete see abate
The malice of the foule vices thre,
That verray foes ben to alle cristentee.

O CRISTEN princes, for the love and awe
Of hym that is kyng of kynges alle,
Softethe your hertes, and to pees you drawe;
Considerethe what goode may thereof falle.
The hony takethe, anf levethe the galle;
The steerne jugge in his juggement
May do not right for his punysshement.

What disobeisance and rebellioun,
What wille unbuxome, what unkyndenesse,
May he preeve in you that distruccioun
Done of men, his hondwerk sothely, I gesse,
It mote need stire his rightwisnesse
Agein you, styntethe at his reverence,
Suethe his grace and his benevolence.

Handbill from the Weavers of Royton (May 1808)[2]

This handbill, issued after Parliament rejected a Bill to guarantee the weavers a minimum wage, shows its authors linked the cause of their economic hardship to the war against Napoleon's France.

At a Meeting of the Weavers and other Inhabitants of the Township of ROYTON, it was agreed to submit the following Statement of our Sufferings, and the Cause thereof, to our Fellow Countrymen:

As we have been called upon to take part with you in your present proceedings, we the said Inhabitants feel it our indispensable duty to address you at this important crisis, upon the subject of our mutual distress; a subject that demands the most serious attention of every one of us, and upon which depends our happiness or misery. While we lament the general distress; we beg leave to suggest that it is our opinion your proceedings are not likely to obtain you relief; for that distress can only be removed, by removing the cause; – which cause we have no hesitation in pronouncing is the WAR: – to prove which we need only refer to our dependence upon Commerce, and how it is obstructed by the War; – and it is our humble opinion that it is impossible for either the Legislature or commercial characters to remedy the evil by any other means than that of the restoration of Peace.

Fellow Countrymen, – We have been misrepresented and treated as enemies to our King and Country; but we can safely say, that our only wish has invariably been, a termination of the contest in which we are unfortunately engaged; and are now convinced, that it is an object equally the wish of the major part of the Country; and which we believe has been withheld from us by those whose Counsels have too long prevailed in this Country. Yet notwithstanding, we are ready at all times to

forward, in any constitutional manner, that which is likely to
be productive of the good we all aim at. But will never lend our
aid to any illegal measure; therefore, by your permission, we
will advise you to desist from your present proceedings – return
to your families and respective employments; as the neglect so
to do, will, we fear, only tend to your misfortune and distress.

John Bright, Speech Against the Crimean War (23 February 1855)[3]

*The Crimean War (1853–6) was responsible for the deaths of 4,600
soldiers in battle, but of 17,500 from disease, as well as 13,000
wounded. The Committee of Inquiry that examined the government's
conduct of the war was so critical that the remaining senior members
of Lord Aberdeen's administration followed his lead in resigning.
The radical MP John Bright (1811–99), who had opposed the war
almost from the beginning, made this speech in the House of
Commons on the day that four senior ministers, including W. E.
Gladstone, announced their resignation over Crimea.*

I shall not say one word here about the state of the army in the Crimea,
or one word about its numbers or its condition. Every Member of
this House, every inhabitant of this country, has been sufficiently
harrowed with details regarding it. To my solemn belief, thousands
– nay, scores of thousands of persons – have retired to rest, night after
night, whose slumbers have been disturbed or whose dreams have
been based upon the sufferings and agonies of our soldiers in the
Crimea. I should like to ask the noble Lord at the head of the
Government – although I am not sure if he will feel that he can or
ought to answer the question – whether the noble Lord the Member
for London has power, after discussions have commenced, and as

soon as there shall be established good grounds for believing that the negotiations for peace will prove successful, to enter into any armistice?

I know not, Sir, who it is that says, 'No, no,' but I should like to see any man get up and say that the destruction of 200,000 human lives lost on all sides during the course of this unhappy conflict is not a sufficient sacrifice. You are not pretending to conquer territory – you are not pretending to hold fortified or unfortified towns; you have offered terms of peace which, as I understand them, I do not say are not moderate; and breathes there a man in this House or in this country whose appetite for blood is so insatiable that, even when terms of peace have been offered and accepted, he pines for that assault in which of Russian, Turk, French and English, as sure as one man dies, 20,000 corpses will strew the streets of Sebastopol? I say I should like to ask the noble Lord – and I am sure that he will feel, and that this House will feel, that I am speaking in no unfriendly manner towards the Government of which he is at the head – I should like to know, and I venture to hope that it is so, if the noble Lord the Member for London has power, at the earliest stage of these proceedings at Vienna, at which it can properly be done – and I should think that it might properly be done at a very early stage – to adopt a course by which all further waste of human life may be put an end to, and further animosity between three great nations be, as far as possible, prevented?

I appeal to the noble Lord at the head of the Government and to this House; I am not now complaining of the war – I am not now complaining of the terms of peace, nor, indeed, of anything that has been done – but I wish to suggest to this House what, I believe, thousands and tens of thousands of the most educated and of the most Christian portion of the people of this country are feeling upon this subject, although, indeed, in the midst of a certain clamour in the country, they do not give public expression to their feelings. Your country is not in an advantageous state at this moment; from one end of the kingdom to the other there is a general collapse of industry. Those Members of this House not intimately acquainted with the trade and commerce of the country do not fully comprehend our position as to the diminution of employment and the lessening of wages. An increase in the cost of living is finding its way to the homes and hearts of a vast number of the labouring population.

At the same time there is growing up – and, notwithstanding what some honourable Members of this House may think of me, no man regrets it more than I do – a bitter and angry feeling against that class which has for a long period conducted the public affairs of this country. I like political changes when such changes are made as the result, not of passion, but of deliberation and reason. Changes so made are safe, but changes made under the influence of violent exaggeration, or of the violent passions of public meetings, are not changes usually approved by this House or advantageous to the country. I cannot but notice, in speaking to Gentlemen who sit on either side of this House, or in speaking to any one I meet between this House and any of those localities we frequent when this House is up – I cannot, I say, but notice that an uneasy feeling exists as to the news which may arrive by the very next mail from the East. I do not suppose that your troops are to be beaten in actual conflict with the foe, or that they will be driven into the sea; but I am certain that many homes in England in which there now exists a fond hope that the distant one may return – many such homes may be rendered desolate when the next mail shall arrive. The Angel of Death has been abroad throughout the land; you may almost hear the beating of his wings. There is no one, as when the first-born were slain of old, to sprinkle with blood the lintel and the two sideposts of our doors, that he may spare and pass on; he takes his victims from the castle of the noble, the mansion of the wealthy, and the cottage of the poor and the lowly, and it is on behalf of all these classes that I make this solemn appeal.

Bertrand Russell, Letter to the *Nation* (12 August 1914)[4]

Shortly after war had been declared on Germany, the Cambridge philosopher Bertrand Russell (1872–1970) set out his objections. Russell was not a general pacifist: he believed that some wars could be justified. But the war against Germany was, he thought, the result of a misguided foreign policy conducted by a government that did not represent the will of the people. Towards the end of the war, Russell was jailed for suggesting that American troops would be used to break up British strikes. During the Second World War, Russell concentrated on his academic work, but he became a leading figure in the Campaign for Nuclear Disarmament, and at the age of eighty-nine was jailed for a week in 1961 for making an illegal protest.

Against the vast majority of my countrymen, even at this moment, in the name of humanity and civilisation, I protest against our share in the destruction of Germany.

A month ago Europe was a peaceful comity of nations; if an Englishman killed a German, he was hanged. Now, if an Englishman kills a German, or if a German kills an Englishman, he is a patriot, who has deserved well of his country. We scan the newspapers with greedy eyes for news of slaughter, and rejoice when we read of innocent young men, blindly obedient to the word of command, mown down in thousands by the machine-guns of Liège. Those who saw the London crowds, during the nights leading up to the Declaration of War, saw a whole population, hitherto peaceable and humane, precipitated in a few days down the steep slope to primitive barbarism, letting loose, in a moment, the instincts of hatred and blood lust against which the whole fabric of society has been raised. 'Patriots' in all countries acclaim this brutal orgy as a noble determination to vindicate the right; reason and mercy are swept away in one great flood of hatred; dim abstractions of unimaginable wickedness

– Germany to us and the French, Russia to the Germans – conceal the simple fact that the enemy are men, like ourselves, neither better nor worse – men who love their homes and the sunshine, and all the simple pleasures of common lives; men now mad with terror in the thought of their wives, their sisters, their children, exposed, with our help, to the tender mercies of the conquering Cossack.

And all this madness, all this rage, all this flaming death of our civilisation and our hopes, has been brought about because a set of official gentlemen, living luxurious lives, mostly stupid, and all without imagination or heart, have chosen that it should occur rather than that any one of them should suffer some infinitesimal rebuff to his country's pride. No literary tragedy can approach the futile horror of the White Paper. The diplomatists, seeing from the first the inevitable end, mostly wishing to avoid it, yet drifted from hour to hour of the swift crisis, restrained by punctilio from making or accepting the small concessions that might have saved the world, hurried on at last by blind fear to loose the armies for the work of mutual butchery.

And behind the diplomatists, dimly heard in the official documents, stand vast forces of national greed and national hatred – atavistic instincts, harmful to mankind at its present level, but transmitted from savage and half-animal ancestors, concentrated and directed by Governments and the Press, fostered by the upper class as a distraction from social discontent, artificially nourished by the sinister influence of the makers of armaments, encouraged by a whole foul literature of 'glory', and by every text-book of history with which the minds of children are polluted.

England, no more than other nations which participate in this war, can be absolved either as regards its national passions or as regards its diplomacy.

For the past ten years, under the fostering care of the Government and a portion of the Press, a hatred of Germany has been cultivated and a fear of the German Navy. I do not suggest that Germany has been guiltless; I do not deny that the crimes of Germany have been greater than our own. But I do say that whatever defensive measures were necessary should have been taken in a spirit of calm foresight, not in a wholly needless turmoil of panic and suspicion. It is this deliberately created panic and suspicion that produced the public opinion by which our participation in the war has been rendered possible.

Our diplomacy, also, has not been guiltless. Secret arrangements, concealed from Parliament and even (at first) from almost all the Cabinet, created, in spite of reiterated denials, an obligation suddenly revealed when the war fever had reached the point which rendered public opinion tolerant of the discovery that the lives of many, and the livelihood of all, had been pledged by one man's irresponsible decisions. Yet, though France knew our obligations, Sir E[dward] Grey refused, down to the last moment, to inform Germany of the conditions of our neutrality or of our intervention . . .

It thus appears that the neutrality of Belgium, the integrity of France and her colonies, and the naval defence of the northern and western coasts of France, were all mere pretexts. If Germany had agreed to our demands in all these respects, we should still not have promised neutrality.

I cannot resist the conclusion that the Government has failed in its duty to the nation by not revealing long-standing arrangements with the French, until, at the last moment, it made them the basis of an appeal to honour; that it has failed in its duty to Europe by not declaring its attitude at the beginning of the crisis; and that it has failed in its duty to humanity by not informing Germany of conditions which would ensure its non-participation in a war which, whatever its outcome, must cause untold hardship and the loss of many thousands of our bravest and noblest citizens.

Siegfried Sassoon, Declaration Against War
(July 1917)[5]

Of those who protested against the First World War, perhaps the most prominent was the poet and officer in the Royal Welch Fusiliers, Siegfried Sassoon (1886–1967). Sassoon wrote this letter, which was read out in the House of Commons, to his commanding officer, while convalescing in England after having been wounded in France. The government had him diagnosed with shell-shock rather than risk a high-profile court martial. Eventually, after time at Craiglockhart War Hospital near Edinburgh, he decided to return to the fighting, and was wounded again in Palestine.

I am making this statement as an act of wilful defiance of military authority, because I believe that the War is being deliberately prolonged by those who have the power to end it. I am a soldier, convinced that I am acting on behalf of soldiers. I believe that this War, on which I entered as a war of defence and liberation, has now become a war of aggression and conquest. I believe that the purpose for which I and my fellow soldiers entered upon this War should have been so clearly stated as to have made it impossible to change them, and that, had this been done, the objects which actuated us would now be attainable by negotiation.

I have seen and endured the sufferings of the troops, and I can no longer be a party to prolong these sufferings for ends which I believe to be evil and unjust. I am not protesting against the conduct of the War, but against the political errors and insincerities for which the fighting men are being sacrificed.

On behalf of those who are suffering now I make this protest against the deception which is being practised on them; also I believe that I may help to destroy the callous complacency with which the majority of those at home regard the contrivance of agonies which they do not share and which they have not sufficient imagination to realise.

Wilfred Owen, 'Disabled' (1917)[6]

Wilfred Owen (1893–1918) is perhaps the best known of the war poets. He was unpublished when he enlisted in 1915, and was sent to the Somme at the end of the following year. His experiences left him with shell-shock and, like Siegfried Sassoon, he was sent to Craiglockhart War Hospital (where they met). Sassoon encouraged Owen to take the war as a subject for his poetry. He returned to France in September 1918, and was killed on 4 November, one week before the Armistice.

He sat in a wheeled chair, waiting for dark,
And shivered in his ghastly suit of grey,
Legless, sewn short at elbow. Through the park
Voices of boys rang saddening like a hymn,
Voices of play and pleasure after day,
Till gathering sleep had mothered them from him.

About this time Town used to swing so gay
When glow-lamps budded in the light-blue trees
And girls glanced lovelier as the air grew dim,
– In the old times, before he threw away his knees.
Now he will never feel again how slim
Girls' waists are, or how warm their subtle hands,
All of them touch him like some queer disease.

There was an artist silly for his face,
For it was younger than his youth, last year.

Now, he is old; his back will never brace;
He's lost his colour very far from here,
Poured it down shell-holes till the veins ran dry,
And half his lifetime lapsed in the hot race,
And leap of purple spurted from his thigh.
One time he liked a bloodsmear down his leg,
After the matches carried shoulder-high.
It was after football, when he'd drunk a peg,
He thought he'd better join. He wonders why . . .
Someone had said he'd look a god in kilts.

That's why; and maybe, too, to please his Meg,
Aye, that was it, to please the giddy jilts,
He asked to join. He didn't have to beg;
Smiling they wrote his lie; aged nineteen years.
Germans he scarcely thought of; and no fears
Of Fear came yet. He thought of jewelled hilts
For daggers in plaid socks; of smart salutes;
And care of arms; and leave; and pay arrears;
Esprit de corps; and hints for young recruits.
And soon, he was drafted out with drums and cheers.

Some cheered him home, but not as crowds cheer Goal.
Only a solemn man who brought him fruits
Thanked him; and then inquired about his soul.
Now, he will spend a few sick years in Institutes,
And do what things the rules consider wise,
And take whatever pity they may dole.
To-night he noticed how the women's eyes
Passed from him to the strong men that were whole.
How cold and late it is! Why don't they come
And put him into bed? Why don't they come?

———————————

Virginia Woolf, *Three Guineas* (1938)[7]

Three Guineas was published as a sequel to A Room of One's Own *(see p. 435). In three extended letters, Virginia Woolf (1882–1941) set out her answers to three questions, posed by a college building fund, a society promoting the employment of professional women, and an anti-war society. This passage is taken from Woolf's answer to the enquiry, 'How should war be prevented?'*

But the educated man's sister – what does 'patriotism' mean to her? Has she the same reasons for being proud of England, for loving England, for defending England? Has she been 'greatly blessed' in England? History and biography when questioned would seem to show that her position in the home of freedom has been different from her brother's; and psychology would seem to hint that history is not without its effect upon mind and body. Therefore her interpretation of 'patriotism' may well differ from his. And that difference may make it extremely difficult for her to understand his definition of patriotism and the duties it imposes. If then our answer to your question, 'How in your opinion are we to prevent war?' depends upon understanding the reasons, the emotions, the loyalties which lead men to go to war, this letter had better be torn across and thrown into the waste-paper basket. For it seems plain that we cannot understand each other because of these differences. It seems plain that we think differently according as we are born differently; there is a Grenfell point of view; a Knebworth point of view; a Wilfred Owen point of view; a Lord Chief Justice's point of view and the point of view of an educated man's daughter. All differ. But is there no absolute point of view? Can we not find somewhere written up in letters of fire or gold, 'This is right. This wrong'? – a moral judgement which we must all, whatever our differences, accept? . . .

But, rhetoric apart, what active method is open to us? Let us consider, and compare. You, of course, could once more take up arms – in Spain, as before in France – in defence of peace. But that presumably is a method that having tried you have rejected. At any rate that method is not open to us; both the Army and the Navy are closed to our sex. We are not allowed to fight. Nor again are we allowed to be members of the Stock Exchange. Thus we can use neither the pressure of force nor the pressure of money. The less direct but still effective weapons which our brothers, as educated men, possess in the diplomatic service, in the Church, are also denied to us. We cannot preach sermons or negotiate treaties. Then again although it is true that we can write articles or send letters to the Press, the control of the Press – the decision what to print, what not to print – is entirely in the hands of your sex. It is true that for the past twenty years we have been admitted to the Civil Service and to the Bar; but our position there is still very precarious and our authority of the slightest. Thus all the weapons with which an educated man can enforce his opinion are either beyond our grasp or so nearly beyond it that even if we used them we could scarcely inflict one scratch.

James Maxton, Speech Against War (4 October 1938)[8]

The Glasgow Labour MP 'Jimmy' Maxton (1885–1946) opposed the First World War as a schoolteacher. In 1938, he opposed the coming war from inside Parliament, as the Member for Bridgeton in Glasgow. This speech was given after the Prime Minister Neville Chamberlain's negotiation of the Munich agreement with Adolf Hitler.

I rise to say a few words on the matters before the House. I and those who sit with me made, more than a week ago, an unequivocal announcement to the country that if war took place we would be in opposition to that war and would take every step that lay within our power to bring it to a speedy end. We did that with much heart-searching, knowing exactly what such a step meant, knowing how we should be derided and chased from pillar to post and misrepresented. We did it because we believe that war is the one great over-riding evil that humanity has to face. We have every sympathy with Czechoslovakia, as much as other people have. We have as much sympathy particularly for the working-class Czechs as other people. We have the same sympathy for them as we had for the people of Belgium in 1914, but we did not see that as the issue. We saw that the war in 1914 was fought for four years as a war to end war; and it did not do that. It was fought as a war to make this land fit for heroes, and it did not do that. It was a war fought for democracy, and it did not do that, because today the big menace with which we are confronted arises from the fact that the aftermath of the last War was not the spread of democracy in Europe but the creation of more dictators. We saw our own country enter into that war as a democracy, and within a short time turned into a military dictatorship – of a necessity. An honourable Member opposite – I am not sure whether it was the right honourable Member for Warwick and Leamington (Mr Eden) or the late First Lord of the Admiralty – said that we ought to copy some of their methods – and democracy would have gone in this country.

The last War lasted four years and produced none of the results it was fought to achieve. It destroyed the lives definitely in battle of ten million men. How many lives should we have lost in this war? We have seen the Japan-China war and the Spanish war lasting two years. There have been estimates assuming that war on the scale envisaged here would have lasted twice as long, and having regard to the tremendous intensification of war-dealing instruments, is it foolish to assume that fifty million people would have lost their lives on this occasion? Is there anything in life which was worth facing that? We were going to live underground as rats. In my own home town I saw trenches being dug, and I pictured dignified and sensible human beings rushing into them to escape some foul death of the skies. I could see it not only in London but in Berlin; I could see it in Prague and in Paris. I could see the terrible degeneration of humanity, and that if we survived we were going to live only if we could make ourselves completely callous to all these horrors. What sort of a new world is to come out of that? What is democracy to get out of that? What sort of new social order is to come out of that?

Whatever happened to me I was against it upon grounds of ordinary common human sense; on every ground of my Socialist philosophy. On every ground of my sympathy and understanding of the aspirations of the working classes of this country I was against it, and said I was against it, and that any effort that was made for peace would receive my support. I said so in this House last Wednesday when the danger was great, and I repeat it now when the danger has somewhat eased. The Prime Minister in that period of time, in that limited period of time, did something that the mass of the common people in the world wanted done. With all my political antagonisms, with all my antagonisms to the political philosophy of the people who stand beside him, I am not going to stand here and lie. Last week he did something which the common people of the world wanted done, and now that we have a breathing-space we can argue and debate and denounce in the good recognised legitimate democratic way.

A very old friend of mine, a Member of the House who many honourable Members will recollect, was the right honourable John Wheatley. Those who were in the House when he was here will recollect that he was a very unorthodox but very gallant Member of the House. I was proud to work in close association with him and we used to have little discussions on things that had happened, a post-mortem examination of what we should have done and how we could have done it much better. He would allow that sort of thing to go on for a certain length of time and then he would say, 'Well, boys, that was last week: what are we going to do next week?'

That seems to me to be the approach that we have to make to the problem. I do not believe that we have got world peace. I do not believe that we have even got as far as the Prime Minister's belief − that we have got the foundations of peace on which the superstructure is to be erected. I believe that what we have got in the world is a possibility of laying the foundations of peace, and it seems to me having regard to the menace of last week, having regard to the clear way in which it was brought hard up against all our minds, that every scrap of human intelligence that can be brought to bear to make this breathing-space a real world peace, must be brought to bear.

I want to say to honourable and right honourable Gentlemen opposite that in the view of those who sit on these benches you cannot get world peace on the basis of a capitalist order of society. You cannot get world peace on the basis of the British Empire − an offence to every other nation in the world. Imperialists here yesterday criticised Herr Hitler for wanting power. But surely that is the basis of capitalist philosophy. Surely that is the British Empire. What ethical or logical reason can you put forward against Herr Hitler wanting power − world-wide power − on the basis of your own social and political philosophy, and what objection can you possibly have to Herr Hitler wanting to defend the people of his own race and of his own nationality wherever they may be? It was the proud boast of the Romans in the Roman Empire that wherever they were they were Roman citizens and their Empire could protect them. It was the proud boast of the British Empire. It was the proud boast of the British Empire when some of its members were in trouble in Russia a few years ago. How can you possibly say to Herr Hitler, 'The philosophy of power, the philosophy of menace, the philosophy of large territories is wrong when you hold it in your heart, but is a right philosophy when we hold it in our hearts and demonstrate it to the world in hard facts'?

We want the world for plain, simple people – not a world for one particular nation, not a world in which it is safe only for Britishers to live or Czechs or Frenchmen, but a world in which it is also safe for Germans to live. The key-point in the whole approach to the breaking of this world entanglement is the German people. The right honourable Gentleman the Member for South Hackney (Mr H. Morrison) made some reference to that. One of the greatest things – I think the greatest thing – in connection with the Prime Minister's visit to Germany, was the fact that it gave the ordinary German people, who are suppressed and denied a voice, an opportunity of demonstrating, under conditions which were not illegal, their desire for peace. That desire for peace demonstrated by the German people is the most hopeful sign in the world today, and that is the point on which everything should be built.

When I am asked to go to war against Germany it is always phrased as 'going to war against Herr Hitler'. But if I went to war against Germany, I should not be going to war against Herr Hitler any more than, on the last occasion, I should have been going to war against the Kaiser. Had I gone to war I should have gone to war against the German working folk who, up to 1934, were my comrades – men whom I met again and again from 1922 to 1931, when they were struggling to build a democratic peaceful republic in Germany, with little help from the peoples of the rest of the world. Those fellows who are crushed now, were the finest Socialists in the world, the best-educated Socialists in the world, the most sincere, and convinced and trained Socialists in the world, and they are still there. [HONOURABLE MEMBERS: 'In concentration camps.'] Some of them in concentration camps, some of them in exile, but the big mass of them in the German population. And I was to go out and slaughter those fellows in the interests of democracy. No!

I admit that for us it is very very difficult, as my right honourable Friend the Member for Bow and Bromley (Mr Lansbury) recognised, to put an alternative to this position, which appeals to the mind of the practical politician who thinks in terms of guns and power politics. But the only way in which world peace can be secured is by the common people of the world stating in no uncertain terms their determination to have peace, their determination to end Imperialism, their determination to construct new forms of social order which shall not have the power ideal as their aim and object but the ideal of human brotherhood and fraternity. That is my Socialist conception, and anything that I can do throughout this world, in Britain or in Germany, to bring that general conception to a point where it becomes practical politics will be done. I congratulate the Prime Minister on the work he did in these three weeks and, in saying that, I do not accept his social philosophy. I do not accept the political philosophy of those who sit behind him. I do not believe that that political philosophy can lead to anything but misery for humanity, and I will use every effort I can to employ the breathing-space that has been vouchsafed to us, not merely to make this nation safe, but to make the world safe, the world secure, the world prosperous, and the world happy.

Charlie Chaplin, Final Speech from *The Great Dictator* (1940)[9]

The Great Dictator *was written, directed, produced by and starred Charlie Chaplin (1889–1977). This was Chaplin's first true talking picture as well as his most commercially successful film. More importantly, it was the first major feature film of its period to satirise Nazism and Adolf Hitler. Chaplin and Adolf Hitler were born in the same year and a few days apart; Hitler's apparent modelling of his appearance on the 'little tramp' character was a source of great annoyance to Chaplin. In the film, he played the Hitler figure, Adenoid Hynkel, and a Jewish barber. Here, the barber speaks.*

I'm sorry, but I don't want to be an Emperor. That's not my business. I don't want to rule or conquer anyone. I should like to help everyone – if possible – Jew, gentile – black man – white.

We all want to help one another. Human beings are like that. We want to live by each other's happiness – not by each other's misery. We don't want to hate and despise one another. In this world there is room for everyone. And the good earth is rich and can provide for everyone.

The way of life can be free and beautiful, but we have lost the way. Greed has poisoned men's souls – has barricaded the world with hate – has goose-stepped us into misery and bloodshed. We have developed speed, but we have shut ourselves in. Machinery that gives abundance has left us in want. Our knowledge has made us cynical; our cleverness, hard and unkind. We think too much and feel too little. More than machinery, we need humanity. More than cleverness, we need kindness and gentleness. Without these qualities, life will be violent and all will be lost.

The airplane and the radio have brought us closer together. The very nature of these things cries out for the goodness in men – cries out for universal brotherhood – for the unity of us all. Even now my voice is reaching millions throughout the world – millions of despairing men, women and little children – victims of a system that makes men torture and imprison innocent people. To those who can hear me I say: 'Do not despair.' This misery that has come upon us is but the passing of greed – the bitterness of men who fear the way of human progress. The hate of men will pass, and dictators die, and the power they took from the people will return to the people. And so long as men die, liberty will never perish.

Soldiers! Don't give yourselves to brutes – who despise you – enslave you – who regiment your lives – tell you what to do – what to think and what to feel! Who drill you – diet you – treat you like cattle and use you as cannon fodder. Don't give yourselves to these unnatural men – machine men with machine minds and machine hearts! You are not machines. You are not cattle. You are men. You have the love of humanity in your hearts. You don't hate! Only the unloved hate – the unloved and the unnatural.

Soldiers! Don't fight for slavery! Fight for liberty! In the seventeenth chapter of St. Luke, it is written that the kingdom of God is within man – not one man, nor a group of men, but in all men! In you! You, the people, have the power, the power to create machines. The power to create happiness! You, the people, have the power to make this life free and beautiful – to make this life a wonderful adventure. Then – in the name of democracy – let us use that power, let us all unite. Let us fight for a new world – a decent world that will give men a chance to work – that will give youth a future and old age a security.

By the promise of these things, brutes have risen to power. But they lie! They do not fulfil their promise. They never will. Dictators free themselves but they enslave the people. Now let us fight to fulfil that promise. Let us fight to free the world – to do away with national barriers – to do away with greed, with hate and intolerance. Let us fight for a world of reason – a world where science and progress will lead to the happiness of all. Soldiers, in the name of democracy, let us unite! . . .

[L]ook up! Look up . . . The clouds are lifting! The sun is breaking through! We are coming out of the darkness into the light! We are coming into a new world – a kindlier world, where men will rise above their greed, their hate and brutality . . . The soul of man has been given wings and at last he is beginning to fly.

———————————

Phil Piratin, Invasion of the Savoy Hotel
(15 September 1940)[10]

The provision of adequate air-raid shelters for Londoners was a subject of dispute before the Second World War, but after the beginning of the Blitz in 1940, it became a matter of life and death. After the war, Phil Piratin (1907–95) was for five years one of only two Communist Party MPs, representing Mile End in Stepney. He had cut his political teeth in the anti-Fascist actions against Oswald Mosley, such as the Battle of Cable Street (see p. 358). During the Blitz, as he recalled in his memoir, Piratin tweaked the nose of the Establishment by invading the Savoy, just as the unemployed had invaded the Ritz before the war (p. 296).

When the Blitz came children and their parents, and many old folk and invalids, left Stepney. Not now in the organised way that had been carried out by the London County Council on Friday, 30 August 1939, but in haste and fear. They had seen death and destruction, and now the children wanted to get away.

Throughout the country billeting officers were hard put to find accommodation for all these Londoners. Many stories, enough to fill a book, could be told of working-class and kindly families who shared their homes and treated the children as their own. Unfortunately, other stories can also be told and, of course, as so often happened during those days, mainly we heard those other stories. Invariably where there was callousness, there was wealth. Many Stepney people, leaving Stepney that first September weekend in haste, went to country towns a relatively short journey from London. A number went to Windsor, where the only accommodation that the Conservative Windsor Council was prepared to provide was a cold hall, where they were told they could sleep on the floor. When they refused they were told by a Conservative Councillor that they could either clear out of the town or get into the fields. Many of them slept out in the open, mothers and children, with nothing to lie on and no covering but their coats.

I remember how in Northampton a billeting officer went to the house of a friend of mine, who, with his family, occupied a six-room house. He immediately offered one room for evacuees and agreed to care for them. This billeting officer described how he had just come away from a house which had nineteen rooms, and was occupied by a young couple whose name is associated with that of a well-known make of shoe. The young lady was in the process of having a baby. She yet had several months to go, but she was able to show a certificate from the doctor, that because of the terrible trials that she was about to face she should not have any evacuees in the house, as they would make a noise. In the light of the medical certificate, the billeting officer was not empowered to take any action. Undoubtedly some mothers thought that children were better off not billeted in such places, but they also thought, 'What kind of war is it?' and they must have had some bitter ideas on the Government's conception of 'equality of sacrifice'.

The Stepney Communist Party was faced with these problems, and in many cases we would get in touch with the authorities, or with the local Communist Party, to help settle matters on behalf of evacuated children and parents. In these towns the Communist Parties did excellent work in this connection, and equally excellent work in exposing those elements who, while talking glibly of the war in the hotel bars, and while 'playing their part' as officers in the Home Guard, refused to give shelter to the blitzed suffering children of East London, who had felt the terror of the bombing which these gentlemen and ladies made sure they never experienced.

The shelters, which until the Blitz were deserted, were now packed to overflowing, and now the conditions were revealed. The trench shelters in the little Stepney parks were a foot deep in water. The benches were half-a-dozen inches above the water. It was quite impossible to use them, and certainly impossible to stay in them night after night. Now the street surface shelters were being put to the test. Many of them were destroyed.

The Communist Party immediately began to organise Shelter Committees in the shelters in order to secure proper conditions and to provide for the feeding and amenities in the shelters. The idea caught on, and within a short while was being carried on throughout Stepney and indeed the whole of London. Later the authorities took over certain responsibilities such as refreshments. The Communist Party was the first to organise entertainments in the shelters. The Unity Theatre did excellent work in this connection; mobile groups went to different shelters to sing songs and perform their lighter sketches. Later, other organisations began to arrange entertainment.

The conditions in the shelters were frightful. Most notorious was the Tilbury shelter, which accommodated several thousand people in conditions which I find it impossible to describe. Many people were without shelter, and every evening there was a trek from Stepney to Central and West London to take shelter in one of the basement shelters of the large buildings there. The next morning thousands of bleary-eyed Londoners were to be seen on the buses and trains coming back to East London from the West End.

The contrast between shelter conditions for the rich and the poor called for exposure. This was done. When the Blitz had continued for some days, we in Stepney took the initiative. One Saturday evening we gathered some seventy people, among them a large sprinkling of children, and we took them to the Savoy Hotel. We had heard from building workers of the well-constructed and luxurious shelter which had been build for their guests. We decided that what was good enough for the Savoy Hotel parasites was reasonably good enough for Stepney workers and their families. We had an idea that the hotel management would not see eye to eye with this proposition, so we organised the 'invasion' without their consent. In fact, there was some effort to stop us, but it was only a matter of seconds before we were downstairs, and the women and children came streaming in afterwards. While the management and their lackeys were filled with consternation, the visitors from East London looked round in amazement. 'Shelters,' they said, 'why we'd love to live in such places!' Structurally, the lower ground floor had been strengthened with steel girders and by other means. But the appearance of the place! There were three sections. In each section there were cubicles. Each section was decorated in a different colour, pink, blue and green. All the bedding, all the linen, was, of course, the same uniform colour. Armchairs and desk chairs were strewn around . . .

We had earlier appointed our marshals to take care of all our people. They immediately made contact with the waiters, and asked for water and other such provisions. The waiters were most helpful. We were expecting trouble; we knew that the management was not going to allow us to sit there, just so easily. After a few minutes the police came. A plain-clothes officer said to me, 'What is it all about?' I explained. He said: 'We will have to get you out.' I said: 'O.K.—I'm curious to see what you do with the women and children.' (The Blitz was on.) I said: 'Some of these men have seen mass murder. God help you if you touch the women and children.' He wasn't very happy. They tried intimidation, such as calling for identity cards, but we sat there.

The management was in a dilemma. They urged the police to throw us out. We were able to impress on the management that any such attempt would meet with some opposition, and that some of his guests in the dining room were likely to be disturbed. The manager left. He agreed to ignore us; that was what we wanted. Then we settled down. The first thing the marshals did was to call for refreshments. Many of our people had sandwiches with them, and we therefore asked one of the waiters to provide tea and bread and butter. The waiter explained that they never served tea and bread and butter, and in any case the minimum price for anything was 2s. 6d. We said to the waiter: 'We will pay you 2d. a cup of tea and 2d. a portion of bread and butter, the usual prices in a Lyons' restaurant.' Three or four of the waiters went into a huddle, with one in particular doing the talking. He was evidently convincing the others. How they convinced the chef and management, I do not know, but within a few minutes, along came the trolleys and the silver trays laden with pots of tea and bread and butter. The waiters were having the time of their lives. They were obviously neglecting their duties, standing around, chuckling and playing with the children.

The next day this news was flashed across the world. The contrast was made in bold headlines between the terrible conditions of the shelters in Stepney and the luxury conditions of the shelters of West London. As a result, the Home Office took special steps to improve the conditions of the Tilbury shelter and others. But this militant action led to further developments. A demand had been made for the Tubes to be made available as shelters. The Home Secretary, Mr Herbert Morrison, said that this was impossible. The only valid reason he gave was that children might fall on to the line and be killed. This was not a very impressive argument, when you consider the hundred who were being killed because they had no shelter. The police were given instructions to allow no one to use the Tubes for shelter. Loiterers were moved on by the police. The Communist Party decided that the Tubes should be open for shelter. This was done.

Two or three days after the Savoy incident preparations were made to break open the gates of the Tubes which the police were closing immediately the air-raid siren was sounded. At a number of stations these actions were taken. Various implements such as crowbars happened to be available, and while the police stood on duty guarding the gates, they were very quickly swept aside by the crowds, the crowbars brought into action, and the people went down. That night tens of thousands sprawled on the Tube platforms. The next day Mr Herbert Morrison, solemn as an owl, rose to make his world-shattering announcement: the Government had reconsidered its opinion in the matter of the Tubes being used as shelters. From now onwards, they would be so employed. They were expected to accommodate 250,000. Arrangements would be made for refreshment and first-aid facilities. Later, bunks were being installed. 'The Government had reconsidered the matter.' They had, indeed! They had been forced to by the resolute action of the people of London which they had been powerless to prevent.

Denis Knight, The Aldermaston Anti-nuclear March (April 1958)[11]

The Campaign for Nuclear Disarmament began protest marches on Easter weekend in 1958, between Aldermaston, home to the UK's Atomic Weapons Establishment, and London. Denis Knight was secretary of the Film and TV Committee for Nuclear Disarmament. Here, he recalls the first march, which he joined with his sons, Christopher, then aged fifteen, and Kevin, thirteen.

The approach and entry into Reading were the gayest part of the whole walk. It was a succession of

> Oh, when the saints, oh, when the saints,
> Oh, when the saints go marching in!
> Oh, Lord, I want to be in that number
> When the saints go marching in!

and

> It's a long, long way to Aldermaston
> It's a long way to go!

and

> Men and women, stand together
> Do not heed the men of war
> Make your minds up now or never
> Ban the bomb for evermore.

All these songs, the variations on old songs and new, the invention of new slogans, and the fun of trying to make them catch on all up and down the column, together with the thought of the approaching town and the knowledge that it was our last night on the march, all helped to quicken the pace and increase the feeling of gaiety and expectancy. In the centre of Reading is a wide and long market street, St Mary's Butts, and this was now packed with people who had turned out to see the fun. It was about half past five as we entered this square at a very fast pace, with every instrument that could play playing, all mixed up with groups shouting or singing. Above our heads the bells of St Mary's were clanging wildly (we heard later that the Vicar was giving his bell-ringers an extra practice), and the marchers, accompanied by occasional police on foot or in cars, were cheering and counter-cheering in turn as they filed past me until gradually the centre of the square was packed tight, though the column of marchers still entering seemed never to be coming to an end.

Finally after the last marcher (and police car) had been cheered, the Salvation Army appeared in full marching order and musical blast. For us, the next thing to do was to find somewhere to sleep . . . I was able to get the name of Mr and Mrs Harold Casey who were among those who had offered their homes to marchers. We found Harold at home with his three young children, his wife being in Reading helping with feeding and sleeping arrangements. Harold gave us a wonderful supper and did everything possible to make us comfortable . . .

Shortly after leaving Burghfield, the fields began to wear an aspect less green and pleasant, as we entered a tract of sandy heath that grew nothing well but gorse and fir. 'Radioactive country,' said Christopher . . . Between the regiments of sour and drab fir, planted up to the very edges of the road, there was moving forward a great mass of men, women and children, four or five or six abreast, in a procession that was probably the longest that English roads have seen these centuries on foot, and was certainly the most purposeful. Its purpose was significant not only for England, but for every other country East and West, because it became clearer with every yard walked that this was more than an old-fashioned peace demonstration, more than a spiritual hunger march. It was felt, as we walked almost in silence through these menacing and monotonous woods, that this was above all a civilising mission, a march away from fear towards normality, towards human standards, towards the real people in the nursery rhyme whose houses are over the hill but not so far away that we will not get there by candlelight, whose hands are set to the plough and the making of things.

Hamish Henderson, 'Freedom Come-All-Ye' (1960)[12]

Hamish Henderson's song 'Freedom Come-All-Ye' was written in the spring of 1960 and dedicated to 'the Glasgow Peace marchers' against nuclear weapons in Scotland. It takes a historical view of Scottish involvement in British imperial wars, before looking forward to global change, invoking the vision of John Maclean (see p. 334), and justice in South Africa (Nyanga is a South African township).

Roch the wind in the clear day's dawin
Blaws the cloods heelster-gowdie ow'r the bay
But there's mair nor a roch wind blawin
Thro the great glen o the warld the day
It's a thocht that wad gar oor rottans
Aa thae rogues that gang gallus fresh an gay
Tak the road an seek ither loanins
Wi thair ill-ploys tae sport an play

Nae mair will our bonnie callants
Mairch tae war when oor braggarts crousely craw
Nor wee weans frae pit-heid an clachan
Mourn the ships sailin doon the Broomielaw
Broken faimlies in lands we've herriet
Will curse 'Scotlan the Brave' nae mair, nae mair
Black an white ane til ither mairriet
Mak the vile barracks o their maisters bare

So come a' ye at hame wi freedom
Never heed whit the houdies croak for doom
In yer hoose a' the bairns o Adam
Can find breid, barley-bree an painted room
When Maclean meets wi's friens in Springburn
Aa the roses an geans will turn tae bloom
An a black boy frae yont Nyanga
Dings the fell gallows o the burghers doon.

———

Adrian Mitchell, 'To Whom It May Concern (Tell Me Lies About Vietnam)' (1964)[13]

Protest against the war in Vietnam became a focus of British activism, as it did across the Western world. Adrian Mitchell (1932–2008) read this poem at an anti-Vietnam war protest in Trafalgar Square, bringing him to national attention. Mitchell continually updated the final lines of the poem to address new political leaders and wars.

I was run over by the truth one day.
Ever since the accident I've walked this way
> So stick my legs in plaster
> Tell me lies about Vietnam.

Heard the alarm clock screaming with pain,
Couldn't find myself so I went back to sleep again
> So fill my ears with silver
> Stick my legs in plaster
> Tell me lies about Vietnam.

Every time I shut my eyes all I see is flames.
Made a marble phone book and I carved out all the names
> So coat my eyes with butter
> Fill my ears with silver
> Stick my legs in plaster
> Tell me lies about Vietnam.

I smell something burning, hope it's just my brains.
They're only dropping peppermints and daisy-chains
> So stuff my nose with garlic
> Coat my eyes with butter
> Fill my ears with silver
> Stick my legs in plaster
> Tell me lies about Vietnam.

Where were you at the time of the crime?
Down by the Cenotaph drinking slime
> So chain my tongue with whisky
> Stuff my nose with garlic
> Coat my eyes with butter
> Fill my ears with silver
> Stick my legs in plaster
> Tell me lies about Vietnam.

You put your bombers in, you put your conscience out,
You take the human being and you twist it all about
    So scrub my skin with women
    Chain my tongue with whisky
    Stuff my nose with garlic
    Coat my eyes with butter
    Fill my ears with silver
    Stick my legs in plaster
    Tell me lies about Vietnam.

Voices of the Greenham Common Women's Peace Camp (1982)[14]

The decision to base US Air Force cruise missiles at Greenham Common, Berkshire, led to a protest camp that lasted for nineteen years. The camp began after a march of 'Women for Life on Earth' from Wales was refused a debate with the camp commander. In 1982, the women's 'Embrace the Base' action gathered thirty thousand women outside Greenham. Some of their experiences were recorded for the Imperial War Museum's archive. The missiles were removed in 1991–2.

Kim Besly

It wasn't until, I suppose it would be 1981, that I read in the paper that there were some women who were going to be marching, walking from Cardiff to a place called Greenham Common near Newbury, to protest about American missiles. I looked at this and I thought, (a) that's a funny thing for women to do, and (b) what on earth are cruise missiles and why are they American, what on earth are they doing in my country? I thought well I ought to go and look at this.

Anyway I managed to put it to the back of my mind quite successfully for some time. I suppose this would have been something like September '81. Anyway this kept niggling away and a month or two later I read that these women were still there. They were sitting in the mud outside Greenham Common protesting at the proposed siting of cruise missiles there. I didn't know what a cruise missile was, but it did get under my skin that Americans were putting their weapons in my country. Again I thought, no, I don't want to get involved. I'd never been involved in anything more dramatic than the Women's Institute. However, this niggled away at my mind and eventually, I think it must have been just after Christmas in December '81, I got in the car and went up to see what was going on. In fact I think it was January. It was a rather sort of cold, drizzly, overcast, what I might call a 'November' day, grey and drizzly. Just outside Newbury I pulled into a lay-by and said, 'You don't want to do this, this means trouble', but somehow or another I found myself going on.

Sarah Hipperson

We just sit down on the ground, or lie down on the ground. The essence of . . . non-violence is that you shouldn't have any violent thing going on between you and the people that are moving you and that's very very difficult. I found that separating it out into that physical thing wasn't enough for me, I actually had to prepare myself before I went into an action. Most women did, really. It's a strange feeling, it's almost like an out-of-body experience. You go into a higher level of some kind of consciousness so you can ignore to some extent the pain that you're suffering. Also you can ignore the comments, you know, nasty things like you being nothing but slags and all sorts of that kind of thing. I can remember one time seeing a woman pick up a stone and about four women rushed to her and said, 'We don't do it that way. We must never do it that way. We're beaten if we ever do it that way. We can stay here for ever provided we're not violent.'

Ann Pettitt

Once it became a women's protest, clearly defined as a women's protest, then all these kind of more imaginative ways of making your protest were able to be released. It was a sort of explosion of imagination that took place. The idea of women webbing themselves up – you know that wonderful photograph of a row of policemen standing there literally scratching their heads, one of them is actually scratching his head, a caricature of puzzlement, as he looks down at two or three women who are lying across ditches.

The work of expanding the camp to take in all the extra personnel to service cruise was still going on and this involved digging ditches across the Peace Camp to take the sewage pipes you see, to take all the extra poo that was going to be generated by all these extra personnel. So this involved all sorts of opportunities for disrupting the work. The women did it by lying in the ditches or lying across them and webbing themselves up, I mean the web had become one of the symbols by then, with wool. All they'd done was just to tie wool around themselves and between themselves, so when a policeman picked one up, she was all tangled up with wool to the next one. All they needed was a pair of scissors for God's sake, but they just didn't know how or where to begin approaching this new thing, you see, and it took them ages to move them away, and they lost a whole day's work and everything because the women were tied up with wool. It was as simple as that. There were so many different ways, I suppose, that you could sort of outwit and startle the authorities, rather than this kind of brutish, unintelligent head-on clash between completely unequal forces, in which you would inevitably be the loser. It never seemed to me to make a lot of sense. I mean non-violent protest, as a form of protest, is much more intelligent, isn't it?

Thalia Campbell

We had this code word, black cardigans, for bolt-cutters and we decided to spread this massive cutting down of the fence by word of mouth only and only amongst women. Somehow the networking managed to keep this from the authorities completely and utterly. They had no idea what black cardigans meant or what we were going to do. So we had a Hallowe'en party with these hats on and fires and witches' broomsticks and then at four o'clock out came all the bolt-cutters and we cut the fence down, miles and miles of it, almost half the fence. That was really hectic and terrifying because the Greenham women who were camped up there had been around the wire for months beforehand, snipping all the wires in unnoticeable little places. So what was left to do on the day was very little, we only had to cut the top wire holding it and the whole fence came down. It was all so haphazard having these picnics and fires and suddenly the word went round, fence at four o'clock, and we all got the bolt-cutters out and we climbed on each other's shoulders and we cut the top wire and the fence just fell. We had no plans to go in, we just stood there by the fallen-down fence and they were on the inside and they had no jurisdiction over us on the outside. This was more infuriating because there they were with us taking the fence down and we stood outside. Most of the police, I think they thought we were going to dress up in black cardigans and go in in the night, so most of the forces of the establishment had been placed on the inside of the base, so there were very few policemen on the outside. There was about one policeman to every sixty or seventy women. So there we were cutting the fence down and it took them about twenty minutes to work out their strategy for coping with this. They would arrest one woman and then there were fifty-nine still cutting the fence down, so they would let her go and grab hold of another one, let that one go and the fence was all being chopped down. Finally, after about twenty minutes, they decided to take the bolt-cutters off us and throw them into the base. By that time so much damage had been done, they got the helicopters out and they were actually flying the helicopters at us, trying to blow us off the fence.

Pettitt

Embrace the Base I always think of as the kind of zenith, the high spot of the whole Greenham story, really, because that was when the original message went thumping round the world. The good that it did was done that day and everything that had gone before seemed to have been entirely necessary to the creation of that day. That was when the message did get through the media and it got through on the mass media in a completely simple, direct way.

The Peace Camp began in September 1981. It was in May, June, it was in summer of the following year, of 1982, that Barbara Doris went to America and took part in a protest around the Pentagon, where women held hands and encircled the Pentagon and she brought back from America this idea to Greenham. She took the idea back to the women at Greenham and they said, 'Oh dear, sounds like far too much,' and they hummed and hawed and I think Lyn Jones turned up and had also heard about the same thing and said, 'Yes, let's do it.' But it was a very kind of last-minute 'Yes, let's do it' decision that was taken some time around, late on in October. I mean you're talking about something to happen on 12 December. Why 12 December? Because it was the date of the decision to bring in cruise missiles.

We organised it by chain letter. You simply sent out ten letters, you photocopied them and sent them out. God knows how many copies of these I got and how many copies I sent out. I mean I sent out about a hundred, loads of other people sent out about a hundred. That was the day when thirty thousand women came. That was the best day of my life, that was brilliant, that was amazing. But what was so exciting was, I just cried, what was so brilliant again was that it was sort a wing and a prayer. You thought, Yes, everybody I know in my area is coming, but are they coming from everywhere else?

We got to Severn Bridge service station at Avon Gorge and the car park was absolutely jammed with coaches. That whole car park was full of coaches that had come up from Devon and Cornwall and all over Wales. The whole of the West Country, women, was in these coaches, you know. Going down the motorway all these coaches were full of women waving their suffragette-coloured ribbons. What was so good about that was that it was in that extraordinary sort of spirit of . . . it was Embrace the Base, it was overwhelm this place with our good vibe. It was still a kind of very naïve, optimistic spirit in a sense. Also you brought a gift. You brought a gift which symbolised the life, how important life was to you. You brought a gift that was important to you and it was a gift to the base to symbolise life. So the whole of the fence was just covered with these, absolutely extraordinary, the whole of the fence covered with things. Again it was this mass of ordinary women and there was a distance between the way that women who considered themselves feminists viewed this. I remember reading in *Spare Rib* a very tut-tutting report of this demonstration about how women had hung pictures of their houses on the fence, you know, 'Oh, goodness me, revelling in domesticity,' or nappies on the fence. One woman had hung her wedding dress on the fence and left it there. She hung her wedding dress on the fence and walked away and left it. To me, I just sort of walked around with tears streaming down my face looking at these things, you know, laughing and crying at the same time.

I remember Carmen telling me that she saw a whole beautiful dinner service clipped to the fence. A lot of things were just left, they were sacrificed, they were left, you know. It was a marvellous day. The whole of that nine-mile fence covered with these things, or with flowers, obviously a lot of paintings, a lot of pictures of babies, a lot of embroidery. Women embroidered, started to embroider the fence and sort of use their own arts in this subversive way. Of course, embroidery became part of the Greenham theme afterwards and the soldiers would become absurdly enraged by embroidery when women would darn the fence. They'd darn huge areas of it in the following years. You know, darning would become something they would do with all multi-coloured wool and everything. They'd darn such enormous areas of it that you couldn't see through it. The military would be sent with scissors to cut through these silly bits of darning and then they'd reappear the next morning.

Mary Compton, Speech at Stop the War Demonstration (15 February 2003)[15]

On 15 February 2003, up to a million people marched in the streets of London to protest at the US and UK invasion of Iraq. Among the speakers that day was Mary Compton, a leader of the National Union of Teachers.

I am speaking as a teacher. As a teacher, I extend my solidarity to the teachers of Iraq and the children of Iraq.

Our union has sent out advice for teachers in the UK about how to deal with the problems faced by our pupils because of this war. This is welcomed. But I cannot even begin to imagine the problems faced by Iraqi teachers when trying to explain to their pupils what is happening and why their country is being targeted.

To the teachers of Iraq, I can only express my deep shame at being in any way associated with this merciless attack on your country.

I ask this government and Tony Blair: how can we teach our

children to tell the truth when this government disguises brutality as liberation?

How can we teach children to care for others when this government is prepared to spend three and a half billion pounds to prosecute their war? When all over the world people are dying of starvation and we stand by and do nothing?

How can we teach our pupils to be fair to one another when one state occupies and brutalises its neighbour, Palestine, and is given a million dollars a day in aid while another is simply judged to have failed to have complied with United Nations resolutions and the whole might of the US Army is unleashed on it?

How can we teach them democracy and respecting other people's point of view when this government is prepared to ignore the views of the majority of its own people and the majority of the nations of the world?

How can we teach them that bullying is wrong when they see our government supporting the biggest, wealthiest and strongest country in the world as it lays into one of the weakest?

Robin Cook, Resignation Speech to Parliament (18 March 2003)[16]

Robin Cook (1946–2005) delivered this speech in the House of Commons debate on the invasion of Iraq, and resigned his position as leader of the House. The speech drew a rare standing ovation, but the vote was for war. Two days later, the invasion began.

This is the first time for twenty years that I have addressed the House from the back benches. I must confess that I had forgotten how much better the view is from here.

None of those twenty years were more enjoyable or more rewarding than the past two, in which I have had the immense privilege of serving this House as Leader of the House, which were made all the more enjoyable, Mr Speaker, by the opportunity of working closely with you.

It was frequently the necessity for me as leader of the House to talk my way out of accusations that a statement had been preceded by a press interview. On this occasion I can say with complete confidence that no press interview has been given before this statement. I have chosen to address the House first on why I cannot support a war without international agreement or domestic support.

The present prime minister is the most successful leader of the Labour Party in my lifetime. I hope that he will continue to be the leader of our party, and I hope that he will continue to be successful. I have no sympathy with, and I will give no comfort to, those who want to use this crisis to displace him.

I applaud the heroic efforts that the prime minister has made in trying to secure a second [UN] resolution. I do not think that anybody could have done better than the foreign secretary in working to get support for a second resolution within the Security Council. But the very intensity of those attempts underlines how important it was to succeed. Now that those attempts have failed, we cannot now pretend that getting a second resolution was of no importance.

France has been at the receiving end of bucket loads of commentary in recent days. It is not France alone that wants more time for inspections. Germany wants more time for inspections; Russia wants more time for inspections; indeed, at no time have we signed up even the minimum necessary to carry a second resolution. We delude ourselves if we think that the degree of international hostility is all the result of President Chirac.

The reality is that Britain is being asked to embark on a war without agreement in any of the international bodies of which we are a leading partner – not NATO, not the European Union and, now, not the Security Council. To end up in such diplomatic weakness is a serious reverse. Only a year ago, we and the United States were part of a coalition against terrorism that was wider and more diverse than I would ever have imagined possible.

History will be astonished at the diplomatic miscalculations that led so quickly to the disintegration of that powerful coalition. The US can afford to go it alone, but Britain is not a superpower. Our interests are best protected not by unilateral action but by multilateral agreement and a world order governed by rules.

Yet tonight the international partnerships most important to us are weakened: the European Union is divided; the Security Council is in stalemate. Those are heavy casualties of a war in which a shot has yet to be fired.

I have heard some parallels between military action in these circumstances and the military action that we took in Kosovo. There was no doubt about the multilateral support that we had for the action that we took in Kosovo. It was supported by NATO; it was supported by the European Union; it was supported by every single one of the seven neighbours in the region. France and Germany were our active allies. It is precisely because we have none of that support in this case that it was all the more important to get agreement in the Security Council as the last hope of demonstrating international agreement. The legal basis for our action in Kosovo was the need to respond to an urgent and compelling humanitarian crisis.

Our difficulty in getting support this time is that neither the international community nor the British public is persuaded that there is an urgent and compelling reason for this military action in Iraq.

The threshold for war should always be high. None of us can predict the death toll of civilians from the forthcoming bombardment of Iraq, but the US warning of a bombing campaign that will 'shock and awe' makes it likely that casualties will be numbered at least in the thousands. I am confident that British servicemen and -women will acquit themselves with professionalism and with courage. I hope that they all come back. I hope that Saddam [Hussein], even now, will quit Baghdad and avert war, but it is false to argue that only those who support war support our troops.

It is entirely legitimate to support our troops while seeking an alternative to the conflict that will put those troops at risk. Nor is it fair to accuse those of us who want longer for inspections of not having an alternative strategy.

For four years as foreign secretary I was partly responsible for the Western strategy of containment. Over the past decade that strategy destroyed more weapons than in the Gulf war, dismantled Iraq's nuclear weapons programme and halted Saddam's medium- and long-range missiles programmes.

Iraq's military strength is now less than half its size than at the time of the last Gulf war. Ironically, it is only because Iraq's military forces are so weak that we can even contemplate its invasion. Some advocates of conflict claim that Saddam's forces are so weak, so demoralised and so badly equipped that the war will be over in a few days.

We cannot base our military strategy on the assumption that Saddam is weak and at the same time justify pre-emptive action on the claim that he is a threat. Iraq probably has no weapons of mass destruction in the commonly understood sense of the term – namely a credible device capable of being delivered against a strategic city target. It probably still has biological toxins and battlefield chemical munitions, but it has had them since the 1980s when US companies sold Saddam anthrax agents and the then British government approved chemical and munitions factories.

Why is it now so urgent that we should take military action to disarm a military capacity that has been there for twenty years, and which we helped to create? Why is it necessary to resort to war this week, while Saddam's ambition to complete his weapons programme is blocked by the presence of UN inspectors?

Only a couple of weeks ago, Hans Blix [head of the United Nations Monitoring, Verification and Inspection Commission in Iraq] told the Security Council that the key remaining disarmament tasks could be completed within months. I have heard it said that Iraq has had not months but twelve years in which to complete disarmament, and that our patience is exhausted. Yet it is more than thirty years since resolution 242 called on Israel to withdraw from the occupied territories. We do not express the same impatience with the persistent refusal of Israel to comply.

I welcome the strong personal commitment that the prime minister has given to Middle East peace, but Britain's positive role in the Middle East does not redress the strong sense of injustice throughout the Muslim world at what it sees as one rule for the allies of the US and another rule for the rest.

Nor is our credibility helped by the appearance that our partners in Washington are less interested in disarmament than they are in regime change in Iraq. That explains why any evidence that inspections may be showing progress is greeted in Washington not with satisfaction but with consternation: it reduces the case for war.

What has come to trouble me most over past weeks is the suspicion that if the hanging chads [the damaged ballot papers in the previous US presidential election] in Florida had gone the other way and Al Gore had been elected, we would not now be about to commit British troops.

The longer that I have served in this place, the greater the respect I have for the good sense and collective wisdom of the British people. On Iraq, I believe that the prevailing mood of the British people is sound. They do not doubt that Saddam is a brutal dictator, but they are not persuaded that he is a clear and present danger to Britain.

They want inspections to be given a chance, and they suspect that they are being pushed too quickly into conflict by a US administration with an agenda of its own. Above all, they are uneasy at Britain going out on a limb on a military adventure without a broader international coalition and against the hostility of many of our traditional allies.

From the start of the present crisis, I have insisted, as Leader of the House, on the right of this place to vote on whether Britain should go to war. It has been a favourite theme of commentators that this House no longer occupies a central role in British politics. Nothing could better demonstrate that they are wrong than for this House to stop the commitment of troops in a war that has neither international agreement nor domestic support.

I intend to join those tomorrow night who will vote against military action now. It is for that reason, and for that reason alone, and with a heavy heart, that I resign from the government.

GENDER AND SEXUAL EQUALITY

———————

'A HUMAN BEING, REGARDLESS
OF THE DISTINCTION OF SEX'

The best-known women's movement in Britain may be the campaign for female suffrage, in particular its militant wing, the 'Suffragettes'. But women's struggle for recognition in the political sphere was only one part of an encompassing battle to be treated as equals in all aspects of life. Women working, cohabiting or even thinking seriously, as well as voting, have all been the subject of debate and of prejudice at different times. Before the eighteenth century, women's voices were rarely recorded, with occasional literary exceptions – mostly aristocratic, like that of the Countess of Pembroke, Mary Herbert. But carried along on the wave of liberty churned up by the American and French Revolutions, which questioned all aspects of social relations, eighteenth-century women such as Mary Wollstonecraft emerged as pioneers of what only became known as 'feminism' a century later.

The trial of Oscar Wilde demonstrated how the establishment was prepared to destroy those who failed to conform to sexual norms. Homosexuality remained illegal until 1967, when homosexual acts between men over twenty-one in private were decriminalised. But sexual prejudice remains in Britain to this day. The fact that Quentin Crisp was eventually treated as a national treasure (though he understandably did not return the nation's lately discovered affection), or that straight audiences sing along to Tom Robinson's 'Glad To Be Gay' cannot conceal the other reality: that it can still be difficult, and sometimes dangerous, to be gay or lesbian or transgender in Britain.

Anonymous, Song on the Labour of Women (*c.* sixteenth century)[1]

Women's voices were rarely recorded so early in British history, but this verse in praise of women is written from a female perspective, and may have been the work of a female poet.

> I am as lighte as any roe
> To preise womene where that I go.

> To onpreise womene it were a shame,
> For a woman was thy dame.
> Our blessed lady bereth the name
> Of all womene where that they go.

> A woman is a worthy thing;
> They do the washe and do the wringe;
> 'Lullay, lullay!' she dothe thee singe;
> And yet she hath but care and wo.

> A woman is a worthy wight;
> She serveth a man both daye and night;
> Thereto she putteth alle her might;
> And yet she hath but care and wo.

The Petition of Divers Well-Affected Women
(5 May 1649)[2]

*In April 1649, a group of women delivered a petition to the
Commonwealth Parliament on behalf of four imprisoned Leveller
leaders, John Lilburne, Richard Overton, William Walwyn and Thomas
Prince. One MP remarked that 'it was not for women to Petition, they
might stay at home and wash their dishes'. This more strongly worded
petition was delivered the following month. The prisoners were
released in November.*

Since we are assured of our creation in the image of God, and of an
interest in Christ equal unto men, as also of a proportionable share
in the freedoms of this commonwealth, we cannot but wonder and
grieve that we should appear so despicable in your eyes as to be
thought unworthy to petition or represent our grievances to this
honourable House. Have we not an equal interest with the men of
this nation in those liberties and securities contained in the Petition
of Right, and other the good laws of the land? Are any of our lives,
limbs, liberties, or goods to be taken from us more than from men,
but by due process of law and conviction of twelve sworn men of the
neighbourhood? And can you imagine us to be so sottish or stupid
as not to perceive, or not to be sensible when daily those strong
defences of our peace and welfare are broken down and trod under-
foot by force and arbitrary power?

Would you have us keep at home in our houses, when men of such
faithfulness and integrity as the four prisoners, our friends, in the
Tower, are fetched out of their beds and forced from their houses by
soldiers, to the affrighting and undoing of themselves, their wives,
children, and families? Are not our husbands, o[u]r selves, our children
and families, by the same rule as liable to the like unjust cruelties as
they? And are we Christians, and shall we sit still and keep at home,
while such men as have borne continual testimony against the

injustice of all times and unrighteousness of men, be picked out and be delivered up to the slaughter? And yet must we show no sense of their sufferings, no tenderness of affections, no bowels of compassion, nor bear any testimony against so abominable cruelty and injustice?

Have such men as these continually hazarded their lives, spent their estates and time, lost their liberties, and thought nothing too precious for defence of us, our lives and liberties, been as a guard by day and as a watch by night; and when for this they are in trouble and greatest danger, persecuted and hated even to the death, should we be so basely ungrateful as to neglect them in the day of their affliction? No, far be it from us. Let it be accounted folly, presumption, madness, or whatsoever in us, whilst we have life and breath we will never leave them nor forsake them, nor ever cease to importune you, having yet so much hopes of you as of the unjust judge (mentioned, Luke 18), to obtain justice, if not for justice's sake, yet for importunity, or to use any other means for the enlargement and reparation of those of them that live, and for justice against such as have been the cause of Mr Lockyer's death.

And therefore again we entreat you to review our last petition in behalf of our friends above mentioned, and not to slight the things therein contained because they are presented unto you by the weak hand of women, it being a usual thing with God, by weak means to work mighty effects.

Anonymous, 'Extraordinary Female Affection', *Saint James Chronicle* (17–20 July 1790)[3]

Lady Eleanor Butler (1739–1829) and Sarah Ponsonby (1755–1831) were two women of aristocratic Irish heritage who refused to live by the sexual norms of their day. Known as the 'Ladies of Llangollen',

> *the couple, who had met when Sarah was still a schoolgirl of thirteen,*
> *'eloped' and set up house together in north Wales, becoming famous*
> *for their unusual partnership. Though there was much gossip about*
> *the form the relationship took, they described it as devoted to*
> *'Pleasures unknown to Vulgar minds'. They died within two years of*
> *each other, and were buried side by side, along with their devoted*
> *maid Mary Carryll. This account of their relationship comes from a*
> *local newspaper.*

Miss Butler and Miss Ponsonby, now retired from the society of men, into the wilds of a certain Welch vale, bear a strange antipathy to the male sex, whom they take every opportunity of avoiding.

Both Ladies are daughters of the great Irish families whose names they retain.

Miss Butler, who is of the Ormond family, had several offers of marriage, all of which she rejected. As Miss Ponsonby, her particular friend and companion, was supposed to be the bar to all matrimonial union, it was thought proper to separate them; and Miss Butler was confined.

The two Ladies, however, found means to elope together. But being soon over-taken, they were each brought back by their respective relations. Many attempts were renewed to draw Miss Butler into marriage. But upon her solemnly and repeatedly declaring that nothing could induce her to wed any one, her parents ceased to persecute her by any more offers.

Not many months after, the Ladies concerted and executed a fresh elopement . . .

The beautiful . . . vale is the spot they fixed on, where they have resided for several years, unknown to the neighbouring villagers by any other appellation than *the Ladies in the Vale.*

About a twelvemonth since, three ladies and a gentleman stopping one night at an inn in the village, not being able to procure beds, the inhabitants applied to the female hermits for accommodation to some foreign strangers. This was readily granted – When lo! in these foreigners they descried some of their own relatives! But no intreaties could prevail on the Ladies to quit their sweet retreat.

Miss Butler is tall and masculine. She wears always a riding-habit. Hangs up her hat with the air of a sportsman in the hall; and appears in all respects as a young man, if we except the petticoat, which she still retains . . .

Miss Ponsonby, on the contrary, is polite and effeminate, fair and beautiful. They live in neatness, elegance and taste. Miss Ponsonby does the duties and honours of the house; while Miss Butler superintends the gardens and the rest of the grounds.

Mary Wollstonecraft, *A Vindication of the Rights of Woman* (1792)[4]

A Vindication of the Rights of Woman is one of the founding texts of modern feminism. It transformed its author, Mary Wollstonecraft (1759–97), from an unknown jobbing writer into one of the famous women in Europe ('the most famous', according to her husband William Godwin). It was partly prompted by her realisation that the revolution in France, which inspired so many radicals, seemed to have done little to improve the situation of women ('fraternité', after all, excluded women). One of her most strongly held views, which she put into practice in her own life, was that women's pretended meekness and lack of intellectual confidence was almost as serious an impediment to taking their rightful place in society as their oppression by men.

My own sex, I hope, will excuse me, if I treat them like rational creatures, instead of flattering their *fascinating* graces, and viewing them as if they were in a state of perpetual childhood, unable to stand alone. I earnestly wish to point out in what true dignity and human happiness consists – I wish to persuade women to endeavour to acquire strength, both of mind and body, and to convince them that the soft phrases, susceptibility of heart, delicacy of sentiment, and refinement of taste, are almost synonymous with epithets of weakness, and that those beings who are only the objects of pity, and that kind of love which has been termed its sister, will soon become objects of contempt.

Dismissing, then, those pretty feminine phrases, which the men condescendingly use to soften our slavish dependence, and despising that weak elegancy of mind, exquisite sensibility, and sweet docility of manners, supposed to be the sexual characteristics of the weaker vessel, I wish to shew that the first object of laudable ambition is to obtain a character as a human being, regardless of the distinction of sex.

Anna Wheeler and William Thompson, Address to Women (1825)[5]

This is an excerpt from Appeal of One Half the Human Race, Women, Against the Pretensions of the Other Half, Men, To Retain Them in Political and Thence in Civil and Domestic Slavery. *Anna Wheeler (1785?–1848) left an alcoholic husband in Ireland to make a transition from upper-class socialite to influential philosopher. With the political economist William Thompson (1775–1833), she produced this pamphlet, which developed the arguments of Mary Wollstonecraft (see p. 417) and applied them in particular to the status of women in marriage. The pamphlet also attacked the argument of James Mill that women's political interests did not need separate representation because they were fully accounted for by husbands and fathers.*

Women of England! women, in whatever country ye breathe – wherever ye breathe, degraded – awake! Awake to the contemplation of the happiness that awaits you when all your faculties of mind and body shall be fully cultivated and developed; when every path in which ye can exercise those improved faculties shall be laid open and rendered delightful to you, even as to them who now ignorantly enslave and degrade you. If degradation from long habitude have lost its sting, if the iron have penetrated so deeply into your frame that it has been gradually taken up into the system and mingles unperceived amidst the fluids of your life; if the prostration of reason and the eradication of feeling have kept pace within you, so that you are insensible alike to what you suffer and to what you might enjoy, – your case were all but hopeless. Nothing less, then, than the sight presented before your eyes, of the superior happiness enjoyed by other women, under arrangements of perfect equality with men, could arouse you. Such a sight, even under such circumstances, would excite your envy and kindle up all your extinct desires. But you are not so degraded. The unvaried despotism of so many thousand years has not so entirely degraded you, has not been able to extinguish within you the feelings of nature, the love of happiness and of equal justice. The united exertions of law, superstition, and pretended morals of past ages of ignorance, have not entirely succeeded. There is still a germ within you, the love of happiness, coeval with your existence, and never to cease but when 'life itself shall please no more', which shall conduct you, feeble as it now is, under the guidance of wisdom and benevolence, to that perfect equality of knowledge, sympathy, and enjoyment with men, which the greatest sum of happiness for the whole race demands.

Sleeps there an infant on your bosom, to the level of whose intellect the systematic despotism and pitiful jealousy of man have not sought, and for the most part successfully sought, to chain down yours? Does no blush rise amongst you – swells no breast with indignation, at the enormous wrong? Simple as ye are, have ye become enamoured of folly? do you indeed believe it to be a source of power and of happiness? Look to your masters: does knowledge in their hands remain idle? is it with them no source of power and happiness? Think ye then indeed that it is of the use of what are called your personal charms alone that man is jealous? There is not a quality of mind which his animal propensities do not grudge you: not one, those only excepted which, like high-seasoned or far-fetched sauces, render you, as objects of sense, more stimulating to his purely selfish desires. Do ye pretend to enjoy with him, at this banquet of *bought* or *commanded* sensuality, the sensuality of prostitution or of marriage? He has a system of domineering hypocrisy, which he calls morals, which brands with the name of vice your enjoyment, while it lauds with the name of virtue, or gilds with that of innocent gratification, his. What quality, worth the possession, and capable of being applied to useful purposes for your own independence and happiness, do you possess, of which ignorant man is not jealous? Strength is his peculiar prerogative; it is *unfeminine* to possess it: hence every expedient is used in what is called your education, to enervate your bodies, by proscribing that activity which is as necessary to health as to preservation from inevitable casualites. Muscular weakness, what is called delicacy of health approaching to disease, helplessness, are by strange perversion of language denominated rather perfections than defects in women, in order to increase their dependence, even their *physical* dependence on man; gratifying by one operation his two ruling animal propensities, sexual desire and love of domination. Hectic delicacy of health – though to yourselves accompanied by torment and followed by death – excites man's appetite; and utter weakness, no matter what personal evils it may entail on the possessor, gratifies his love of domination, by rendering his aid on every trivial occasion indispensable for your protection or for your most trifling exertions. Not satisfied with the inferiority of strength which your comparative size and structure, under the name of nature, give you, his poor jealousy increases it a hundredfold by all the resources of a vicious and partial physical training: and for this weakness and helplessness you are subsequently reproached, as a mark of your natural physical inferiority! Of strength of mind in you the ignorant amongst men, that is to say, the bulk of men, are still more jealous than of strength of body. Cowardice, that is to say, dread without reason, and in consequence of that dread, incapacity of using the means of preservation in your power against the most trifling attacks of the most contemptible animals or even insects or petty accidents, is by the sexual system of morality rather a virtue than a vice in you. No matter what inconveniences you personally suffer from this pernicious quality, no matter how your minds through life are tormented by it; it is of much more importance that man's vanity should be perfumed with his comparative hardihood than that you should be happy. Not on benevolence, but on antipathy, or malignant jealousy of your good, is the cursed system of sexual morality founded. Strength, without which there can be no health, both of body and mind, would cause you to approach too nearly to those high prerogatives in your masters, with whom to aim at an equality is the summit of female audacity, if not of wickedness. Prudence for the management of your affairs, wisdom for the guidance of your voluntary actions, the same unrelenting jealousy of ignorance proscribes. An education of baby-clothes, and sounds, and postures, you are given, instead of real knowledge; the *incidents* are withheld from you, by which you could learn, as man does, the management of affairs and the prudential guidance of your own actions; and thus factitiously incapacitated, man interposes, seizes on your property, leaves you none to manage, and assumes the despotic guidance of your actions, as the right of his superior wisdom and prudence! Every moral and intellectual quality of which you might be possessed is thus deliberately and systematically sacrificed at the shrine of man's all-devouring jealousy, of his most immoral love of superiority, deriving pleasure where if benevolent he could not avoid feeling pain, from the contemplation of the weaknesses, vices, or privations, thus entailed upon you his fellow-creatures. That no intellectual faculties may be by you developed, it is *immoral* that you should exercise even the faculty of speech (though it is a quality at times of the highest virtue, exciting the utmost admiration in *man*), to address in public, that is to say; to address any where, numbers of your fellow-creatures; this high and exciting source of influence and intellectual improvement, man's universal jealousy having also monopolised. On the stage, as servants, as *despised* servants, you may act and receive his payment to flatter his eye and ear; but for your own interest in life, to turn to any serious use those powers of graceful and reasoning eloquence, which these illicit occasions have shown you to possess, and with which they have enabled you to thrill man's overpowered faculties, his cowardly and malignant jealousy forbids the exercise. An excluding law would be in this case superfluous. Though super-human wisdom were to be gleaned by woman, as grains from the well reaped fields of men, and in spite of their exclusions, your lips, the vehicle of such wisdom, would be closed, in spite of the vain permissions of law, by the superior strength of men, even by open force! . . .

To be respected by [men], you must be respectable in your own eyes; you must exert more power, you must be more useful. You must regard yourselves as having equal capabilities of contributing to the general happiness with men, and as therefore equally entitled with them to every enjoyment. You must exercise these capabilities, nor cease to remonstrate till no more than equal duties are exacted from you, till no more than equal punishments are inflicted upon you, till equal enjoyments and equal means of seeking happiness are permitted to you as to men . . .

Demand with Confidence and dignity your portion of the common rights of all.

Anonymous, Letter on Prostitution
(24 February 1858)[6]

In 1858, The Times *backed a campaign to suppress street prostitution in London. Two 'unfortunates' – prostitutes – wrote to give their side of the story. The first had fallen on hard times, having started out as 'governess in a highly respectable family'. The second wished to make clear that prostitution provided the prospect of a decent living to those with few others. The following day, an editorial on 'The Great Social Evil, as it is not unfairly called' assured readers that 'we are not endeavouring to palm off a cunningly executed literary imposture on our readers. The letter is, to the best of our belief, a revelation of the feelings of the class to which the writer openly declares she belongs.' Faced with such intransigence,* The Times *could only suggest that 'the night houses be brought into the same orderly condition as the ordinary public houses'.*

Now, what if I am a prostitute, what business has society to abuse me? Have I received any favours at the hands of society? If I am a hideous cancer on society, are not the causes of the disease to be sought in the rottenness of the carcass? Am I not its legitimate child; no bastard, Sir? Why does my unnatural parent repudiate me, and what has society ever done for me, that I should do anything for it, and what have I ever done against society that it should drive me to a corner and crush me to the earth? I have neither stolen (at least since I was a child), nor murdered, nor defrauded. I earn my money and I pay my way, and I try to do good with it, according to my ideas of good. I do not get drunk, nor fight, nor create uproar in the streets or out of them. I do not use bad language, I do not offend the public eye by open indecencies. I go to the opera, I go to Almack's, I go to the theatres, I go to quiet, well-conducted casinos. I go to all the places of public amusement, behaving myself with as much propriety that society can exact. I pay business visits to my trades people, the most fashionable of the West End. My milliners, my silk mercers, my bookmakers, know, all of them, who I am and how I live, and they solicit my patronage as earnestly and as cringingly as if I were Madame of the right reverend patron for the Society of the Suppression of Vice. They find my money as good and my pay better than that of Madame, and if all circumstances and conditions of our lives had been reversed, would Madame have done better or been better than I?

I speak of others as well as myself, for the very great majority, nearly all the real undisguised prostitutes in London, spring from my class. We come from the dregs of society. What business has society to have dregs – such dregs as we? You – the pious, the moral, the respectable-who stand on your smooth and pleasant side of the great gulf you have dug and keep between yourself and the dregs, why don't you bridge it over or fill it up, and by some urban or generous process absorb us into your leavened mass, until we become interpenetrated with goodness? What have we to be ashamed of, we who do not know what shame is – the shame you mean?

I conduct myself prudently, and defy you and your policemen too, Why stand you there mouthing with sleek face about morality? What is morality? Will you make us responsible for what we never knew? We who are the real prostitutes of the true natural growth of society and no impostors will not be judged by 'One More Unfortunate', not measured by her standard. She is a mere chance intruder in our ranks and has no business there.

Like 'One more Unfortunate' there are other intruders among us – a few, very few 'victims of seduction'. But seduction is not the root of the evil – scarcely a fibre of the root. A rigorous law should be passed to punish seduction, but it will not perceptibly thin the ranks of prostitution. Seduction is the common story of numbers of well brought up, who were never seduced, and who are voluntary and inexcusable profligates. Vanity and idleness send us a large body of recruits. Servant girls who wish to ape their mistresses' finery, and whose wages won't permit them to do so honestly – these set up seduction as an excuse. Married women, who have no respect for their husbands, and are not content with their lawful earnings, these are the worst among us. They have no principle of any kind and are a disgrace to us. If I were a married woman, I would be true to my husband. I speak for my class, the regular standing army of the force.

Gentlemen of philanthropic societies may build reformatories and open houses of refuge and may save, occasionally, a 'fallen sister' who can prevail on herself to be saved; but we who were never sisters – who never had any relationship, part or interest or communion with the large family of this world's virtues, moralities and proprieties – we, who are not fallen, but were always down – who never had any virtue to lose – we who are the natural growth of things and are constantly ripening for the harvest – what do they propose to do with us?

Hurling big figures at us, it is said that there are 80,000 of us in London alone – which is a monstrous falsehood – and of those 80,000, poor hard-working sewing girls, sewing women, are numbered in by the thousands and called indiscriminately prostitutes, writing, preaching, speechifying, that they have lost their virtue too.

It is a cruel calumny to call them in mass prostitutes; and as for their virtue, they lose it as one loses his watch who is robbed by the highway thief. Their virtue is the watch, and society is the thief. These poor women toiling on starving wages, while penury, misery, and famine clutch them by the throat and say, 'Render up your body or die.'

Admire this magnificent shop in this fashionable street; its front, fittings and decorations cost no less than a thousand pounds. The respectable master of the establishment keeps his

carriage and lives in his country house. He has daughters too; his
patronesses are fine ladies, the choicest impersonations of society.
Do they think, as they admire the taste and the elegance of that
tradesman's show, of the poor creatures who wrought it, and what
they were paid for it? Do they reflect on weary toiling fingers, on
eyes dim with watching, on the bowels yearning in hunger, on
the bended frames, the broken constitutions, on poor human
nature driven to its coldest corner and reduced to its narrowest
means in the production of these luxuries and adornments? This
is an old story! Would it not be truer and more charitable to call
these poor souls 'victims'? What business has society to point its
finger in scorn, to raise its voice in reprobation of them? Are they
not its children, born of cold indifference, of its callous selfish-
ness, its cruel pride?

Sir, I trespassed on your patience beyond limit, and yet much
remains to be said . . .

The difficulty of dealing with the evil is not so great as society
considers it. Setting aside 'the sin', we are not so bad as we are
thought to be. The difficulty is for society to set itself, with the
necessary earnestness, self-humiliation and self-denial, to the
work. To deprive us of proper and harmless amusements, to
subject us in mass to the pressure of force – of force wielded, for
the most part, by ignorant, and often brutal men – is only to
add the cruelty of active persecution to the cruelty of passive
indifference which made us what we are.

Josephine Butler, *An Appeal to the People of England, On the Recognition and Superintendence of Prostitution by Governments* (1870)[7]

The Contagious Diseases Acts, first enacted in the 1860s, legislated for 'common prostitutes' to be registered and forcibly examined for venereal disease. This measure was first applied in garrison towns, where prostitution was viewed as an unavoidable adjunct to military life. Later, it was extended to other towns. In 1869, the feminist Josephine Butler (1828–1906) was asked to become honorary secretary of the Ladies' National Association for the Repeal of the Contagious Diseases Acts, which she fronted unstintingly until the repeal of the Acts in 1886.

I write in the name of the thoughtful and Christian women of England, and I beg leave to draw your attention to the attempt now being made by a vigorous and active association, calling itself an 'Association for promoting the extension of the Contagious Diseases Act to the Civil Population', to bring into action generally throughout the country measures which provide for the legislation of prostitution. We are deeply convinced that such legislation is opposed to the interests of morality; while it will prove, as it has proved in other countries, ineffectual to stamp out disease. Its effect upon those large classes of men to whom, in default of religious principle or a high moral training, the laws of the country are a guide to conscience, is to teach them to look upon fornication not as a sin and a shame, but as a necessity which the State takes care that they shall be able to practise with impunity. In increasing the facilities to vice, you must certainly increase its noxious results. Such is found to be the consequence of the systematising and recognition of prostitution in Paris, and in many Continental cities . . .

Further, the proposed measures, politically considered, are without precedent in the history of our country in their tyranny, and their defiance of all which has ever been considered by Englishmen as *justice*. If you will study the provisions of the Acts of 1866 and 1869, and the evidence given last session before the Select Committee of the House of Commons, you will see how distinctly the introduction of such a law tends to the creation of a bureaucracy in England, which would be intolerable to a free people. It resembles the Spanish Inquisition in its system of paid spies, and the admission of anonymous whispers as evidence not to be rebutted. Contrary to the entire spirit of English Law, the whole burden of proof is thrown not upon the accuser, but upon the accused; there is a complete absence of all fair and open court – to say nothing of jury; and the accused, in this case, are the weakest, the most helpless, and most friendless of the community.

By this law a crime has been *created* in order that it may be severely punished; but observe, that has been ruled to be a crime in women which is not to be considered a crime in men. There are profligate men who are spreading disease everywhere, but the law does not take effect on *these*.

I have said that a crime has been created – which is to be severely punished. The alternative for every woman accused is either to appear before the Magistrates, or to submit to a torture which to any woman with a spark of feeling left in her is worse than death. Refusing to submit to the torture she is imprisoned. There is no escape from the one penalty or the other. An innocent woman who is accused may escape the torture, but she cannot escape the appearance before the Magistrates, and that very appearance means ruin to the character and prospects of a poor and virtuous woman. The tortures to which these poor fallen women (to whom, if there be an acknowledged *necessity* on the side of men for their existence, the State ought to be grateful and tender) are subjected by this Law, has no parallel except in the darkest and foulest forms of persecution practised on helpless women in the cruellest ages of history.

Edmund Kell, 'Effects of the Acts Upon the "Subjected" Women' (January 1871)[8]

Edmund Kell (1800–74) was a Unitarian minister in Southampton who campaigned against the hypocrisy and humiliation that the Contagious Diseases Acts represented. The Shield, *subtitled* The Anti-Contagious Diseases Acts Association's Weekly Circular, *to which Kell wrote this letter, was edited by Josephine Butler (see p. 427).*

SIRS – I am heartily rejoiced to hear of so many successful public meetings against the Contagious Diseases Acts at Edinburgh, Liverpool, Manchester, Newcastle-upon-Tyne, Bradford &c. Whilst every *effort* must be made in the South of England and in the subjected districts, still the most potent assistance on this great conflict must come from the North, where there have always been the most independent and energetic bands of reformers for every valuable work. My especial object in writing is to show the importance of immediate and strenuous efforts to stem the mischief of these Acts on the poor victims themselves, which my late attendance at the magistrates courts when their cases have been tried, has more particularly led me to deplore. In the subjected districts these Acts are, except with the spirited few, more and more reducing these poor slaves of man's sin to a helpless and degrading submission. In the garrison towns, generally, this prostrate submission of the women to the Acts, soon became more or less conspicuous. They were already from their contact with the military, in a more subdued and hardened state than prostitutes among a merely 'civil population'. In Southampton, the first 'civil population' where this fearful experiment has been essayed, the women held out against the Acts in larger numbers, and for a much longer time. About a dozen successively went to prison rather than submit to the

examination. One woman, Annie Clarke, submitted to a second
incarceration for a month rather than endure it, saying, she
would rather go to prison a dozen times, than suffer such an
examination. To elude the dreaded police spies, these women
resorted to all sorts of ruses, showing unmistakably how deeply
they hated the indignity. Lately, no less than 29 women were
summoned before the magistrates in one day, because they had
refused to go up to examination. The week previous to Christmas
was, with cruel tact, chosen for this large issue of summonses.
It is true that after several condemnatory verdicts, the magistrates declined to call the remaining number before them,
possibly in the hope that the terrors of the prison, with its wint-
erly cold, would do the work and subdue the girls into submission. And in fact larger numbers have gone up for examination
than formerly. If this law is to continue in force, it is to be feared
that these girls will be gradually seduced to the wretched condition of the French unfortunates. Thus it is that these infamous
Acts have worked, and are working, an evil change even in this
already degraded class of the population. And what an exhibition
is afforded of our magistracy through those Acts. For the last
four months, have been seen in England, gentlemen of position
and character, sitting hour after hour, added by the Admiralty
solicitor, sentencing women to prison. For what? Nor for the sin
of *prostitution*. No! for as long as the prostitute would say she
would submit to the atrocious examination, she was rather
patronised by the Pro-Act magistrates, her summons cancelled,
and she was sent free on her errand to 'go and sin more'. But
the poor women who resisted examination were sent to prison
for refusing to commit another sin, viz., that of acting contrary
to the dictates of all modesty and decency. It is gratifying to state
that not a few of these magistrates are opposed to the Acts, and
unwillingly gave way to a majority (often a small one) to send
these girls to prison, but the Acts themselves are now imperative,

and unless they are abolished, the Bench, as a rule, will ultimately commit all such women who have any modesty left to gaol. This is then to be a British magistrate's future vocation in this Christian country, to *harden* sinners by *law* thus opposing a ban to the efforts of those who are trying to reclaim the less hardened of the class. One fact, these trials at Southampton have elicited without a doubt, it is, that the unfortunate women here hate and abominate the Acts. They frequently half intoxicate themselves before they go to examination, thus paving the way to habits of drunkenness, more difficult, it is said, to eradicate than the habits of prostitution. The examination may doubtless, through this *hardening* process, after a time become less odious to them, but this shows all the more, the need of a prompt arrest of the Acts. There is indeed a small class of women, supported by richer men, driving themselves to the examination house, elegantly attired, who go through the examination methodically and unhesitatingly. To them and to some others, the Acts are a boon, for they enable them to obtain a higher price for their market. No wonder, moreover, that in the towns where those Acts are introduced, there are a number of rich unprincipled men, who support the Acts, besides those, who from ignorance or inadvertence, give them their sanction. I conclude with expressing my earnest hope that the intelligent and high-spirited population of the North will come to our rescue in the South. In the garrison towns not a few of the tradesmen are so much mixed up in business with the officers and soldiers, that they are hardly free to give that opposition to the Acts they would desire. And how difficult is it for a few such towns to withstand the combined influence of the Admiralty and their satellites.

Oscar Wilde, Second Trial for 'Gross Indecency' (26 April 1895)[9]

In 1895, Oscar Wilde (1854–1900) was put on trial for multiple counts of 'gross indecency' and conspiracy to commit 'gross indecency', after a failed libel action against the Marquess of Queensberry. During the trial, the prosecuting counsel, Charles Gill, asked Wilde to explain the title of a poem written by Lord Alfred Douglas, Queensberry's son, 'The Love That Dare Not Speak Its Name'. This is his reply.

'The love that dare not speak its name' in this century is such a great affection of an elder for a younger man as there was between David and Jonathan, such as Plato made the very basis of his philosophy, and such as you find in the sonnets of Michelangelo and Shakespeare. It is that deep, spiritual affection that is as pure as it is perfect. It dictates and pervades great works of art like those of Shakespeare and Michelangelo, and those two letters of mine, such as they are. It is in this century misunderstood, so much misunderstood that it may be described as the 'love that dare not speak its name', and on account of it I am placed where I am now. It is beautiful, it is fine, it is the noblest form of affection. There is nothing unnatural about it. It is intellectual, and it repeatedly exists between an elder and a younger man, when the elder man has intellect, and the younger man has all the joy, hope and glamour of life before him. That it should be so the world does not understand. The world mocks it and sometimes puts one in the pillory for it.

Helen Gordon Liddle, *The Prisoner* (1911)[10]

From 1905 until the outbreak of war in August 1914 about a thousand British women were sent to prison because of their suffrage activities (see Emmeline Pankhurst, p. 355). In 1907, Helen Gordon Liddle was imprisoned for a month after breaking a window. She demanded to be treated as a political prisoner and protested against prison regulations and food. Like many imprisoned suffragists she was forcibly fed. This is from her account of her experiences, The Prisoner, *published four years later.*

The prisoner is at her weakest this morning – her physical powers are at their lowest ebb – her mouth, which has been so tortured, is ulcerated, and shrinking from the slightest touch.

In his right hand the man holds an instrument they call a gag, partly covered with India rubber, which part the prisoner never feels, and the moment of battle has come.

The prisoner refuses to unclose her teeth – the last defence against the food she out of principle refuses to take – the doctor has his 'duty' to perform – his dignity also to maintain before five women and a tall junior doctor. His temper is short – has already been ruffled. So he sets about his job in a butcherly fashion – there is no skill required for this job – only brutality. He puts his great fingers along her teeth – feels a gap at the back, rams the tool blindly and with evident intention to hurt her, and cause the helpless woman to wince – along the shrinking flesh – how long will it take before superior strength triumphs? Tears start in the prisoner's eyes – uncontrollable tears – tears she would give anything to control.

It is still dark in the cell and the man strains at her mouth blindly, without result. 'Can you see?' asks the junior doctor. 'No,' blusters the other, 'better bring a light.' But he does not wait until the taper is brought – ah – at last he has forced the tool in, and with leverage the jaw opens.

He has still to hold it for twenty minutes or so while the food is being poured or pushed or choked down her throat – unluckily the gag has been forced in so carelessly that it has caught in the cheek, between it and the sharp teeth below.

The pain is maddening – she strains at her hands – her feet are in a vice – her head is held – she tries to speak – her jaw is forced to its widest. They pour the food down – it is a mince of meat and brown bread and milk – too dry – too stiff – they hold her nose [so] that she cannot breathe, and so she must breathe with her mouth and swallow at the same time, the doctors helping it in with hot hands that have handled a pipe and heaven knows how many patients – scraping their fingers clean on her teeth from the horrible mess.

It would seem they are not doctors, for they force it down so heedlessly that the prisoner chokes and gasps for breath, the tears pouring from her eyes. The young doctor is called away – the pain is too much for her – she moves her head – the doctor gives another twist, and the nurse, to get it over with sooner, pours the food quicker.

The limit is reached, and for the first time the prisoner gives way – great sobs of pain and breathlessness come fast and faster – she cannot bear it – she tries to call out 'Stop!' with that tortured wide-open mouth – and with one wrench she frees her hand and seizes the gag.

The doctor says to the officers – 'She says it is hot.' 'No,' they cry – the horror of the scene upon them – 'she said stop.'

He waits, gloomily with irritation, and in a moment free from the restraint of his fellow physician, without a word he drags her head back and she is held down again.

A short quick thrust and her mouth is gagged again – the prisoner tries to control herself – her sobs increase – her breathlessness also – there is nothing but the pain and the relentless forcing of food down her throat – her choking despair, and the bitter draught of tonic and digestive medicine which is also poured down her throat.

Virginia Woolf, Two Passages from *A Room of One's Own* (24 October 1929)[11]

For women throughout British history, being deprived of education has been a common form of discrimination. The novelist and critic Virginia Woolf (1882–1941) originally wrote the essays that were published under the title A Room of One's Own *as papers to be read at two Cambridge colleges in 1928. In the first passage here, Woolf muses on the fact that men have been the principal commentators on and arbitrators of the condition of women. In the second, with its sadly prophetic vision of a writer's suicide, she sets out the historical constraints on women who have aspired to be artists, imagining the fate of 'Shakespeare's sister'.*

Professors, schoolmasters, sociologists, clergymen, novelists, essayists, journalists, men who had no qualification save that they were not women, chased my simple and single question – Why are some women poor? – until it became fifty questions; until the fifty questions leapt frantically into midstream and were carried away. Every page in my notebook was scribbled over with notes. To show the state of mind I was in, I will read you a few of them, explaining that the page was headed quite simply, WOMEN AND POVERTY, in block letters; but what followed was something like this:

> Condition in Middle Ages of,
> Habits in the Fiji Islands of,
> Worshipped as goddesses by,
> Weaker in moral sense than, Idealism of,
> Greater conscientiousness of,
> South Sea Islanders, age of puberty among,
> Attractiveness of,
> Offered as sacrifice to,
> Small size of brain of,

    Profounder sub-consciousness of,
    Less hair on the body of,
    Mental, moral and physical inferiority of,
    Love of children of,
    Greater length of life of,
    Weaker muscles of,
    Strength of affections of,
    Vanity of,
    Higher education of,
    Shakespeare's opinion of,
    Lord Birkenhead's opinion of,
    Dean Inge's opinion of,
    La Bruyère's opinion of,
    Dr Johnson's opinion of,
    Mr Oscar Browning's opinion of . . .

Here I drew breath and added, indeed, in the margin, Why does
Samuel Butler say, 'Wise men never say what they think of women'?
Wise men never say anything else apparently. But, I continued,
leaning back in my chair and looking at the vast dòme in which I
was a single but by now somewhat harassed thought, what is so
unfortunate is that wise men never think the same thing about
women. Here is Pope:

    Most women have no character at all.

And here is La Bruyère:

    Les femmes sont extrêmes, elles sont meilleures ou pires que les hommes

— a direct contradiction by keen observers who were contemporary.
Are they capable of education or incapable? Napoleon thought them
incapable. Dr Johnson thought the opposite. Have they souls or have

they not souls? Some savages say they have none. Others, on the contrary, maintain that women are half divine and worship them on that account. Some sages hold that they are shallower in the brain; others that they are deeper in the consciousness. Goethe honoured them; Mussolini despises them. Wherever one looked men thought about women and thought differently. It was impossible to make head or tail of it all, I decided, glancing with envy at the reader next door who was making the neatest abstracts, headed often with an A or a B or a C, while my own notebook rioted with the wildest scribble of contradictory jottings. It was distressing, it was bewildering, it was humiliating. Truth had run through my fingers. Every drop had escaped.

*

[I]t would have been impossible, completely and entirely, for any woman to have written the plays of Shakespeare in the age of Shakespeare. Let me imagine, since the facts are so hard to come by, what would have happened had Shakespeare had a wonderfully gifted sister, called Judith, let us say. Shakespeare himself went, very probably – his mother was an heiress – to the grammar school, where he may have learnt Latin – Ovid, Virgil and Horace – and the elements of grammar and logic. He was, it is well known, a wild boy who poached rabbits, perhaps shot a deer, and had, rather sooner than he should have done, to marry a woman in the neighbourhood, who bore him a child rather quicker than was right. That escapade sent him to seek his fortune in London. He had, it seemed, a taste for the theatre; he began by holding horses at the stage door. Very soon he got work in the theatre, became a successful actor, and lived at the hub of the universe, meeting everybody, knowing everybody, practising his art on the boards, exercising his wits in the streets, and even getting access to the palace of the Queen. Meanwhile his extraordinarily gifted sister, let us suppose, remained at home. She was as adventurous, as imaginative, as agog to see the world as he was. But she was not sent to school. She had no chance of learning grammar and logic, let alone of reading Horace and Virgil. She picked up a book now and then, one of her brother's perhaps, and read a few pages. But then her parents came in and told her to mend the stockings or mind the stew and not moon about with books and papers. They would have spoken sharply but kindly, for they were substantial people who knew the conditions of life for a woman and loved their daughter – indeed, more likely than not she was the apple of her father's eye. Perhaps she scribbled some pages up in an apple loft on the sly, but was careful to hide them or set fire to them. Soon, however, before she was out of her teens, she was to be betrothed to the son of a neighbouring wool-stapler. She cried out that marriage was hateful to her, and for that she was severely beaten by her father. Then he ceased to scold her. He begged her instead not to hurt him, not to shame him in this matter of her marriage. He would give her a chain of beads or a fine petticoat, he said; and there were tears in his eyes. How could she disobey him? How could she break his heart? The force of her own gift alone drove her to it. She made up a small parcel of her belongings, let herself down by a rope one summer's night and took the road to London. She was not seventeen. The birds that sang in the hedge were not more musical than she was. She had the quickest fancy, a gift like her brother's, for the tune of words. Like him, she had a taste for the theatre. She stood at the stage door; she wanted to act, she said. Men laughed in her face. The manager – a fat, loose-lipped man – guffawed. He bellowed something about poodles dancing and women acting – no woman, he said, could possibly be an actress. He hinted – you can imagine what. She could get no training in her craft. Could she even seek her dinner in a tavern or roam the streets at midnight? Yet her genius was for fiction and she lusted to feed abundantly upon the lives of men and women and the study of their ways. At last – for she was very young, oddly like Shakespeare the poet in her face, with the same grey eyes and rounded brows – at last Nick Greene the actor-manager took pity on her; she found herself with child by that gentleman and so – who shall measure the heat and violence of the poet's heart when caught and tangled in a woman's body? – killed herself one winter's night and lies buried at some crossroads where the omnibuses now stop outside the Elephant and Castle.

That, more or less, is how the story would run, I think, if a woman in Shakespeare's day had had Shakespeare's genius.

Peter Wildeblood, *Against the Law* (1955)[12]

Peter Wildeblood (1923–1999) was a journalist and later television producer who was convicted for conspiracy to incite acts of gross indecency (the first use of the charge since the trials of Oscar Wilde, see p. 432) on 24 March 1954. This was part of the home secretary David Maxwell-Fyfe's 'new drive against male vice'. The case became notorious because Lord Montagu of Beaulieu was also convicted, and sent to gaol. Wildeblood's frankness in the dock and in his memoir seemed to mark a change in public attitudes to homosexuality. He gave evidence to the Wolfenden Committee, whose report led to the decriminalisation of homosexual behaviour between adults in private, the first reform of its kind in the twentieth century, and one that in time led to further movement towards equalising the law in Britain.

While Superintendent Jones was going through the contents of my wallet he found a number of visiting cards and telephone numbers, mainly belonging to business 'contacts'. Noticing one well-known name among them, he asked: 'I suppose he's queer too?' I said that if they really wanted a list of homosexuals from me I would be happy to oblige, beginning with judges, policemen and members of the

Government. I was beginning to feel slightly better. Very faintly, as though at the end of a tunnel, I could see what I must do. I would make a statement, but it would not be of the kind which Superintendent Jones was expecting. Far from incriminating Edward Montagu and Michael Pitt-Rivers, as he hoped, I would simply tell the truth about myself. I had no illusions about the amount of publicity which would be involved. I would be the first homosexual to tell what it felt like to be an exile in one's own country. I might destroy myself, but perhaps I could help others.

Two Recollections of Lesbian Life in Brighton in the 1950s and 1960s (1950–60s)[13]

Brighton Ourstory collects and preserves the lesbian, gay and bisexual history of a town that the project describes as the 'Gay Capital of the South'. In the 1920s, Brighton came to be recognised as a more liberal environment for lesbian and gay lifestyles, but as these two recollections from the 1950s and 1960s show, even many years later, prejudice was still very common.

Vicky

The dice is really loaded against you, in many respects. I mean, you couldn't get a loan from a bank without a man to guarantee you. You couldn't buy anything on HP [hire purchase] without having a man to guarantee you. I mean, a woman was definitely a second-class citizen, without a doubt. They talk about inequality nowadays, but you've got no real conception of what inequality was unless you lived then.

We had awful trouble, Jean and I, borrowing money for a business. It was purgatory. They automatically assumed that there's always got to be a man somewhere. I mean, a salesman would come into the shop, for instance, and he would call you 'Lovey' or 'Dearie' or 'Duckie' and, 'Where's your guv'nor, love?' I'd say, 'What do you want him for?' 'Oh, just to talk some business.' 'Well you're talking to the owner, is that good enough for you?' But then, I'm a bolshie, you see. I am that way. I mean a man's only got to give an indication that I couldn't possibly be in charge and my back goes up a mile.

But that's what it was all the time. You were fighting, all the time, because we were women in what they saw as a man's world. And to even borrow money to buy a car . . . I went into the bank to borrow money to buy a car and they said, 'Of course, you'll get your husband to sign again.' 'No, I'm not married, I'm divorced.' 'Well, haven't you got a brother or a . . .' I said, 'Why should I have anybody to guarantee me? I've got my own business, I guarantee myself.' I mean, to buy a car, Barclays Bank actually wanted me to give the deeds of my house and I said, '*I'm only buying a car!*'

Janice

When I was twenty, I actually had a nervous breakdown because of pressure and all sorts of things. I ended up going into Graylingwell, which was a very prominent nuthouse down in Chichester at the time. I had agoraphobia, that's what form the breakdown took, and I was really bad with it. I couldn't walk from one room to another.

Anyway, I went into the mental hospital a total wreck, but pleased to be there because anything to get away from home would have been wonderful. All the women there were very nice to me and they said, 'You've got to keep away from this woman called Stella, you must keep away from her.' I said, 'Well, why?' Now Stella was a very attractive thirty-year-old, very old, I thought, very pretty, married with two children. They would say, 'Keep away from her 'cause she likes young girls.'

Well, I tell you what, I have never manipulated things so much in all my life. I thought, 'This has got to be it now.' Ill as I was, I thought, 'I've got to get in tow with this Stella, I've got to start talking to her.' And I did just that. A lot of people used to go home at the weekends there because nobody was ill to the point of being physically violent or anything like that – we were all just doped up to the eyeballs – and Stella actually made a pass at me finally. I've never felt so happy and elated in all my life. This was what I'd been looking for, this was it, this was the missing piece of the puzzle and my health improved dramatically, oh, yes, very much so, it definitely did, I never looked back really.

I did see a psychiatrist, obviously, as everyone did while you were there and I told the psychiatrist of my feelings about this and I am very very angry to this day about that. I was under twenty-one then and the age of consent for anything was twenty-one and the actual psychiatrists had to see your parents in those days, if you were in hospital like that. And they told them, the psychiatrist told my parents about me being lesbian, and this resulted in me being forced, against my will, to have aversion treatment in the hospital, which to this day I will never forgive them for.

It was appalling to have to go through something like that. The treatment went over six weeks and the idea is you are given injections and made to feel physically ill at the sight of women doing anything. For about three months I felt dreadful about it, I mean, I couldn't face being anywhere near the proximity of women. But what it doesn't do, you see, is make you like men any more. It can't actually make you like something. It can put you off something you do like but it certainly can't work the other way around.

So, poor Stella, I mean, once the hospital realised what was happening, we were separated at the speed of light and Stella was then discharged. But it didn't stop it really, because all it did, once the treatment wore off, I'd learnt to be crafty. I no longer told the truth in these sessions. I said what they wanted me to say, really, in order to get better, in order to get out and see her. So in actual fact, she instigated my recovery quite a lot, without realising it.

I stayed in touch with Stella even though she had been discharged from Graylingwell. Illicit phone calls and coded letters and all sorts, yes. She used to write to me and call herself the Reverend Newstead. 'Cause all your letters were read just in case, you know. I suppose it was a bit like being in prison really.

Fortunately I haven't had a nervous breakdown since and I haven't had to go back anywhere like this, but I know that when I left there, I was still a wreck. You don't get over these things in five minutes, it took about three years, I suppose. And one of the psychiatrists I saw after that said, 'The only way you'll ever get better is to live the sort of life you need to live. You can't be so restrained and bottle things up the way you are.' And I mean it wasn't as if I was a child molester or something. But you were then, in fact, put in the same category.

Selma James and Women's Liberation Workshop, 'Women Against the Industrial Relations Act' (1971)[14]

Selma James was born Selma Deitch in New York in 1930, and first came to prominence in 1952 as the author of A Woman's Place. *She moved to Britain in the 1950s and married C. L. R. James (see p. 193), and campaigned for West Indian independence and racial equality. As part of the Women's Liberation Workshop in London she co-wrote this leaflet in response to the Industrial Relations Act, passed by the Conservative government of Edward Heath. The following year, James founded the International Wages for Housework Campaign. The Industrial Relations Act was repealed in 1974.*

This is an attack on the whole working class, and that includes women. But women in industry have almost no representation on the shop floor. They have always been ignored by men who call themselves militants. Now that we are all attacked these men expect us to join in defence of our class.

And we will join. The question is: are they going to join with us? When women are under attack, then the whole working class is under attack. When women are forced to accept low wages, this threatens the higher wages that men have won through struggle.

If the man's pay packet doesn't feed the family, the first to suffer is the woman.

She is the first to go without everything, from food to medical care.

She is the one who has no choice but to work not only at home for no pay but also in factories and offices for low pay.

This Act is the spearhead of an attack upon the working class. Unemployment is next. They have already begun to throw us out of jobs. They tell us women don't 'need' to work.

First, that is their excuse for offering women only the lowest paid jobs. And because we are discriminated against, we have no choice but to accept.

Second, what they think we 'need' is only enough to survive on. Women in the last years have gone out to work for what our rulers call 'extras', to bring into our homes a few of the comforts that are THE RIGHT OF EVERYONE. Even so, because of inflation, we have been forced to stay in industry to cover the family's basic survival needs.

Third, millions of women are fed up with the isolation and boredom of their unpaid work at home. We *NEED* to live a social existence. We *NEED* to be free of financial dependence on men. But our only escape has been to be exploited worse than men in factories or, harem-like, in typing pools. Black women especially are confined to the lowest paid jobs, and for us nursing is one of the few alternatives to factory work. Once the Immigration Bill becomes law, any struggle we wage will be in spite of the threat of deportation. Whatever work outside the home a woman does, she still has another job waiting for her when she gets home.

We have often had to wage our struggle for equal pay alone. As a result, the government was able to pass an act which gives us equal pay (if it does) only on condition that we are night and day at the disposal of industry. *If men had supported us this would never have happened.* As it is now, in order to work we have to abandon our children.

We can only defeat the Industrial Relations Act if we are a united force. The only basis for that unity is that the needs of *every* section of the working class is respected and fought for. The defeats of women have been the defeats of the whole class.

THE TIME HAS COME WHEN MEN MUST REALIZE THAT UNLESS THEY SUPPORT US IN OUR STRUGGLE FOR LIBERATION, THEY WILL NEVER BE FREE THEMSELVES.

We want men for the first time to share with us the raising of our children. We therefore demand A SHORTER WORK WEEK FOR ALL. Then *nobody* has to be sacked.

THE TIME HAS COME WHEN WOMEN MUST NOT WAIT FOR TRADE UNIONS OR ANYBODY ELSE TO WAGE THEIR STRUGGLE.

We must organize in the community, in the factory, in the hospital, in the office – wherever we are.

OUR STRUGGLE IS AGAINST THIS ACT AND BEYOND IT, AGAINST THE WHOLE STRUCTURE OF THIS SOCIETY.

———————

Tom Robinson, 'Glad To Be Gay' (1976)[15]

Long after homosexual acts between consenting adults had been legalised in Britain, in 1967, prejudice and violence were a common feature of gay life. Tom Robinson wrote this song for a Gay Pride march in London in 1976, and it was released as a single two years later. Like Adrian Mitchell with ('Tell Me Lies About Vietnam)' (see p. 396), Robinson has regularly updated the lyrics to reflect changing circumstances, such as the AIDS epidemic. He has explained, 'I never wanted it to become a fossilised museum piece about ancient injustices.'

The British Police are the best in the world
I don't believe one of these stories I've heard
'Bout them raiding our pubs for no reason at all
Lining the customers up by the wall
Picking out people and knocking them down
Resisting arrest as they're kicked on the ground
Searching their houses and calling them queer
I don't believe that sort of thing happens here

Sing if you're glad to be gay
Sing if you're happy that way

Pictures of naked young women are fun
In *Titbits* and *Playboy*, page three of the *Sun*
There's no nudes in *Gay News* our last magazine
But they still find excuses to call it obscene
Read how disgusting we are in the press
The *News of the World* and the *Sunday Express*
Molesters of children, corruptors of youth
It's there in the paper, it must be the truth

Sing if you're glad to be gay
Sing if you're happy that way

Don't try to kid us that if you're discreet
You're perfectly safe as you walk down the street
You don't have to mince or make bitchy remarks
To get beaten unconscious and left in the dark
I had a friend who was gentle and short
Got lonely one evening and went for a walk
Queerbashers caught him and kicked in his teeth
He was only hospitalised for a week

Sing if you're glad to be gay
Sing if you're happy that way

So sit back and watch as they close all our clubs
Arrest us for meeting and raid all our pubs
Make sure your boyfriend's at least twenty-one
So only your friends and your brothers get done
Lie to your workmates, lie to your folks
Put down the queens and tell anti-queer jokes
Gay Lib's ridiculous, join their laughter
'The buggers are legal now, what more are they after?'

Sing if you're glad to be gay
Sing if you're happy that way

———————————

Quentin Crisp, *How to Become a Virgin* (1981)[16]

Quentin Crisp (1908–99) sprang to fame when the first volume of his memoirs, The Naked Civil Servant, *was published in 1968. It detailed without self-pity the constant abuse Crisp endured for choosing not to hide his homosexuality.* How to Become a Virgin *was a sequel.*

I myself have often wondered why it took so long for anyone to get around to 'taking me in for questioning', considering that I used to waltz along the streets of the West End totally unaware that they were infested by plain-clothes coppers. Though they did not arrest me till 1943, they knew that I was in a weak position and constantly threatened me for their own and one another's amusement. Their condescension towards me on these occasions will never fade from my mind. Even now I could never wittingly become acquainted with a policeman; nor would I, except under torture, betray anyone to the authorities. Life is so hard for poor little crooks at the best of times. I imagine that these opinions which I hold so intensely are, in a milder form, fairly common. As a former police chief has himself said, 'If the police were popular there would be something wrong somewhere.'

Ian McKellen, Stonewall Equality Dinner Keynote Speech (3 April 2008)[17]

The actor Ian McKellen delivered this keynote speech at a dinner for the gay rights group Stonewall, looking back on the effects of the introduction of anti-gay legislation to the Local Government Act by

the Conservative government in 1988. It was during a radio debate
on the law that McKellen first came out publicly as gay. The campaign
against Section 28 lasted until its final repeal in 2003.

It was twenty years ago.

The biggest story regarding gay people in this country was about AIDS, and our lives were beginning to become a matter of public discussion. The media began to consider gay sex seriously and for the first time started publishing the truth about gay people's lives.

And then the bombshell of Section 28: 'A local authority shall not intentionally promote homosexuality or promote the teaching in any school of the acceptability of homosexuality as a pretended family relationship.' Some people in government saw Section 28 as part of the battle to try and prevent the disease. 'Don't talk to teenagers about sex, in case they might try it,' seemed to be the theory.

In truth Section 28 was part of a wider argument between the centralising government and local authorities, who were beginning to spend modest sums on small ventures such as gay youth groups. Margaret Thatcher's view, I think, was we could have homosexuality but not on the rates, and that encouraged us to stick up for ourselves.

It was the suggestion of a lesbian friend of mine that I join the Arts Lobby, which was chaired by the director of Gay Sweatshop at the time, and he had the astounding idea of damning Section 28 not just with regard to gay people but freedom of speech. We were part of a historic initiative in that group in which gay men took things into their own hands. They argued and insisted that right was on their side and it was a righteous response to ensure the outlawing of brutish law. Unwittingly Section 28 gave gay activists determination and campaigning against it gave us hope.

It was about this time we stopped wearing pink triangles, the symbol of oppression, and started to wear the rainbow, the symbol of hope. And the idea for a permanent professional lobby, which would prevent the government ever again making a mess of gay lives, was suggested to me by the unlikely figure of one of Mrs Thatcher's chief whips. It appealed to me because coming out had politicised me.

When I'd come out I'd heard about a whole group of people I would never have met with whom I had something in common. I had joined a community. And Michael Cashman had the idea of a permanent lobby too, and so did the twenty or so family members, all of whom were much more talented at drawing up constitutions and making them work than I was, or ever will be.

Under John Major we didn't progress very much. Major's vision, I think, was to quietly placate us so that we would all quietly get along with each other as well as we could. He was an enabler but he only had a small majority, and when he invited me to come and meet him in Downing Street, it was seen to be a first, and some of his supporters were apoplectic. 'Meeting that terrible homosexual actor,' was Norman Tebbit's summary of the situation.

I, too, for my part, got into trouble with Derek Jarman for appearing to take on single-handedly the representation of all gay people in this country, which wasn't my idea at all. At our meeting John Major promised nothing and simply delivered nothing, except possibly a sign of good intent.

Six years later I was back in serious politics again, with a brief from Stonewall under my arm and set to meet the leader of the opposition, three months before he became prime minister. Blair had his jacket off and we sat together on the sofa. He had a pad and pencil and I reeled off the demands of Stonewall: there should be a review of Section 28, there should be an equal age of consent, there should be gays immediately admitted into the military, and he wrote them all down with a tick by each one of them and said, 'We'll do all that.' And he said: 'Further to that, we're going to put you in the script.' 'What script is this?' I asked, and he replied: 'This is the script of the world I want to see for my grandchildren.' And I said, 'I'm sorry . . . but we can't wait that long.'

And fortunately we didn't have to and what's more he threw civil partnerships into the bargain. As for our current Prime Minister, I've only met him once but it was on a good occasion, at the marriage between Michael Cashman and Paul Cottingham, who is here this evening.

So what is left to be done? I think that's the question I really want to ask. There is certainly equality needed and I think we could leave Stonewall to get on with it as it's done so well in the past. Angela Mason set the agenda, which is achieved, and Ben Summerskill and his fantastic team are continuing in exactly the same spirit. But what about social equality? Don't they have it? Isn't it established?

Paul O'Grady, John Barrowman, Alan Carr: they're never off the box. Everything's right with the world. Well, not quite, because there's always those sly subtle jocks on the radio who think of sexuality as a joke and a dirty one at that.

Freedom to be out in public. Old Compton Street and the gay scene is terrific, but I can't help but think that the young and not so young revellers at Heaven or even at my local, the White Swan, actually go back to closeted lives and closeted workplaces. And it's a brave couple that walks outside on the streets of the East End where I live. Dramatically and tragically in 2003 Jodi Dubrowski was beaten to death on Clapham Common. Thirty-five injuries, which meant he could only be recognised by his fingerprints. His murderers are in prison now for twenty-eight years apiece.

Barack Obama has said of blacks in the United States something that I think may be true of the gay people in the United Kingdom. The laws have changed in our favour. Indeed civil partnership made us the only country that discriminates in favour of gay people as straights are not allowed to have a civil partnership. But there is an undercurrent culture that emerges . . .

And from the pulpit, homophobia is preached, by some arrogant religious leaders who think that their beliefs are superior to our inborn and some would say God-given nature.

The Anglican communion rejects a democratically elected openly gay bishop in North America because of the evangelical wing of the Anglican communion in Africa, but couldn't they listen to Archbishop Desmond Tutu? Our Anglican Church is almost obsessed with questions of human sexuality – why doesn't the Archbishop of Canterbury demonstrate the particular attribute of God which is that God is a welcoming God?

Last month the Bishop of Motherwell addressed his flock and told them how appalled he was that I had received an honour and that a hundred years ago I would have been imprisoned like Oscar Wilde. He feels that the Roman Catholic Church is beleaguered in some way. We neglect the gay lobby at our peril, he said. And when a mother asked him what he would do if his child said that he had a mission to be gay, the Bishop of Motherwell replied, sympathising with the mother but not the child, 'I would try to handle it with a degree of compassion but would not tolerate it.'

You can go on the Internet and identify active gay groups of all religions. One of the first couples to take out a civil partnership were two Muslim lesbians dressed in *hijab*s. The head of the Muslim Council of Britain denounced their partnership as harmful to society. 'It is something we would certainly not in any form encourage the community to be involved in.'

Incidentally things are, I hope, looking good for Mehdi Kazemi, whom I wanted to be my partner here this evening, my date, but could not be because he is still in detention until the Home Office has reconsidered its decision to send him back to a very possible public execution in Iran, because he is gay.

In a sense these are internal theological arguments but they do affect the rest of us and God help those being educated at faith schools where the instances of homophobic bullying is higher than in other schools. Stonewall's next major campaign will be in schools, encouraging them to treat their gay members of staff and their gay pupils with understanding. They have come up with ten suggestions to deal with homophobia in schools and will start a league table rather like the diversity champions for companies.

Stonewall asked, what are we going to do with these billboards we have been offered around the country and the kids were asked and came up with the slogan 'Some people are gay, get over it.' To coin a phrase, 'Sex education, sex education, sex education.'

In the future, what can any of us do as individuals? You can contact your old school and ask them if it isn't about time they started helping their gay students and staff. Ask them about their policies; they won't have one. You could vote for Mayor of London; one of the leading candidates, an openly gay man, is here this evening. You could vote for the gay-friendly straight man, or you could vote for the self-declared polymorphous pervert. You choose. If you don't have a firm that understands LGBT employees are of importance, tell them why they are. And if you are the member of such a firm, why don't you sponsor a young gay student through college? Why don't you contact the Albert Kennedy Trust, who look after homeless kids who have been thrown out by their families because they are gay?

Anything you do is of use. We all do what we can. None of us can do anything more important for ourselves and then for our friends and our family and the community at large than to come out of the closet completely. Complete that long journey that took me nearly fifty years and is these days taking teenagers a third of that time.

Where are all the high-profile lesbians in the United Kingdom? They are all sitting on these three tables! It is great you are here but we are not enough. Where are the sports people who will brave the ragging in the changing rooms and the heckling from the terraces?

1945–2012

———

BATTLING THE STATE

After the Second World War, the introduction of the welfare state, the nationalisation of some industries and the apparently secure place of trade unions in the political establishment all seemed to presage a less combative political and social scene. But entrenched prejudices, economic realities and what Harold Macmillan called 'Events, dear boy, events,' all conspired to make post-war politics every bit as dramatic as what had gone before.

One theme that emerged was a general mistrust of Parliament, whether it was supporting or participating in foreign wars or introducing unpopular taxes. Turnout in general elections declined, if not steadily, from a high of 83 per cent in 1950 to an all-time low of 59 per cent in 2001. But the conclusion that British society was generally 'apathetic' about politics is difficult to sustain when confronted with the evidence of extra-parliamentary marching, campaigning, song-writing, and now tweeting and Facebook group-making that have also characterised these decades. The numbers and commitment of young people turning out to protest against university fees are a demonstration that the student activist spirit of the 1960s is still alive and kicking.

Tariq Ali, 'The Street Is Our Medium' (27 October 1968)[1]

This editorial by Tariq Ali was published unsigned in Black Dwarf, *the paper of the Vietnam Solidarity Campaign, of which Ali was a leader. The VSC had been a moving force in the demonstrations against the Vietnam war outside the US Embassy in Grosvenor Square in March and October 1968.* Black Dwarf *took its name from the radical paper published around the time of the Peterloo Massacre, between 1817 and 1824. On the same page as Ali's editorial appeared the handwritten lyrics Mick Jagger sent to the paper of the Rolling Stones' new song 'Street Fighting Man', which radio stations were then refusing to play (see p. 459). Ali later called his memoirs* Street Fighting Years. *He continues to campaign prominently against the wars of the United States and its allies, and to challenge mainstream politicians.*

Demonstrations against the war in Vietnam have, throughout Western Europe and the United States, played a vital role in radicalising large numbers of young people and bringing them into direct contact with revolutionary politics. Wherever we look we see that the epic resistance of the Vietnamese people has galvanised the revolutionary left, or, at any rate, a large section of it into direct action.

Britain has been no exception. The familiar tactics of left-reformists typified by a refusal to take sides in public and a reliance on parliamentary cretinism have been swept away by militants throughout the country. We do not want any more teach-ins on Vietnam – our minds are made up. We support the National Liberation Front of South Vietnam and want it to defeat United States imperialism. We do not want any more petitions to Parliament. The House of Commons is as irrelevant as those who sit inside it. The political beliefs some of the left MPs claim to profess have not been put into practice and can NOT be within the existing social structure. The brand of social democracy preached by Mr Harold Wilson has shown all who care to see that the main function of the Labour government is to preserve the existing social structure at all costs. That is why the racist Home Secretary [James] Callaghan describes us as political 'hooligans'.

We say that the hooligans in this country are those who support American hooliganism in Vietnam; who pandered to [Enoch] Powellism and prevented the Asian immigrants from entering Britain; who have been trying to bash the working-class organisations of this country by sneers and innuendoes which were employed by Goebbels. We say that the hooligans are those who are negotiating with the racialist White settler Ian Smith behind the backs of the black leaders of Zimbabwe; who have recognised the Fascist regime of Greece; who are by remaining in NATO helping to crush the rebel lions in Mozambique, Angola and Guinea.

And when these hooligans reject successive resolutions passed by the annual conferences of their own party then we say that they leave us no alternative but the streets. At the moment they are merely irritated by us but when large groups of workers on strike take to the street or start occupying their places of work then we shall begin to see the real, ugly face of the ruling class in this country. It will be as brutal as any other ruling class. There should be no doubt about that and militants should prepare for this.

October 27 will be an important day on the calendar of socialist protest in this country whatever the outcome. The point is, however, to look beyond October. The *Black Dwarf* believes that all left-wing groups should get together and set up a joint co-ordinating committee to be called the Extra-Parliamentary Opposition. Apart from dealing with issues at home this body could lay the basis for the construction of a proper revolutionary socialist party, the need for which has been felt for a long time. Such a party cannot be built in isolation from those who are active on the streets against the Vietnam war because they are a practised vanguard and will of necessity form the cadres of a new party.

The movement is completely fed up with the sectarianism for which the British left is so notorious. We are fed-up with those who devote more time to attacking other socialists than capitalism itself or those who spend most of their time in accusing each other of being 'police agents'. The time has come to stop this internal wrangling and to move forward after October 27 and set up an Extra-Parliamentary Opposition. October 27 should not be seen as an end in itself but as the beginning of a new movement which will finally overwhelm those trying to destroy it.

Mick Jagger's handwritten lyrics to 'Street Fighting Man', sent to *Black Dwarf*

Paul Foot, Speech on the Murder of Blair Peach (13 June 1979)[2]

On 23 April 1979, St George's Day, the National Front decided to hold a meeting in Southall, west London, an area with a high Asian population. This was viewed as a deliberate provocation by anti-racist groups, who turned out in force to protest against the meeting. Five thousand police were drafted in to keep order. Violence broke out hours before the meeting was due to start, and in the running battles between police and demonstrators Blair Peach, a schoolteacher from Hackney, was knocked unconscious by police, and subsequently died. The journalist and socialist historian Paul Foot (1937–2009) spoke at a memorial soon after his murder.

From Manchester to Tolpuddle, the martyrs of our movement have been humble people. They neither sought the limelight nor found it. They were unknown except to a close circle of friends and family. They became famous not because of their ambitions nor their vanity, but because of their deaths.

Such was a man called Alfred Linnell. No one knows very much about him. He earned a pittance by copying out legal documents. On 21 November 1887 he went down to Trafalgar Square to join the fighters for free speech in the week after Bloody Sunday, when a great demonstration had been broken up by police truncheons.

While he was standing unarmed and unsuspecting, by the side of the crowd, a posse of police, who had orders to keep Trafalgar Square free of demonstrators 'by whatever force was necessary', charged straight into him, breaking his neck with horses' hoofs. The police openly despised the people they were charging. They saw them, as the *Times* leader put it on the day after Bloody Sunday, as 'all that is weakest, most worthless and most vicious in the slums of a great city'. These were the 'sweepings', which deserved only to be swept.

But the poor of London flocked to commemorate Alfred Linnell.

Tens of thousands of socialists, Irish Republicans, radicals, feminists and working people of no party and no persuasion joined in what Edward Thompson described as 'the greatest demonstration which London had seen'. The streets were lined all the way to Bow Cemetery with crowds of sympathetic onlookers. The few rather shamefaced policemen who dared to appear were greeted with cries of 'That's your work!' Very, very few of that mighty crowd knew Alfred Linnell. Yet they hailed him, in the words of William Morris at Linnell's funeral, as 'our brother and our friend'. He was a representative of all the tens of thousands who had nothing, and when they took to the streets to demand something were ridden down and battered by the forces of law and order.

That was nearly a hundred years ago and can easily be dismissed as 'the sort of thing which happened in the bad old days'. The killing of Blair Peach proves that the same things are still going on today. He was attacked at a demonstration by policemen who, as at Bloody Sunday and its aftermath, were licensed to clear the streets by brutality and violence.

In Southall, as in Trafalgar Square a hundred years ago, the police were driven on by a contempt for the demonstrators – 'black scum', as one mounted police officer so politely put it. No doubt the savagery of the blow which ended Blair Peach's life was prompted at least in part by the fact that his skin was dusky. And Blair Peach, like Alfred Linnell, has been hailed as a brother and friend by thousands of working men and women who did not know him.

On 28 April fifteen thousand of the Asian people of Southall marched in his memory. They stood with clenched fists over the place where he was murdered. And they chanted a single triumphant slogan: 'BLAIR PEACH SINDABAD – LONG LIVE BLAIR PEACH.' It was perhaps the greatest demonstration of solidarity between people of different colours but with similar interests and similar purpose that the town had ever seen.

Why? Because Blair Peach, like Alfred Linnell, is a representative of all the people all over Britain who see in the strutting perverts of the National Front the broken bodies of black people battered in the street; who can detect further off but no less horrible the awful spectre of Fascism looming over all society, and who stand up and say NO.

To me, and all members and supporters of the Socialist Workers Party, Blair Peach means even more than that. I never knew him personally. But I knew him as one of the party members who kept socialist organisation alive and well during the worst times. These are not the great speechmakers; they organise meetings and demonstrations, but are not to be seen on the platforms; they enjoy the big party occasions, but do not take the credit for them; the meetings they speak in are the vital ones, the little groups of twos and threes who meet to organise this or argue about that, and from whose arguments and ceaseless activity the very existence of socialist organisation depends. They're not very good, these people, at the quick quip or noble turn of phrase. But they know how to sustain the Anti-Nazi League in an area where two or three delegates turn up to a meeting to which twenty people had promised to come.

They have endless patience and endurance and they try to excite others into political activity without straining too hard at their patience and endurance. They seem to be at all the meetings and all the demonstrations. They are not in the front line when the press cameras are clicking, but they are in the front line when the SPG [police Special Patrol Group] wade in with their coshes. In the last three years – the period, by the way, in which Blair Peach joined the Socialist Workers Party – these people have been strained to breaking point as more and more of the burden of the organisation of the Left has fallen upon them. Blair Peach was killed in the process, and that above all is why we honour him.

We march at his funeral not just in sympathy with the people who loved him, nor just out of respect for all he did for us, but in anger.

———————

The Clash, 'Know Your Rights' (23 April 1982)[3]

The Clash were among the most politically engaged punk bands. Like most punks, they also had a good line in sarcasm, on display in this song, written by Joe Strummer and Mick Jones, which opened their Combat Rock *album in 1982.*

This is a public service announcement
With guitar
Know your rights all three of them

Number 1:
You have the right not to be killed
Murder is a CRIME!
Unless it was done by a
Policeman or aristocrat
Know your rights

And Number 2:
You have the right to food money
Providing of course you
Don't mind a little
Investigation, humiliation
And if you cross your fingers
Rehabilitation

Know your rights
These are your rights
Wang! Young offenders!

Know your rights

Number 3:
You have the right to freeeee
Speech as long as you're not
Dumb enough to actually try it.

Know your rights
These are your rights
All three of 'em
It has been suggested
In some quarters that this is not enough!
Well . . .

Get off the streets
Get off the streets
Run
You don't have a home to go to
Smush

Finally then I will read you your rights

You have the right to remain silent
You are warned that anything you say
Can and will be taken down
And used as evidence against you

Listen to this
Run

_____

Elvis Costello, 'Shipbuilding' (5 August 1982)[4]

The singer and songwriter Declan MacManus, better known as Elvis Costello, wrote this song during the Falklands war. As he later explained of the song, 'Ships were being lost. More ships would soon be needed. So welcome back the discarded men of Cammell Laird, Harland & Wolff . . . Boys are being lost. We need more boys. Your sons will do . . .'

Is it worth it
A new winter coat and shoes for the wife
And a bicycle on the boy's birthday
It's just a rumour that was spread around town
By the women and children
Soon we'll be shipbuilding
Well I ask you
The boy said 'Dad they're going to take me to task
But I'll be back by Christmas'
It's just a rumour that was spread around town
Somebody said that someone got filled in
For saying that people get killed in
The result of this shipbuilding

With all the will in the world
Diving for dear life
When we could be diving for pearls

It's just a rumour that was spread around town
A telegram or a picture postcard
Within weeks they'll be reopening the shipyards
And notifying the next of kin
Once again

It's all we're skilled in
We will be shipbuilding

With all the will in the world
Diving for dear life
When we could be diving for pearls

———————————

Pensioner Nellie Discusses the
Poll Tax Revolt (1990)[5]

*The community charge, better known as the poll tax, was one of the
most unpopular measures introduced by Margaret Thatcher's
Conservative government. Demonstrations were combined with a widespread refusal to pay; it was claimed that, four months after its introduction, up to a fifth of the population had not paid the tax. The poll
tax was eventually scrapped in 1991, but not before Thatcher, whose
flagship policy it was, had been ousted by her party. One more source
of resentment about the tax was that it was introduced in Scotland
before the rest of the country, apparently to test the waters. Nellie was
a sixty-nine-year-old pensioner who had been active in the Gorgie/
Dalry anti-poll tax union in Edinburgh for more than two years. She
appeared in court on 8 January 1990, along with sixteen others, for
occupying the sheriff's offices in Edinburgh to protest against the use
of warrant sales, a method of debt collection. Here she speaks to a
reporter about her involvement in the protest.*

All my children are dead now. Richard died when he was five from
meningitis and Annie died five months later; she was three. Ellen
had pneumonia and died when she was twelve weeks old. Then my
other son died three years ago; he was pulled out of the canal.

When the miners went on strike it was quite simple: you just supported them. I went on all the marches. But I had no real political involvement until the poll tax. I've had a hard life and you had to be hard yourself.

But now the pits have closed. This factory and that have closed. The health service is in a bad state. She's not getting away with it, even if I have to go to Downing Street myself; I would as well.

The poll tax is the final straw. I've worked all these bloody years, paid my insurance, my man's paid it as well and for what? A wee skittery pension.

I was one of the first to join my anti-poll tax union. I go to the stall on Saturday with Jamie, my dog. He's always got his 'Pay no poll tax' placard round his neck. I've been on all the demonstrations.

I've always voted Labour, but Kinnock hasna' got a clue. I've been and lobbied the Labour council here. They should be representing us, but they aren't doing anything. One of them came to our meeting ages ago and said there was no way he was paying the poll tax but now he's paying it.

The sheriff's office occupation was a good thing to do but there wasn't any hassle like they're accusing us of.

Warrant sales happened all the time when I was young but there's no way in this day and age we should let them happen. I don't regret the occupation. I'd do anything to beat the poll tax and we'll definitely win.

I won't be paying my poll tax, no way, even if I had to go to jail. They can't do that to you, but if they could, I'd go, no bother at all.

————————

Jeremy Hardy, 'How To Be Truly Free' (7 October 1993)[6]

The comedian Jeremy Hardy has given a regular series of comedy lectures on Radio 4, Jeremy Hardy Speaks to the Nation, *since 1993. This is one of his first commentaries.*

In the course of this brief talk, I shall be focusing on the ways in which we can achieve that rarest of commodities, freedom. Of course, the only reason that I am able to discuss this issue at all is that, in our country, we have absolute freedom of expression up to a point. But even here in Britain, speaking to you today, there are things I can't say. I can't say I've read any of Melvyn Bragg's books, for example. And there are legal restraints on my freedom of speech. For example, the police could prosecute me if I were to say something which is an incitement to racial hatred, although it's much more likely that they'd write it down and use it later. Moreover, anyone addressing a gathering of more than five persons is forbidden by law to call on the armed forces to mutiny, to demand an uprising against the Queen, to divulge an official secret, to commit blasphemy or to tell the hamster joke.

It is doubtful whether anyone can have total freedom. When a man says he is free, does he really mean that he is wholly independent in thought and deed, or does he simply mean that he's not doing anything at the moment? But even if complete freedom is an unattainable goal, there are things we can do to maximise the amount of freedom which we enjoy. These things fall into three categories.

1. throwing off all forms of oppression;

2. staying out of prison; and

3. achieving inner freedom through breathing and relaxation.

In order to liberate ourselves from oppression, we first have to know that we are being oppressed. The great thing about Margaret Thatcher was that she left us in absolutely no doubt. But, as I intimated in my introduction, even after all our years of Conservatism, there are places far more oppressive than Britain. There are regimes in the world so vile and tyrannical that they make us look like a mere trading partner. Let us look for a moment at Iraq.

In 1991, the Western Allies went to war against Iraq, with the stated claim of freeing Kuwait. Because, of course, when we talk about being free, we mean free not only as an individual or a group but as a nation-state. Therefore, the Western Allies liberated Kuwait and handed it back to its rightful dictators.

In the years which have followed the war, many have asked why we supplied arms to Saddam Hussein, a man who was obviously an evil, bellicose tyrant. The answer is that, by and large, evil, bellicose tyrants are our best customers: you don't shift much hi-tech weaponry to kindly old souls who haven't got a bad word to say about anyone. You have to know your market: starving Africans get the dodgy baby milk; psychopaths get the weapons. That is what we mean by Free Trade.

But what are the options for people living under oppression? Briefly, there are three: they can knuckle under, rebel, or leave the country. Some people have fled the regimes in their own countries to come here. The British government does all it can to make asylum seekers feel at home – by treating them as badly as they were treated where they came from. The Home Office does, however, deport anyone whom it considers to be an economic migrant, along with anyone facing a death sentence or torture when they get back.

But what can we in Britain do to avoid being oppressed? The best way not to be oppressed yourself is not to belong to an oppressed group. It is frankly reckless to be female, gay or black in a society so clearly fraught with prejudice and discrimination. If you must belong to one of these groups, it's best to become rich and a Tory, like Joan Armatrading, who is female, gay and black. Curiously, the tabloids have for years told us that left-wing councils give all their money to black lesbians. If that were true, you'd think Joan would have sufficient gratitude to vote Labour.

Liz Crow, 'Catching Buses' (19 June 1999)[7]

Liz Crow is a disabled audio-visual artist and activist in Bristol. Her direct-action campaign to highlight the inaccessibility of public transport is part of a disability activist movement that came to prominence during the 1990s, when disabled protesters led high-profile direct actions against welfare-reform proposals by Tony Blair's government.

I'm waiting at the bus stop on a cold and blustery day. Down a sweep of road comes a double-decker, lumbering towards us. It draws closer and I move into the road, into its path, arms outstretched to greet it, until the bus roars and hisses to a stop. And round the base of the front wiper blade I slip a handcuff and clip the bracelet home. I have caught a bus. I turn to face the street and join the chants echoing from the buildings, 'We will ride. We will ride.'

We are told by the powers-that-be to wait another thirty years for a transport system that is accessible. Two more generations! And so when decades of letter-writing, lobbying MPs and talking to transport operators fail to bring the results we need, we must turn up the heat.

We use non-violent direct action – handcuffing to buses, traffic stoppages, railway blockades and other tactics – to draw attention to our issue and win changes. We make a public spectacle of their shame.

Our demands are simple: we take action to demand universal access to public transport – that's buses, trains, trams, coaches and taxis that can be used efficiently, safely, independently and with dignity by everyone.

And we do it because someone's got to, because there's no time to lose, because change isn't won comfortably – and because it works.

When I go on an action I sometimes taste fear, and the night before, my stomach churns. For all the months of planning and recce and safety checks, there's still the unknown.

There's the man who tells us we're scum of the earth and the woman who thinks we should have been killed at birth. There are days when it's hard – fast moving, adapting to change, fielding abuse and waiting around for hours in the rain and chill.

And then there are moments – many moments – of exhilaration. A woman puts down her shopping bags to join us, others promise to write to their MPs, a group of kids asks to hand out leaflets and a bloke who saw us on yesterday's news comes down with his disabled daughter and her school friends.

It must seem to you that our sole aim is to make life difficult for everyone else, but your morning's inconvenience is, for us, a day-in day-out lifetime's exclusion. We break the smoothness of other people's routines so that we can drive the message home. And the message is getting there.

We chant until we're hoarse and we explain our purpose so many times it feels we must have converted a nation by now. 'If you support us, go home, tell your friends and family, go to work, tell your colleagues, talk about us and talk about the issue.'

I once read somewhere that it is not direct action that convinces the decision-makers so much as public opinion. Through direct action we shape that opinion and we point to solutions, but it's your response to us that wins the day.

How strange it is to see on the news and read in the press of the wheelchair warriors, the radicals and the militants. It's me and it's us! And it's not so much militancy as sheer, rock-bottom necessity. For all that it costs in time, money, health and arrests, doing nothing costs us all far more.

Because two and a half million people in the UK are being disabled by the transport systems – that's 2.5 million with their earning power reduced and their contribution to their communities restricted. And for every disabled person, there is a whole network of family, friends and colleagues held back.

And here in Bristol, you can wade through official statements of intent, policies and broken promises, but you still can't get on the bus. We live in a city that boasts of its international reputation as a 'centre for progressive transport policies', but it's got just one accessible bus route, difficult access to trains and not a single accessible public coach.

Just think for a moment why you use transport – and where you would be without it. How would you get to work, earn a living, see friends, shop for your family, visit relations? Most of the activities outside your home and most of the activities within it are made possible by your access to transport. Your freedom, your sense of belonging and your everyday function depend on it.

For a whole century now, there has been public transport – except that it isn't actually public. Travel to the United States, to Australia, Germany or to Scandinavia, and you'll find another story. They have proved that accessible transport works – some of them have had systems operating for years – and have found that, rather than being too expensive, transport operators' profits are up.

Back home, we are making progress. When we started direct action, the response to our demands from government and the transport operators was predominantly 'No way'. Now, a decade later, we're on the verge of legislation that might allow us to end our transport actions. It's too soon to rest yet, but there will be a future when we can all travel freely.

Harold Pinter, 'Art, Truth and Politics' (7 December 2005)[8]

The playwright Harold Pinter (1930–2008) was politically engaged throughout his career, and took a particular interest in the machinations of US foreign policy, from South America in the 1970s to the Middle East in this century. In 2005, he was awarded the Nobel Prize for Literature. Unable to attend the ceremony because he was receiving hospital treatment, he recorded his speech to be broadcast to the prize audience in Stockholm. This is a selection from that address.

Early in the invasion there was a photograph published on the front page of British newspapers of Tony Blair kissing the cheek of a little Iraqi boy. 'A grateful child,' said the caption. A few days later there was a story and photograph, on an inside page, of another four-year-old boy with no arms. His family had been blown up by a missile. He was the only survivor. 'When do I get my arms back?' he asked. The story was dropped. Well, Tony Blair wasn't holding him in his arms, nor the body of any other mutilated child, nor the body of any bloody corpse. Blood is dirty. It dirties your shirt and tie when you're making a sincere speech on television . . .

I have referred to death quite a few times this evening. I shall now quote a poem of my own called 'Death'.

Where was the dead body found?
Who found the dead body?
Was the dead body dead when found?
How was the dead body found?

Who was the dead body?

Who was the father or daughter or brother
Or uncle or sister or mother or son
Of the dead and abandoned body?

Was the body dead when abandoned?
Was the body abandoned?
By whom had it been abandoned?

Was the dead body naked or dressed for a journey?

What made you declare the dead body dead?
Did you declare the dead body dead?
How well did you know the dead body?
How did you know the dead body was dead?

Did you wash the dead body?
Did you close both its eyes?
Did you bury the body?
Did you leave it abandoned?
Did you kiss the dead body?

When we look into a mirror we think the image that confronts us is accurate. But move a millimetre and the image changes. We are actually looking at a never-ending range of reflections. But sometimes a writer has to smash the mirror – for it is on the other side of that mirror that the truth stares at us.

I believe that despite the enormous odds which exist, unflinching, unswerving, fierce intellectual determination, as citizens, to define the real truth of our lives and our societies is a crucial obligation which devolves upon us all. It is in fact mandatory.

If such a determination is not embodied in our political vision we have no hope of restoring what is so nearly lost to us – the dignity of man.

————————

Mark Thomas, Put People First G20 Protest (28 March 2009)[9]

The comedian Mark Thomas made this speech in Hyde Park at a rally called by protesters before the G20 summit meeting for leaders of the world's richest economies in London.

Thank you very much. It's brilliant to be here. And I want to say thank you, it's lovely to be introduced by Tony Robinson. What you can't see is that Tony has actually got a *Time Team* dig going on under the stage, and we're looking for a Labour Party socialist policy.

We're here because we want to say our job is to set out to kill neo-liberal capitalism. That's our task. And if anyone thinks the situation we're in is going to get any better, by just hunkering down and hoping it will blow over, you come and see me 'cos I've got some shares in Enron I still wanna sell.

We're going to have to get out and fight. We know we're in the crap. You know you're in the crap when Iceland the company is worth more than Iceland the country. You know . . . we're in the crap. You know you're in the crap – I was in Hackney the other day and Primark had a sale! They had stuff on at half price, which is against the laws of physics. We are facing a huge struggle. We are gonna face things getting worse, we are gonna face redundancies, an increase in poverty. We are gonna face bankruptcy, and a re-formed Spandau Ballet. We've got a lot of hard work.

But we're here because we have a unique moment. We have a chance to see *laissez-faire* capitalism as it struggles on its knees. We've got a chance to get in there and kill it, and kill it dead.

This is a struggle for democracy over capitalism, and we haven't got an option, we've got to win!

We've paid for the banks, we've subsidised the banks. People have said we've nationalised them, but we haven't – we've just subsidised them. We're not in control – well, that changes. We've got to get in those banks and we've got to take control of them. We've got to start putting social policy through the Royal Bank of Scotland. It's our bank, so let's have it. Let's get in there. The Royal Bank of Scotland has got £16 billion worth of investment in carbon extractive industries. £16 billion worth of investment in climate change. It's our bank, let's get in, let's shut that down.

The European Union said the Royal Bank of Scotland has the account for arms dealers who are arming Mugabe. It's our bank – let's get in there and shut that down.

The Royal Bank of Scotland operates a series of offshore tax havens and companies. Tax dodgers. Spongers. Corporate filth. It's our bank, let's get in there and shut them down.

You know, while we're at it we might as well take back the PFI [private finance initiative] contracts, and we'll have that for starters and we'll take the bankers' bonuses and we're on a roll. We'll get the HQ for council housing. We've got to fight. I should also explain one very important thing, which is part of the reason for this housing explosion and all of that is a very simple one. That Labour has overseen the destruction and depletion of council houses. Last year we saw three hundred council homes built. There are 444 councils. We couldn't even build a single council house in each council and that is a disgrace! It seems to me that Labour ministers don't care about state money going for housing, unless it's Jacqui Smith claiming her expenses.

We have to remember that, while we're bashing bankers let me tell you – Gordon Brown loves Fred Goodwin. He loves him, because Gordon Brown must love it to wake up each morning and know that the man who is most hated in this country is Fred Goodwin and Gordon Brown only gets the silver medal. Gordon Brown, his light regulatory touch, has been the cause of this crisis. Gordon Brown is a free marketeer. Gordon Brown had Margaret Thatcher into Number 10 and he gave her tea! If you get Margaret Thatcher in a room you put a stake in her heart and put her under the patio! . . .

Every time they blame working people and the poor. They spend millions chasing people who have the audacity to work and actually claim dole, when they ignore the billions of pounds that leave our country each year in corporate tax dodging and sponging. The Tax Justice Network estimate that each year, we, Britain, lose in corporate tax avoidance and corporate tax evasion £100 billion. Well, those days are over now. Those days are over.

Peter Mandelson said, and Peter Mandelson, I don't know how we're ever going to get rid of him, we have to cover him in salt or something, I don't know. But Peter Mandelson said that New Labour were seriously relaxed about people getting stinking filthy rich. And everything was OK if people made billions, and signed a direct debit for Oxfam to alleviate a bit of poverty. Those days are over. Those days . . . are over. New Labour is over! They're over and good riddance to the war-loving, liberty-hating free marketeers!

We've got a very simple message here, which is this. When people say, 'What's the alternative?' we are! We are the alternative. We have to build a movement that will fight and fight and fight, and fight for decades to win! To reclaim democracy. To reclaim our lives from capitalism. That is our task. That is the job that we start today – to fight and kill neo-liberal capitalism!

Thanks very much for coming along, folks. Oh, and if there are any police who are around over the week in the city, just remember it was Jacqui Smith who cut your pay.

Euan Booth, 'Subversively Move Tony Blair's Memoirs to the Crime Section in Bookshops' (3 September 2010)[10]

The publication of Tony Blair's memoirs, in which he wrote about the decision to go to war along with US forces in Iraq, generated protests and boycotts across the world. This campaign, launched on Facebook, was one of the wittiest, and a demonstration of the power of new media.

Be part of a literary movement. Literally.

Subversively move Tony Blair's memoirs to the crime section in bookshops

Make bookshops think twice about where they categorise our generation's greatest war criminal.

Go on . . . do it.

NON-VIOLENT DIRECT ACTION

Please invite your friends to do it too!

Barnaby Raine, Speech on Student Protests (27 November 2010)[11]

The announcement by the Conservative-Liberal Democrat Coalition government of the introduction of tuition fees for higher education in England and Wales was met with some of the biggest student protests since the 1960s. Anger was particularly high against the Liberal Democrats, who had made a manifesto commitment not to bring in the fees. The next generation of college and university students, still at school at the time of the marches in November 2010, was also well represented. Barnaby Raine, a fifteen-year-old school pupil, took part in the march on Whitehall, and three days later, on 27 November 2010, he addressed the Coalition of Resistance Conference.

Well, I might be in detention for a week, and the school might not be very happy, but we sure showed something much bigger last Wednesday. You know, this was meant to be the first post-ideological generation, right? This was supposed to be the generation that never thought of anything bigger than our Facebook profiles and our TV screens. This was meant to be the generation where the only thing that Saturday night meant was *X Factor*. I think now that claim is quite ridiculous. I think now that claim is quite preposterous. I think now we have shown that we are as ideological as ever before. Now we've shown that solidarity and comradeship, and all those things that used to be associated with students, are as relevant now as they've ever been.

You know, the most incredible thing that happened on Wednesday, I went down and I thought I was going to go down for lunch break and then get back for lessons. Perhaps I should have known they'd put the guy in charge of the G20 in charge. Perhaps I should have been more concerned for my life than with whether I was going to get down for lessons . . .

You know, when I was kettled in there I was with thousands and thousands of school students who'd come down with their ties around their heads in their school uniforms, and, yeah, they were cold, who'd come down, who'd never been at a protest before, who'd never joined a political party or been involved in a political movement before, who didn't have any economic knowledge or political degrees. But they were there because they believed in something. They were there because they believed in something bigger. And they were there because they knew that either – you know there weren't a million choices, there were two choices – either they lay down and took everything the government threw at them, or they stood up and fought back.

And so those school students who'd never been involved in anything before stood up, and they fought back. And when they were in that kettle, being kettled in by police, you know, the word that went around as we were sitting huddling around fires sharing around what little food we had, and the word went around, people said, 'We know what they're up to. We know that they don't think we're a danger to the public.' I'm fifteen years old; people there were as young as thirteen. We know they don't think we're going to run riot through the streets of London. We know what they're up to. They think that if they kettle us now we're not going to come to a demonstration ever again.

'Well, let the word go out from today,' people said, 'let the word go out about [the planned demonstration] next Tuesday, let the word go out about next week and next month and next year, that they can't stop us demonstrating. They can't stop us fighting back.'

And however much they try to imprison us in the streets of London, those are our streets and we will always be there to demonstrate. We will always be there to fight. People who had always thought that the police were just those people at the other end of the telephone line to help if there was a burglary, people who thought that the media were just those friendly newspaper men who were there to give them that unbalanced picture of the facts – people learned a lot last Wednesday. People learned a lot as they huddled around fires, and then emerged from that kettle to see headlines like 'Vandals' on the *Evening Standard* that afternoon. People learned a lot when a police van was left in the middle of the road so that the police could tow it away and show the whole public, look what vandals these people are. People learned a lot.

So the message that goes out from last Wednesday is pretty clear. We are no longer that post-ideological generation. We are no longer that generation that doesn't care. We are no longer that generation that's prepared to sit back and take whatever they give us. We are now the generation at the heart of the fight back. We are now the generation that will stand with everyone that's fighting back.

The most inspiring thing, I think, was that just after Wednesday hundreds of people joined a Facebook group, school students joined a Facebook group, in solidarity with tube members on the strike. Those people had previously thought that tube strikes were something annoying because they stopped them from getting into school. Now they think they've got to link arms and fight back with everyone.

So we want to show solidarity with everyone who's fighting back. We hope you show solidarity with us and send a strong message to this government that they can't throw their cuts at us. We're going to stand up and we're going to fight back.

Zadie Smith, Library Closures (30 March 2011)[12]

Cuts in central government grants to local government from 2011 have led to reductions in various local services. Many councils decided to close or amalgamate public libraries. By March 2012, it was estimated that 397 libraries were under threat, already closed or had left council control since the previous April, out of a total of around 4,600. The prizewinning novelist Zadie Smith gave a radio talk about what the local library had meant to her when she was growing up in west London.

I grew up in a council flat decorated with books; hundreds of them. I never paused to wonder where my mother found all these books, given the tightness of money generally. I just read them. A decade later we moved into a maisonette, where she filled the extra space with yet more books, arranged in a certain pattern. Second-hand Penguin paperbacks together, then the Women's Press books, then Virago. Then several shelves of Open University textbooks on social work, psychotherapy, feminist theory. Busy with my own studies and oblivious the way children are, I didn't noticed that my brothers and I were not the only students in that flat. By the time I did, my mother had a degree. We were reading because our parents and teachers told us to. My mother was reading for her life.

About two-thirds of those books had a printed stamp on the inside cover explaining their provenance: property of Willesden Green Library. I hope I'm not incriminating my family by saying that during the mid-eighties it seems as if the Smiths were covertly trying to move the entire contents of that library into the living room. It was a happy day when my mother spotted a sign pinned to a tree in the High Road: Willesden Green Library Amnesty. Next day we filled two black bin bags with books and returned them. Just in time – I was about to start my GCSEs.

I've spent a lot of time in libraries since then but I remember the spring of 1990 as the most intense study period of my life, probably because it was the first.

To choose to study with no adult looking over your shoulder and any other students for support and company: this was a new experience for me. I think it was a new experience for a lot of the kids in there. Until that spring, we'd come to the library primarily for the café or the cinema or to meet various love prospects of whom our immigrant parents would not approve, under the cover of that all-purpose immigrant-parents-silencing sentence: 'I'm going to the library.'

When the exams came we stopped goofing off. There's no point in goofing off in the library: you're acutely aware that the only person's time you're wasting is your own. We sat next to each other at the long white tables and used the library computers and did not speak. Now we were reading for our lives.

Still it's important not to overly romanticise these things: Willesden Green Library was not to be confused with the British Library. Sometimes whole shelves of books would be missing, lost, defaced or torn. Sometimes people would come in just to have a conversation while I bit my biros to pieces in frustration. Later I learnt what a monumental and sacred place a library can be.

I spent my adult life in libraries that make a local library look very small indeed; to some people clearly quite small enough to be rid of without much regret. But I know I never would've seen a single university carrel if I had not grown up living a hundred yards from the library in Willesden Green.

Local libraries are gateways not only to other libraries but to other lives. Of course I can see that if you went to Eton or Harrow, like so many of the present cabinet, you might not understand the point of such lowly gateways or be able to conceive why anyone would crawl on their hands and knees for the privilege of entering one. It's always

been, and always will be, very difficult to explain to people with
money what it means not to have money. 'If education matters to
you,' they ask, 'and if libraries matter to you, well, why wouldn't you
be willing to pay for them if you value them?' They're the kind of
people who believe value can only be measured in money. At the
extreme end of which logic lies the dangerous idea that people who
fail to generate a lot of money for their families cannot possibly value
their families the way people with money do.

My own family put a very high value on education, on bookish-
ness. Like many people without money, we relied on our public
services, not as a frippery, not as a pointless addition, not as an excuse
for personal stagnation, but as a necessary gateway to better opportunities. We paid our taxes in the hope that they'd be used to establish shared institutions from which all might benefit equally. We
understood very well that there are people who have no need of these
services, who make their own private arrangements, in health care,
and education, and property, and travel, and lifestyle, and have a
private library in their own private houses.

Nowadays, I also have a private library in my own private house
and a library in the university in which I teach. But once you've
benefited from the use of shared institutions, you know that to
abandon them when they're no longer a personal necessity is like
Wile E. Coyote laying down a rope bridge between two precipices,
only to blow it up once he's reached the other side so that no one
might follow.

But no matter how many individuals opt out of it, community
exists in Britain. And the commons of British life will always be the
greater force practically and morally. Community is a partnership
between government and the people and it's depressing to hear the
language of community, the so-called 'Big Society', being used to
disguise the low motives of one side of that partnership as it attempts
renege on the deal. What could be better than handing people back
the power so that they might build their own schools, their own

libraries? Better to leave people to the already onerous tasks of building their lives and paying their taxes. Leave the building of infrastructure to government and the protection of public services to government, that being government's mandate and the only possible justification for its power. That the grotesque losses of the private sector are to be nationalised, cut from our schools and libraries, our social services and our health care, in short from our national heritage, represents a policy so shameful I doubt this government will ever live it down.

Perhaps it's because they know what the history books will make of them, that our politicians are so cavalier with our libraries. From their point of view, the fewer places you can find a history book these days, the better.

———————————

NOTES

1. Monty Python, *Monty Python and the Holy Grail*, dir. Terry Gilliam (Python (Monty) Pictures/EMI Films, 1975).

1066–1450: COMMONERS AND KINGS

1. *The Ecclesiastical History of Orderic Vitalis*, vol. 2: Books III and IV, ed. and trans. Marjorie Chibnall (Oxford: Clarendon Press, 1969), p. 203.
2. *Liber Eliensis: A History of the Isle of Ely from the Seventh Century to the Twelfth, Compiled by a Monk of Ely in the Twelfth Century*, trans. Janet Fairweather (Suffolk: Boydell Press, 2005), pp. 205–6.
3. British Library, http://www.bl.uk/treasures/magnacarta/translation/mc_trans.html.
4. Thomas Wright, ed., *The Political Songs of England: From the Reign of John to that of Edward II* (London: Printed for the Camden Society by John Bowyer Nichols and Son, 1839), trans. David Horspool, pp. 72–3, 75, 116, 121.
5. From *The Anonimalle Chronicle, 1333 to 1381: From a MS. Written at St Mary's Abbey, York* (Manchester: University of Manchester Press, 1972), pp. 146–7; taken from the translation in Charles Oman, *The Great Revolt of 1381* (Oxford: Clarendon Press, 1906), pp. 200–1.
6. John Froissart, *Chronicles of England, France, Spain, and the Adjoining Countries from the Latter Part of the Reign of Edward II*, trans. Thomas Jones (New York: American Book Exchange, 1880), p. 283.
7. *The Chronica Maiora of Thomas Walsingham, 1376–1422*, trans. David Preest (Suffolk: Boydell Press, 2005), p. 159.

Disunited Kingdoms: 'Our English Enemies'

1. National Archives of Scotland, http://www.nas.gov.uk/about/090401.asp. Translation compiled by Alan Borthwick.

2. J. Gwynfor Jones and Dylan Reed, eds., *Thomas Matthews's Welsh Records in Paris* (Cardiff: University of Wales Press, 2010), trans. David Horspool, pp. 105–6.

3. *The Complaynt of Scotlande Wyth ane Exortatione to the Thre Estaits to Be Vigilante in the Deffens of Their Public Veil, 1549 ad*, ed. James A. H. Murray (London: English Early Text Society, 1872), trans. Neil Davidson, p. 123.

4. *The Works of Jonathan Swift*, vol. 2 (London: Henry Washburne, 1841), pp. 99–102.

5. *'Guilty or Not Guilty?': Speeches from the Dock, Or, Protests of Irish Patriotism* (Dublin: 1867), pp. 19, 20, 21, 22. The court did not allow Tone to read the paragraph beginning 'I have laboured to create a people in Ireland . . .' This paragraph is included out of order on p. 22. We have restored the probable order.

6. Ibid., pp. 41, 42, 43–4, 45–6, 47.

7. Angharad Llwyd, *A History of the Island of Mona, or Anglesey* (Ruthin: R. Jones, 1833), pp. 39–40.

8. G. T. Evans, ed., *Rebecca and Her Daughters: Being a History of the Agrarian Disturbances in Wales Known as The Rebecca Riots* (Cardiff: Educational Publishing Company, 1910), pp. 52–3, 66.

9. William Patrick O'Brien, *The Great Famine in Ireland: And a Retrospect of the Fifty Years 1845–95* (London: Downey, 1896), pp. 77–9, 80–81.

10. *Fenian Heroes and Martyrs*, ed. John Savage (Boston: Patrick Donahoe, 1868), pp. 281–2.

11. Pádraig Pearse, *The Best of Pearse*, eds Proinsias Mac Aonghusa and Liam Ó Réagáin (Cork: Mercier Press, 1967), pp. 1323.

12. Lewis Grassic Gibbon, *Sunset Song* (Cambridge: Penguin Classics, 2011), pp. 260–62.

13. Mike Burns, 'This Week', 13 April 1969, RTÉ Libraries and Archives, http://www.rte.ie/laweb/ll/ll_t18b.html.

14. R. A. R. Wade, 'A Travelling Traders' Guild?' in *Journal of the Gypsy Lore Society*, Third series, vol. 47 (January–April 1968), pp. 29–31.

15. Silvester Gordon Boswell, *The Book of Boswell: Autobiography of a Gypsy*, ed. John Seymour (London: Victor Gollancz, 1970), pp. 33–4.

16. The Dubliners, *Revolution* (EMI/Columbia, 1970).

17. Don Mullan, ed., *Eyewitness Bloody Sunday: The Truth* (Dublin: Wolfhound Press, 1997), pp. 97–8.
18. Roger Rawcliffe, *No Man Is An Island: 50 Years of Finance on the Isle of Man* (Douglas: Manx Heritage Society, 2009), p. 171.
19. Bobby Sands, Prison Diary, http://www.bobbysandstrust.com/writings/prison-diary.
20. *The Dragon Has Two Tongues: A History of the Welsh* (BBC, 1985).

FREEDOM OF WORSHIP: 'TOUCHING OUR FAITH'

1. *Letters and papers, Foreign and Domestic, of the Reign of Henry VIII: Preserved in the Public Record Office, The British Museum, and Elsewhere in England*, vol. 12, Part 1 (London: Eyre and Spottiswoode, 1890), pp. 38–9.
2. M. L. Bush, *The Pilgrims' Complaint: A Study of Popular Thought in the Early Tudor North* (Surrey: Ashgate, 2009), pp. 268–29, 270.
3. Mary Bateson, 'The Pilgrimage of Grace and Aske's Examination', *English Historical Review*, no. 5 (1890), pp. 561–2.
4. John Foxe, *Acts and Monuments* (1563 edition), pp. 1699–1700. See *The Unabridged Acts and Monuments Online* (Sheffield: HRI Online Publications, 2011), http//www.johnfoxe.org.
5. Hyder E. Rollins, ed., *Old English Ballads, 1553–1625, Chiefly from Manuscripts* (Cambridge: Cambridge University Press, 1920), p. 54. A different version of his statements appears in 'The city of Norwich, chapter 27: Of the city in Queen Elizabeth's time', *An Essay towards a Topographical History of the County of Norfolk: volume 3: The History of the City and County of Norwich, part I* (1806), pp. 277–360: '[O]n May 20, 1579, Matthew Hamount was burned for having said that "the New Testament and Gospel of Christ is but mere foolishness, a mere fable; that Christ is not God or the Saviour of the world, but a mere man, a shameful man, and an abominable idol; that he did not rise again from death or ascend unto Heaven; that the Holy Ghost is not God; and that baptism is not necessary, nor the sacrament of the body and blood of Christ."'
6. *The Troubles of Our Catholic Forefathers Related by Themselves, Third Series*, ed. John Morris (London: Burns and Oates, 1877), p. 416–17.
7. Daniel Defoe, *The Shortest-Way with the Dissenters: Or, Proposals for the Establishment of the Church* (London: 1702).
8. Joseph Jekyll, *Letters of the Late Ignatious Sancho: An African, To Which Is Prefixed, Memoirs of His Life* (London: William Sancho, 1802), pp. 269–73.

9. *The Complete Poetry and Prose of William Blake*, ed. David V. Erdman (New York: Anchor Books, 1988), pp. 53, 95, 200.
10. *Chambers's Miscellany of Useful and Entertaining Tracts*, vol. 18 (Edinburgh: William and Robert Chambers, 1847), pp. 15–16, 17–18.
11. Nadia Valman, 'Aguilar, Grace (1816–1847)', *Oxford Dictionary of National Biography* (Oxford University Press: 2004).
12. George Jacob Holyoake, *The History of the Last Trial by Jury for Atheism in England: A Fragment of Autobiography, Submitted for the Perusal of Her Majesty's Attorney General and the British Clergy* (London: James Watson, 1850), pp. 80–82.
13. Jim Etherington, *Lewes Bonfire Night: A Short History of the Guy Fawkes Celebrations* (Sussex: SB Publications, 1993), pp. 44–5.
14. Victoria Brittain, *The Meaning of Waiting* (London: Oberon Books, 2011), pp. 48–51.

1642–1789: REPRESENTING THE PEOPLE

1. 'The Humble Petition of Elizabeth Lilburne' (London, 1646), British Library, Wing L2077.
2. *An Arrow Against All Tyrants and Tyranny, Shot from the Prison of Newgate into the Prerogative Bowels of The Arbitrary House of Lords, and All Other Usurpers and Tyrants Whatsoever* (1646).
3. *Puritanism and Liberty: Being the Army Debates (1647–9) from the Clarke Manuscripts with Supplementary Documents*, ed. A. S. P. Woodhouse (Chicago: University of Chicago Press, 1951).pp. 52–3.
John Lilburne, *The Young Men's and the Apprentices' Outcry. Or an Inquisition after the Lost Fundamental Laws and Liberties of England* (London, 1649), in Andrew Sharp, ed., *The English Levellers* (Cambridge: Cambridge University Press, 1998), pp. 198–9.
4. *A Complete Collection of State-Trials and Proceedings for High-Treason, And Other Crimes and Misdemeanors from the Earliest Period to the Year 1783, with Notes and Other Illustrations, Volume II*, ed. T. B. Howell (London: T. C. Hansard, 1816), pp. 879–81.
5. William Andrews, *Bygone Punishments* (London: William Andrews, 1899), pp. 89–92.
6. 'Rude Britannia: British Comic Art', Tate Britain, London, 9 June to 5 September 2010.
7. Thomas Paine, *The Political Works of Thomas Paine* (Chicago: Belford Clarke, 1882), pp. 16–17.

8. The Declaration of Independence, US National Archives and Records Administration, http://www.archives.gov/exhibits/charters/declaration.html/.

9. Thomas Paine, *The Political Works of Thomas Paine*, pp. 275, 277–8.

10. Samuel Taylor Coleridge, *The Complete Poems*, ed. William Keach (London: Penguin Books, 1997), pp. 11–12.

11. *Aris's Birmingham Gazette*, 11 July 1791, Birmingham Central Library, Aris-1791-07-11-0001a (9/2268).

12. *The Parliamentary History of England from the Earliest Period to the Year 1803*, Volume 29 (London: T. C. Hansard, 1817), p. 1446.

LAND AND LIBERTY: 'THE EARTH IS A COMMON TREASURE'

1. Diarmaid MacCulloch and Anthony Fletcher, *Tudor Rebellions* 5th edn (Edinburgh: Pearson Education, 2008), pp. 156–58.

2. *The Works of Gerrard Winstanley, With an Appendix of Documents Relating to the Digger Movement*, ed. George H. Sabine (New York: Russell & Russell, Inc., 1965), pp. 269–77.

3. *A Declaration of the Grounds and Reasons Why We The Poor Inhabitants of the Town of Wellingborrow, in the County of Northampton, Have Begun and Give Consent to Dig Up, Manure and Sow Corn upon the Common, and Waste Ground, Called Bareshanke Belonging to the Inhabitants of Wellinborrow, by Those That Have Subscribed and Hundreds More That Give Consent* (London: Giles Calvert, 1650).

4. Also commonly rendered as 'Bonnie Portmore'. As this song dates from the oral tradition, we have not been able to find an authoritative version.

5. *Quarterly Review*, vol. 16, no. 31 (October 1816), p. 263.

6. *John Clare: Selected Poetry and Prose*, ed. Merryn and Raymond Williams (London: Methuen, 1986), pp. 90–93.

7. Arthur Clayden, *The Revolt of the Field: A Sketch of the Rise and Progress of the Movement Among the Agriculural Labourers, Known as the 'National Agricultural Labourers' Union'* (London: Hodder and Stoughton, 1874), pp. 146, 147, 151.

8. Victoria Street Society for the Protection of Animals from Vivisection, National Anti-Vivisection Society, *Zoophilist*, Volume 2, Issue 4 (1 August 1883), p. 145.

9. Henry S. Salt, *Animals' Rights Considered in Relation to Social Progress, With a Bibliographical Appendix* (London: Macmillan, 1894), pp. 36–41.

10. Ernest A. Baker, *The Forbidden Land: A Plea for Public Access to Mountains, Moors, and Other Waste Lands in Great Britain* (London: Witherby, 1924),

pamphlet, Archives of the Union of Post Office Workers, MSS.148/UCW/6/13/1/4.

11. Benny Rothman, Statement at the trial of the Kinder Scout Mass Trespass leaders, (Working Class Movement Library.)

12. Nick Broomfield, *A Time Comes: The Story of the Kingsnorth Six* (Bright Green Pictures, 2009), http://www.guardian.co.uk/environment/2009/may/31/kingsnorth-activists-climate-change-coal.

EMPIRE AND RACE: 'ALL SLAVES WANT TO BE FREE'

1. David C. A. Agnew, *Protestant Exiles from France in the Reign of Louis XIV: Or, The Huguenot Refugees and Their Descendants in Great Britain and Ireland* (London: Beeves and Turner, 1874), pp. 10–11. The translations of the Latin quotes in this passage are as follow. *Omnes omnium charitates una Patria complexa est*, 'All affections to all men are embraced in country alone' (Cicero, *De Officiis* I, 57); *Punctum est indivisibile*, 'A point is indivisible' (Thomas Aquinas, *Summa Theologica*, 1., Q52.2); *Caput tanquam radicem infixum caelo*, 'The head as much as the root fixed by heaven; *tum artibus, tum opera, tum facultatibus, devincire hominum inter homines societatem*, 'Both by arts, by works, as by every means, to bind together the society of men among men' (Cicero, *De Officiis*, I. 6).

2. *The Book of Sir Thomas More*, British Library, Harley MS. 7368, f. 9.

3. Lucy Aiken, *The Works of Anna Lætitia Barbauld: With a Memoir*, vol. 2 (London: Longman, Hurst, 1825), pp. 400–2, 403–4, 405.

4. 1910; Oxford: Bodleian Library MS Asquith 25, fol. 130

5. Ian Donnachie and Carmen Lavin, eds, *From Enlightenment to Romanticism: Anthology I* (Manchester: Manchester University Press, 2003), pp. 170–73.

6. *The History of Mary Prince, a West Indian Slave. Related by Herself. With a Supplement by the Editor. To Which Is Added, the Narrative of Asa-Asa, a Captured African*, 3rd edn. (London: F. Westley and A. H. Davis, 1831), pp. 21–3.

7. Ibid., pp. 42–4.

8. Henry Richard, *Memoirs of Joseph Sturge* (London: S. W. Partridge, 1865), pp. 115, 116–17.

9. *Conscience Versus Cotton: Or, The Preference of Free Labour Produce*, 2nd edn, condensed, Newcastle Anti-Slavery Series, no. 10 (*c.* 1860), University of Manchester, John Rylands University Library, Wilson Anti-Slavery Collection, Box 7, no. 6, pp. 1–4.

10. *The People's Paper,* 5 September 1857. In *Ernest Jones: Chartist,* ed. John Saville (London: Lawrence & Wishart, 1952), pp. 219–20.

11. John Morley, *The Life of Richard Cobden* (London: T. Fisher Unwin, 1903), pp. 675, 676–7.

12. Peter Fryer, *Staying Power: The History of Black People in Britain* (London: Pluto, 1984), pp. 278–9, 277. See pp. 561–2 for details on sources.

13. Society for the Study of Labour History, *Bulletin,* issue 12 (March 1966), pp. 16, 17, 18–19, 20.

14. Henry Woodd Nevinson, 'The Slave-Trade of Today', *Harper's Monthly Magazine,* vol. 112, no. 669 (February 1906), pp. 335–7.

15. Important Documents of the Ghadar Movement, India Relief and Education Fund (IREF), Fremont, California, http://iref.homestead.com/GadarDocs.html.

16. *Workers' Republic,* 9 October 1915. Transcribed by the James Connolly Society.

17. *Dr Babasaheb Ambedkar, Writings and Speeches,* vol. 12, ed. Vasant Moon (Bombay: Education Department, Government of Maharashtra, 1993), pp. 53–9.

18. Lajpat Rai, England's Debt to India, p. 7, New York (1917)

19. ibid., p. 7.

20. Fryer, *Staying Power,* Appendix E, p. 415.

21. Shahid Bhagat Singh Research Committee, Ludhiana, Letter, Writings and Statements of Shaheed Bhagat Singh and his Copatriots, http://www.shahidbhagatsingh.org/bharat_sabha.asp.

22. *The Collected Works of Mahatma Gandhi* (Electronic Book), *Volume 83: 7 June, 1942 - 26 January, 1944* (New Delhi, Publications Division Government of India, 1999), pp. 181–82, 183–84.

23. C. L. R. James, *Beyond a Boundary* (1963), pp. 29–30, 21–2, 25–6, 41–2.

24. Derek Humphry, *The Cricket Conspiracy* (National Council for Civil Liberties, May 1975), Doc. No.1975.001.NFB, pp. 117–19.

25. Linton Kwesi Johnson, *Mi Revalueshanary Fren* (London: Penguin Books, 2002), pp. 36–9.

26. Sinéad O'Connor, *I Do Not Want What I Haven't Got* (Ensign/Chrysalis Records, 1990).

27. Campaign Against Racism and Fascism, *CARF,* August/September 2001, http://www.irr.org.uk/carf/feat53.html.

28. Benjamin Zephaniah, *Too Black, Too Strong* (Northumberland: Bloodaxe Books, 2001), pp. 20–21.

29. Roger Huddle and Lee Billingham, 'Anti-Fascism: That Was Then, This is Now', *Socialist Review* (London), June 2004.

30. Chagos Gulag Watch, 25 January 2010, http://chagosgulagwatch.blogspot. com/2010_01_01_archive.html. The original statement appears to have been issued on 11 March 2008.

31. Mark Steel, *Independent*, 9 September 2009, http://www.independent.co.uk/ opinion/commentators/mark-steel/mark-steel-the-poles-might-be-leaving- but-the-prejudice-remains-1783815.html.

1790–1860: One Man, One Vote

1. 'An account of the arrest of Thomas Hardy', 12 May 1794, National Archives, Catalogue ref: TS 24/3/33, http://www.nationalarchives.gov.uk/education/ politics/transcript/g2s2t.htm.

2. Anonymous, 'Declaration of the Political Protestants of Newcastle Upon Tyne and Neighbourhood' (20 July 1818).

3. Letter from Mr W. R. Hay, a magistrate from Lancashire, to Lord Sidmouth, 16 August 1819, catalogue ref: ZHC 2/41 pp. 259–62, National Archives, http://www.nationalarchives.gov.uk/education/politics/g4/source/g4s3a. htm.

4. Percy Bysshe Shelley, *The Masque of Anarchy: A Poem*, ed. Thomas J. Wise (London: Shelley Society, 1892), pp. 43–7.

5. William Hone, *The Political House That Jack Built* (London: William Hone, 1819), n.p.

6. *A Complete Collection of State Trials and Proceedings for High Treason and Other Crimes and Misdemeanors from the Earliest Period to the Year 1783: With Notes and Other Illustrations,* vol. 33 (London: Longman, Rees, 1826), pp. 1549–50, 1551.

7. Charles Wilkins, *The History of Merthyr Tydfil* (Merthyr Tydfil: Joseph Williams and Sons, 1908), pp. 408–10.

8. Henry Vincent, 'Life and Rambles', *Western Vindicator*, no. 7 (6 April 1839), pp. 3–4.

9. Dorothy Thompson, *The Early Chartists* (London: Macmillan, 1971), pp. 222–5.

10. Thomas Ainge Devyr, *The Odd Book of the Nineteenth Century, Or, 'Chivalry' in Modern Days* (New York: Thomas Ainge Devyr, 1882), pp. 179–80.

11. *The Writings of Charles Dickens: Plays, Poems, and Miscellanies* (Boston: Houghton, Mifflin, 1894), pp. 101–2.

12. George J. Barnsby, *The Working Class Movement in the Black Country: 1750 to 1867* (Wolverhampton: Integrated Publishing Services, 1977), pp. 98–9.

MONEY AND CLASS: 'THE RANK IS BUT THE
GUINEA'S STAMP'

1. *Roger of Wendover's Flowers of History, Comprising the History of England from the Descent of the Saxons to ad 1236: Formerly Ascribed to Matthew Paris, vol. 2*, trans. J. A. Giles (London: Henry G. Bohn, 1849), pp. 146–7.

2. Andrews, *Bygone Punishments*, pp. 22–3.

3. The Thomas Gray Archive, http://www.thomasgray.org/cgi-bin/display.cgi?text=elcc.

4. Robert Burns, *The Poetical Works of Robert Burns: Edited with a Memoir by George A. Aitken*, vol. 3 (London: George Bell & Sons, 1893), pp 215–17.

5. *Ballads and Songs of Lancashire, Ancient and Modern, ed. John Harland and T. T. Wilkinson*, 3rd edn (London: John Heywood, 1882), pp. 193–5.

6. An Account of Machine-Breaking at Linthwaite, Yorkshire, March 1812. Catalogue ref: HO 40/1/1, part 2, f.6, National Archives, http://www.nationalarchives.gov.uk/education/politics/g3/source/g3s1a.htm.

7. Kevin Binfield, ed., *Writings of the Luddites*, (Baltimore: Johns Hopkins University Press, 2004) pp. 234–6.

8. Binfield, *Writings of the Luddites*, pp. 135–6.

9. George Gordon Byron, *The Works of Lord Byron; In Verse and Prose* (Hartford: Silas Andrus & Son, 1851), pp. 278–79.

10. *The Complete Poetical Works of Byron*, ed. Paul Elmer More (Boston, MA: Houghton Mifflin, 1905), p. 1281.

11. Handbill, printed by J. Pitts, 14, Great St Andrew Street, Seven Dials (London). Bodleian Library, University of Oxford, The *allegro* Catalogue of Ballads, Harding B 17(321a).

12. Thomas Carlyle, *Past and Present* (London: Chapman and Hall, 1843), pp. 5–6.

13. Frederick Engels, *The Condition of the Working Class in England,* trans. Florence Kelley Wischnewetsky (London: Swan Sonnenschein, 1892), pp. 114–18.

14. Karl Marx and Frederick Engels, *The Communist Manifesto: A Road Map to History's Most Important Political Document*, ed. Phil Gasper (Chicago: Haymarket Books, 2005), pp. 37–8, 59–67, 68, 71.

15. *Morning Chronicle*, 23 October 1849, reprinted in *The Farmer's Magazine* (London), second series, vol. 21, no. 1 (January 1850), pp. 39–41, 42.

16. Ellen Johnston, *Autobiography, Poems and Songs of Ellen Johnston, The 'Factory Girl'* (Glasgow: William Love, 1867), pp. 100–1.

17. *The Works of Thomas Hardy in Prose and Verse, Volume 1: Wessex Poems and Other Verses* (London: Macmillan, 1912), pp. 179–80.

18. Jack Dash, *Good Morning Brothers!* (London: Lawrence & Wishart, 1969), pp. 44-45.
19. George Orwell, *My Country Right or Left, 1940–1943, Volume 2: Essays, Journalism, and Letters* (New York: Harcourt, 1968), pp. 84–6.
20. John Lennon, *John Lennon/Plastic Ono Band* (Apple/EMI, 1970).
21. Archive of the University of Glasgow.
22. Dick Gaughan, *Call It Freedom* (Celtic Music, 1988).

Workers United: 'Labour's "No" Into Action'

1. *Trials for High Treason, in Scotland, Under a Special Commission, Held at Stirling, Glasgow, Paisley, and Ayr, in the Year 1820*, vol. 1 (Edinburgh: Manners and Miller, 1825), pp. 46–8.
2. Samuel Kyd, *The History of the Factory Movement: From the Year 1802, to the Enactment of the Ten Hours' Bill in 1847*, vol. 1 (London: Simpkin, Marshall, 1857), pp. 98–102.
3. *The Book of the Martyrs of Tolpuddle, 1834–1934* (London: Trades Union Congress General Council, 1934), pp. 100–1.
4. Jonathan French Scott and Alexander Baltzly, eds, *Readings in European History Since 1814* (New York: F. S. Crofts & Co., 1930), pp. 88–89.
5. Thomas and George Allan, *Allan's Illustrated Edition of Tyneside Songs and Readings: With Lives, Portraits, and Autographs of the Writers, and Notes on the Songs* (Newcastle upon Tyne: Thomas & George Allan, 1891), pp. 558–9.
6. The William Morris Internet Archive, http://www.marxists.org/archive/morris/works/1885/trade.htm.
7. The William Morris Internet Archive, http://www.marxists.org/archive/morris/works/1886/means.htm.
8. *The Link: A Journal for the Servants of Man*, no. 21 (23 June 1888).
9. Samuel Webber interview, British Library, recorded by Roy Palmer, 29 October 1971, 1CDR0007263 (copy of C1023/31), http://sounds.bl.uk/World-and-traditional-music/Traditional-music-in-England/025M-C1023X0031XX-1300V0#.
10. Ben Tillett, 'The Great Dock Strike of 1911', *The Clarion*, no. 1028 (18 August 1911), p. 1.
11. John Maclean, *In the Rapids of Revolution: Essays, Articles and Letters, 1902–23*, ed. Nan Milton (London: Allison and Busby, 1978), pp. 100–2, 112, 114.
12. 'B. W.', quoted in *Sheetmetal Workers' Quarterly* (October 1926), in Raymond

William Postgate, Ellen Cicely Wilkinson and James Francis Horrabin, *A Workers' History of the Great Strike* (London: Plebs League, 1927), pp. 34–5.

13. Lyrics supplied by the author. For a fine recording, we recommend Various Artists, *Whaur the Pig Gaed On the Spree: Scottish Recordings by Alan Lomax, 1951–1957* (Global Jukebox, 2011).

14. See 'The Unthanks perform "The Testimony of Patience Kershaw"', *Guardian*, 2 October 2009, http://www.guardian.co.uk/music/video/2009/oct/02/folk-the-unthanks-performance.

15. Raphael Samuel, Barbara Bloomfield and Guy Boanas, eds, *The Enemy Within: Pit Villages and the Miners' Strike of 1984–5* (London: Routledge & Kegan Paul, 1986), pp. 118–19, 177–9.

16. Mark Serwotka, Public and Commercial Services Union, News and Events, http://www.pcs.org.uk/en/news_and_events/news_centre/index.cfm/id/B591C03A-50FD-4530-9FA4AD11A3D03CF1.

1890–1945: EQUAL RIGHTS

1. Oscar Wilde, *The Essays of Oscar Wilde* (New York: Cosmopolitan Book Corporation, 1916), pp. 5–11.

2. *Speeches and Trials of the Militant Suffragettes: the Women's Social and Political Union, 1903–1918*, ed. Cheryl R. Jorgensen-Earp (Madison, New Jersey: Fairleigh Dickinson University Press, 1999), pp. 313, 314.

3. George Orwell, *Shooting an Elephant and Other Essays* (London: Secker and Warburg, 1953), pp. 13–14.

4. Cable Street Group, *The Battle of Cable Street* (Nottingham: Five Leaves Publications, 1995), pp. 32–41.

5. Aneurin Bevan, *In Place of Fear* (London: William Heinemann, 1952), pp. 25–6.

WAR AND PEACE: 'WHAT PEOPLE HAVE YOUR BATTLES SLAIN?'

1. Thomas Hoccleve, *De Regimine Principum: A Poem* (London: J. B. Nichols, 1860), pp. 191, 193–4.

2. 'Royton' (Manchester: W. Cowdroy, 1808), catalogue ref. HO 42/95 f.375, National Archives, http://www.nationalarchives.gov.uk/education/politics/transcript/g3s5t.htm.

3. John Bright, *Speeches on Questions of Public Policy*, vol. 1, 2nd edn, ed. James E. Thorold Rogers (London: Macmillan, 1869), pp. 488–90.

4. *Nation* (London), 15 August 1914.

5. House of Commons, 30 July 1917, as read into the record by Hastings Bertrand Lees-Smith. See also *The Times* (London), 31 July 1917. Facsimile of the letter available at: http://www.lettersofnote.com/2011/04/finished-with-war-soldiers-declaration.html.

6. Wilfred Owen, 'Disabled', *The War Poems of Wilfred Owen,* ed. Jon Stallworthy (London: Chatto & Windus, 1994), pp. 32–3.

7. Virginia Woolf, *Three Guineas* (New York: Harcourt, 1936), pp. 12–13, 15–16.

8. Commons Debates, 4 October 1938.

9. *The Great Dictator* (United Artists, 1940), 124 min. Transcript based on Eric L. Flom, *Chaplin in the Sound Era: An Analysis of the Seven Talkies* (Jefferson, North Carolina: McFarland, 1997), pp. 141–2.

10. Phil Piratin, *Our Flag Stays Red* (London: Thames, 1948), pp. 71–5.

11. Christopher Driver, *The Disarmers: A Study in Protest* (London: Hodder & Stoughton, 1964), pp. 56–8.

12. Lyrics supplied by the author.

13. Adrian Mitchell, *Adrian Mitchell's Greatest Hits: His 40 Golden Greats* (Northumberland: Bloodaxe Books, 1991), pp. 48–9. In later versions, Mitchell updated the poem to include the following lines:

> Tell Me Lies about Iraq
> Burma
> Afghanistan
> BAE Systems
> Israel
> Iran
> Tell me lies, Mr Blair
> Tell me Lies about Vietnam.

From personal correspondence with Celia Hewitt, 16 September 2010.

14. Imperial War Museum Sound Archive, Greenham Common: The Women's Peace Camp, 1981–2000, available at: http://archive.iwm.org.uk/upload/package/22/greenham/.

15. Innovative Minds, 22 March 2003, http://www.inminds.com/antiwar-rally-22mar03.html. Compton is misidentified in the audio clip and on the website as 'Lady Hampton'.

16. 'Cook's resignation speech', BBC News, 18 March 2003, http://news.bbc.co.uk/2/hi/2859431.stm.

GENDER AND SEXUAL EQUALITY: 'A HUMAN BEING REGARDLESS
OF THE DISTINCTION OF SEX'

1. E. K. Chambers, *Early English Lyrics: Amorous, Divine, Moral and Trivial*
    (London: A. H. Bullen, 1907), p. 197.
2. *To the Supreme Authority of England, the Commons Assembled in Parliament.
    The Humble Petition of Divers Well-Affected Women of the Cities of London and
    Westminster, the Borough of Southwark, Hamlets and Parts Adjacent. Affecters
    and Approvers of the Petition of Sept. 11 1648* (London, 1949), British Library,
    Wing T1724.
3. Rictor Norton, ed., 'Extraordinary Female Affection, 1790', Homosexuality
    in Eighteenth-Century England: A Sourcebook, 22 April 2005, updated 15
    June 2005 http://rictornorton.co.uk/eighteen/1790extr.htm.
4. Mary Wollstonecraft, *A Vindication of the Rights of Woman: With Strictures
    on Moral and Political Subjects* (London: T. Fisher Unwin, 1891), p. 34.
5. William Thompson, *Appeal of One Half of the Human Race, Women, Against
    the Pretension of the Other Half, Men, to Retain Them in Political, and Thence
    in Civil and Domestic, Slavery* (London: Richard Taylor, 1825), pp. 187–92,
    193, 210.
6. 'The Great Social Evil', *The Times* (London), 24 February 1858.
7. 'An English Mother' [Josephine Butler], *An Appeal to the People of England,
    On the Recognition and Superintendence of Prostitution by Governments*
    (Nottingham: Frederick Banks, 1870), pp. 3, 4–5.
8. *Shield*, 4 February 1871.
9. H. Montgomery Hyde, *Oscar Wilde: A Biography* (London: Methuen, 1977),
    p. 329.
10. Eleanor S. Riemer and John C. Fout, eds., *European Women: A Documentary
    History, 1789–1945* (Brighton: Harvester Press, 1983), pp. 73–74.
11. Virginia Woolf, *A Room of One's Own* (New York: Mariner Books, 1989), pp.
    27–30, pp. 46–8.
12. Peter Wildeblood, *Against the Law* (London: Weidenfeld and Nicolson, 1955),
    p. 55.
13. Peter Dennis, Beccie Mannall and Linda Pointings, eds., *Daring Hearts:
    Lesbian and Gay Lives of 50s and 60s Brighton* (Brighton: Brighton Ourstory
    Project, 1992), pp. 27, 35–6.
14. Leaflet of the Notting Hill group, Women's Liberation Workshop. It was
    reprinted in the issue of *Shrew* edited by the Notting Hill group in September
    1971. In Selma James, *Sex, Race and Class – The Perspective of Winning: A*

Selection of Writings 1952–2011 (Oakland: PM Press/Common Notions, 2012), pp. 41–2.

15. Lyrics supplied by the author.

16. Quentin Crisp, *How to Become a Virgin* (London: Duckworth, 1981), p. 49.

17. Sir Ian McKellen, http://www.mckellen.com/writings/activism/080403 stonewall.htm.

1945–2012: BATTLING THE STATE

1. Unsigned editorial in *The Black Dwarf*, vol. 14, no. 7 (27 October 1968), p. 2.

2. Paul Foot, *Words as Weapons: Selected Writing 1980–1990* (London: Verso, 1990), pp. 155–7.

3. The Clash, 'Know Your Rights' (CBS, 1982).

4. Elvis Costello, *Punch the Clock* (F-Beat, 1983).

5. *Militant,* 12 January 1990.

6. Jeremy Hardy, *Jeremy Hardy Speaks to the Nation* (BBC Radio 4, 7 October 1993).

7. 'A Life in Chains', *Evening Post* (Bristol), 19 June 1999.

8. Harold Pinter, 'Art, Truth and Politics', The Nobel Prize in Literature 2005, 7 December 2005, Swedish Academy, Stockholm, Sweden, http://www. nobelprize.org/nobel_prizes/literature/laureates/2005/pinter-lecture.html.

9. IFIwatchnet, http://www.ifiwatch.tv/en/video/2009/03/mark-thomas-put-people-first-g20-protest.

10. Facebook, http://www.facebook.com/group.php?gid=150746811621277.

11. Barnaby Raine, Coalition of Resistance, 27 November 2010, Camden, http:// www.youtube.com/watch?v=CrgzpPvJxmQ.

12. BBC Radio 4, *Today,* 30 March 2011.

Acknowledgements

Very, very special thanks to David Horspool, who was our invaluable partner on bringing this project from the stage to the printed page, as well as the remarkable Canongate team: Jamie Byng (who can take the blame for us doing this book), Nick Davies, Tif Loehnis, Norah Perkins, Jenny Todd, Lindsay Terrell, and others. Hazel Orme, our excellent, meticulous copy editor, saved us from numerous errors in the text.

Special thanks, for all their support, to Brenda Coughlin, Livia Firth, Julia Bueno, Jude and Johan Horspool.

We owe a huge debt to many librarians, archivists, oral historians, editors, authors, researchers, chroniclers, singers, folklorists, and people's historians (many of whom are acknowledged in the permissions section below). But we wish especially to thank the British Library, London Library, Stoke Newington Library, and Marx Memorial Library.

We are immensely grateful to the brilliant cast of our original stage production and television documentary: Nonso Anozie, Saffron Burrows, John Castle, Anna Chancellor, Noel Clarke, Omid Djalili, Rupert Everett, Tom Hickey, Celia Imrie, Ben Kingsley, Keira Knightley, Laura Marling, Kelly Macdonald, Ian McKellen, Stephen Rea, Tom Robinson, Arundhati Roy, Colin Salmon, Mark Steel, Juliet Stevenson,

Joss Stone, Mark Strong, Owen Teale, Teddy Thompson, the Unthanks, Benjamin Zephaniah. All of them inspired us to continue this project, and many helped us find the voices in this book.

The team at History UK/AETN – Tom Davidson, James Pestell, Delissa Needham, Miriam Lyons – also were vital to bringing this project from the United States, with the support of Christian Murphy and the wonderful people at History/AETN in the United States, to the United Kingdom. We are especially indebted to the original research team for that project: Miles Taylor, Helen Picridas, Martha Vandrei, and Katherine Louise Jones. We also were greatly aided on that project by Isabel Freer, Paul Lyon-Maris, Jessica Kolstad, Nick Forgacs and Carey Mulligan.

We received important translation, research and editorial advice from Neil Davidson, Mike Marqusee, Samantha Fingerhut, Carl Bromley, Jessie Kindig, Arundhati Roy, S. Anand, Shaun Harkin, Ahmed Shawki, Paul D'Amato, Scott McLemee, Paul Laverty, William Keach, James McKusick, Vanessa Redgrave, Saffron Burrows and Tariq Ali. We were especially inspired by Michael Rosen's excellent *Chatto Book of Dissent*, which is a must for any library.

Howard Zinn's family, particularly Myla Kabat-Zinn and Jeff Zinn, have been especially encouraging of our work, as has Ike Williams. And, of course, none of this would have been possible without the work, vision and example of Howard Zinn.

Permissions Acknowledgements

For help with permissions, we would also like to thank: Ady Cousins; Alison Light; Alistair Cartwright of Stop the War Coalition; Ann Cattrall; Ann Pettitt; Anne Sears; Association for Cultural Equity; Barbara Levy of the Barbara Levy Literary Agency; Barnaby Raine; Benjamin Zephaniah; Bernadette McAliskey; Celia Hewitt; Charles Finch; Charles Guard of the Manx Heritage Foundation; Claire Daniel, Rachael Egan and Emma Yan of University of Glasgow Archive Services; Clare Fermont; Daneka Norman and Rachael Simmonds of The Bevan Foundation; Danny Morrison of the Bobby Sands Trust; Diane Schumacher of The Gandhi Foundation; Darrell Gilmour and Elvis Costello; Geoffrey Goodman and Lawrie Nerva of the Aneurein Bevan Society; Hamish Henderson; Harmit Athwal of the Campaign Against Racism and Fascism; Helen Wilson at the *Guardian*; Ian McKellen; Jeremy Hardy; Jil Cove and the members of The Cable Street Group; John Barrow; Joanne Kent and Suzanne Carey at Universal Music, Shari Wied at Hal Leonard Corporation, and Matt Cansick at Music Sales; Jon Stallworthy, Trustee of the Wilfred Owen Estate; Jonas E. Herbsman; Jonna Petterson of The Nobel Foundation; Kate Murphy; Kätzel Henderson; Ken Loach; Laurence Holmes of Liberty (formerly National Council for Civil Liberties); Lee Billingham; Linda Pointing of Brighton Ourstory; Liz Crow; Lynette Cawthra of the Working Class Movement Library; Martin Sanders of the University of Warwick Modern Records Centre; Margaret Bennett ; Mark Steel;

Mark Thomas; Mark L. Thomas of Socialist Review; Mary Compton; Nick Broomfield; Oxford University Digital Archives; Peter Rothberg; Peter Ruhe of GandhiServe Foundation; Phillip Ward; Ramsey Kanaan; Richard Simcox of the Public and Commercial Services Union; Richard Hughes, Vicky Northridge, Rita ODonoghue and Parveen Sodhi of the Imperial War Museum; Rob Marsden of Red Mole Rising; Rochelle Harris; Roger Huddle; Stuart D. Lee; Sue Brearley; Susan Usher of Bodleian Libraries, University of Oxford; Tariq Ali; Tina Becker; Tom Robinson; Tony Simpson of the Bertrand Russell Peace Foundation; Umar Farooq; Victoria Brittain; Yoko Ono; and Yvonne Morris of the Wilfred Owen Association.

Permissions Credits

Every effort has been made to trace copyright holders and obtain their permission for the use of copyright material. The publisher apologises for any errors or omissions and would be grateful if notified of any corrections that should be incorporated in future reprints or editions of this book.

Adrian Mitchell, 'To Whom It May Concern (Tell Me Lies About Vietnam)'. Used by permission of United Agents.

Aneurin Bevan, *In Place of Fear*. Used by permission of the Aneurin Bevan Society.

Anonymous Tanzanian Asylum Seeker. Used by permission of Campaign Against Racism and Fascism.

Benny Rothman, *The Kinder Trespass*. Reproduced with the kind permission of Harry & Marian Rothman and the Working Class Movement Library.

Bertrand Russell, Letter to the *Nation*. Used by permission of The Bertrand Russell Peace Foundation Ltd.

Bobby Girvan and Christine Mahoney, The 1984 Miners' Strike. Used by permission of the Estate of Raphael Samuel.

Bobby Sands, Prison Diary. Used by permission of the Bobby Sands Trust. © Bobby Sands Trust.

Chagos Protest by the People's Navy. Used by permission of Diego Garcia.

Charlie Chaplin, Final Speech from *The Great Dictator.* © Roy Export S.A.S.

C.L.R. James, *Beyond a Boundary.* Published by Yellow Jersey Press. Use by permission of The Random House Group Limited.

Elvis Costello, 'Shipbuilding'. Words & Music by Elvis Costello & Clive Langer © 1982 BMG Music Publishing Limited. Universal Music Publishing MGB Limited. All Rights Reserved. International Copyright Secured. Used by permission of Music Sales Limited.

Ernest A. Baker, *The Forbidden Land*. This extract is taken from a copy of the pamphlet held at the Modern Records Centre (http://www2.warwick.ac.uk/services/library/mrc/) in the archive of the Union of Post Office Workers (reference: MSS.148/UCW/6/13/1/4).

George Orwell, 'A Hanging'. © 1931. Used by permission of Bill Hamilton as the Literary Executor of the Estate of the Late Sonia Brownell Orwell and Seck & Warburg Ltd.

George Orwell, *The Lion and the Unicorn.* © 1941. Used by permission of Bill Hamilton as the Literary Executor of the Estate of the Late Sonia Brownell Orwell and Seck & Warburg Ltd.

Hamish Henderson, 'Freedom come-all-ye'. Used by permission of Kätzel Henderson.

Hamish Henderson, 'John MacLean March'. Used by permission of Kätzel Henderson.

Harold Pinter, 'Art, Truth and Politics'. Used by permission of The Nobel Foundation 2005.

Jack Dash, *Good Morning Brothers!* Used by permission of Lawrence & Wishart.

Jimmy Reid, Inaugural Speech as Rector of Glasgow University. Used by permission of University of Glasgow Archive Services, James Reid collection, GB0248 DC455/1/1/9.

Linton Kwesi Johnson, 'Inglan is a Bitch'. Used by permission of the author.

Monty Python, *Monty Python and the Holy Grail.* Used by permission of Methuen Publishing Ltd.

Paul Foot, Speech on the Murder of Blair Peach. First published in *Socialist Worker*, June 1979. Reprinted in Paul Foot, *Words as Weapons: Selected Writing 1980–1990*, p. 155–57. London: Verso, 1990.

Pensioner Nellie Discusses the Poll Tax Revolt. Used by kind permission of the Socialist Party, www.socialistparty.org.uk.

Peter Wildeblood, *Against the Law.* Used by permission of J.M. Dent, an imprint of Orion Publishing. © Peter Wildeblood, 1955.

Phil Piratin, *Our Flag Stays Red.* Used by permission of Lawrence & Wishart.

Quentin Crisp, *How to Become a Virgin.* © 2012 by Quentin Crisp. All rights reserved. Used by permission. Courtesy of Crisperanto: The Quentin Crisp Archives (crisperanto.org).

Siegfried Sassoon, Declaration Against War. © Siegfried Sassoon. Used by kind permission of the Estate of George Sassoon.

Sinéad O'Connor, 'Black Boys on Mopeds'. Words & Music by Sinead O'Connor © 1990 Nettwerk One Music Limited. All Rights Reserved. International Copyright Secured. Used by permission of Music Sales Limited.

Images

CHRONOLOGICAL INDEX

INDEX

CHANNELLING GREAT CONTENT FOR YOU TO WATCH, LISTEN TO AND READ.

canongate.tv